The Theological and Ecological Vision of *Laudato Si'*: Everything is Connected

The Theological and Ecological Vision of *Laudato Si'*: Everything is Connected

Edited by Vincent J. Miller

t&tclark

LONDON · NEW YORK · OXFORD · NEW DELHI · SYDNEY

T&T CLARK
Bloomsbury Publishing Plc
50 Bedford Square, London, WC1B 3DP, UK
1385 Broadway, New York, NY 10018, USA

BLOOMSBURY, T&T CLARK and the T&T Clark logo are trademarks of
Bloomsbury Publishing Plc

First published 2017
Reprinted 2020

A catalogue record for this book is available from the British Library.

A catalog record for this book is available from the Library of Congress.

ISBN: HB: 978-0-5676-7318-3
PB: 978-0-5676-7315-2
ePDF: 978-0-5676-7317-6
eBook: 978-0-5676-7316-9

Typeset by Deanta Global Publishing Services, Chennai, India
Printed and bound in Great Britain

To find out more about our authors and books visit www.bloomsbury.com
and sign up for our newsletters.

To our children and students.
"Hope would have us recognize that there is always a way out,
that we can always redirect our steps,
that we can always do something to solve our problems."
Pope Francis Laudato Si', §160

CONTENTS

Part Three: Responding in care for our common home

COPYRIGHT ACKNOWLEDGMENTS

Figure 1 in Chapter 3 is from David Olson et al., "Terrestrial Ecoregions of the World: A New Map of Life on Earth," *BioScience* 51 (2001), 934. Used with permission of Oxford University Press and the American Institute of Biological Sciences.

Chapter 10 originally appeared as Ottmar Edenhofer and Christian Flachsland, "Laudato Si': Die Sorge um die globalen Gemeinschaftsgüter," in *Stimmen der Zeit* 9 (September 2015): 579–91. It was published in English translation as "Laudato Si': Concern for Our Global Commons" in *Thinking Faith*, the online journal of the Jesuits in Britain. The essay and translation have been revised for this book. Used with permission of *Stimmen der Zeit* and *Thinking Faith*.

The "Ecological Examen" in Chapter 12 is used with permission of Joseph P. Carver, S.J.

Figure 1 in Chapter 13 is from Jonathan A. Patz, et al., "Climate Change and Global Health: Quantifying a Growing Ethical Crisis," *EcoHealth* 4 (2007): 397–405. © Ecohealth Journal Consortium 2007. Used with permission of Springer.

ACKNOWLEDGMENTS

This book emerged from a conference at the University of Dayton in March of 2015 cohosted by the Hanley Sustainability Institute and the Gudorf Chair in Catholic Theology and Culture. We thank Ken and Evelyn Gudorf and George and Amanda Hanley for their support of this scholarship. Monti Moyer handled the myriad administrative details of implementing the conference. Without her work, this project would not have been possible. Bob Brecha, Sister Leanne Jablonski FMI, Don Pair, and Maura Donahue contributed to the steering committee for the conference. Members of my doctoral seminar "Theology, Ecology and U.S. Culture" read and discussed all of the chapters in draft form. My graduate assistants contributed many hours of labor to this project. Laura Eloe read the first drafts of the chapters and mapped their citations of the encyclical. Jens Mueller helped with research, translation, and logistics for the conference. Anne Huey and Gillian Halusker provided assistance in preparing the final manuscript: checking citations, correcting formatting, and attending to the seemingly endless small details required to unite 13 essays into one book. I would like to thank the authors for their patient willingness to contribute not simply essays to a collection, but chapters to a book. This project required more dialogue and reworking than collected volumes usually entail. Finally, my thanks to Eileen, whose love and support are present in all of my labors.

NOTES ON CONTRIBUTORS

Anthony Annett is the Climate Change and Sustainable Development Advisor at the Earth Institute, Columbia University. He received his doctorate degree in economics from Columbia University. He is also a knight commander of the Equestrian Order of the Holy Sepulchre of Jerusalem, a papal order of chivalry. Working closely with Religions for Peace, he leads the Earth Institute's initiative to strengthen the engagement of the world's religious communities in the climate change and sustainable development agenda. Trained as an economist, he has a keen interest in Catholic social teaching and in the intersection of ethics and economics more broadly.

Robert Brecha is Professor of Physics, a member of the Renewable and Clean Energy Program and Research Director of the Hanley Sustainability Institute at the University of Dayton. He was founding director of the Sustainability, Energy, and the Environment (SEE) minor from 2007 to 2015. Since 2006 he has been a regular visiting scientist at the Potsdam Institute for Climate Impact Research (PIK) in Germany, including a sabbatical in 2010–11 partially sponsored by the Fulbright Commission. His research publications focus on energy efficiency in buildings, climate change mitigation strategies, fossil-fuel resource limits, integration of fluctuating renewable energy sources, and energy needs for sustainable development.

Daniel Castillo is Assistant Professor of Theology at Loyola University Maryland. His expertise lies at the nexus of liberation theology and ecological theology. His work has been published in the journals *Theological Studies, Political Theology*, and *Koinonia*. While completing his Ph.D. at the University of Notre Dame, Dan was the recipient of a Global Linkages of Biology, Environment, and Society (GLOBES) Fellowship, funded by the National Science Foundation. He teaches courses in liberation theology and environmental ethics at Loyola University Maryland, where he is an assistant professor of theology and a Bunting Peace and Justice Fellow. He is the author of *An Ecological Theology of Liberation: Salvation and Political Ecology*, forthcoming from Orbis Press.

Douglas Christie is Professor of Theological Studies at Loyola Marymount University. He earned his doctorate degree in Christian spirituality at the Graduate Theological Union, Berkeley. He is the author of *The Word in the*

Desert: Scripture and the Quest for Early Christian Monasticism (Oxford) and *The Blue Sapphire of the Mind: Notes for a Contemplative Ecology* (Oxford). He was the founding editor of the journal *Spiritus* and recently returned from living for two years in Córdoba, Argentina, where he served as codirector of LMU's Casa de la Mateada Program.

María Teresa Dávila is an associate professor of Christian ethics at Andover Newton Theological School. Her scholarship focuses on the option for the poor, especially in the context of US civil society. She has published in the areas of public theology, Latino/a ethics, the ethics of the use of force, the use of the social sciences in ethical reflection, racial justice, and immigration. She is currently working on a volume on the option for the poor in the United States as a key to transcending the culture wars.

Daniel R. DiLeo is Ph.D. candidate in theological ethics with a minor in systematic theology at Boston College. He is also Project Manager of Catholic Climate Covenant, which works to support and complement the Environmental Just Program of the U.S. Conference of Catholic Bishops. His work on this chapter comes out of his research into how Catholic Christian ethics can help persons and communities address climate change and better care for God's creation.

Ottmar Edenhofer is Professor of the Economics of Climate Change, TU Berlin-Berlin Institute of Technology, and Deputy Director as well as Chief Economist at the Potsdam Institute for Climate Impact Research. He currently leads Research Domain III—Sustainable Solutions—which is focusing on research in the field of the economics of atmospheric stabilization. In 2012 he was appointed director of the newly founded Mercator Research Institute on Global Commons and Climate Change (MCC). From 2008 to 2015 he served as Cochair of Working Group III of the Intergovernmental Panel on Climate Change (IPCC). His research work concentrates on strategies to mitigate climate change, questions of growth and development theory, public finance, questions of distributional effects of climate policy instruments, game theoretic aspects of designing international agreements and, last but not least, energy economic aspects. He specializes in the economics of atmospheric stabilization, social cost-benefit analysis, sustainability theory, economic growth theory, environmental economics, welfare theory, and general intertemporal equilibrium theory.

Christian Flachsland is Head of the working group on "Governance" at the Mercator Research Institute on Global Commons and Climate Change (MCC) and Assistant Professor for Climate and Energy Governance at the Hertie School of Governance.

Terrence Ehrman, C.S.C., is the assistant director for life science research and outreach at the Center for Theology, Science, and Human Flourishing and concurrent professional specialist in the theology department at the University of Notre Dame. He investigates the relationship between theology and science, particularly the life sciences of ecology and evolution. His interests include understanding who God is as Creator, who we are as creatures, and what our relationship is to God, ourselves, and the natural world. He teaches a course in the theology department entitled "Science, Theology, and Creation."

Elizabeth T. Groppe is Associate Professor of Theology at Xavier University. Her area of expertise is Roman Catholic systematic theology. Her recent publications include "Seed that Falls on Fertile Ground (Mt 13:1–9): Catholic Higher Education and the Renewal of Agrarianism" published in the journal *Horizons* and "The Way of Wisdom" in *Environmental Justice and Climate Change: Assessing Pope Benedict XVI's Ecological Vision for the Catholic Church in the United States*, edited by Jame Schaefer and Tobias Winright. She serves on the Climate Change Task Force of the Archdiocese of Cincinnati, and her work in progress includes a book that will be a theological response to the ecological crisis.

Erin Lothes is Assistant Professor of Theology at the College of Saint Elizabeth, Morristown, New Jersey, and a former Earth Institute Fellow at Columbia University. She is the author of *Inspired Sustainability: Planting Seeds for Action* (Orbis 2016) and *The Paradox of Christian Sacrifice: The Loss of Self, the Gift of Self* (Herder and Herder, 2007). Dr Lothes's numerous articles on energy ethics include "Catholic Moral Traditions and Energy Ethics for the Twenty-First Century," *Journal of Moral Theology* 5:1, a coauthored, peer-reviewed, and scientifically reviewed article. Dr Lothes actively participates in interfaith environmental coalitions such as the Catholic Climate Covenant, the Global Catholic Climate Movement, and GreenFaith as a scholar, speaker, and advocate.

Vincent Miller is the Gudorf Chair in Catholic Theology and Culture at the University of Dayton. He is the author of *Consuming Religion: Christian Faith and Practice in a Consumer Culture* (Bloomsbury) and a frequent contributor to *America Magazine*. His theological research focuses on the interplay between the church and cultural structures such as the economy, media, and technology. He coedited with Robert Schreiter a volume of *Theological Studies* on "Theology and Globalization" in June 2008 and is currently writing a book on the topic entitled *Theology and Neoliberal Globalization: Solidarity in a World Made Indifferent*.

Sandra Yocum is University Professor of Faith and Culture at the University of Dayton. Her area of expertise is historical theology. She has served on the boards of the American Historical Association, American Society of Church History, and the College Theology Society as a president. She was Director of Graduate Studies in Religious Studies and the chair of the Department of Religious Studies and is currently the coordinator of undergraduate studies in religious studies. She is the author of *Joining* *the Revolution in Theology: The College Theology Society, 1954-2004* (Sheed and Ward, 2007), is coeditor of *Clergy Sexual Abuse: Social Science Perspectives,* and is writing a history of the US Catholic women's entrance into the formal study of theology in the twentieth century, currently titled *A Strange Impulse: Roman Catholic Women Enter the Court of the Queen of Science.*

Introduction

Vincent Miller

This book provides an introduction to Pope Francis's encyclical *Laudato Si'*. It offers expositions of its major theological and ethical themes, introductions to the science of climate change and ecology, and engagements with economic and policy debates about how to realistically change our path in order to avert extreme climate disruption. The book is designed to help nonspecialist readers understand the elements of the encyclical's argument. Chapters on the encyclical's theological and moral teachings explore Francis's teachings and locate them within the Christian theological tradition and previous papal teaching. Science and policy chapters, in addition to engaging the encyclical, provide introductions to the Fifth Assessment Report of the Intergovernmental Panel on Climate Change (IPCC). The book is designed to provide an introductory guide for those wishing to explore more fully the issues raised by *Laudato Si'* but who lack the specialist knowledge required to know where to begin.

Seeking hope in ominous times

As this book goes to press, the September 2016 carbon dioxide (CO_2) readings from Mauna Loa Observatory registered 401.02 parts per million (ppm).[1] This marks an important threshold. Coming at the end of the Northern Hemisphere growing season, September is the annual low point for atmospheric CO_2. Thus, we are unlikely to see a reading below 400 ppm for generations to come. The preindustrial average was 280 ppm. Global temperature averages have followed the increase in CO_2. August 2016 was the hottest month on record, tied with July 2016. This marked the 11th straight month to break the record for global monthly average temperature.[2] The average temperature for the first half of 2016 was 1.3°C above the nineteenth-century average.[3] The IPCC has concluded that 2°C above preindustrial levels is the highest we dare go to avoid catastrophic effects. The amount of CO_2 already released will continue to raise temperatures for some time, and we release millions of tons more each day. To stay below 2°C, we must not exceed 450 ppm. We do not have much time to act. At our current emission rate, we will pass 450 ppm in less than 30 years.

There is good news as well. In December 2015 the members of the United Nations reached a landmark agreement. The Paris Agreement set a goal of keeping global warming below 2°C and vowed to pursue keeping it below 1.5°C. The agreement calls for net zero greenhouse gas emissions after 2050. It went into effect on November 4, 2016 after the countries responsible for 55 percent of greenhouse gas emissions, including the United States and China, the two largest emitters, publicly ratified the agreement.[4] Shortly thereafter, the United States elected a president who had vowed to withdraw from the Paris Agreement.

We face more problems than climate change. Thus, this book speaks of ecological crises in the plural. In addition to climate change, CO_2 emissions are acidifying the oceans, changing the chemistry upon which the largest ecological system on the earth depends. We are overdrawing our supplies of fresh water, losing top soil, overharvesting numerous species for food and commercial use, and destroying the habitat of millions of other species with whom we share the world. By one account, overall, 50 percent of the vertebrate wildlife population has disappeared in the past 40 years.[5]

Much is being lost, and much more is in danger of being lost. What we face, however, is not a challenge to "save the planet." The planet will survive. What is more in question is the survival of *homo sapiens* and the millions of other species along for the ride in the planet we have remade. Natural processes will likely return atmospheric CO_2 to preindustrial levels over the next several hundred thousand years. If this does not happen, then evolution will continue over millions of years and new species will thrive in the altered environment humans bequeath to their successors. But the current ecosystem, of which we are a part, cannot adapt to the pace of climate disruption we have begun to unleash. We humans have already unwittingly changed the atmosphere and thus, the climate, beyond the conditions in which we evolved. When we began burning fossil fuels, we didn't know that this would be the consequence. Now we do know. Can we change?

From a technical standpoint, we have what we need to make a major start in transforming our energy system to delink our economy and society from carbon fuels. If we start in earnest now, we will quite likely have time to develop the further technical breakthroughs that will be necessary to end carbon emissions later this century. What we lack is awareness, concern, and will.

The contribution of Pope Francis's encyclical

Pope Francis's encyclical *Laudato Si': On the Care of Our Common Home* was greeted with more attention and enthusiasm than any previous papal letter. It was most commonly understood as an act of advocacy that brought the moral authority of the Catholic Church to bear on the climate crisis. It is true that *Laudato Si'* was timed to encourage the negotiations leading up to the Paris Climate Agreement. Its contribution, however, goes beyond advocacy.

Laudato Si' continues the tradition of papal social encyclicals that engage the public moral challenges of the day. Pope Benedict XVI described the Church's social doctrine as a "search for truth" that seeks to recognize and synthesize truth "from whichever branch of knowledge it comes."[6] *Laudato Si'* likewise calls for an interdisciplinary dialogue. "If we are truly concerned to develop an ecology capable of remedying the damage we have done, no branch of the sciences and no form of wisdom can be left out."[7] Francis lists philosophy, the various sciences, different religions, cultures, the arts, and poetry as necessary conversation partners (§63, 199, 201). This book aims to further that conversation with contributions on the physical science of climate, ecology, theology, economics, and policy.

But what is the specific contribution of religion in this conversation? The chapters of this book will explore many: theologies of creation, the nature of the human person, liturgy, spiritual transformation, and ethical principles. There is, however, one major contribution interwoven within all of these. It concerns the problem of anthropocentrism—our tendency to reduce the value of everything to its usefulness to humans—that is so central to questions of ecological ethics. How can we imagine, value, and act in a way that doesn't reduce the importance of all other species to how we can use them or what they can do for us? This is a decidedly difficult question. How can human knowledge avoid being centered on human interests? Even a broad concern for the complex interconnections of ecosystems can implicitly be reduced to valuation based on human needs.

Theology has long wrestled with the problem of anthropocentrism for its own reasons: the bedrock belief that God is creator not creature, and thus, God is fundamentally unlike any existing thing. Theologians and spiritual authors in all three Abrahamic religions—Judaism, Christianity, and Islam—have always been attentive to what God *is not*, in order to limit the human tendency to remake and reduce God to our own image. For this reason, theology, as a specific form of thought, has a distinctive, substantial contribution to make.

This difference between creator and creature is presumed throughout *Laudato Si'*, beginning with its title. The phrase is drawn from St Francis of Assisi's great "Canticle of the Sun." The opening lines of the encyclical quotes St Francis: "Praise be to you, my Lord, through our Sister, Mother Earth, who sustains and governs us, and who produces various fruit with colored flowers and herbs" (§1, 87). God is praised through and with our myriad sister and brother creatures: sun, moon and stars, fire, and water. The virtues of each are celebrated, but not merely because they are useful to humans. They all manifest the goodness of God, and, in their harmony, they all contribute to the praise of the Creator. The title phrase *Laudato Si'* translates as "Praised be." Thus, this explicitly religious act—praise of God—provides a form of knowledge that can understand the diversity of creation in a manner that is not centered on humans. This non-anthropocentric form of knowledge is no small thing.

This theological framing of knowledge is not a completed answer, but rather a necessary contribution to a shared dialogue about how to respond to the crises we face. We desperately need to deepen our knowledge of our connections with the world around us. But knowledge is never value-free. Indeed, Pope Francis, echoing twentieth-century critical theorists, argues that it is precisely a certain kind of objectifying and instrumental reason that has given rise to the ecological crises we face. This is the knowledge that sees mountains as obstacles to be removed in order to obtain the coal they contain, that views rivers as places to dump waste and that considers animals as protein concentrating mechanisms. We need a different kind of knowledge.

Here, another dimension of the encyclical's theological contribution emerges. We do not simply need more knowledge, but a change of heart that impacts the form of knowledge we create. Catholic theology sees humans as working under two limits: finitude and sin. The first is a frustrating, but fundamental, aspect of our creaturehood. Our knowledge is limited. The second limit, sin, corrupts the knowledge we create. The book of Genesis portrays sin as a rejection of communion with God that shatters our communion with other humans and the rest of creation. We make ourselves the center of the world—leading to interhuman strife and alienation from nature. Thus the encyclical calls both for a deepening of knowledge about ecology and for an "ecological conversion," a change of heart, so that we can learn to understand the depth of our interrelations with other creatures and act as responsible brothers and sisters, as members of an ecological family, not its masters. Too often faith and science are portrayed as opposing views of the world. Francis is calling instead for a truly deep conversation between them. What would a non-anthropocentric science and technology look like? The whole world desperately needs to find out.

On September 26, 2016, "Toughie," the last surviving Rabbs' fringe-limbed tree frog, died in a zoo in Atlanta. He was a refugee from Panama where up to 85 percent of amphibians have died and numerous species have gone extinct; part of what scientists are calling the sixth great extinction.[8] From the perspective of *Laudato Si'* we can perhaps begin to comprehend this extinction as more than say, a loss of a pest-eating animal or a potential source of pharmaceuticals. Toughie was one of the endangered species whose image was projected onto St Peter's Basilica in December 2015, in the exhibition "Fiat Lux: Illuminating Our Common Home."[9] To watch that video and to hear Toughie's forever unanswered call as the last member of his species is to encounter the dizzying abyss of extinction, to hear a voice of creation's harmony and, indeed, of its praise of God that has fallen silent forever.

Overview of the text

The 13 chapters of the book are divided into three parts. Part I focuses on the central theme of the encyclical—"everything is connected"—from the perspective of theology and science. Chapter 1, by Vincent Miller, introduces Francis's notion of "integral ecology." This concept applies the theological belief in God's triune nature to a way of seeing and acting in the world that is attentive to and concerned for our ecological interconnections. If, as Francis argues, there is a theological and moral imperative to attend to these connections, we need to deepen our knowledge of them.

The scientific chapters in this section seek to provide the general reader with essential basic literacy in the science of climate and ecology. In Chapter 2, Robert Brecha explores the biggest system of interconnection in which humans currently act: the world climate system. It explores how the earth's temperature is maintained, what human emission of greenhouse gases have done to this system and what the consequences are. This chapter also serves as a guide to the major conclusions of the IPCC Fifth Assessment Report on climate change.

Chapter 3, by Terrence Ehrman, turns to the dense system of relationships that the science of ecology aims to study. It provides an introduction to the study of the interconnection of life, considers the relationship between evolution and ecological interconnection, and reflects upon the consequences of the profound changes humans have worked upon our ecosystems. These scientific chapters both provide essential knowledge about the topics discussed in *Laudato Si'* and participate in the dialogue that the encyclical has begun.

Part II unpacks the major theological themes of *Laudato Si'*. These chapters both provide the deeper theological foundation to understand the encyclical and illuminate the ecological relevance of traditional theological themes in light of the encyclical's teaching. Chapter 4, by Elizabeth Groppe, explores the Christian understanding of creation. This chapter discusses different conceptions of the relationship between religious and scientific knowledge, contrasting Francis's dialogical and aesthetic understanding of the unity of knowledge with the conflictual relationship more commonly assumed. Groppe explores aspects of Dante's *Divine Comedy* quoted in the encyclical to evoke the relationship between Christian understandings of creation and sacrificial love.

Chapter 5, by Daniel Castillo, explores the major themes of "theological anthropology," that is, how Catholicism understands the human person. It employs Ignatius of Loyola's "Principle and Foundation" of the *Spiritual Exercises* as a key for understanding Pope Francis's thought in regard to what human persons should "know, love and serve." It considers, in particular, the problems of anthropocentrism and the human vocation to care for both fellow human beings and the rest of creation.

Chapter 6, by Douglas Christie, considers the spirituality of "painful awareness" in *Laudato Si'*. Integral ecology is not simply a call for an intellectually broad epistemology; it is also a call for a transformation of heart and awareness. Christie introduces us to the ancient contemplative traditions of Christian spirituality which have long experience in cultivating loving presence. This chapter considers the cultivation of awareness, including its painful aspects such as mourning the environmental destruction we have wrought and accepting the "gift of tears" in which the piercing of our hearts plays a fundamental role in spiritual transformation. Christie considers the many distractions that enable us to avoid openness to the world and points us toward a revolution of slow, contemplative awareness of our place within the whole of creation.

In Chapter 7, Sandra Yocum considers the sacramental and liturgical dimensions of Francis's encyclical. *Laudato Si's* concern for all creation helps illuminate the omnipresence of nature in Christian sacramental life. Yocum offers an introduction to Catholic liturgy through an ecological reading of the liturgies of the Easter Triduum: Holy Thursday, Good Friday, and the Easter Vigil.

Chapter 8, by María Teresa Dávila, considers one of the central connections in *Laudato Si'*—the link between ecological and social justice. Often, the first and greatest human victims of environmental destruction are the poor and minority communities. Dávila discusses the history of the doctrine of the "preferential option for the poor" in Catholic moral teaching and considers how Pope Francis has developed this in *Laudato Si'* as well as in his earlier document *Evangelii Gaudium*—"The Joy of the Gospel." She then explores the many contemporary circumstances—from industrial pollution to "fast fashion" in which we are implicated in both environmental destruction and exploitation of the poor and marginalized.

In Chapter 9, the economist Anthony Annett considers Pope Francis's economic vision which has been developed throughout his papacy and plays a central role in *Laudato Si'*. Francis, like his predecessors John Paul II and Benedict XVI, has been profoundly critical of the structural excesses of contemporary capitalism. Annett helpfully shows the roots of this critique in Christian doctrine—namely, a theological understanding of the human person that cannot accept the individualistic assumptions of modern economics. He contrasts the relational vision of the human person at the foundation of Catholic social thought with the individualistic *homo economicus* of post-enlightenment economics. The chapter draws evidence from contemporary economic research on happiness and human development to show that the principles of Catholic social teaching are supported by empirical research into development and human flourishing.

Section III turns to a practical response. What, given these theological and moral arguments and the state of our scientific knowledge, can we do? In Chapter 10, economists Ottmar Edenhofer and Christian Flachsland consider *Laudato Si'* as a development of Catholic social teaching. The problem of atmospheric disposal of CO_2 emissions involves what economists refer to as "common pool resources" which cannot be adequately managed by liberal procedures concerning private property. They must be managed as "global commons." Edenhofer and Flachsland explore the resources in Catholic social thought for addressing this problem.

Chapter 11, by Robert Brecha, explores the economic and technological options at our disposal for mitigating carbon emissions and the resultant climate disruption. It considers the need to transform our energy system within the context of the historical relationship between energy and development. The chapter draws from and supplements the IPCC report on the mitigation of climate change. It considers economic options for pricing carbon emissions, a range of technological means for zero emissions energy, CO_2 capture from power plant emissions and the atmosphere, and more radical climate interventions.

In Chapter 12, Daniel DiLeo explores the personal dimension of care for creation. While individual actions alone will not be enough to solve our crises, the fact remains that the choices of first world consumers have a significant impact on a planetary scale. Beyond this practical impact, DiLeo offers a theological account of the importance of individual choice for the development of virtue and for contributing to broader social change.

Chapter 13, by Erin Lothes, explores collective action for structural change. This chapter explores the religious dimensions of collective action in terms of "social love." Lothes recounts how some congregations have sustained collective action for ecological change. The chapter outlines the basic policies proposed for reducing carbon emission. As historical agreements are negotiated on the international level, their success will be made or broken on the federal and state policy level. This chapter provides knowledge essential for moral literacy in the *Laudato Si'* era.

As this book was in production persistent concerns were expressed concerning possible plans of the new US administration to remove climate change data and information from government websites.[10] Several chapters make substantial use of these data and publications. Like any publication, we cannot warrant the persistence or continued accuracy of URL links after publication. Should these websites be removed from government servers, references can be pursued at the End of Term Web Archive site.[11]

Notes

1   http://www.esrl.noaa.gov/gmd/ccgg/trends/.

2   http://data.giss.nasa.gov/gistemp/news/20160912/.

3   http://www.giss.nasa.gov/research/news/20160719/.

4   http://newsroom.unfccc.int/paris-agreement/.

5   Christine Dell' Amore, "Has Half of World's Wildlife Been Lost in Past 40 Years?" http://news.nationalgeographic.com/news/2014/09/1409030-animals-wildlife-wwf-decline-science-world/.

6   Benedict XIV, *Caritas in veritate* [Encyclical On Integral Human Development in Charity and Truth] (2009), §9.

7   Francis, *Laudato Si'* [Encyclical On the Care of Our Common Home] (2015), §63. Further references to *Laudato Si'* will be noted with a parenthetical reference to the paragraph number in the text.

8   Elizabeth Kolbert, *The Sixth Extinction: An Unnatural History* (Picador, 2015).

9   http://news.nationalgeographic.com/2016/09/toughie-rabbs-fringe-limbed-tree-frog-dies-goes-extinct; http://news.nationalgeographic.com/2015/12/151208-vatican-photo-ark-wildlife-photos-cop21/. The Fiat Lux exhibition is viewable at http://ourcommonhome.world.

10 Brady Dennis, "Scientists are frantically copying U.S. climate data, fearing it might vanish under Trump," The Washington Post, December 13, 2016; available online: https://www.washingtonpost.com/news/energy-environment/wp/2016/12/13/scientists-are-frantically-copying-u-s-climate-data-fearing-it-might-vanish-under-trump/?utm_term=.e780bb36925c. Valerie Volcovici, "Trump administration tells EPA to cut climate page from website: sources," Reuters.com, January 25, 2017. Available online: http://www.reuters.com/article/us-usa-trump-epa-climatechange-idUSKBN15906G.

11 http://eotarchive.cdlib.org.

PART ONE

Everything is connected

1

Integral ecology: Francis's spiritual and moral vision of interconnectedness

Vincent Miller

ENCYCLICAL READING GUIDE

Francis discusses "integral ecology" in Chapter IV of *Laudato Si'*

- Environmental, Economic and Social Ecology, §137–142
- Cultural Ecology, §143–146
- Ecology of Daily Life, §147–155
- The Principle of the Common Good, §156–158
- Justice Between the Generations, §159–162

The "Gaze of Jesus" is discussed in Chapter II §96–100.
"Ecological Conversion" is discussed in Chapter VI §216–221

Integral ecology is the central theme of *Laudato Si'*. It can be understood on three levels: as an understanding that interconnection is the essence of reality, as a way of seeing that can perceive interconnections among humans and the rest of creation and as a moral principle for acting in harmony with them. The concept serves as both the foundation of Pope Francis's analysis of the ecological crises we face and the basis for his proposals about how to respond. Francis contrasts integral ecology with shallow analyses that dominate our understanding of the world: forms of economics concerned only with short-term profit and technology focused on narrow solutions.

Integral ecology proposes a path of transformation that might be surprising. It suggests that moral change comes not only from will and self-control but also from attentiveness to the world around us. Francis presents responsibility as originating in a loving response to our brothers and sisters with whom we share creation, rather than on self-sacrifice for abstract ideals. In Francis's vision, love is the beginning and root of responsibility and action.

This chapter explores the meaning of Francis's term "integral ecology." We will consider integral ecology as a set of beliefs, as a way of seeing the world, and as a moral principle. We will then turn to obstacles to seeing and acting upon the interconnectedness of the world that integral ecology desires. We will consider Francis's analysis that certain forms of economics and types of technology train us to see things in a disconnected and shallow manner.

Integral ecology in *Laudato Si'*

Francis's understanding of "integral ecology" is developed throughout the encyclical where the term itself is discussed and in the many uses of the phrase "everything is connected" in its various forms. The fourth chapter of the encyclical, which begins Francis's positive response to the ecological crisis, is entitled "integral ecology." The treatment of integral ecology opens noting the need for a "vision capable of taking into account every aspect of the global crisis" including its "human and social dimensions" (§137).

Here we will discuss three interrelated aspects of Francis's treatment of integral ecology: (1) integral ecology as a set of beliefs about the nature of the world, (2) integral ecology as a way of seeing and perceiving the world, and (3) integral ecology as a moral principle to guide action.

Believing each creature is a "caress of God"

As a "vision," integral ecology is an understanding, an imagination that enables us to perceive the interconnections among all things. This understanding is based upon specific doctrines, beliefs, and scriptural themes that teach these interconnections. Francis traces this understanding to the Hebrew Scriptures or the Old Testament.

> The creation accounts in the book of Genesis contain, in their own symbolic and narrative language, profound teachings about human existence and its historical reality. . . . Human life is grounded in three fundamental and closely intertwined relationships: with God, with our neighbour and with the earth itself. (§66)

Francis notes that the "laws found in the Bible dwell on relationships, not only among individuals but also with other living beings," such as the obligation to help fallen beasts of burden, the prohibition on simultaneously hunting mothers and their young, even eggs, and Sabbath requirements that even donkeys and oxen be given rest (§68).

This vision is rooted in the Doctrine of Creation (discussed more fully in Chapter 4), that is, belief in God as the creator of all things and that all created things thus are members of one family in God. Francis cites St Thomas Aquinas's (1224–76) argument that the diversity of creatures expresses the infinite goodness of God, "which could not be represented fittingly by any one creature." The diversity of creatures in their "multiple relationships" together convey the goodness of the Creator (§86). Thus, "each creature has its own purpose. None is superfluous. The entire material universe speaks of God's love, his boundless affection for us. Soil, water, mountains: everything is, as it were, a caress of God" (§84).

The ultimate foundation of this vision of the interrelatedness of all things is the triune God who creates all things. In a passage that can be read as the spiritual core of the encyclical, Francis connects the three levels of integral ecology being discussed here with the relational nature of the triune God.

> The divine Persons are subsistent relations, and the world, created according to the divine model, is a web of relationships. Creatures tend towards God, and in turn it is proper to every living being to tend towards other things, so that throughout the universe we can find any number of constant and secretly interwoven relationships. (§240)

This understanding that all creation reflects God's triune, and relational nature gives rise to a way of perceiving the world that is attentive to interconnection.

> This leads us not only to marvel at the manifold connections existing among creatures, but also to discover a key to our own fulfilment. (§240)

We humans don't simply notice these interrelations in the world around us; we participate in them socially and ecologically. We learn from the triune God and the created world that reflects that God, that our fulfillment, and indeed our sanctification, is found not in isolation, but in embracing and deepening relationship through human solidarity and care for creation.

> The human person grows more, matures more and is sanctified more to the extent that he or she enters into relationships, going out from themselves to live in communion with God, with others and with all creatures. In this way, they make their own that trinitarian dynamism which God imprinted in them when they were created. Everything is interconnected, and this invites us to develop a spirituality of that global solidarity which flows from the mystery of the Trinity. (§240)

Our alienation from this trinitarian truth of our being is not simply a matter of ignorance or confusion. It also arises from sin: the brokenness of the world in which we all share. We are born into a world marked by division, domination, and exploitation. We do not know our interconnectedness and we are encouraged to ignore it, to think of ourselves as separated individuals. Thus the fullness of relationship to which we are called requires both a conversion of heart and a deepening of understanding. On the positive side, the triune God is not simply a distant model of relationship, a lost truth which we must discover. God is actively working in the world to draw all things into communion, "in the unity of the Holy Spirit." Salvation is God's gracious opening of our hearts to see, love, and care for all our sibling creatures.

If Pope Francis's understanding of interconnection is rooted in the triune God and trusts in the power of the Holy Spirit to bring all things into communion, he understands this vision to be accessible and available to people of any faith or none at all. Following in the footsteps of Pope John XXIII who addressed his 1963 encyclical *Pacem in Terris* on war and peace to "all men and women of good will," Francis presents *Laudato Si'* as a "dialogue with all people about our common home" (§3). Catholicism does not separate faith and reason. Both describe the same universe. Honest openness to the world will find interconnection regardless of faith commitment or lack thereof.

Laudato Si' clearly engages the other Abrahamic faiths—Judaism and Islam—in developing this understanding of reality. As we have seen, Francis roots integral ecology in the text of the book of Genesis. It is noteworthy that the papal encyclical quotes the Sufi Muslim mystical writer Ali al-Khawas's call to recognize the mystical encounter with the divine be found in listening "to what is being said when the wind blows, the trees sway, water flows, flies buzz, doors creak, birds sing, or in the sound of strings or flutes, the sighs of the sick, the groans of the afflicted."[1] Surprisingly similar teachings can be found in other faith traditions as well. Key among these is the Buddhist notion of *Pratītyasamutpāda* or "interdependence." David McMahan describes contemporary Buddhist understandings of "interdependence" as combining "empirical description, world-affirming wonder, and an ethical imperative."[2] These are striking parallels with Pope Francis's notion of integral ecology.

A way of seeing: Integral ecology as a gaze of serene attentiveness

These beliefs about God and the nature of creation inspire a way of seeing, a certain kind of gaze that seeks to perceive the interconnections in creation. Francis speaks of it as "an attitude of heart . . . which approaches life with

serene attentiveness, which is capable of being fully present to someone."
Jesus is the supreme example of this loving gaze.

> Jesus taught us this attitude when he invited us to contemplate the lilies
> of the field and the birds of the air, or when seeing the rich young man
> and knowing his restlessness, "he looked at him with love" (Mk 10:21).
> He was completely present to everyone and to everything, and in this way
> he showed us the way to overcome that unhealthy anxiety which makes
> us superficial, aggressive and compulsive consumers. (§226)

This gaze of Jesus is very important to Pope Francis. The scene of Jesus's
encounter with another rich young man—the calling of Matthew the tax
collector—is the basis for the motto on his papal coat of arms "miserando
atque eligendo." The phrase can be roughly translated as "by having mercy
and choosing him." Francis likes that the Latin word "miserando" has no
easy modern translation. It means "by having mercy" or as he prefers to say
"mercying."[3] Jesus's gaze is "mercying"; he looks upon people and things
with a love that sees the fullness of what they are and might be.

There is always more to someone or something than meets the eye. In
Matthew's case, the something more is that a wealthy tax collector for
the Roman occupiers (at that time a position closer to an extortionist
than a bureaucrat) might become a great apostle. In the case of integral
ecology, it is the patient openness to imagine and to understand the many
interconnections among the other creatures with whom we share the
world. All things around us—soil, trees, bees—are so much more than the
simple objects that meet our eyes. They are interconnected in ways that
have profound importance for our lives.

Consider soil. We know that it is more than dirt, of course. It is where
plants grow. But it is teaming with microscopic life—bacteria, fungi,
microscopic animals—all essential for supporting plant life. In ecologist
Aldo Leopold's analysis, it is the foundation of "a fountain of energy" that
flows from the sun through plants and animals which gives us life and is a
community to which we give back through care as well as our own death
and decay.[4] No soil, no humans. Curiously, the Hebrew name of the first
human in the Bible—*Adam*—is a play on words that means "being of the
soil." Integral ecology inspires us to gaze with the patient openness to learn
these connections.

This attentive and loving gaze is not limited to Jesus. The model for
integral ecology is Saint Francis of Assisi, whose great prayer-poem the
"Canticle of the Sun" provides the title for the encyclical. "Francis helps
us to see that an integral ecology calls for openness to categories which
transcend the language of mathematics and biology, and take us to the
heart of what it is to be human." Saint Francis was open to all of creation.
He responded to it, not with mere "intellectual appreciation or economic

calculus" but with love. "Just as happens when we fall in love with someone, whenever he would gaze at the sun, the moon or the smallest of animals, he burst into song, drawing all other creatures into his praise." For St Francis "each and every creature was a sister united to him by bonds of affection. That is why he felt called to care for all that exists" (§11).

Pope Francis's choice of St Francis has an important referent in debates about the ecological crisis. In 1967, the historian of science and technology, Lynn White, wrote an enormously influential essay on "The Historical Roots of Our Ecological Crisis," in which he argued that Christian anthropocentrism and belief in human dominion over creation was the historical source of the understanding of nature as object in modern secular science and technology. Thus, Christian belief is the ultimate source of the environmental destruction that began in the West. White ended his article with a curious turn. He invoked Francis of Assisi, "the greatest Radical in Christian history since Christ," as an exemplar of an alternative Christian tradition that viewed other creatures not as objects, but as brothers and sisters. He extolled St Francis's extension of humility from the individual to the entire human species so that humans could praise God together with "Brother Ant and Sister Fire."[5] White called for Francis to be named the patron saint of ecologists. Pope John Paul II declared him such in 1979, and Pope Francis made him the central figure of this first papal encyclical devoted entirely to ecological responsibility.[6]

St Francis's biography is full of stories in which he joyfully engaged other creatures, such as by preaching the Gospel to fish and birds. If you want a wild story of a human being reconciled with the rest of creation, look up the story of the St Francis and the Wolf at Gubbio, in which the saint tames a fierce wolf terrorizing the town. It sounds like a Catholic fairy tale, were it not for the decidedly odd fact that in 1872 the bones of a very large canine were found during an excavation of the town chapel San Francisco della Pace.[7]

Pope Francis argues that there is more here than "naïve romanticism." Our attitudes of love and attentiveness affect what we see and, thus, what we are able to value. This is a path of transformation worth noting. For Francis, awareness of our relationships is a path to moral transformation. Seeing can precipitate moral conversion. It is not simply a matter of our priorities following what we love; rather, it is that love enables us to see more of reality. If "we feel intimately united with all that exists, then sobriety and care will well up spontaneously." On the other hand,

> If we approach nature and the environment without this openness to awe and wonder, if we no longer speak the language of fraternity and beauty in our relationship with the world, our attitude will be that of masters, consumers, ruthless exploiters, unable to set limits on their immediate needs. (§11)

Integral ecology is a way of seeing that opens our eyes to the myriad creatures with whom we are interrelated. It helps us to understand our interdependence and thus to value the rest of creation.

This serene gaze is not something we gain all at once, rather it is something that is cultivated and developed. "Nature is filled with words of love, but how can we listen to them amid constant noise, interminable and nerve-wracking distractions, or the cult of appearances?" Francis lists several spiritual practices that can help develop our capacity for "serene harmony with creation" taking time for quiet, "reflecting on our lifestyle and ideals," and "contemplating the Creator who lives among us and surrounds us" (§225).

Openness requires developing concrete skills of attention and perception. A "serene gaze" is literally a way of seeing—open, engaged, attentive to creatures with whom we share the world. Integral ecology engages all the senses: it is looking another person in the eye; attentively listening to what they have to say; feeling the solidity of a tree and the warmth of the soil in the sun, hearing the rush of the wind in the grass, the call of a bird or the murmur of a brook; smelling the warm scent of healthy soil, the fecund muck of a wetland or the sharp message of a fox's musk.

When we see the world with an eye to these connections, we see more and differently. Coal, oil, and natural gas appear as more than hidden resources to be extracted and burned. We can see their fuller dimensions as part of the earth's climate system that has maintained the temperatures in which humans have evolved and civilization has flourished by removing carbon from the atmosphere and sequestering it underground. We can see wild animals as more than predators, nuisances, and potential game. We can attend to their myriad ecological interconnections upon which we depend. In the words that Aldo Leopold famously coined to describe what he *did not* understand as a youth when he worked to eliminate wild wolves from the American West, we can learn to think "like a mountain."[8]

Laudato Si' argues that we are made for this attention, much the way the great naturalist E. O. Wilson argues that humans have evolved an intrinsic interest in other creatures and life processes, which he terms "biophilia."[9] Openness to the rest of creation is a value shared beyond the church. The positive relationship between religion and science is a recurring theme in *Laudato Si'*. Although Francis is quite critical of the limited, narrow gaze of contemporary economics and technology, it is noteworthy that he generally portrays integral ecology and science as mutually enriching ways of seeing the world. He opens the chapter on integral ecology with a discussion of the science of ecology. Ecology studies the relationships between organisms and their environment. (See Chapter 3.) Francis expands this scientific insight from biological ecology to human society, noting that the existence of human society is as much a matter of relationship with other species as it is a matter of economic development (§137).

Francis presents this dialogue with science as one of the central projects of the encyclical. He notes in the introduction that he will draw "on the results of the best scientific research available today, letting them touch us deeply and provide a concrete foundation for the ethical and spiritual itinerary that follows" (§15). Again, ethical responsibility is a matter of being able to see what the problem is as much as possessing the will to respond to it. This incorporation of scientific knowledge into the vision of integral ecology has a profound spiritual depth. "Our goal is not to amass information or to satisfy curiosity, but rather to become painfully aware, to dare to turn what is happening to the world into our own personal suffering and thus to discover what each of us can do about it" (§19). These themes are developed further in the discussion of spirituality in Chapter 6.

Integral ecology draws from scientific attentiveness to creation. Francis believes that integral ecology can, in turn, contribute to science as well. He argues repeatedly that our current crises can only be solved if all dimensions of human wisdom are brought to bear. Faith has much to contribute to the scientific task, not least is the loving and attentive gaze of integral ecology to seek to know and love the depths of things in their complex relationships. Whereas religious fundamentalists too often provoke a conflict between faith and science (see Chapter 4), Pope Francis views them as mutually enriching ways of seeking the truth. In that regard, he quotes at length from *Lumen fidei*, the encyclical he wrote with his predecessor Benedict XVI:

> The gaze of science thus benefits from faith: faith encourages the scientist to remain constantly open to reality in all its inexhaustible richness. Faith awakens the critical sense by preventing research from being satisfied with its own formulae and helps it to realize that nature is always greater. By stimulating wonder before the profound mystery of creation, faith broadens the horizons of reason to shed greater light on the world which discloses itself to scientific investigation. (*Lumen fidei*, §34)

A guide for action: Integral ecology as a moral principle

We have discussed integral ecology as a belief that everything in the world is interconnected, which inspires us to see and seek to understand these connections. This understanding gives rise to the desire to hallow and to preserve these interconnections.

It is helpful to think of integral ecology as an expansion of the Catholic social imagination and moral framework. Catholicism has long cultivated a vision that sees social connections and the social dimensions of morality. Catholicism is a communal religion. If some forms of Christianity emphasize the individual soul's encounter with its "Personal Lord and Savior," Catholicism speaks of shared sacraments and the "communion of saints."

Pope Saint John Paul II spoke of this social imagination through his teachings on the virtue of "solidarity." Solidarity is the social dimension of love. As a virtue, it describes the ability to see the social dimension of problems and the courage to stand together in community to confront injustice and build shared flourishing. In John Paul II's words, solidarity is the "firm and persevering determination to commit oneself to the common good. That is to say to the good of all and of each individual, because we are all really responsible for all."[10] For John Paul II, solidarity is based on the underlying fact of human interdependence. We are not born self-sufficient individuals; we are born into families and communities, sheltered and nourished, educated and encouraged. All of us depend on others not only for our survival, but for our flourishing. A full human life involves accepting support from our communities and in, turn, contributing back.

Integral ecology can be thought of as the expansion of solidarity from social interdependence with other human beings, to human interdependence with the rest of creation. Just as an infant grows into an adult and learns to contribute to the society in which he or she was nurtured, so humankind must now develop a vision that allows it to perceive, appreciate, and cultivate its interconnections with the rest of creation.

Pope Francis uses integral ecology to discuss other sorts of moral connections as well. One of these is the relationship between our treatment of the poor and vulnerable and the environment. Francis has labeled disregard for the poor and vulnerable as the "culture of indifference." Described here as a "sin" (§246), indifference is the opposite of integral ecology. It is the same self-centered attitude that leads us to ignore both the poor and the ecology which sustains us. They are two sides of the same coin of indifference.

The poor are the greatest victims of climate change. Globally, the poor rely more directly "on natural reserves and ecosystemic services such as agriculture, fishing and forestry" (§25). When their ecologies are disrupted, their livelihoods collapse and they are forced to become migrants. Many of the mass migrations taking place today are linked to environmental crises caused by climate change. The International Organization for Migration reports that projections for the number of "environmental migrants" by 2050 range from 200 million to 2 billion—that is one-fifth of the projected human population.[11] Even in more developed countries, the poor and marginalized bear a disproportionate burden of environmental damage and pollution. In the United States, there is the widespread reality of "environmental racism" as major sources of industrial pollution are located disproportionately near poor communities of color (see Chapter 8).

Another set of moral connections that Francis addresses concern "the relationship between human life and the moral law" (§155). Ecological matters are connected with "life" issues. Indifference to abortion is of a piece with indifference to the rest of creation. "How can we genuinely teach the importance of concern for other vulnerable beings, however troublesome or inconvenient they may be, if we fail to protect a human embryo, even when its presence is uncomfortable and creates difficulties?" (§120) Francis challenges us to confront the mistreatment of life in "all its forms" (§230). He also speaks of attentiveness to the meaning of our own bodies:

> It is enough to recognize that our body itself establishes us in a direct relationship with the environment and with other living beings. The acceptance of our bodies as God's gift is vital for welcoming and accepting the entire world as a gift from the Father and our common home, whereas thinking that we enjoy absolute power over our own bodies turns, often subtly, into thinking that we enjoy absolute power over creation. Learning to accept our body, to care for it and to respect its fullest meaning, is an essential element of any genuine human ecology. Also, valuing one's own body in its femininity or masculinity is necessary if I am going to be able to recognize myself in an encounter with someone who is different. (§155)

Francis concludes the chapter on integral ecology with a discussion of its relationship with the common good—a foundational principle in Catholic social and political ethics. The common good is defined in Catholic social doctrine as "the sum total of social conditions which allow people, either as groups or as individuals, to reach their fulfillment more fully and more easily."[12] The common good is not simply the aggregate of individual flourishing; rather, it refers to goods that can only be achieved by humans together in society. Examples include language, culture, and justice. None of these human goods can be achieved privately. To exclude anyone from the flourishing sought by the common good undermines it. The common good is not common if it is restricted to the privileged. It concerns matters that affect all and require the contribution of all members of society in order to be achieved.[13]

The common good is in direct tension with the "rampant individualism" and concern for "instant gratification" that marks contemporary consumer societies. The environmental impact of the lifestyles we take for granted in developed nations is profoundly unsustainable and often presupposes radical inequality (§162). If every person on the earth were to live the average American lifestyle—a single-family home, transportation by car, a high-meat diet—it would require the resources of more than four times the capacity of the planet earth.

In addition to the common good among those alive now, integral ecology forces us to face the question of sustainability and the question of justice between generations. "What kind of world do we want to leave to those who come after us, to children who are now growing up?" (§160)

Laudato Si' expands the common good to include all creation. In this sense, it is similar to a key principle of Aldo Leopold's "Land Ethic." Leopold argued, "A thing is right when it tends to preserve the integrity, stability, and beauty of the biotic community. It is wrong when it tends otherwise."[14]

Integral ecology is the central theme of *Laudato Si'*. It is a transformative way of seeing that opens us up to the interconnections with the rest of creation that sustains us. By opening ourselves to the world around us, attending to it deeply, we can be moved to respond to these connections with respect, love, and care. The path of transformation begins by opening our eyes and attending to the world around us.

Obstacles to integral ecology

We have described integral ecology as a set of beliefs about the nature of reality, as a way of seeing the world that is attentive to our interdependence with the rest of creation and as a moral principle that guides us to act in a way that respects and nurtures these interconnections. Obstacles to integral ecology exist on all levels. There are many powerful belief systems that imagine human beings as independent individuals who are not bound to society or to nonhuman creatures. We are deeply influenced by moral systems that ignore our interconnections and focus only on matters of individual choice and preference. These beliefs and values can and should be criticized and debated. However, they have their greatest impact not as explicit beliefs that are used to justify actions but as implicit lenses through which we encounter the world. These ways of seeing the world are built into the structures and systems of everyday life. Often, they aren't presented to us as ideologies or values we must accept. Rather they influence us by narrowing what we can see and by limiting the ways we have to act.

These obstacles are sinful prejudices woven into the fabric of our culture, society, and economy. They are part of the sin of the world, which marks each of us deeply. Like racial and gender prejudices they often remain implicit. Yes, they appear in anger, violence, and exploitation, but they often do more of their work quietly, in unremarked judgments about what is valuable, or in even what we succeed or fail to notice. The opposite of a "gaze of serene attentiveness" is often simply unconscious indifference.

There are three major obstacles to seeing the interconnections around us. Two are explicitly discussed in *Laudato Si'*: an economic system focused on short-term profit through the production of consumer goods and a form of technology that views nature as a set of resources to be exploited. Note that Francis is not criticizing market economics or technology per se, but their narrow forms that dominate contemporary life. The third obstacle to seeing the complex interconnections in the world around us is their very complexity and the fact that the full consequences of human environmental damage takes place on spatial and timescales far beyond the perceptions of ordinary people.

All of these obstacles are woven from the two limits humans face: finitude and sin. As finite creatures our perception and knowledge are limited. We cannot see and comprehend all things. On top of that, we face the sinful struggle with self-centeredness and willful ignorance. There are things we avoid knowing because they might require change from us or demand moral action. We must be careful to distinguish the two. We should not feel guilty for what we do not know and cannot change. But we cannot allow that to insulate us from the call to lovingly attend to the crises humans have unwittingly unleashed on the rest of creation. The central call of the encyclical is to develop loving awareness: "to become painfully aware, to dare to turn what is happening to the world into our own personal suffering and thus to discover what each of us can do about it" (§19).

Economic barriers to the vision of integral ecology

Laudato Si' offers a sustained criticism of the way the contemporary global economy is conducted. Francis' critique is quite specific. He does not condemn or reject capitalism or market economies in themselves, but rather offers a powerful criticism of the contemporary economic focus on short-term growth and consumer production, while long-term economic questions of sustainability and environmental degradation are ignored. (The economic teaching of the encyclical is discussed more fully in Chapter 9.) Here we will focus on how this limited economic focus obscures the broad vision that integral ecology requires.

Market economic systems can provide very efficient means to allocate scarce resources. But they can only address issues that are priced into the cost of production. One of the biggest problems with contemporary capitalism is that so many of the full costs of resources and waste production are kept off the books. These are known as "external costs" or market "externalities"—costs associated with production that are not paid by the producer and thus not factored into the cost to consumers. The classic example of an externality is unregulated pollution from a factory. Every item that a polluting factory produces results in pollution. Thus, pollution is part of the cost of production. But this cost is not paid by the factory owner or the purchaser, but in the sickness of those who live near the factory. (See the discussion of "environmental racism" in Chapter 8.) The market fails because a part of the cost of the product is shifted onto victims outside of the market exchange. If, on the other hand, the factory owner pays to capture the pollution and includes that price in the cost of the good produced, then it ceases to be an externality. The market can then function properly to process the true price of the product.

Carbon dioxide (CO_2) emissions from the burning of fossil fuels are the most pressing form of externality in the current market. Every pound of additional CO_2 we emit into the atmosphere has a current and future cost in climate disruption. But these costs are not currently factored into the prices we pay. The same problem is present in many other forms of pollution as well as unsustainable fishing, farming, and timber harvesting.

Is it realistic to hope that those who are obsessed with maximizing profits will stop to reflect on the environmental damage which they will leave behind for future generations? Where profits alone count, there can be no thinking about the rhythms of nature, its phases of decay and regeneration, or the complexity of ecosystems which may be gravely upset by human intervention (§190).

The problem of externalities challenges the dominance of short-term measurements of economic growth. If you overfish the oceans, overharvest timber, and don't properly maintain cropland, you may make more money in the short term. But from a fuller and wiser economic perspective it is apparent that medium- and long-term growth will suffer. Fish populations will collapse, we'll run out of forests to cut down and our farmland will become less productive. Our children and grandchildren will be forced to pay these costs we have ignored. Long-term economic thinking can see that the concerns of integral ecology are a necessary part of any truly rational economic calculus. A systemic focus on short-term profits prevents business people from taking seriously the interconnections upon which future growth depends. "Efforts to promote a sustainable use of natural resources are not a waste of money, but rather an investment capable of providing other economic benefits in the medium term. If we look at the larger picture, we can see that more diversified and innovative forms of production which impact less on the environment can prove very profitable" (§191).

The limited focus of the current economic system trains consumers in shallow thinking as well. Because the market ignores most broader ecological costs, they are absent from our daily decisions as consumers. Our system of commodity exchange systematically hides the origins of the goods we consume. All we are shown is the cup of coffee, the juicy cheeseburger, and the latest gadget. We are not shown their impact in resource depletion and CO_2. Unless consumers are willing to do additional difficult work to find out the origins of the products they consume, their decisions will likely be limited to cost, appearance, and fashion. It is not that we are shallow and only care about these things. Rather it is that these are the only things shown to us. Our daily lives as consumers in this system train us to ignore the broader connections of integral ecology.[15] We are endlessly taught that everything *is not* connected.

The technocratic paradigm as an obstacle to the vision of integral ecology

Francis offers an extended critique of a certain form of technology in *Laudato Si'*. As with economics, he is not rejecting all technology.

Technology has remedied countless evils which used to harm and limit human beings. How can we not feel gratitude and appreciation for this progress, especially in the fields of medicine, engineering and communications? How could we not acknowledge the work of many scientists and engineers who have provided alternatives to make development sustainable? Technoscience, when well directed, can produce important means of improving the quality of human life. (§102–103)

Francis does, however, offer a sustained critique of a certain approach to technology, which he names the "technocratic paradigm." This modern approach to technology presumes a strong separation between the human subject and the rest of creation. Nature is viewed as "something formless, completely open to manipulation," with no intrinsic meaning in itself. This form of technology reduces nature to a purely passive object for human manipulation. Francis contrasts this modern approach to technology with earlier epochs. "Men and women have constantly intervened in nature, but for a long time this meant being in tune with and respecting the possibilities offered by the things themselves. It was a matter of receiving what nature itself allowed, as if from its own hand." The technocratic paradigm is different. "Now, by contrast, we are the ones to lay our hands on things, attempting to extract everything possible from them while frequently ignoring or forgetting the reality in front of us" (§106). This paradigm gradually expands from our treatment of nature around us, to the way we treat our fellow human beings and even ourselves (§107).

For this reason, modern "technological products are not neutral" (§107). They train us in a narrow, exploitative vision of the world whenever we use them. Technology constructs a system in which the objectification and exploitation of nature is taken for granted. The switch on my wall trains me in an entire view of the world and my role in it. I write in Southwest Ohio, where much of the electricity is provided by coal mined by the methods of mountaintop removal in the Appalachian Mountains. Every time I enter a room and turn on the lights, I'm acting within a system that presumes that our desire for light after the sun goes down justifies the destruction of the complex ecological systems of the Appalachian Mountains. Few people would openly agree, but that value judgment is built into our electrical system. But since I seldom reflect on this technocratic paradigm, the more influential lesson is disconnect. Mountaintops are destroyed, but I'm seldom confronted with my connection to that. I see only the light switch. Again, this system trains us to think that everything *is not* connected.

Francis's critique of the technocratic paradigm extends to the way in which technological analyses of problems tend to be one dimensional. Here the necessary specialization required in technical fields can cause a narrowing of analysis. "The specialization which belongs to technology makes it difficult to see the larger picture. The fragmentation of knowledge proves helpful for concrete applications, and yet it often leads to a loss of appreciation for the whole, for the relationships between things, and for the broader horizon, which then becomes irrelevant."

In its extreme, technological solutionism can silence ethical analyses and calls for radical systemic change. "Life gradually becomes a surrender to situations conditioned by technology, itself viewed as the principal key to the meaning of existence" (§110). Precisely because of its great strength, this approach to technology can become a trap which leads us to ignore the complexities of problems and the full range of human moral response that they demand. "Technology, which, linked to business interests, is presented as the only way of solving these problems, in fact proves incapable of seeing the mysterious network of relations between things and so sometimes solves one problem only to create others" (§20).

The limits of human perception

Integral ecology challenges us to expand our awareness to the relationships around us. We miss much of what is happening because of the limits of our senses and lack of knowledge. The human attention span and moral focus are honed for immanent threats. We're wired to connect a bump in the dark with a predator or enemy; to imagine moral responsibility as primarily occurring within the range of our sight and reach of our hands. But humans impact the world in ways that far exceed our immediate sense perception. Human history is sadly full of examples in which humans simply had no idea of the environmental destructiveness of their actions until it was too late—such as when soil erosion and degradation from poor agricultural practices lead to a collapse in food production. This is a story that has been replayed over and over again in the collapse of once-vital civilizations.

The interconnections between species that constitute ecosystems are so complex that even highly trained ecologists only know a small percentage of what is happening around us. E. O. Wilson discusses the thousands and thousands of species present in just one cubic foot of soil—most of them unstudied by science.[16]

Ecological destruction is similarly beyond our easy perception. Loss of biodiversity and climate change are happening very rapidly on geological timescales, but are still far too slow for most humans to notice. Species are going extinct at ten to a hundred times the normal rate, yet the pace is still too slow for us to easily perceive. In my childhood, monarch butterflies were so common as to be unremarkable. My children grow up in a world where we might see a handful a summer. My grandchildren could very well never see one, but they won't notice the disappearance. Each generation sees its situation as normal.

Here we need not only to cultivate our attention, but augment our perception. Atmospheric scientists and ecologists have developed the tools for seeing things not visible to the human eye or on spatial and timescales humans cannot directly perceive. Humans can only perceive CO_2 in very high concentrations and in the current moment. But the instruments at the Mauna Loa Observatory and the laboratory evaluation of ice cores from Antarctica enable us to perceive crucial facts about a shift in concentrations of a few hundred parts per million that are having effects now and will have growing and dire consequences for our children's and grandchildren's lives. We cannot easily perceive the interconnections among the plants and animals around us, but ecologists study the links and can alert us to the increasingly frayed ecologies upon which we depend.

Integral ecology describes the sort of sustained attention we need to develop in order to survive as a species. We need to both overcome the structures around us that train us to ignore connections and hone our ability to see and understand the ecological interconnections essential for both the survival of our species and its flourishing.

Conclusion

> Many things have to change course, but it is we human beings above all who need to change. We lack an awareness of our common origin, of our mutual belonging, and of a future to be shared with everyone. This basic awareness would enable the development of new convictions, attitudes and forms of life. A great cultural, spiritual and educational challenge stands before us, and it will demand that we set out on the long path of renewal. (§202)

Integral ecology is one of the major contributions of *Laudato Si'*. It develops the long-standing Catholic moral valuing of relationships from the social to the ecological level. Integral ecology is not simply a moral principle; it is a way of seeing that seeks to be alert and attentive to interconnections. Rather than accept a simplistic appraisal of the world as a collection of dead objects available for human manipulation, integral ecology inspires us to probe deeper, to seek to understand the complex and delicate interconnections that sustain the life of creation, including our own. Once we begin to know the complexity of creation, we can more deeply love and protect it. Knowing, loving, and caring are all part of the communion to which the triune God is drawing all creation.

Questions

1 What specific Christian beliefs and scriptural teachings does integral ecology depend upon?

2 What does it mean to say that integral ecology is a way of seeing?

3 How does Pope Francis's teaching in *Laudato Si'* build upon previous papal teaching?

4 What is the relationship between integral ecology and science?

5 How is "integral ecology" an expansion of Catholic social concern, especially the notion of solidarity?

6 This chapter argues that integral ecology provides a different path of transformation. Pope Francis suggests that the path to change begins not with self-control or denial, but with lovingly attending to the world around us. Reflect on this. How does what you love affect your actions? Have you ever witnessed someone change because their eyes were opened to something new?

Notes

1 *Laudato Si'*, §233, n. 159.

2 David L. McMahan, *The Making of Buddhist Modernism* (Oxford: Oxford University Press, 2009), 150. Thich Nhat Hanh is among the most influential teachers on this topic, which he terms "interbeing." See *The Heart of Understanding: Commentaries on the Prajnaparamita Heart Sutra* (Berkeley, CA: Parallax Press, 1988, 2009). Joanna Macy is an important voice connecting this doctrine with ecological consciousness and action. See *Mutual Causality in Buddhism and General Systems Theory: The Dharma of Natural Systems* (Albany, NY: State University of New York Press, 1991). Her practical teachings are available at http://www.joannamacy.net.

3 "A Big Heart open to God," *America* 209, no. 8 (September 30, 2013): 16. http://americamagazine.org/pope-interview.

4 Aldo Leopold, *A Sand County Almanac and Sketches Here and There* (Oxford: Oxford University Press, 1968), 216.

5 Lynn White, "The Historical Roots of Our Ecologic Crisis," *Science* 155, no. 3767 (March 10, 1967): 1203–07.

6 John Paul II, *Bula Inter Sanctos Proclaiming Saint Francis of Assisi as Patron of Ecology*, November 29, 1979.

7 Adrian House, *Francis of Assisi* (Paulist Press, 2003), 181. House discusses many different accounts of St Francis's interaction with animals, 177–82.

8 Leopold, *Sand County Almanac*, 129–32.

9 Edward O. Wilson, *Biophilia* (Cambridge, MA: Harvard University Press, 1984).

10 John Paul II, *Sollicitudo rei socialis* [Encyclical: On Social Concern](1987), §38. See the extended discussion of solidarity in the Vatican's "catechism" of the Church's social teaching: *The Compendium of the Social Doctrine of the Church*, §192–196. Available at: http://www.vatican.va/roman_curia/pontifical_councils/justpeace/documents/rc_pc_justpeace_doc_20060526_compendio-dott-soc_en.html

11 https://www.iom.int/complex-nexus#estimates.

12 Second Vatican Council, *Gaudium et spes* [Pastoral Constitution on the Church in the Modern World], §26.

13 See the *Compendium of the Social Doctrine of the Church*, §164–170.

14 Leopold, *Sand County Almanac*, 224.

15 See Vincent Miller, "Slavery and Commodity Chains: Fighting the Globalization of Indifference," *America Magazine*, January 2, 2014. http://americamagazine.org/content/all-things/slavery-and-commodity-chains-fighting-globalization-indifference. For a more comprehensive treatment of commodification, see Vincent Miller, *Consuming Religion: Christian Faith and Practice in a Consumer Culture* (New York: Continuum, 2004).

16 E. O. Wilson, "Within One Cubic Foot," *National Geographic,* 217, no. 2 (February 2010), 62–83, http://ngm.nationalgeographic.com/2010/02/cubic-foot/wilson-text/1.

2

The physical science of climate change

Robert Brecha

ENCYCLICAL READING GUIDE

- Ch. 1 What is Happening to Our Common Home?
- Esp. "Pollution and Climate Change," §17–26

"Ecological Conversion" is discussed in Chapter VI §216–221

This chapter provides a primer of how the earth's climate works and presents some of the evidence for past and current climate change. The key point is that there is a qualitative difference between current changes in climate and those of the distant past—things are changing much more rapidly now. It is precisely for this reason that we are concerned about how humans have contributed to recent climate change and that we have come to the realization that our societies must make conscious decisions about how to proceed toward the future.[1]

It should be noted that the papal encyclical does not claim to pronounce on the truth of scientific matters. Rather, in Francis's words, it draws "on the results of the best scientific research available today, letting them touch us deeply and provide a concrete foundation for the ethical and spiritual itinerary that follows" (§15). *Laudato Si'* presumes that scientists have a good understanding of the basic functions of the earth's physical systems. Francis offers a brief summary of the scientific consensus on climate change:

A very solid scientific consensus indicates that we are presently witnessing a disturbing warming of the climatic system. In recent decades this warming has been accompanied by a constant rise in the sea level and, it would appear, by an increase of extreme weather events, even if a scientifically determinable cause cannot be assigned to each particular phenomenon . . . a number of scientific studies indicate that most global warming in recent decades is due to the great concentration of greenhouse gases (carbon dioxide, methane, nitrogen oxides and others) released mainly as a result of human activity. (§23)

This consensus is reflected in the overwhelming body of scientific literature on climate change.[2] That is not to say that there are no open questions. Scientists around the world are constantly seeking to better understand many details of how our planet's systems work.

The earth system

At its heart, the climate system of the earth is very simple. Our sun is the main driving force that makes everything work and that has been understood for a very long time. From the start of the nineteenth century, scientists began investigating some of the details of earth's climate. This introductory section will review the historical development in thinking about climate, look at basic scientific principles needed to explain why our planet is comfortably habitable, and explain what scientists mean when they put together models of the earth system. Although not all scientists would agree with this characterization, the idea that there is a "climate science" somehow separate from other fields of science is misleading. Fundamentally, physics, chemistry, biology, and geology are the fields of scientific inquiry that come together in studying the earth's climate as one application of their theoretical and experimental investigations.

Intuitively we know that the sun shines on the earth and the earth's surface (including the oceans) heats up. The more subtle question is how the earth "knows" when to stop heating up and how this level changes.

All objects radiate energy, and the amount radiated increases very strongly as the temperature of the object increases. Furthermore, the color of an object (think of an electric stove burner) can give us information about its temperature. The sun itself has a temperature of about 6000°C on its surface and gives off (radiates) mainly the visible light we know through the spectrum of colors of the rainbow, as well as some infrared and ultraviolet light. Your stove burner starts out giving off only infrared radiation which we sense as heat—we know the burner is on when we get close to it. As an object heats up even more, we begin to see it turn reddish orange; we know it is much hotter than it had been simply by looking at its color. Still, most of the energy given off by the burner is in the infrared part of the spectrum.

With that background, we can explain the temperature of the earth as being a balance between incoming solar radiation and the outgoing radiation given off by the earth in the form of heat or infrared radiation. The earth will itself heat up until the incoming and outgoing energies balance. Since incoming and outgoing radiation must remain in balance, if the sun were to cool down slightly and less sunlight would reach the earth, the earth would in turn adjust by cooling down slightly and its outgoing radiation would decrease.

A good source for much of the historical context that follows is Spencer Weart's book *The Discovery of Global Warming* and its accompanying detailed webpage. Beginning around 1800, scientists such as Joseph Fourier realized that the atmospheric layer was key to understanding the earth's energy balance and what keeps the planet warm.[3] Without an atmosphere, one would expect the temperature of any part of the surface to plummet as soon as the rotation of the earth moved that part away from direct sunlight. In fact, the energy balance condition allows us to calculate that the earth's temperature as seen from space to be about –18°C; without an atmosphere the earth would behave like the moon: warm in direct sunlight and freezing cold on the dark side.[4] Fourier realized that the thin atmospheric layer acted like a blanket holding energy near the surface and slowing down the escape of energy into space. The comparison is often made to the functioning of a greenhouse, and for that reason, the gases contributing to trapping heat near the earth's surface are referred to as greenhouse gases. The major anthropogenic greenhouse gases in the earth's atmosphere are carbon dioxide (CO_2), methane (CH_4), halocarbons (CFCs and HCFCs), and nitrous oxide (N_2O). It is important to recognize that scientists consider the "forcing" of climate due to *excess* amounts of these gases emitted to the atmosphere beyond natural occurrences. Water vapor also plays a key role in the greenhouse effect, but quantities of this gas react to the temperature, increasing as the temperature rises due to other greenhouse gases increases.[5]

WEATHER VS. CLIMATE

We can think of the difference between *weather* (day-to-day fluctuations in temperature, precipitation, barometric pressure, etc.) and *climate* as being one of timescales. The climate is an average over weather conditions; for example, when considering the surface temperature of the earth, climate scientists usually look at a 30-year average to define the baseline, and look at deviations with respect to that longer-term average, not concerned much by year-to-year fluctuations. Those who claim that climate projections 50 years into the future are not to be believed because we cannot even predict the weather one week in advance are mixing these concepts.

Jumping ahead to the middle of the nineteenth century, John Tyndall in England carried out a long series of laboratory experiments to investigate how infrared radiation is transmitted through or absorbed by various gases.[6] Note that these were physics and chemistry laboratory experiments carried out under controlled conditions. Tyndall found that both visible and infrared radiation passed easily through the main atmospheric constituents, nitrogen and oxygen. In contrast, gases such as CO_2 and water vapor (he tested many others as well) strongly absorbed infrared radiation in ways that he could quantify. Therefore, he concluded, the gases making up 99 percent of the atmosphere could not be responsible for the warming-blanket effect, but rather that minority constituents are very strong absorbers of infrared radiation, and thus act to trap energy (heat) near the earth's surface.

The implication of Tyndall's laboratory work was an understanding that increasing the amount of infrared-absorbing gases in the atmosphere could change the overall energy balance temporarily. Tyndall provided the basic knowledge of how the planetary temperature level works, which guides our understanding today. As seen from above the atmosphere, the outgoing and incoming radiation must be equal in the long run. As the atmosphere gets "thicker" with gases like CO_2 and CH_4, the surface has to heat up more to be able to push enough infrared radiation out through the atmosphere to provide that necessary balance. However, as the earth warms near the surface, more water vapor will be present in the atmosphere; since water vapor is a strong greenhouse gas, the earth must heat up even more to overcome this additional blanketing—a feedback loop is created.

Moving ahead to the end of the nineteenth century, Svante Arrhenius[7] was interested in understanding the relationship between the amount of CO_2 in the atmosphere and the occurrence of ice ages. Whereas Tyndall was probably more motivated to explain the dampening effect of atmosphere on what would otherwise be extreme temperature swings from day to night, Arrhenius was looking at "climate change" as we would understand the term today. Using the background experimental work of Tyndall on the absorption of infrared radiation by CO_2 and water vapor, Arrhenius painstakingly calculated how the energy balance of the earth would change if the amount of CO_2 were to be cut in half, or if it were to be doubled. More absorbing gas would, on the one hand, mean that the surface temperature would rise; less absorbing gas would, on the other hand, lead to a decrease in temperature. It is hard to convey today how difficult his work must have been. With only pencil and paper, he not only figured out how temperatures would be altered for different gas concentrations, but also calculated how average temperatures would change for different latitudes, realizing that high latitudes (near the poles) would be significantly more sensitive to perturbations than lower latitudes—a phenomenon we clearly observe today.

Arrhenius is notable not only because his results are still reasonably accurate, but also because he created what was really the first climate model.

Scientists use the word "model" to describe how they put together known mathematical equations of relevant physics and chemistry, and then solve those equations for variables of interest. A climate model today can range from ones that are even more basic than what Arrhenius used, to extremely complex global climate models that must be run for long periods of time on supercomputers before output answers are found. At every level, models must include approximations and simplifications; the important point is the purpose a given model is meant to serve. To calculate simple radiation balance, one equation with well-known parameters may suffice; specific local effects due to long-term climate change are more difficult to project with a great degree of confidence. However, regional trends, for example, that Mexico and the US Southwest will likely face a decrease in precipitation, while the US Northwest can expect increases in annual precipitation, are possible to make.[8]

The scientific explorations of Fourier, Tyndall, and Arrhenius, as well as many others not mentioned in this short summary, are important in that they laid the foundations for how we understand the most fundamental processes of the earth's climate even today. What makes these discoveries all the more remarkable is that much of the fundamental physics and chemistry of molecular structure (the properties of molecules that exactly determine how effectively they absorb radiation) and of blackbody radiation (the distribution of wavelengths and amount of energy being emitted by objects) were not well understood until the early twentieth century. Without delving too deeply into areas of philosophy and history of science, the episodes described in this section provide a nice illustration of the steady incremental progress that was made over a long period of time in probing nature and trying to build connections between observations and theory, much of which having been developed independently of modern considerations of anthropogenic influence on the earth's climate.

Past climate change

The earth's climate is always changing—so why should we worry about consequences of a changing climate now? One could take a geological view of the earth that, since humans are part of the earth system, changes that we produce are also just an extension of natural processes and will therefore be "taken care of" through natural adaptation. In this section, we will examine the record of past changes to get a sense of the range of natural fluctuations in climate. Along the way we will learn a bit about how we know what we know about climate in the distant past. Finally, we will also look at relevant timescales over which climate changes have occurred in the past, an important piece of information that will carry over into the subsequent section.

The earth system is both incredibly robust and exquisitely sensitive. We return to the latter below when looking at how small changes in the earth's orbit around the sun can have large consequences. As for robustness, we can look at the question of why the level of CO_2 in the atmosphere is what it is. Indirect data from the past several tens of millions of years show that concentrations of CO_2 haven't varied by more than about a factor of two or three[9]; oxygen concentrations have also remained very constant. Why should that be so, and why couldn't CO_2 suddenly rise to 20 percent concentration in the atmosphere and oxygen decrease to a fraction of a percent? The statement that the earth system is sensitive comes from realizing that currently the concentration of CO_2 is about 400 ppm (parts per million) or 0.04 percent. Before industrialization, this level was about 280 ppm. These may seem like vanishingly small quantities of gases, but an increase of only a few hundred parts per million is precisely the amount scientists estimate will change the earth's climate dramatically. Returning to the work of Tyndall, it is these small concentrations of greenhouse gases that are responsible for absorbing the infrared radiation trying to escape from the earth's surface.

A quick answer is that over very long periods of time, on the order of hundreds of thousands to millions of years, a naturally stabilizing feedback cycle serves to keep CO_2 fairly constant, with the essential processes being volcanic activity and the weathering of rocks. Volcanoes emit relatively small amounts of CO_2 into the atmosphere and thus contribute to enhancing the greenhouse effect.[10] As CO_2 concentrations increase, temperatures rise (slightly, and over thousands of years), leading to more precipitation since the warmer atmosphere can hold more moisture. More precipitation means more erosion of rock with runoff into the oceans; it is this process that completes the cycle, since the effect of erosion is to remove CO_2 indirectly and through surface chemical reactions and bury that CO_2 in compounds deep in the ocean. Thus, the negative feedback loop operates to stabilize CO_2—more CO_2 leads to more precipitation and weathering, which results in removal of CO_2. The opposite process occurs as well, with lower temperatures resulting in less weathering and slower removal of CO_2 from the atmosphere into the deep oceans.

This stabilizing feedback was not understood until fairly recently. As early as eighteenth century, however, scientists began to realize the earth has experienced major deviations from the world as we know it today, including periods of much greater glacial coverage (e.g., far south of today's Great Lakes in the United States). One can only imagine the consternation that might be caused by knowing *that* such changes had occurred, but in not having any idea as to *why* it had happened. It was in an attempt to answer this question that led Arrhenius to look at CO_2 concentrations in the atmosphere. We now know that the most recent deglaciation happened from about 12,000 years ago.

Not until the late twentieth century did scientists find clever ways of measuring not only CO_2 levels from the distant past, but also local temperatures and sea levels. The key to these measurements was that snow and ice in Antarctica is permanent and constantly accumulating, as new snow falls each year. The ice therefore builds up layers, with older layers being further from the surface. In addition, the layers of ice trap small bubbles of air, and that air contains the same mixture of molecular gases that was present in the atmosphere when the snow originally fell. CO_2 is well mixed in the atmosphere, that is, overall the concentration is the same everywhere on the earth. This is obviously not the case for temperature, so the samples of air in Antarctic ice can only give information about the historical temperature on that continent.

Figure 2.1 shows data from an Antarctic ice core—scientists drill down into the ice and extract a cylindrical core of ice that can then be thinly sliced, and each slice can be analyzed for the percentage of CO_2 and other gases.[11] The tests used to determine temperature and relative sea levels are more complicated but have been increasingly refined over the past few decades. In Figure 2.1 the present (year 0) is on the left-hand edge of the plot. The top half of the graph is a set of data points for CO_2 concentrations in "parts per million volume (ppmv)." We see that over the past 400,000 years atmospheric CO_2 has varied between about 180 and 300 ppmv (0.018%–0.030 concentration). Similar data sets go back even further, to at least 800,000 years.[12]

Although somewhat irregular, a clear pattern can be seen in the data with a periodicity of approximately 100,000 years between peaks in CO_2 concentrations, times which we now identify as interglacial, or relatively warm, periods. After each peak in CO_2 (here, that means moving from right

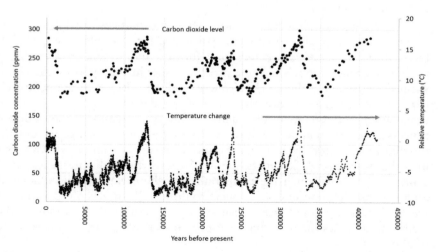

FIGURE 2.1 *Ice core data from Antarctica showing (global) carbon dioxide levels and (local) temperature changes over time. Data available at ftp://ftp.ncdc.noaa. gov/pub/data/paleo/icecore/antarctica/vostok/*

to left) the concentration begins to drop again. In the bottom half of Figure 2.1, the relative deviation in temperature (in °C) is shown; it is clear that temperature and CO_2 concentrations are strongly correlated. That is, over more than 400,000 years, high CO_2 levels have been accompanied by high temperatures.

These observations lead to several questions. First, since correlation is not the same as causation, can we unravel from these data which came first, the temperature change or the CO_2 change? Second, whichever one came first, what was the cause of that initial change? Third, since the two move along together, is there simply a causality in one direction, or is there a feedback mechanism that leads to a mutual reinforcement of temperature and CO_2 levels? Finally, how does the process reverse direction instead of just continuing in the direction of increase (or decrease) of both temperature and CO_2?

As it turns out, there is a relatively straightforward set of interconnected answers to these questions. We have already learned that Arrhenius found a link between CO_2 levels and temperature. In the mid-twentieth century, it was realized that over long periods of time the shape of the earth's orbit around the sun changes very slightly, becoming more or less elliptical. At the same time the north-south axis of the earth bobs up and down slightly, and wobbles around like a spinning top on a table. The times over which these changes occur are tens of thousands of years, and although the overall yearly average amount of sunlight falling on the earth does not change, its distribution between the hemispheres changes slightly. That small change in how sunlight falls through the seasons (the Northern Hemisphere appears to be particularly important for this process) is enough to trigger the growth and retreat of glaciers.[13]

With changes in temperature, however, come changes in CO_2 levels; as oceans warm, they absorb CO_2 less efficiently, for example. Then, as CO_2 levels increase, temperature increases further, and so on, in a so-called positive feedback loop. The same process works in the opposite direction, with decreased Northern Hemisphere sunlight, lowered temperatures, lowered CO_2, etc. Therefore, the cause of the glacial cycles is triggered by input sunlight and temperature changes. However, because of the feedback processes, the earth system will react to either an initial change in sunlight distribution (natural cycles) or a perturbation in the amount of CO_2 put into the atmosphere. Scientists speak of the earth's "climate sensitivity," a measure of how much the temperature of the surface would change if atmospheric CO_2 concentrations were to double. Without consideration of feedback processes, the "bare" sensitivity would be about 1°C; adding in the feedback increases the warming to approximately 3°C, with an uncertainty of about ±1°C.[14]

Returning to Figure 2.1 we can see that the upper limit for CO_2 concentrations over the past 400,000 years has been about 300 ppmv; the current concentration of CO_2 is 400 ppmv, well outside of natural cyclic levels, with the excess arising from human combustion of fossil fuel carbon to create CO_2. Human activities are pushing the earth into a new state that has certainly not been experienced by our species during its 200,000 years of existence.

Temperature changes are not the only indicator of a changing climate. However, we look one more time at a composite record of both indirect (proxy) and direct temperature measurements to emphasize some key points. In Figure 2.2 we show the temperature deviation from a reference level over the period since the last deglaciation about 12,000 years ago.[15] Global average temperatures have remained within a fairly narrow range of approximately ±0.5°C. This is to be compared with the goal set by the international community of not exceeding a temperature change of 2°C with respect to nineteenth-century values, a change that would be well off the top edge of the plot in Figure 2.2. That is, the expressed international goal implies accepting an average change in temperature four times larger than any natural deviations experienced during all of human civilization.

More worrisome to many scientists is the other feature shown in Figure 2.2. The temperature anomalies in Figure 2.2 show a relatively slow rise emerging from the last glacial maximum, followed by a plateau lasting about 5,000 years, and then a slow decrease for nearly another 5,000 years. Natural processes due to orbital variations and the natural CO_2 regulation cycle operate at a very slow rate of change on a timescale of many thousands of years. The sharp upward spike at the end of the temperature anomaly record is the change imposed on the system by human activity. While not

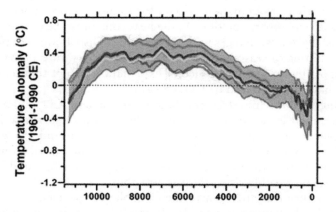

FIGURE 2.2 *Global average surface temperature anomaly (deviation) from a reference level. Time moves forward toward the right, that is, "today" is at the right-hand edge of the graph. Note the (relatively) slow change in temperature over the past 11,000 years except for the rapid change within the past hundred years or so. From Shaun Marcott et al., "A Reconstruction of Regional and Global Temperature for the past 11,300 Years," Science 339, no 6124 (March 7, 2013):1198-1201." Reprinted with permission from AAAS.*

in and of itself conclusive, these disparate rates of change seem to indicate strongly that the anomalous temperature behavior of the past decades is not just part of a normal natural cycle.

Before moving on to discuss indicators of a changing climate that are observed today, we can summarize the key points of this section. While the earth's climate has indeed always changed through natural processes, there is abundant evidence from records of past climate that the magnitude and rapidity with which climate is changing now are qualitatively different. This strongly suggests that we are in a different epoch now, one often referred to as the "Anthropocene" due to the dominance of human influence on global changes.

Evidence of current climate change

In this section we will briefly discuss some of the evidence that leads to the conclusion that the earth's climate system is changing in observable ways. No single piece of data can be sufficient to prove that the climate is changing, and it is even more difficult to attribute with 100 percent certainty any given changing physical parameter to a specific bit of CO_2 emissions. However, as we have seen above, scientists predicted over a century ago that adding excess CO_2 to the atmosphere would lead to an enhanced greenhouse effect and therefore to warming of the surface of the planet. When we put together the fact that humans have been burning fossil fuels at an ever-increasing rate for the past two centuries (but most emissions have occurred in the past half century!) with an examination of data for things like ocean acidity, which increases due to absorption of CO_2, the heat content of the oceans, sea-level rise, mass of glaciers, changes in the geographical distributions of plants and animals, shifting of seasons, as well as average temperatures, it has thus far been impossible to find any coherent explanation except that temperature changes have been induced by CO_2 emissions.

Starting with the industrial revolution, atmospheric CO_2 concentrations have been increasing due to fossil-fuel combustion (a slow rise had been taking place previously due to net deforestation around the globe). In Figure 2.3 we see the complete data set for directly measured monthly CO_2 levels from 1958, already starting well above the "background" value of 280 ppmv, and steadily rising to over 400 ppmv.

We now turn our attention to the cryosphere—glaciers, sea ice and ice sheets, and links between ice and sea levels. When ice floating on the ocean begins to melt, such as around the North Pole in the Arctic, it may be an indicator of warmer temperatures, but the meltwater will have no effect on sea levels. (When ice cubes in a glass of water melt, the level of water in the glass does not change.) But most of the frozen water on our planet is stored in Antarctica (primarily) and Greenland, with much smaller amounts in other land-based glaciers. During the last ice age, when glaciers were much more extensive than at present, sea levels were 150 m lower than today; conversely, if all of the ice on the planet were to turn to water, sea levels would be about 70 m higher compared to today.

Satellites have been constantly measuring the extent of the frozen areas of the Arctic over the past few decades. There are very large annual variations, with a maximum extent typically occurring in March of each year, and a corresponding minimum each September. In Figure 2.4 we show the September minimum Arctic sea ice extent over the past few decades

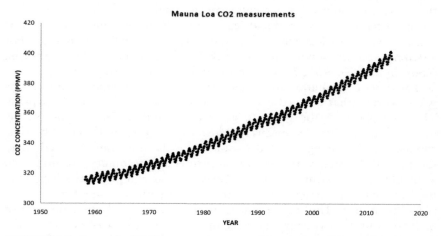

FIGURE 2.3 *Record of CO_2 measurements at Mauna Loa Observatory in Hawai'i. Data available from http://www.esrl.noaa.gov/gmd/ccgg/trends/full.html*

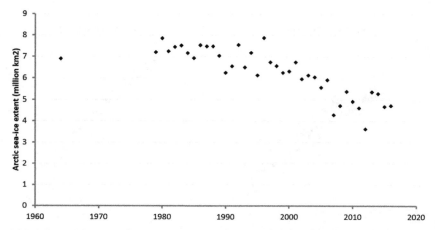

FIGURE 2.4 *Extent of Arctic sea ice in the month of September, as measured by satellites. Sea ice, unlike land-based ice sheets or glaciers, does not contribute to rising sea levels. Data from National Snow and Ice Data Center (NSIDC) http://http://nsidc.org/data/seaice_index/archives.html*

(with one rougher independent estimate from early satellite photos in 1964). There is a clear decline in sea ice, and in fact the rate is significantly faster than what had been predicted by scientists just a decade or two ago.

More worrisome from the point of view of both sea-level rise and land-based glaciers, often the source of fresh water for many societies, is the increasing pace of melting of ice sheets and glaciers over time. As shown in Figure 2.5 for Antarctica and Greenland, exquisitely sensitive measurements using a pair of satellites named GRACE show a significant ongoing loss of mass from these ice sheets, resulting in increasing sea levels. In each case, these represent only a tiny percentage of the total mass of the ice sheet (360 Gt of melted ice raise the global sea level by about one millimeter), but as warming increases, it is expected that the rate of melt will also increase. (For a striking account of what this looks like on the ground, see the multimedia report in the *New York Times*, "Greenland is Melting Away."[16])

The other contribution to sea-level rise is due to thermal expansion—as water warms (that trapped energy or heat we saw earlier) it will expand. The only place for the water to go is in expanding the "height" of the ocean, although that also means that lower-lying spots on the coast become submerged. The change in global sea level has been measured directly over the past 100 years, with different measurement techniques having been available over the course of time.[17] Coastal areas and port cities have long used manual tidal gauges; now satellite measurements supplement these older techniques. The main point to note here is exactly that the rate of increase is itself increasing—there is an acceleration in sea-level rise as the data curve bends more strongly upward.

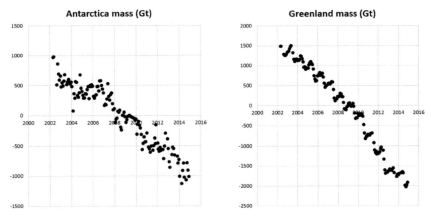

FIGURE 2.5 *Measurements of changes in mass of Antarctica and Greenland, representing loss of ice due to melting. The meltwater translates directly to sea-level rise. Data from the GRACE satellites available at http://grace.jpl.nasa. gov/mission/grace/*

Finally, we arrive at temperature as one measure of our changing climate. Several groups around the world have been monitoring global temperatures directly, and many efforts have been made to use "proxy" measurements to determine historical temperatures more indirectly. Examples of the latter include tree rings, bore holes in the earth, and even glacier extents and written records. The left-hand side of Figure 2.6 shows a compilation of proxy records going back over 1,000 years together with more modern direct temperature measurements. As would be expected, there is an increasing amount of uncertainty in measurements going further back in time; in spite of that, it is very unlikely that global average temperatures have been as high as they are now in the past thousand years. We mentioned earlier the qualitatively different character of temperature anomalies over the past several decades compared to the long-time record; current rates of change are about ten times larger than when the planet emerged from the last ice age.

On the right-hand side of Figure 2.6 we zoom in to look at more recent changes in global average temperature. There is no apparent stop to warming over time, as is sometimes claimed by those who doubt the existence of climate change.[18] On the other hand, there is a fairly large natural variability within the climate system, which should not surprise us, given the complexity of processes involved in both trapping energy near the surface and distributing that energy both around the earth's surface and between the land, atmosphere, and the oceans.

One final point should be made about signals of climate change. When we read that, "2015 was the warmest year on record," the reference is to surface air temperature, which changes more easily than water temperature. However, the ocean actually plays the largest role in absorbing the heat

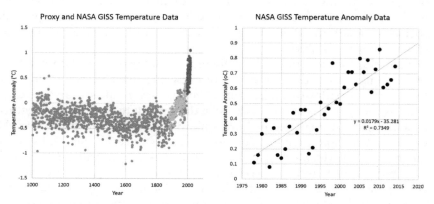

FIGURE 2.6 *Combined "proxy" and directly measured temperature data for the past millennium (left-hand side) and a zoomed-in version (right-hand side) for the past four decades showing a relatively continuous rise in temperature. Temperatures are global averages and given with respect to the average value of the 1960s–1990s. Data from http://data.giss.nasa.gov/gistemp/*

trapped by greenhouse gases—over 90 percent of the total, as has been confirmed by observations of temperatures at different depths in the oceans. It is precisely this stored ocean energy, a small fraction of which is released in El Niño years such as 1983, 1998, and 2015, that can then change the entire global average atmospheric temperature significantly.[19]

How will climate change in the future?

There are two fundamentally different sources of uncertainty in determining future climate change. First, although the basic physical principles of the climate are well understood, there is still plenty of complexity left when it comes to understanding exactly how the earth system will respond to a given amount of additional CO_2 or CH_4 being added to the atmosphere. A typical example of this uncertainty was referenced above with respect to the so-called "climate sensitivity," which expresses the amount of temperature increase to be expected if the CO_2 level were to double from the preindustrial levels of about 280 ppmv to 560 ppmv, with the best estimate being 3.0°C ± 1.5°C.

The second fundamental source of uncertainty is in projecting exactly how much CO_2 human societies will emit over the next several decades— that is, a socioeconomic uncertainty. Put simply, we have under our collective control the ability to determine how much CO_2 will be emitted. Over the past few years a set of scenarios has been developed as a standardized input to international climate change computer modeling efforts. These scenarios are referred to as Representative Concentration Pathways or RCPs. Each RCP considers a set of plausible pathways for population and economic growth, as well as for technological developments. The relevant output is yearly CO_2 emissions, as well as the cumulative concentration of CO_2 in the atmosphere. The goal of the RCP exercise is to bracket possible socioeconomic futures, matching each with a set of outcomes for relevant climate system variables.

Scenarios for the future will be discussed in more detail in Chapter 11 of this volume dedicated to mitigation of climate change. Here, it is sufficient to say that the pathways range from a "business-as-usual" scenario (referred to as RCP8.5) with emissions increasing throughout the twenty-first century, to a scenario with emissions decreasing to zero in the second half of the century (RCP2.6). These two scenarios are illustrated by the solid lines in Figure 2.7a, in which other RCPs are also shown.[20] We will use these two examples in what follows here. Each of the emission pathways ends up corresponding to a concentration of atmospheric CO_2 by the end of the century, which in turn leads to a temperature change that can be determined within the range of scientific uncertainty discussed above.

One of the interesting scientific results that has come to light in the past few years is that, for all of its inherent complexity, temperature change is expected to respond in a fairly simple way to the total cumulative CO_2

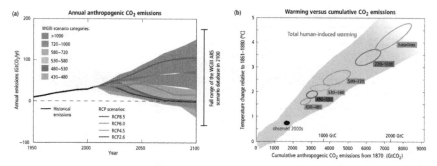

FIGURE 2.7 *(a) Annual CO_2 emissions under different scenarios for future energy use and economic development. Currently we are following most closely the higher-emission pathways. (b) Expected eventual global average temperature increase depends on the total cumulative amount of CO_2 emissions (shown here from 1870 on into the future). From IPCC AR5 Synthesis Report Fig. SPM.5 Used with Permission.*

emissions since the beginning of the industrial age. Choosing a given amount of total emissions is equivalent to choosing a final average temperature at which the earth reaches equilibrium. On the graph shown in Figure 2.7, following a chosen CO_2 amount upward from the horizontal axis (say, 3700 Gt CO_2, which is equivalent to 1000 Gt Carbon) one would intersect the (fuzzy) curve around the oval labeled "530-580 ppmv." Moving horizontally to the left from there, the vertical axis is intercepted at about 2.5°C, which would be the expected equilibrium temperature for that amount of emissions. This concept is referred to as a "carbon budget"; if you choose your desired end-temperature, there is a corresponding budget for total emissions that must be maintained so as not to exceed that temperature.[21]

We finish up this section by looking at the expected changes for various physical variables under different climate change scenarios.[22] In the upper left of Figure 2.8, we see the global average surface temperature change going forward toward the end of the century under the RCP8.5 (business-as-usual; emissions keep increasing) and the RCP2.6 (emissions peak soon and decrease to zero by the end of the century) scenarios. Under the latter scenario, temperature change is maintained at below 2°C with respect to late-nineteenth-century values with a reasonably high level of probability; this is the goal to which the nations of the world have made a commitment, at least in principle. Many scientists involved in climate studies believe that this 2°C target, while not guaranteed to be safe, is an upper limit beyond which we should not push the earth system, precisely because there is a fair degree of certainty that most consequences would be negative, and because there is a significant possibility of catastrophic consequences. One example of the latter would be a shift into irreversible decline of the Antarctic and Greenland ice sheets, leading to ever-accelerating sea-level rise, with all of the impacts that would then have on communities around the world.

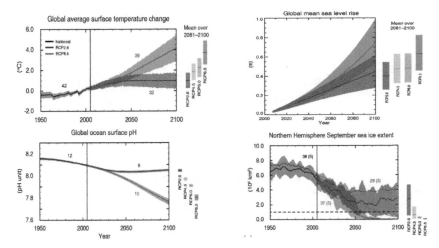

FIGURE 2.8 *Projected impacts of climate change under two different scenarios. Upper left: Global average temperature change with respect to the late-twentieth-century average. Upper right: Global mean sea-level rise. Lower left: Global near-surface ocean pH. Lower right: September Arctic sea ice extent. All plots represent a compilation of a large number of climate model projections under two different scenarios for future greenhouse gas emissions. In the upper two graphs, high-emission scenarios result in the upper curves; in the lower two plots, high-emission scenarios yield the lower curves. Figures from IPCC AR5 WG I Summary for Policymakers, Fig. SPM.7 and SPM.9. Used with permission.*

In the remaining panels of Figure 2.8 we see (lower left) that ocean pH levels continue to decline (meaning the oceans become more acidic) in the RCP8.5 scenario, whereas an RCP2.6 scenario allows the changes to halt and even begin to recover slightly. Arctic sea ice extent (lower right) collapses to zero at the September minimum for RCP8.5, but in the RCP2.6 scenario the decline at least stops and perhaps can begin to recover further in the future. Finally, in the upper right panel of Figure 2.8 the evolution of sea-level rise is seen to be the variable that responds most slowly to change. Even under the RCP2.6 scenario sea levels will continue to rise past the end of the century; for an RCP8.5 scenario the increase is faster and would continue for even a much longer time.

It is important to keep in mind that many changes set in motion by our current emissions will continue beyond this century. Furthermore, a significant fraction of any CO_2 emitted today will remain in the atmosphere for many centuries, affecting generations of people far into the future. Decisions made today are not just about us and our children, and unfortunately, if we take actions today, or refuse to take mitigative actions in the near future, many of the consequences are irreversible on timescales over which human societies typically operate. We saw at the beginning of this chapter that there is a natural stabilizing cycle for CO_2 within the earth system—but these processes operate on timescales of tens and hundreds of thousands of years.

There is no objectively well-defined upper limit to temperature changes (or other climate change effects) below which we are "safe" and above which we are "doomed. We have already reached globally averaged temperature increases of about 1°C compared to nineteenth-century levels, and a range of climate change impacts have already begun to occur. If changes continue to occur gradually, human civilization can perhaps adapt to the changes. However, scientists also note the very real possibility of "tipping points" in the earth system.[23] These are major elements of the climate system: ocean currents, ice sheets or forests that can move quickly and irreversibly into a new state after a relatively small shift in temperature. Many of these have the effect of then setting off a chain reaction to further accelerates warming (e.g., massive forest fires in dried-out tropical forests, or CH_4 releases from thawing permafrost). Thus we cannot be certain that even small additional increases in temperature will not massively disrupt ecological systems and human civilization which depends on them. When international leaders agreed in Paris in December 2015 to aim for a temperature target of 2°C, or if at all possible, 1.5°C, they were heeding the best evidence of scientists that indicates caution in pushing the earth system beyond those limits.[24] Missing the 2°C target and going to 4°C, for example, could be much, much more than simply two times worse.

These caveats lead to a final point, one that may seem overly pessimistic, but which remains well within the realm of possibility. The very exercise of constructing scenarios, and as we will see in more detail in Chapter 11, weighing costs and benefits of actions based on assumptions of equally well-informed human beings acting rationally within the framework of perfectly functioning social systems, might be called into question. Since the early 1970s scientists have been aware of models of complex systems that can lead to societal collapse.[25] More recently, a large body of literature has addressed questions of fossil-fuel resource scarcity and the potential hardships this would create for a society addicted to coal, natural gas, and oil.[26] It might seem at first glance that limits to the availability of fossil fuels would be a blessing in disguise when it comes to climate change mitigation, and that may indeed prevent us from following the extreme RCP8.5 scenario to its bitter end. However, it is now clear that even the amounts of fossil fuels we are certain can be recovered will be more than enough to push the climate well beyond the 2°C limit.

Impacts of climate change

If it were not for the potential impacts of a changing climate on both human and other natural systems, we would not be so concerned with the topic. As pointed out earlier in this chapter, a key point is that current increases in greenhouse gases, and then the resulting temperature changes, are occurring ten to one hundred times faster than those changes to which humans have been forced to adapt throughout history. In this section some of the key messages of the most recent IPCC Working Group II (impacts and adaptation) are presented.

In Figure 2.9 the projected temperature changes with respect to early-twentieth-century levels are shown for two different scenarios (as described above).[27] The right-hand side of the figure shows a qualitative set of potential impacts that depend on global average temperatures. The "thermometer" on the far right sets the scale relevant for agreements to limit warming to 2°C, taken with respect to average temperature in the early industrial period of the nineteenth century. Darker shading in the bars refers to stronger impacts; it is clear that a business-as-usual scenario, represented by RCP8.5, would lead to severe impacts for all indicators.

It is important to get a sense of some of the more specific features of these impacts.[28] For example, unique and threatened systems include those as varied as tropical coral reefs and Arctic sea ice, the latter of which has already been mentioned. Coral reefs are often considered to be the ocean's analogy to tropical rain forests, remarkably biodiverse and supplying critical habitat for an entire food chain upon which, ultimately, many coastal societies depend. Global average temperatures are already 1°C above preindustrial levels. Even with an additional 1°C of warming beyond today's level, these systems will likely be severely threatened.

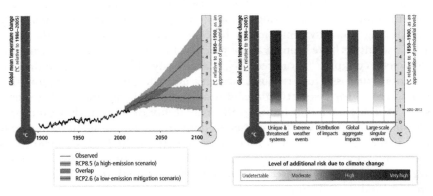

FIGURE 2.9 *Illustration of two representative scenarios for future temperature change, based on the emission pathway that is followed for the future (left-hand side). The right-hand side describes qualitatively some of the potential impacts resulting from different temperature changes. Many of these impacts will be geographically variable in intensity and timing. Figure from IPCC AR5, WG2 Summary for Policymakers. Assessment Box SPM.1, Figure 1 Used with Permission.*

It can already be stated with relatively high confidence that a climate change signature in some extreme weather events is detectable. For example, extreme heat waves such as those in Russia in 2010 and in Europe in 2003 would have been extremely unlikely without the background changes due to increasing global average temperatures. Likewise, large precipitation events and coastal flooding also demonstrate the "fingerprints" of climate change.

As a final example from Figure 2.9 of the potential impacts of climate change on human societies, as global average temperatures rise beyond the 2°C range, the distribution of impacts will become even more noticeable, with those around the world who are already disadvantaged, primarily those in developing countries, suffering the greatest damages. It is perhaps this point that provides one important motivation for *Laudato Si'*—the message that climate change is not simply an issue for the distant future and a symbol of "anthropogenic interference in the earth system," but also that we must respond to the "cry of the earth and the cry of the poor" (§49).

Conclusions

Pope Francis's encyclical *Laudato Si'* is written as a message to all of humanity that we must be concerned about both the impacts of societies on the natural world and the potential impacts of a climate-changed world on the well-being of those already in poverty and on generations in the future. Natural science is a powerful tool for understanding the functioning of our earth's biogeochemical and physical systems, but a more holistic approach is necessary for developing strategies to both mitigate climate change and to enable sustainable development for the future. This chapter has presented the basic science behind the climate, with evidence for past and present changes, both natural and anthropogenic. The majority of contributions to this text consider the much more difficult aspects of how we as humans react and adapt to the challenges before us.

Questions

1   Describe the greenhouse effect. Why are gases such as nitrogen and oxygen, which make up 99 percent of the earth's atmosphere, not greenhouse gases?

2   If you are told by a relative that the earth has always experienced natural cycles of warming and cooling, how would you make a convincing argument that warming as currently experienced is qualitatively different?

3   Which impacts of climate change do you think will be the most serious, and most difficult to adapt to? Why, and does your answer depend on the area of the world in which you live?

4   Which one of the many lines of evidence for anthropogenic climate change resonates particularly with you? That is, if you had to choose one set of data as being most convincing, which would it be?

5   Climate does change over time, between ice ages and interglacial periods, and has done so over longer than our species *Homo sapiens* has been around. Why can't we simply adapt to the changing climate as we have obviously done in the past?

6   From Figures 2.1 and 2.3 estimate the rate of change in CO_2 in the atmosphere around 10,000 years ago and the current rate of change. Do these rates differ significantly? Do the same for the rates of temperature change shown in Figures 2.2 and 2.6, comparing rates 11,000–10,000 years ago with those of today. How different are these rates?

Notes

1   IPCC, "Summary for Policymakers," in *Climate Change 2013: The Physical Science Basis. Contribution of Working Group I to the Fifth Assessment Report of the Intergovernmental Panel on Climate Change*, ed. Thomas F Stocker et al. (Cambridge, UK, and New York, USA: Cambridge University Press, 2013).

2   Naomi Oreskes, "The Scientific Consensus on Climate Change," *Science* 306, no. 5702 (December 03, 2004): 1686.

3   Spencer Weart, "The Carbon Dioxide Greenhouse Effect", *The Discovery of Global Warming*, https://www.aip.org/history/climate/co2.htm (accessed April 27, 2016).

4   Weart, "The Carbon Dioxide Greenhouse Effect." Weart's full hyperlinked website is a good source of information on the science of climate change and the history of our understanding of that science.

5   IPCC, "What is the Greenhouse Effect?" *Climate Change 2007: The Physical Science Basis. Contribution of Working Group I to the Fourth Assessment Report of the Intergovernmental Panel on Climate Change*, ed. S. Solomon, D. Qin, M. Manning, Z. Chen, M. Marquis, K. B. Avery M. Tignor and H. L. Miller (Cambridge, UK, and New York, USA: Cambridge University Press, 2007), http://ipcc.ch/publications_and_data/ar4/wg1/en/faq-1-3.html.

6   Weart, "The Carbon Dioxide Greenhouse Effect."

7   Ibid.

8   IPCC, *Climate Change 2014: Impacts, Adaptation, and Vulnerability: Working Group II Contribution to the Fifth Assessment Report of the Intergovernmental Panel on Climate Change*, ed. C. B. Fields, V. R. Barros, D. J. Dokken, K. J. Mach, M. D. Mastrandrea, T. E. Bilir, M. Chatterjee, K. L. Ebi, Y. O. Estrada, R. C. Genova, B. Girma, E. S. Kissel, A. N. Levy, S. MacCracken, P. R. Mastrandrea, and L. L.White (Cambridge, UK, and New York, USA: Cambridge University Press, 2014), 1454.

9   V. Masson-Delmotte, M. Schulz, A. Abe-Ouchi, J. Beer, A. Ganopolski,
    J. F. González Rouco, E. Jansen, K. Lambeck, J. Luterbacher, T. Naish,
    T. Osborn, B. Otto-Bliesner, T. Quinn, R. Ramesh, M. Rojas, X. Shao, and
    A. Timmermann, "Information from Paleoclimate Archives" in *Climate
    Change 2013: The Physical Science Basis. Contribution of Working Group
    I to the Fifth Assessment Report of the Intergovernmental Panel on Climate
    Change*, ed. T. F. Stocker, D. Qin, G.-K. Plattner, M. Tignor, S. K. Allen,
    J. Boschung, A. Nauels, Y. Xia, V. Bex and P. M. Midgley (Cambridge:
    Cambridge University Press, 2013), 395.

10 When a large volcano erupts now, the overwhelming climatic effect is to
    decrease temperatures temporarily due to aerosol particles tending to block
    sunlight from arriving at the earth's surface.

11 J. R. Petit, et al., "Vostok Ice Core Data for 420,000 Years," *IGBP PAGES/
    World Data Center for Paleoclimatology Data Contribution Series #2001-076*
    (Boulder CO, USA NOAA/NGDC Paleoclimatology Program, 2001).

12 Dieter Lüthi, et al., "High-Resolution Carbon Dioxide Concentration Record
    650,000–800,000 Years before Present", *Nature* 453, no. 7193 (May 15,
    2008): 379–82, doi:10.1038/nature06949.

13 Spencer Weart, *"Past Climate Cycles: Ice Age Speculations," The Discovery
    of Global Warming*, https://www.aip.org/history/climate/cycles.htm (accessed
    April 27, 2016).

14 IPCC, "Summary for Policymakers, 16; Spencer Weart, 'Basic Radiation
    Calculations'," *The Discovery of Global Warming*, https://www.aip.org/
    history/climate/Radmath.htm (accessed April 27, 2016).

15 Shaun A. Marcott, et al., "A Reconstruction of Regional and Global
    Temperature for the Past 11,300 Years", *Science* 339, no. 6124 (March 7,
    2013): 1198–1201, doi:10.1126/science.1228026.

16 Http://www.nytimes.com/interactive/2015/10/27/world/greenland-is-melting-
    away.html.

17 IPCC, "Summary for Policymakers," 11.

18 Data are updated on a monthly basis and available at http://data.giss.nasa.gov/
    gistemp/.

19 See for example explanations of El Niño at http://www.pmel.noaa.gov/elnino/
    what-is-el-nino.

20 Figure SPM.3; Figure SPM.7; Figure SPM.9 from IPCC, *Climate Change 2014:
    Mitigation of Climate Change. Contribution of Working Group III to the
    Fifth Assessment Report of the Intergovernmental Panel on Climate Change*.
    ed. O. Edenhofer, R. Pichs-Madruga, Y. Sokona, E. Farahani, S. Kadner,
    K. Seyboth, A. Adler, I. Baum, S. Brunner, P. Eickemeier, B. Kriemann,
    J. Savolainen, S. Schlömer, C. von Stechow, T. Zwickel and J. C. Minx
    (Cambridge, UK, and New York, USA: Cambridge University Press, 2014).

21 Figure 7 reproduced with permission from IPCC, "Summary for
    Policymakers," (2013). Figure SPM.5 IPCC, *Climate Change 2014: Synthesis
    Report. Contribution of Working Groups I, II and III to the Fifth Assessment
    Report of the Intergovernmental Panel on Climate Change*, ed. R. K. Pachauri
    and L. A. Meyer (IPCC, Geneva, Switzerland, 2014), 9.

22 Figure 8 reproduced with permission from Figure SPM.7; Figure SPM.9 from IPCC, "Summary for Policymakers", *Climate Change 2013: The Physical Science Basis. Working Group I Contribution to the Fifth Assessment Report of the Intergovernmental Panel on Climate Change*, ed. T. F. Stocker, D. Qin, G.-K. Plattner, M. Tignor, S. K. Allen, J.Boschung, A.Nauels, Y. Xia, V. Bex and P. M. Midgley (Cambridge, UK, and New York, USA: Cambridge University Press), 21 and 26, respectively.

23 Timothy M. Lenton, Hermann Held, Elmar Kriegler, Jim W Hall, Wolfgang Lucht, Stefan Rahmstorf and Hans Joachim Schellnhuber, "Tipping Elements in the Earth's Climate System," *Proceedings of the National Academy of Sciences* 105, no. 6 (2008): 1786–93.

24 http://unfccc.int/paris_agreement/items/9485.php.

25 D. Meadows, et al., *Limits to Growth* (New York: Universe Books, 1972).

26 R. Heinberg, The Party's Over (Gabriola Island, British Columbia: New Society Publishers, 2005).

27 Figure 9 reproduced with permission from Assessment Box SPM.1, Figure 1 from IPCC, "Summary for Policymakers, " in *Climate Change 2014: Impacts, Adaptation, and Vulnerability. Contribution of Working Group II to the Fifth Assessment Report of the Intergovernmental Panel on Climate Change*, ed. C. B. Fields, V. R. Barros, D. J. Dokken, K. J. Mach, M. D. Mastrandrea, T. E. Bilir, M. Chatterjee, K. L. Ebi, Y. O. Estrada, R. C. Genova, B. Girma, E. S. Kissel, A. N. Levy, S. MacCracken, P. R. Mastrandrea, and L. L. White (Cambridge, UK, and New York, USA: Cambridge University Press, 2014), 12.

28 IPCC, "Summary for Policymakers, " in *Climate Change 2014: Impacts, Adaptation, and Vulnerability. Part A: Global and Sectoral Aspects. Contribution of Working Group II to the Fifth Assessment Report of the Intergovernmental Panel on Climate Change*, ed. C. B. Fields, V. R. Barros, D. J. Dokken, K. J. Mach, M. D. Mastrandrea, T. E. Bilir, M. Chatterjee, K. L. Ebi, Y. O. Estrada, R. C. Genova, B. Girma, E. S. Kissel, A. N. Levy, S. MacCracken, P. R. Mastrandrea, and L. L. White (Cambridge, UK, and New York, USA: Cambridge University Press, 2014), 13.

3

Ecology: The science of interconnections

Terrence P. Ehrman, C.S.C.

Life is a wondrous gift. Christians profess belief in "God the Father, almighty, maker of heaven and earth." St Basil the Great, bishop in the fourth century, preached on the six days of creation from Genesis, "I want creation to penetrate you with so much admiration that everywhere, wherever you may be, the least plant may bring to you the clear remembrance of the Creator."[1] The natural world radiates with divine splendor, but do we respond to it with delight and wonder? Pope Francis calls for ecological awareness, conversion and responsibility by which we would see ourselves in relationship to God, one another, and the natural world (§66). Care for our human community is not compartmentalized and isolated from care for the natural world: everything is interconnected (§91). We require a new "far sighted" vision to see both our identity—as ecological citizens of a global ecosystem and biotic community—and our mission to care for earth's ecosystems (§36, 211).

All organisms on the earth are interconnected with one another. When Earth formed 4.5 billion years ago, it was void of life. The earliest fossil evidence for life dates to bacterial stromatolite colonies from 3.5 billion years ago. Currently, we identify six kingdoms of living beings: four eukaryotic—animals, plants, fungi, protists—and two prokaryotic—bacteria and archaea. The major moments of the history of life over geologic and evolutionary time are summarized in Table 3.1. Since life's origin, living beings have descended with modification over time and diversified through evolutionary processes to our current community of 1.5 million named species and the even greater number, perhaps 8.7 million, of unnamed species (Table 3.2).[2] However, 99 percent of the species that have ever lived are extinct. Five major extinction events have occurred, marking the boundaries of some of the geologic periods. After each event, recovery to prior levels required ten million years. Scientists identify a possible sixth extinction event, this one currently under way and caused directly and indirectly by human interactions and transformations of the ecosystem and community. The rate of extinction measured today is ten to one hundred times higher than background rates.[3]

At the planetary scale, the earth is one ecosystem of a global community of all species that are interconnected and that transform the community and the environment at varying temporal and spatial scales. The human population is 7.4 billion, and we are transforming the earth's geology, ecosystems, and biotic community on a global scale. Many scientists think that the anthropogenic changes to geological processes and sedimentation is so distinct from what characterizes the Holocene epoch as to warrant the classification of a new geological epoch, the Anthropocene.[4] But prior to the Anthropocene and the Holocene, humans have been agents of ecological disturbance, drastically affecting biotic communities and ecosystems. At the end of the Pleistocene (50,000–10,000 years ago), two-thirds of the world's largest mammal species, such as North American mastodons and saber-toothed cats, went extinct as a combined interactive result of human influence and climatic changes.[5]

What is our relationship to the natural world, especially as Christians? Technology and urban life can distance us from the natural world of God's creation so that it becomes an unappreciated backdrop to our human activities. St Basil wanted to wean his Christian community away from their fascination with their own cultural entertainments so that they could contemplate the amphitheater of creation.[6] Today, Pope Francis calls all people, especially Christians, to a serene attentiveness to the Creator and to all of creation (§226). He also calls for a greater research commitment to the study of ecosystems and their modifications (§42). Ecologists have the privilege of immersing themselves in the ecological theater of creation, getting to know the cast members and how they interact with each other and with the physical theater itself. What follows is an introduction to the science of ecology and a guided tour through the wondrous theater of God's creation, with attention drawn to the interconnections of all living beings, including ourselves, as we all interact with one another and transform the natural world at different scales of time and space. Ecologists also draw our attention to the reality that many of our interactions can disrupt ecosystem function and destroy the theater and participants—including ourselves.

Ecology and evolution

Ecology can be defined as the scientific study of the biotic and abiotic interactions that determine the abundance and distribution of organisms; it is the science of interconnections. Etymologically, ecology is the study of the *oikos*, the Greek word for house. Ecology is the study of the household of living beings in relation to their environment. The Earth is home for all its living beings, a perspective Pope Francis promotes as he repeatedly refers to "our common home" throughout *Laudato Si'*. However, the solar system and even entire universe are our home. The energy from the sun and the meteorites originating beyond the solar system affect the abundance and distribution of organisms on the earth on different timescales. The meteorite that struck Earth 65 million years ago is widely thought to have contributed both to the extinction of the dinosaurs and to the emergence of mammals. The present distribution and abundance of organisms can be partly explained by past evolutionary history, but even the evolutionary origin of species has an ecological component.

Ecology and evolution are intimately related. Ernst Haeckel, the German biologist, coined the term "ecology" (*Oecologie*) as the science of the interrelationships among organisms and their environment.[7] Haeckel connected ecology, with its study of the organic and inorganic, to Darwin's "conditions of existence" that would bring about new species through natural selection. Almost 100 years later, in 1965, prominent ecologist G. Evelyn Hutchinson wrote *Evolutionary Play, Ecological Theater*, which expresses in metaphor the intimate relationship between evolution and ecology.

Darwin and the modern synthesis

In 1859, Charles Darwin laid out his argument for natural selection as the primary mechanism of evolution in *The Origin of Species by Means of Natural Selection or the Preservation of Favoured Races in the Struggle for Life*. His argument was rather concise: (1) variation exists within a population of organisms; (2) some of this variation is heritable, or passed on to offspring; (3) in each generation, more offspring are produced than can survive and reproduce; and (4) survival and reproduction are not random. Heritable variation confers a fitness advantage such that those individuals will be more likely to survive and leave more offspring. In the 1930s and 1940s, Darwin's theory was combined with advances in genetics, paleontology, and systematics (the study of the diversity of life). This reformulation is known as the modern synthesis or neo-Darwinism. Evolution can now be described

Table 3.1 Origin and extinction of various kinds of organisms over geologic and evolutionary time

Era	Period	Epoch	MYA		
Cenozoic	Quaternary	Anthropocene?			
		Holocene	0.01		
		Pleistocene	2.6	*Homo* arises; glacial-interglacial megafauna extinction	
	Neogene	Pliocene	5.3	Hominins	tundra; decreased plant diversity;
		Miocene	23.0	grazing mammals	aster/composite plants
	Paleogene	Oligocene	33.0	apes	forests replaced by savannas, grasslands, or dry scrublands
		Eocene	56.0	pollinating insects	earth covered by forests
		Paleocene	66.0	radiation of mammalian orders	
5th Major Extinction (40% genera, 76% species went extinct)					
Mesozoic	Cretaceous		145	1st placental mammals	1st angiosperms
	Jurassic		201	1st bird; diverse dinosaurs	worldwide expansion of conifer forests
4th Major Extinction (47% genera, 80% species went extinct)					
	Triassic		252	1st mammals; 1st dinosaurs	radiation of conifers

		3rd Major Extinction (56% genera, 96% species went extinct)		
Paleozoic	Permian	299	radiation of reptiles	rise of gymnosperms
	Carboniferous	359	mammal-like reptiles 1st reptiles	forests expand fern radiation 1st seed plants
	2nd Major Extinction (35% genera, 75% species went extinct)			
	Devonian	419	amphibians 1st winged insects 1st insects	1st trees/forests spore plants
	Silurian	444	jawed fish	expansion of land plants
	1st Major Extinction (57% genera, 86% species went extinct)			
	Ordovician	485	bryozoans 1st vertebrates (jawless fish)	1st land plants early lichens and liverworts
	Cambrian	541	most animal phyla first chordates	marine algae
Pre-Cambrian	Neoproterozoic	1000	planktonic microalgae	
	Mesoproterozoic	1600	1st multicellular algae	
	Paleoproterozoic	2500	1st unicellular algae	

Adapted from Douglas Futuyma, *Evolutionary Biology*, 2nd ed. (Sunderland, MA: Sinauer Associates, 1986), 320; Felix Gradstein et al., *The Geologic Time Scale 2012*, vol. (Oxford: Elsevier, 2012), 236; and Anthony Barnosky et al., "Has the Earth's Sixth Mass Extinction Already Arrived?" *Nature* 471 (2011): 51.

Table 3.2 Present abundance of identified species by group

Kingdom	Phyla	Sub-phyla	Class	Order	species
Animalia	Chordata	Vertebrata	Mammalia		4,800
			Aves (birds)		9,900
			Reptilia		7,800
			Amphibia		4,800
			Osteichthyes (bony fish)		24,000
			Chondrichthyes (sharks, rays, skates)		1,000
			Agnatha (jawless fish: lampreys)		100
	Porifera (sponges)				5,000
	Ctenophora (comb jellies) and Cnidaria (jellyfish, corals, anemones)				9,000
	Platyhelminthes (flatworms)				12,200
	Nematodes (roundworms)				12,000
	Annelida (segmented worms)				12,000
	Arthropoda		Crustaceans (crabs, barnacles, shrimp)		50,000
			Chelicerata (spiders, scorpions)		73,000
			Insecta (750,000 species)	Orthoptera (grasshoppers, crickets)	20,000
				Hemiptera (true bugs)	90,000

			Taxon	Number
			Coleoptera (beetles)	350,000
			Hymenoptera (bees, wasps, ants)	125,000
			Lepidoptera (butterflies, moths)	150,000
			Diptera (true flies)	120,000
			Mollusca (snails, clams, oysters, mussels, scallops, octopuses, squids)	50,000
Plantae	Angiosperms		Dicotyledons (oaks, maples, sunflowers, roses)	170,000
			Monocotyledons (grasses, grain crops, orchids, lilies)	50,000
	Gymnosperms (pines, firs, spruces, junipers, araucarias, ginkgos, cycads)			500
	Pteridophytes (ferns)			13,000
	Bryophytes (mosses)			10,000
Fungi				100,000
Protista	Protozoans			31,000
	Algae			28,000
Bacteria				10,00
Archaea				500

Based on data from Camilo Mora et al., "How Many Species Are There on Earth and in the Ocean?" *PLoS Biology* 9 (2011): 1–8. E. O. Wilson, *The Diversity of Life* (Cambridge, MA: Harvard University Press, 2010). Neil A. Campbell, *Biology: Third Edition* (San Francisco: Benjamin-Cummings Pub Co, 1993).

as descent with modification and defined most succinctly as the change in allele (character trait) frequency in a population over time. A population is a group of interbreeding individuals of a particular species sharing a common geographic area. An understanding of populations is important, because populations evolve, not individuals.

Evolution is central to understanding all of biology. One of the principal scientists to establish the modern synthesis was Russian Orthodox population geneticist Theodosius Dobzhansky. In 1973, he presented a paper entitled "Nothing in Biology Makes Sense except in the Light of Evolution."[8] The theory of evolution gives form and coherence to biological phenomena and patterns such as the unity of life, molecular similarities among species, comparative anatomy, embryology, adaptation to unique environments, and biodiversity. Evolution provides an explanatory framework to account for all of these phenomena. But just as nothing makes sense in biology apart from evolution, one might also say that nothing in evolution makes sense apart from ecology. Unlike fundamentalist forms of Christianity, Roman Catholicism has long accepted the validity of evolution as a scientific account of the origins of species.[9]

Niche

At the intersection of ecology and evolution is the concept of the niche. The niche is fundamentally about interrelationships between one species and its environment, including other species. As an ecological concept, it has evolutionary consequences, such as extinction or speciation. Based on the competitive exclusion principle, two species cannot occupy the same niche, and if two competing species coexist in a stable environment, they do so as a result of niche differentiation. G. Evelyn Hutchinson laid the modern foundation for niche theory in its relation to natural selection. He defined the niche as an n-dimensional hypervolume of all the requirements and conditions of an organism. Each environmental requirement or condition (e.g., temperature, light, humidity, salinity, water, oxygen, nutrients, food and nest sites) for a species to survive is one dimension. The niche, however, is not merely physical habitat but the conceptual space of all the abiotic and biotic dimensions. Hutchinson further delineated the fundamental niche—the potentiality of a species—from the realized niche—the actual niche constrained by biotic interconnections among species, such as competition for shared resources, herbivory (e.g., an animal consuming a plant) and predation (e.g., one animal trying to eat another). Some species can so constrain the fundamental niche of another that its realized niche disappears, and the species goes locally or globally extinct. The niche concept has continued to develop and now recognizes that species not only have requirements in terms of conditions and resources, but they also have an impact on the world by their culling of resources and by their trophic interactions (*troph=* Greek for nourishment, food).

The biosphere we see around us and in which we are immersed exists in and through interconnections. The presence of different species creates new potential niches for organisms. For example, pitcher plants (*Sarracenia purpurea*) are carnivorous plants that obtain their nutrients not from photosynthesis but from the digestion of animals that fall into the plant's liquid reservoir and cannot escape. The pitcher plant mosquito, *Wyeomia smithii*, has evolved in a specialized ecological niche: the mosquito larvae live only within the liquid of these plants, feeding on the organisms in the reservoir. The distribution of *W. smithii* is limited by the range of pitcher plants which grow primarily in bogs in North American temperate forests.

Temperate forests are one type of biome or major category of biological communities. David Olson identified 14 terrestrial biomes, 7 freshwater biomes, and 5 marine biomes (Table 3.3).[10] Terrestrial biomes are largely identified by plant growth forms that are determined primarily by climate, specifically annual precipitation and annual temperature.[11] Generally, species richness or diversity increases with precipitation and temperature and decreases with increasing latitude and elevation. Biotic interactions also influence richness. Tropical rainforests, which are wet and warm, harbor half of the planet's species.[12] In total, 68 percent of all angiosperm species occur

Table 3.3 Types of terrestrial, aquatic, and marine biomes in the world

Terrestrial	Freshwater
Tropical and Subtropical Moist Broadleaf Forests	Large Rivers
Tropical and Subtropical Dry Broadleaf Forests	Large River Headwaters
Tropical and Subtropical Coniferous Forests	Large River Delta
Temperate Broadleaf and Mixed Forests	Small Rivers
Temperate Coniferous Forests	Large Lakes
Boreal Forests (Taiga)	Small Lakes
Tropical and Subtropical Grasslands, Savannas, & Shrublands	Xeric Basins
Temperate Grasslands, Savannas, and Shrublands	
Flooded Grasslands and Savannas	**Marine**
Montane Grasslands and Shrublands	Polar
Tundra (Artic and Alpine)	Temperate Shelf and Seas
Mediterranean Forests, Woodlands, and Scrub	Temperate Upwelling
Deserts and Xeric Shrublands	Tropical Upwelling
Mangroves	Tropical Coral

Based on David Olson and Eric Dinerstein, "The Global 200: Priority Ecoregions for Global Conservation," *Annals of the Missouri Botanical Garden* 89 (2002): 199–224.

in the tropics and subtropics.[13] The diversity found in tropical rainforests results partly from the species promoting abiotic conditions (temperature and rainfall) but also from the abundance of specialized niches available from the community of organisms. Such specialized niches and the species dependent upon them, however, are vulnerable to extinction from human activities.

Pope Francis focuses attention on the Amazon and Congo River basins (§38), which, along with the Mekong river basin in Asia, are home to one-third of the world's freshwater fish species, many of which are endemic or found only in that location.[14] All three areas are endangered from ongoing habitat destruction, including deforestation and dam construction. Freshwater ecosystems are particularly imperiled from human use; they cover only 0.8 percent of the earth's surface but contain 100,000 species, or 6 percent of the planet's biodiversity.[15]

Species richness in biomes has also been shaped over geologic time by evolutionary processes. At the global scale, biomes are nested within eight biogeographic realms: Nearctic, Neotropical, Palearctic, Afrotropic, Indo-Malay, Australasia, Oceania, and Antarctic (Figure 3.1). These boundaries are determined by several factors, including paleoclimate, continental drift, dispersal barriers, and evolutionary history. These realms and biomes are the ecological theaters where the evolutionary play has been performing

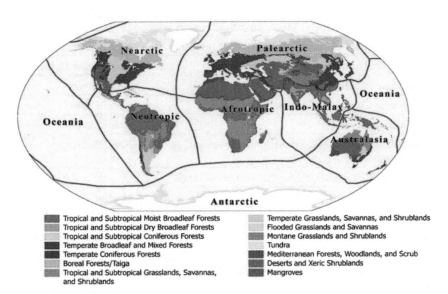

Tropical and Subtropical Moist Broadleaf Forests
Tropical and Subtropical Dry Broadleaf Forests
Tropical and Subtropical Coniferous Forests
Temperate Broadleaf and Mixed Forests
Temperate Coniferous Forests
Boreal Forests/Taiga
Tropical and Subtropical Grasslands, Savannas, and Shrublands

Temperate Grasslands, Savannas, and Shrublands
Flooded Grasslands and Savannas
Montane Grasslands and Shrublands
Tundra
Mediterranean Forests, Woodlands, and Scrub
Deserts and Xeric Shrublands
Mangroves

FIGURE 3.1 *The distribution of the seven biogeographic realms of the planet. From David Olson et al., "Terrestrial Ecoregions of the World: A New Map of Life on Earth," BioScience 51 (2001): 934. Used with permission of Oxford University Press and the American Institute of Biological Sciences.*

over geologic time and the interacting cast members are interconnected with one another across biomes and time in one global theater. The whole community and each of its members has an "irreplaceable and irretrievable beauty" (§34) revelatory of the divine director and worthy of our awareness and care.

Levels of ecology

Pope Francis partially connects the awareness and care for our common ecological home to a call for more research into "understanding more fully the functioning of ecosystems" (§42). The science of ecology studies interconnections of life at four different levels: autecology, population ecology, community ecology, and ecosystem ecology. Through their scientific study, ecologists have a privileged encounter of and attentiveness to these cast members.

Autecology

Walking by a small lake in a beech-maple temperate forest, you may see a Blue Dasher dragonfly (*Pachydiplax longipennis*) patrolling its territory and searching for prey to eat. Dragonflies have an immature aquatic stage (nymph/naiad) before molting to a winged terrestrial adult. Blue Dasher nymphs live in the littoral zone (=shore) of freshwater lakes and ponds or slow depositional areas of streams where they are sit-and-wait predators that use a jet propulsion system to quickly lunge at unsuspecting prey grabbed with prehensile mouthparts. An autecologist studies how a single species, such as the Blue Dasher, interacts with the environment: life cycle and development from egg, to aquatic nymph, to adult; rate and pattern of reproduction; physiology and anatomy (response to oxygen, temperature, current); habitat selection; dispersal; mating behavior; and foraging behavior.

Population ecology

Population ecologists study the abundance and distribution of Blue Dasher dragonflies in a given area and how they interact with their environment, conspecifics, and with other species. New properties and dynamics emerge in a population, such as density, age structure, sex ratios, birth and death rates, and immigration and emigration. Is the population growing or declining and why? What do the density-dependent (e.g., fish eating nymphs) or density-independent (oxygen level in water) factors involve? Is there intra- or interspecific competition? What are the predator—prey or host—parasitoid interactions?

Community ecology

Autecology and population ecology study primarily only one species and its interactions with only one or a couple other species, but the natural world is much more complex and interconnected than that. Beyond population ecology, ecology divides into two major areas: community ecology and ecosystem ecology. Community ecology studies an assemblage of species populations that occur together. For the Blue Dasher dragonfly, the researcher could select the entire pond with all the organisms present within it as the community. This would include all the benthic (=bottom dwelling) macroinvertebrates (e.g., insects, snails, crayfish), bacteria and fungi in the sediment and water column, algae, zooplankton, macrophytes (= large plants such as cattail, arrowhead, and bladderwort), fish, frogs, turtles, birds (e.g., Great Blue Heron) and mammals (e.g., muskrat). Or the ecologist could focus on some subset of organisms, for example just the entire assemblage of different dragonfly species. Properties of a community studied by ecologists include the following: biodiversity, spatial, and temporal patterns of species, food webs or trophic interactions, the structure, stability, and resilience of the community, and productivity and biomass.

Ecosystem ecology

An ecosystem is an organizational concept for ecology that unites population—community ecology, abiotic factors, and a systems approach to transformations of energy and matter. Ecosystem ecology studies the structure and function of the biotic and abiotic components of a given area over time. Though ecosystems are natural units of all the organisms interacting with the abiotic factors, there is no uniform size. The ecosystem ecologist selects the scale at which to study an ecosystem, which can range in size from the pond of the Blue Dasher dragonfly, to the temperate forest containing the pond, to one of the Great Lakes and its surrounding watershed, to the entire planet. Typically, however, ecosystems refer to the basic community types or biomes.

An ecosystem ecologist would examine the transformation of energy and matter, caused by the living and nonliving components of the community, and its flow through the system, in this case, the pond of the Blue Dasher dragonfly. The sun is the ultimate source of energy for the ecosystem, and primary producers (or autotrophs), such as phytoplankton (e.g., algae) in the open water and macrophytes, convert sunlight into chemical energy stored in organic molecules. Primary producers require nutrients (carbon, nitrogen, phosphorus, etc.) and water for this process. All other organisms are heterotrophs; they must consume primary producers. Primary consumers (herbivores) eat producers: zooplankton (e.g., *Daphnia*) eat the phytoplankton and various herbivores consume the macrophytes (e.g., chrysomelid beetles graze on water lily leaves). Secondary consumers (predators) eat primary consumers and so on to an upper limit: planktivorous fish (minnows) eat zooplankton, Blue Dasher dragonfly nymphs eat other insects and piscivorous fish (bass) eat other fish. Decomposers and detritivores consume waste material or dead organic matter and release nutrients back to the environment to be used by primary producers. At each trophic level, however, the conversion of energy is not efficient, and only about 10 percent of the energy is converted into biomass at the next level. Because of this, most—but not all—trophic systems are pyramidal in structure with a higher biomass or abundance of primary producers at the base and decreasing biomass and numbers of successive consumer levels. Because of this energy loss, most ecosystems cannot have more than four or five trophic levels, and ecosystems support fewer top predators, such as tigers, killer whales, and muskies, than lower-level consumers.

Energy is transferred through trophic levels, but organisms also generate biomass when they grow by transforming matter. A principal focus of ecosystem ecology is the study of the uptake, use and biogeochemical cycling of the chemical elements and molecules incorporated into biotic tissue, particularly the major nutrients (carbon, nitrogen, phosphorus, sulfur), and water required by all organisms. For example, nitrogen is an essential element for life as it is a component of proteins, nucleic acids, and vitamins. At a metabolic level, we humans eat fish that ate dragonflies that ate insects that ate zooplankton that ate phytoplankton in order to obtain the nitrogen necessary for cellular structure and processes. The same nitrogen molecule is sequentially incorporated into the tissue of the next trophic level, but it all starts with primary producers. The biodiversity of life is interconnected through trophic dynamics and the transformation of energy and matter. The 1.2 million identified species of consumers and decomposers depend upon the 300,000 species of plants, but the terrestrial plants are interconnected and flourish because of the decomposer and detritivore soil community. The process by which nitrogen becomes available to the community of organisms reveals the inherent interconnectivity of life.

Just as ice is not a form of water available for plant root uptake, nitrogen must be in the proper molecular form to be available to organisms. The major reservoir of nitrogen on the planet is the atmosphere, which is 78 percent nitrogen gas (N_2) by volume, but this molecular form is not biologically available for most organisms. Nitrogen fixation, the transformation of gaseous nitrogen (N_2) to ammonia (NH_3), occurs through two natural processes, one abiotic (lightning) and the other biotic. Biological nitrogen fixation is accomplished primarily by microorganisms, such as bacteria and blue-green algae. Bacteria are also the primary metabolizers of ammonia, and through the process of nitrification transform ammonia (NH_3) into nitrate (NO_3^-), which plants readily absorb and convert into organic form (e.g., amino acids). Heterotrophs and decomposers obtain nitrogen by consuming plants or other animals or their remains. Decomposers and detritivores convert nitrate (NO_3^-) to ammonia (NH_3) in a process of ammonification. Denitrifying bacteria reduce nitrate (NO_3^-) back to gaseous nitrogen (N_2).

The availability of nitrogen to algae in the pond is a function of abiotic factors—underlying geologic rock type, precipitation, leaching of soil, temperature, and oxygen concentration; and biotic factors—uptake and processing by terrestrial soil microorganisms and algal communities. The pond is part of the larger terrestrial watershed, and trophic cascades cross ecosystem boundaries that have effects on nutrient cycling and species abundance. Greater fish predation upon dragonfly nymphs in a pond can increase plant reproduction on land.[16] With a smaller population of adult dragonflies to prey upon plant pollinators (such as bees), seed and fruit production is more successful. If you happen upon the wild raspberry bush with abundant fruit beside the pond, you can benefit from this trophic cascade.

Humans are not mere spectators to this play and theater but participants as well. Pope Francis's call for ecological conversion entails "a loving awareness that we are not disconnected from the rest of creatures, but joined in a splendid universal communion" (§220). However, because we are interconnected, we can also disrupt the global biotic communities and ecosystems. The ecological crisis and threat of climate change are results of our interactions and usurpation of the stage, often acting against the director's commands.

The precariousness of interconnection

Vulnerability of biodiversity

Pope Francis directs attention to biodiversity, the interconnections among biota and abiotic factors that foster and cause it to be, and the theological significance of the created world. "Because all creatures are connected, each must be cherished with love and respect, for all of us as living creatures are dependent on one another" (§42). Not only are we to love creatures because of our interconnections with each other but because of their interconnection with God as their Creator. Species are more than resources to be exploited; they have "value in themselves" (§33). Extinction is a natural process, but since the rise of humankind, we have caused extinctions through our interactions and are doing so today at an accelerating rate that threatens a sixth mass extinction. "Because of us, thousands of species will no longer give glory to God by their very existence, nor convey their message to us" (§33). We imperil our own human flourishing by our destruction of the ecological theater and the interconnections within the biotic communities to which we belong.

One group of researchers has developed a framework based on planetary ecosystem function and the stability or resilience of the earth system to define "safe operating space" for human societal development and flourishing (Figure 3.2).[17] They identify nine interdependent planetary boundaries with

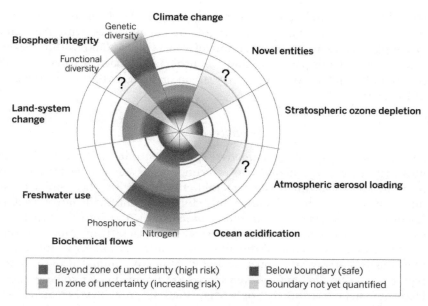

FIGURE 3.2 *Planetary Boundaries. The safe operating space is represented by the inner dark circle. The next dark circular line represents the beginning of the high-risk zone. From Will Stefan, et al. "Planetary Boundaries: Guiding Human Development on a Changing Planet," Science 347, no. 6223. Reprinted with Permission from AAAS.*

thresholds indicating safety for, or danger to, sustained human societal flourishing. They contend that we have already far exceeded the safety threshold for three areas—climate change, biogeochemical change, and rate of biodiversity loss—and have entered the dangerous level for each, which carries with it a high risk of serious impact not only for humans but for the global theater and its biodiversity.

For the last two decades, entomologist E. O. Wilson has heralded a warning against the human threat to biodiversity. He has identified five factors ranked in order of destructiveness that threaten the irreversible extinction of species: habitat destruction, invasive species, population growth, pollution and overexploitation (acronym HIPPO).[18] To this list has been added climate change (HIPPCO). Within this framework, let us look at a few examples that show the vulnerability of biodiversity.

Human disruption of interconnections

Habitat destruction

Humans have so transformed natural biomes that 75 percent of the terrestrial ecosystems are considered anthropogenic biomes or "anthromes."[19] In the

United States, a satellite landscape analysis of the land use and land cover reveals a nearly ubiquitous pattern of human influence with the major "exemplar landscapes" being rectangular fields, farmland within cleared forests, shrublands/pastures, and suburbs.[20] Humans deforest ~2,500 square miles of Amazon forest per year, an area about the size of the state of Delaware.[21]

Invasive species

An invasive species is a nonnative species introduced (intentionally or not) into an ecosystem that causes economic or environmental harm or harm to human health.[22] The threefold effects identified here point to the interconnection of life with human life. Humans intentionally introduced the Javan mongoose (*Herpestes auropunctatus*) from Asia into the Caribbean to control other invasive species, Norway and Black (roof) rats. Not only has the mongoose increased the abundance of the pestiferous roof rats by reducing its Norway rat competitor, but it has nearly eliminated all the native reptile species on the islands; seven species are already known to be extinct.[23] Here, human intervention has only aggravated the problem we created (§34). Of the 50,000 nonnative species that have been introduced into the United States, which has a native described species number of nearly 370,000, some are beneficial (e.g., crop species such as corn and wheat), whereas others are extremely harmful, causing $100 billion of damage.[24] One beneficial, exotic species is the honey bee (*Apis mellifera*). Without this species, yields of some fruit, seed, and nut crops decrease by 90 percent.[25] Human flourishing depends on our interconnections with insect pollinators, such as bees whose populations are threatened by Colony Collapse Disorder whose cause is uncertain but attributed to another exotic species—Asian ectoparasitic mites (*Varroa destructor*), exotic pathogens, and possibly pesticides.[26]

Population growth

Human population growth plays a significant role in the magnitude of the other five factors that lead to biodiversity loss, but population alone cannot be blamed without considering other factors such as "extreme and selective consumerism" (§50). Decision making about human procreation is a moral issue that reveals the interconnectivity between human ecology and general ecology. Pope Francis reiterates Catholic teaching about responsible parenthood whereby parents make decisions about family size based on their "duties towards God, themselves, their families and human society."[27] In the United States, the most common form of birth control is hormonal contraceptives. However, even this can have deleterious effects upon aquatic ecosystems. The synthetic estrogen 17α-ethinylestradiol (EE_2) used in birth control pills passes through women's bodies, enters aquatic ecosystems, and has been shown to adversely affect fish development and behavior that can cause declines and even collapse of some fish populations.[28] (Similar effects have been mapped for many other pharmaceuticals.[29])

Pollution

Trophic dynamics have important consequences for humans and the biotic community itself, especially in relation to pollution. Mercury is a heavy metal that is a neurotoxin in humans. It is produced naturally (e.g., volcanoes), but anthropogenic emissions of mercury as a by-product of fossil-fuel combustion far exceed the former. Aquatic ecosystems are particularly vulnerable to mercury poisoning through bioaccumulation and biomagnification. In an Arctic marine food web, the biologically active form of methylmercury is taken up by and accumulates in phytoplankton. With each successive trophic level (zooplankton, fish, seal, human/polar bear), consumers not only accumulate methylmercury, but the concentration is magnified tenfold or more. Seafood consumption is the primary source to humans of methylmercury, and communities such as the Northern Peoples (e.g., Inuit), who rely on seafood and marine mammals, are particularly at risk to mercury poisoning. In the Arctic, methylmercury levels exceed toxic threshold levels in both wildlife and humans.[30]

Furthermore, human disruption of the nitrogen and phosphorus cycles shows well the local and global interconnections of ecosystems and communities and our participation in that cycle. Plant and animal growth are limited primarily by nitrogen and phosphorus. Thus, humans fertilize crops with these nutrients, but our activity has greatly altered the global biogeochemical nitrogen cycle. Humans have nearly doubled the rate of nitrogen fixation through industrial fertilizer production. The effects of the altered nitrogen cycle are not local but can reach hundreds of miles downwind or downstream, such as with the annually recurring toxic algal blooms in Lake Erie that have contaminated the drinking water supply of Toledo, Ohio, with microcystin (a liver toxin). The cyanobacteria or blue-green algal blooms (e.g., *Microcystis*) are primarily driven by high levels of phosphorus in run off from fertilized crop fields that cover 73 percent of the watershed drained by the Maumee River that empties into Lake Erie. Nitrogen loads exacerbate the blooms by shifting algal composition to more aggressive and toxic species. Unprecedented warmer temperatures and more extreme high temperatures over the last two decades most likely facilitate the toxic blooms.[31]

Overexploitation

Trophic cascades and keystone species exemplify the interconnectivity of life. A trophic cascade is the ripple effect that the removal or addition of a trophic level has upon the rest of the food web structure. A keystone species now refers to organisms whose effect upon the community or ecosystem is disproportionate to its abundance.[32] Sea otters (*Enhydra lutris*) live in the kelp forests of the Pacific Ocean along the west coast of North America and consume herbivorous sea urchins. By the end of the eighteenth century, European hunters had nearly extinguished the sea otter population which allowed sea urchins to proliferate and consume the kelp, reducing the productive marine forest tenfold to so-called sea-urchin barrens. This trophic cascade was most likely the cause of the extinction of the Steller's sea cow (*Hydrodamaline sirenians*), relatives of Manatees that grew to 30 feet in length and whose primary food source was kelp.[33] Our impact on keystone species has led scientists to classify humans as hyperkeystone species. Humans negatively impact keystone species (orcas, sea otters, starfish, salmon, bears, and eagles) across several habitats (ocean, intertidal, freshwater, and terrestrial) in the Pacific Northwest ecosystems that lead to changes in community structure and ecosystem processes.[34] For so long, humans have lived in ignorance of these interconnections upon which we depend. Pope Francis's notion of "integral ecology" is a call to attend to, to respect, and to preserve these interconnections.

Climate change

Climate change affects the entire community of life at a global scale. The increase in the abiotic factor CO_2 leads to increases in temperature and greater ocean acidity that immediately affect the realized niches of terrestrial and marine organisms. Changes in climate affect the fundamental drivers (temperature and rainfall) that determine global level biomes. All of the preceding examples above cover a large range of spatial scales at a relatively short temporal scale, but the distribution of organisms may require thousands of years to adjust to changes in climate. For example, when the glaciers receded from southern Alaska and warmer temperatures returned ~13,000 years ago, dispersal of spruces, pines, cedars, and hemlocks across the Pacific Northwest and southern Alaska lagged 1,500 years behind the climate changes. Various interconnected abiotic and biotic factors were at play that constrained the niche of the trees: lack of mycorrhizal fungi in the soil, soil moisture, precipitation pattern and abundance, and competition from alder and birch trees.[35] A single species does not just disperse on its own, independent of its niche with its biotic and abiotic interconnections. For past rates of climate change, species migration is constrained by the presence or absence of other species. For example, insects that are host-specific to a certain plant are constrained in their migration by the presence of their host, and species with similar fundamental niches may show correlated migration.[36] However, the predicted rates of climate change—caused by increased greenhouse gases—for the latter twenty-first century may exceed the ability of many species to move quickly enough to maintain their own fundamental niche, and thus, they and all the species that depend on them face the risk of extirpation or extinction (Figure 3.3).[37]

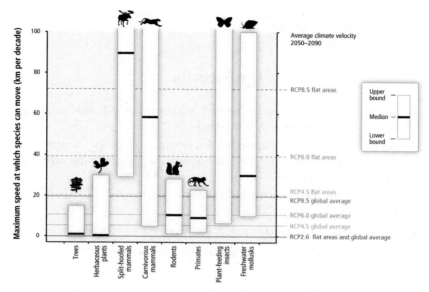

FIGURE 3.3 *The vertical columns are the upper and lower bounds of the maximum dispersal rate of various types of species. These are shown against average rates of climate velocity under various scenarios of levels of CO_2. Species whose maximum movement rate is below the climate velocity are not expected to survive without human intervention. (For a description of the RCP scenarios, see Chapter 2, Figure 7.) From IPCC AR5 WG2 Summary for Policy Makers, Figure SPM.5. Used with permission.*

Conclusion

From our guided tour through the ecological theater of God's creation, we can see more clearly our interconnection with the ecosystems and community of life as well as our impacts upon our common home and fellow cast members. The short list of ecological threats described here reveal how we are altering and disturbing our beautiful home that can be seen more like "an immense pile of filth" (§21). Our impact is much broader than obvious despoiling of the environment. The science of ecology enables us to see the manifold interconnections of all life on the earth of which we are a part, although, as we have seen, change is nothing new. Francis observes the profound impact of the "rapidification" of human impacts on ecological systems. "Although change is part of the working of complex systems, the speed with which human activity has developed contrasts with the naturally slow pace of biological evolution" (§18).

Pope Francis first calls Christians and all people of goodwill to "ecological awareness" about our "ecological citizenship." For Christians, in particular, this awareness is directed to ecological conversion by which their encounter with Jesus Christ should "become evident in their relationship with the world around them" (§217).[38]

Questions

1   What is the Anthropocene Epoch? What evidence do scientists cite who propose this new designation?

2   What does the author mean by describing ecology as "theater"? As the "theater of creation"? What does this way of framing ecology imply about humans' role?

3   What are the elements of the "modern synthesis" in biology?

4   Define niche and biome.

5   What are the four levels of ecological study?

6   List and describe the major threats to biodiversity.

Notes

1   St. Basil the Great, *Hexaemeron*, ed. Paul Böer, Sr. (Veritas Splendor, 2012), 5.2.

2   Camilo Mora, Derek P. Tittensor, Sina Adl, Alastair G. B. Simpson, and Boris Worm, "How Many Species Are There on Earth and in the Ocean?" *PLoS Biology* 9 (2011): 1–8.

3   Anthony Barnosky, Nicholas Matzke, Susumu Tomiya, Guinevere O. U.Wogan, Brian Swartz, Tiago B. Quental, Charles Marshall, Jenny L. McGuire, Emily L. Lindsey, Kaitlin C. Maguire, Ben Mersey, and Elizabeth A. Ferrer, "Has the Earth's Sixth Mass Extinction Already Arrived?" *Nature* 471 (2011): 51–57.

4   Colin Waters, Jan Zalasiewicz, Colin Summerhayes, Anthony D. Barnosky, Clément Poirier, Agnieszka Gałuszka, Alejandro Cearreta, Matt Edgeworth, Erle C. Ellis, Michael Ellis, Catherine Jeandel, Reinhold Leinfelder, J. R. McNeill, Daniel deB. Richter, Will Steffen, James Syvitski, Davor Vidas, Michael Wagreich, Mark Williams, An Zhisheng, Jacques Grinevald, Eric Odada, Naomi Oreskes, and Alexander P. Wolfe, "The Anthropocene is Functionally and Stratigraphically Distinct from the Holocene," *Science* 351 (2016): aad2269:1–10.

5   Paul Koch and Anthony Barnosky, "Late Quaternary Extinctions: State of the Debate", *Annual Review of Ecology, Evolution, and Systematics* 37 (2006): 215–50.

6   St. Basil, *Hexaemeron*, 4.1.

7   Ernst Haeckel, *Generelle Morphologie der Organismen: Allegemeine Grundzüge der organischen Formen-wissenschaft, mechanisch begründet durch die von Charles Darwin reformirte Descendenz-Theorie* (Berlin: Georg Reimer, 1866), B.236.

8 Theodosius Dobzhansky, "Nothing in Biology Makes Sense Except in the Light of Evolution," *The American Biology Teacher* 35 (1973): 125–29.

9 Pius XII, *Humani generis* (1950) §36; John Paul II, Address to Pontifical Academy of Sciences, October 22, 1996; Pope Benedict XVI directly challenged the assumption that evolution conflicts with the Doctrine of Creation: "Currently, I see in Germany, but also in the United States, a somewhat fierce debate raging between so-called 'creationism' and evolutionism, presented as though they were mutually exclusive alternatives: those who believe in the Creator would not be able to conceive of evolution, and those who instead support evolution would have to exclude God. This antithesis is absurd because, on the one hand, there are so many scientific proofs in favor of evolution which appears to be a reality we can see and which enriches our knowledge of life and being as such. But on the other, the doctrine of evolution does not answer every query, especially the great philosophical question: where does everything come from?" Benedict XVI, Meeting of the Holy Father Benedict XVI with the Clergy of the Dioceses of Belluno-Feltre and Treviso, July 24, 2007.

10 David Olson and Eric Dinerstein, "The Global 200: Priority Ecoregions for Global Conservation," *Annals of the Missouri Botanical Garden* 89 (2002): 199–224.

11 Glenn Moncrieff, Thomas Hickler, and Steven I. Higgins, "Intercontinental Divergence in the Climate Envelope of Major Plant Biomes," *Global Ecology and Biogeography* 24 (2015): 324–34.

12 Olson and Dinerstein, "The Global 200," 199.

13 E. O. Wilson, *The Diversity of Life* (Cambridge, MA: Harvard University Press, 2010), 197. Angiosperms are all of the flowering plants.

14 K. O. Winemiller, P. B. McIntyre, L. Castello, E. Fluet-Chouinard, T. Giarrizzo, S. Nam, I. G. Baird, W. Darwall, N. K. Lujan, I. Harrison, M. L. J. Stiassny, R. A. M. Silvano, D. B. Fitzgerald, F. M. Pelicice, A. A. Agostinho, L. C. Gomes, J. S. Albert, E. Baran, M. Petrere Jr., C. Zarfl, M. Mulligan, J. P. Sullivan, C. C. Arantes, L. M. Sousa, A. A. Koning, D. J. Hoeinghaus, M. Sabaj, J. G. Lundberg, J. Armbruster, M. L. Thieme, P. Petry, J. Zuanon, G. Torrente Vilara, J. Snoeks, C. Ou, W. Rainboth, C. S. Pavanelli, A. Akama, A. van Soesbergen, L. Sáenz, "Balancing Hydropower and Biodiversity in the Amazon, Congo, and Mekong," *Science* 351 (2016): 128–29.

15 David Dudgeon, Angela H. Arthington, Mark O. Gessner, Zen-Ichiro Kawabata, Duncan J. Knowler, Christian Lévêque, Robert J. Naiman, Anne-Hélène Prieur-Richard, Doris Soto, Melanie L. J. Stiassny, and Caroline A. Sullivan, "Freshwater Biodiversity: Importance, Threats, Status, and Conservation Challenges," *Biological Reviews* 81 (2006): 163–82.

16 Tiffany M. Knight, Michael W. McCoy, Jonathan M. Chase, Krista A. McCoy, and Robert D. Holt, "Trophic Cascades across Ecosystems," *Nature* 437 (2005): 880–83.

17 Will Steffen, Katherine Richardson, Johan Rockström, Sarah E. Cornell, Ingo Fetzer, Elena M. Bennett, Reinette Biggs, Stephen R. Carpenter, Wim de Vries, Cynthia A. de Wit, Carl Folke, Dieter Gerten, Jens Heinke, Georgina M. Mace, Linn M. Persson, Veerabhadran Ramanathan, Belinda Reyers, Sverker Sörlin,

"Planetary Boundaries: Guiding Human Development on a Changing Planet," *Science* 347 (2015): 1259855: 1–10, http://science.sciencemag.org/content/347/6223/1259855.

18 E. O. Wilson, *The Creation: An Appeal to Save Life on Earth* (New York: W. W. Norton and Co., 2006), 75.

19 Erle Ellis, "Sustaining Biodiversity and People in the World's Anthropogenic Biomes," *Current Opinion in Environmental Sustainability* 5 (2013): 368–72.

20 Jeffrey Cardille and Marie Lambois, "From the Redwood Forest to the Gulf Stream Waters: Human Signature Nearly Ubiquitous in Representative US Landscapes," *Frontiers in Ecology and the Environment* 8 (2010): 130–34.

21 Antonio Regaldo, "Brazil Says Rate of Deforestation in Amazon Continues to Plunge," *Science* 329 (2010): 1270.

22 K. George Beck, Kenneth Zimmerman, Jeffrey D. Schardt, Jeffrey Stone, Ronald R. Lukens, Sarah Reichard, John Randall, Allegra A. Cangelosi, Diane Cooper, and John Peter Thompson, "Invasive Species Defined in a Policy Context: Recommendations from the Federal Invasive Species Advisory Committee," *Invasive Plant Science and Management* 1 (2008): 414–21.

23 Francis Howarth, "Environmental Impacts of Classical Biological Control," *Annual Review of Entomology* 36 (1991): 485–509.

24 David Pimentel, Lori Lach, Rodolfo Zuniga, and Doug Morrison, "Environmental and Economic Costs of Nonindigenous Species in the United States," *BioScience* 53 (2000): 53–65.

25 Alexandra-Maria Klein, Bernard E. Vaissière, James H. Cane, Ingolf Steffan-Dewenter, Saul A. Cunningham, Claire Kremen, and Teja Tscharntke, "Importance of Pollinators in Changing Landscapes for World Crops," *Proceedings: Biological Sciences* 274 (2007): 303–13.

26 Benjamin Dainat, Jay D. Evans, Yan Ping Chen, Laurent Gauthier, and Peter Neumann, "Predictive Markers of Honey Bee Colony Collapse," PLoS 7 (2012): e32151:1–9.

27 Francis, *Amoris Laetitia* [Apostolic Exhortation On the Love of the Family] (2016), §68.

28 Minna Saaristo, John A. Craft, Kari K. Lehtonen, and Kai Lindström, "Sand Goby (*Pomatoschistus minutus*) Males Exposed to an Endocrine Disrupting Chemical Fail in Nest and Mate Competition," *Hormones and Behavior* 56 (2009): 315–21.

29 C. G. Daughton and T. A. Ternes, "Pharmaceuticals and Personal Care Products in the Environment: Agents of Subtle Change?" *Environmental Health Perspectives*, 107 Supplement 6 (1999): 907–38.

30 Igor Lehnherr, "Methylmercury Biogeochemistry: A Review with Special Reference to Arctic Aquatic Ecosystems," *Environmental Reviews* 22 (2014): 229–43.

31 George S. Bullerjahn, Robert M. McKay, Timothy W. Davis, David B. Baker, Gregory L. Boyer, Lesley V. D'Anglada, Gregory J. Doucette, Jeff C. Ho, Elena G. Irwin, Catherine L. Kling, Raphael M. Kudela, Rainer Kurmayer, Anna M. Michalak, Joseph D. Ortizm, Timothy G. Otten, Hans W. Paerl, Boqiang Qin,

Brent L. Sohngen, Richard P. Stumpf, Petra M. Visser, and Steven W. Wilhelm, "Global Solutions to Regional Problems: Collecting Global Expertise to Address the Problem of Harmful Cyanobacterial Blooms. A Lake Erie Case Study," *Harmful Algae* 54 (2016): 223–38.

32 Mary E. Power, David Tilman, James A. Estes, Bruce A. Menge, William J. Bond, L. Scott Mills, Gretchen Daily, Juan Carlos Castilla, Jane Lubchenco, and Robert T.Paine, "Challenges in the Quest for Keystones," *BioScience* 46 (1996): 609–20.

33 James A. Estes, Alexander Burdin, and Daniel F. Doak, "Sea Otters, Kelp Forests, and the Extinction of Steller's Sea Cow," *Proceedings of the National Academy of Sciences* 113 (2016): 880–85.

34 Boris Worm and Robert Paine, "Humans as a Hyperkeystone Species," *Trends in Ecology and Evolution* 31 (2016): 600–07.

35 Scott Elias, "The Problem of Conifer Species Migration Lag in the Pacific Northwest Region since the Last Glaciation," *Quaternary Science Reviews* 77 (2013): 55–69.

36 Stephen Jackson and Jonathan Overpeck, "Responses of Plant Populations and Communities to Environmental Changes of the Late Quaternary," *Paleobiology* 26 (2000): 208, 212.

37 Figure 3 reproduced with permission from Figure SPM.5, IPCC, *Climate Change 2014: Impacts, Adaptation, and Vulnerability: Summary for Policymakers*, ed. Christopher B. Field, Vicente R. Barros, Michael D. Mastrandrea, Katharine J. Mach, Mohamed A.-K. Abdrabo, W. Neil Adger, et. al. (Cambridge, UK, and New York, USA: Cambridge University Press, 2015), 15, http://ipcc.ch/pdf/assessment-report/ar5/wg2/ar5_wgII_spm_en.pdf.

38 I would like to thank Celia Deane-Drummond, Gary Lamberti, Jessica Hellmann, and Vincent Miller for their critical reviews of prior versions of this manuscript.

PART TWO

Theological and ethical themes in *Laudato Si'*

4

"The Love that moves the sun and the stars": A theology of creation

Elizabeth T. Groppe

ENCYCLICAL READING GUIDE

- All of Chapter 2 is devoted to the 'The Gospel of Creation', §62–100
- Religions in Dialogue with Science, §199–201

"When I had journeyed half of our life's way, I found myself within a shadowed forest, for I had lost the path that does not stray."[1] These are the opening lines of Dante Alighieri's *Divine Comedy*, widely considered a masterpiece of world literature and the greatest poem ever written in the Italian language. This story of a pilgrimage down into the underworld, through Purgatory, and finally up into Paradise begins on Good Friday and culminates in an Easter Sunday vision of "the Love that moves the sun and the stars." Pope Francis cites this famous verse from Dante's *Paradiso* in *Laudato Si'*, and it provides a key to understanding the encyclical's theology of creation. In this chapter, I will introduce Pope Francis's integral and dialogical approach to knowledge of creation, explore the Dante passage that he draws to our attention and outline the encyclical's theology of a created order that is grounded in sacrificial love.

An integral and dialogical approach to knowledge of creation

The natural sciences have given us breathtaking views of a vast cosmos and detailed knowledge of atoms we cannot even see with the naked eye. They have also enabled us to understand some of the ways in which human activity is profoundly changing the character of the biosphere on the one planet in the universe known to support life. We *homo sapiens* have altered the chemistry of the atmosphere and triggered a change in the Earth's climate, acidified the oceans, eroded soils, leveled forests, polluted waters with chemicals toxic to ourselves and other creatures, and precipitated a mass extinction of species. As a team of scientists explain in the coauthored study "Planetary Boundaries: A Safe Operating Space for Humanity" published in the journal *Nature* in 2009 and then updated in *Science* in 2015, humanity has overstepped four of the nine boundaries of the life systems that make the planet a place that we can call home.[2] (See the discussion in Chapter 3.) At this point of crisis in human civilization, we need an intensification of scientific research and also a renewed vision of the origin and purpose of creation and the vocation of the human person within the created order. We need both scientific knowledge and a compelling theological vision. Indeed, Pope Francis reflects, if we are to begin to repair the damage we have done, we are going to need every form of wisdom—including not only science and theology but also philosophy, the fine arts, poetry, literature, and the humanistic sciences (§63).

In *Laudato Si'*, Pope Francis draws from multiple sources of knowledge to articulate a vision for the care of our common home. In a similar fashion, Dante Alighieri (1265–1321) integrated the truths of Christian faith with the philosophy and science of his era in the *Divine Comedy*. This synthesis of Christian faith and philosophical and scientific reason was an ideal of medieval Christian culture. In our own era, the sapiential vision of Dante and Pope Francis offers an alternative to two influential approaches to the knowledge of creation: Christian biblical fundamentalism and secular scientism.

Christian fundamentalism arose in the late nineteenth century in response to Modernism. It affirms five religious fundamentals, including the belief that every word of the Bible is directly inspired by God and that Scripture is therefore inerrant in every and all respects, not only in regard to theology and ethics but also in respect to astronomy, geology, biology, and history. Most Christian fundamentalists reject evolutionary science's account of the slow emergence of diverse life forms through natural selection. They affirm either a "young-earth creationism" that maintains that the Earth and all living things were created in six literal days about 10,000 years ago or an "old-earth creationism" that accepts the scientific dating of the age of the Earth (4.5 billion years) but maintains that living organisms were created directly by God.[3]

Scientism, in contrast, is an approach to knowledge that assumes that the scientific method of testing hypotheses through experimental observation is the only path to truth. This approach is evident in the work of the popular author Richard Dawkins, who writes that either God "exists or he doesn't. It is a scientific question: one day we may know the answer, and meanwhile we can say something pretty strong about the probability."[4] The title of Dawkins' best-selling book *The God Delusion* indicates the degree of probability he ascribes to God's existence in the light of contemporary scientific knowledge.

In distinction from both Christian fundamentalism and secular scientism, Pope Francis speaks from the Catholic tradition's conviction that all truths participate in the divine truth and that a dialogue and integration between Scripture, tradition, and reason is not only possible but essential to the human quest for knowledge. Catholicism approaches Scripture as a text inspired by God that witnesses to divine revelation in a form shaped by human language and cultures.[5] Even prior to the advent of modern cosmology and evolutionary science, theologians read the Genesis narrative in a sophisticated manner that did not interpret the text as a physical description of how the heavens and the earth came to be. In interpreting the account of creation in the first chapter of Genesis, for example, the third-century theologian Origen of Alexandria (ca. 185–254) noticed that light exists (Gen. 1.3) and that morning and evening mark the first "day" (Gen. 1.5) even before the sun, the moon and the stars are created on "day" three (Gen. 1.16). Why, he wonders, does Genesis speak of the cycles of day and dusk even before the sun and moon, have been created? Pondering this and other anomalies in the biblical texts, Origen concludes that "much effort and toil" must be exercised in reading Scripture, for it has multiple layers of meaning, including a bodily, moral, and spiritual sense.[6] The first chapter of Genesis, comments Origen scholar John Cavadini, is not intended as a chronological account of creation. Rather, the anomaly of "days" that take place before the sun and the moon exist leads to the insight that God's act of creation is ineffable and cannot be observed by human beings nor described in human terms.[7]

Catholicism's affirmation of the ineffability and mystery of creation is a dimension of the mystical tradition that Pope Francis emphasizes in *Laudato Si'*. "The universe unfolds in God," he writes, "who fills it completely. Hence, there is a mystical meaning to be found in a leaf, in a mountain trail, in a dewdrop, in a poor person's face" (§233). This mysticism does not mean that Catholicism is antiscientific. To the contrary, the Catholic theological tradition embraces reason as a gift that participates in the wisdom of the Creator. Indeed, historians note that it was precisely a religious faith in a divine wisdom creating and sustaining the cosmos that fostered the development of empirical science, for it inspired scientists to probe the created order. "It is widely recognized," writes Christopher Kaiser, "that many of the founders of modern Western science were Christians not merely incidentally, but were inspired in creative ways by their Christian faith."[8] Among these Christian scientists he names Johannes Kepler, Robert Boyle, Isaac Newton, and James Clerk Maxwell. Gregor Mendel (1822–94), whose mathematical analyses of experiments with plant hybridization led to the founding of the science of genetics, was an Augustinian monk. Georges-Henri Lemaitre (1894–1966), who developed a hypothesis about an initial expansion of the universe that his critics derisively dubbed the "big bang theory," was both a physicist and a priest.[9] His theory is now an axiom of astrophysics and cosmology. Pope Francis himself holds a *título* in chemistry from a technical secondary school in Argentina.

The well-known saga of the Italian philosopher, astronomer, and mathematician Galileo Galilei (1564–1642) has given some the impression that Catholicism opposes scientific findings that challenge convictions of faith.[10] When Galileo's research on the nature of motion and his telescopic discoveries led him to affirm Copernicus's theory of the Earth's movement around the sun, he was accused of heresy by the Catholic Church and forbidden to hold or defend Copernican geokineticism. When he published the book *Dialogue* (1632) that presented but did not personally endorse geokineticism, he was summoned to Rome to stand trial and then placed under house arrest from 1633 until his death in 1642. Less well known is that Galileo was vindicated in the papacy of John Paul II, who affirmed that "Galileo formulated important norms of an epistemological character, which are indispensable to reconcile Holy Scripture and science."[11] Catholicism's commitment to scientific research is also evident in the existence of the Pontifical Academy of Science, established by Pope Pius IX in 1847. Today, the Academy is comprised of 80 scientists from many countries who conduct studies in their own disciplines and undertake interdisciplinary collaboration. In principle, albeit not always in historical practice, Catholicism is open to all that can be learned through dialogue with scientific observation and analysis.[12]

In distinction from secular scientism, however, Catholicism affirms that the natural sciences are one dimension of knowledge, not the only source of wisdom. Liturgical and contemplative prayer, music, poetry, art, literature, philosophy, and theology mediate and give expression to beauty, goodness, and truth in a manner that is not irrational but that is different from and complementary to the scientific method and mathematical computation. "It cannot be maintained," Pope Francis emphasizes, "that empirical science provides a complete explanation of life, the interplay of all creatures and the whole of reality. This would be to breach the limits imposed by its own methodology. If we reason only within the confines of the latter, little room would be left for aesthetic sensibility, poetry, or even reason's ability to grasp the ultimate meaning and purpose of things" (§199). Francis traces the roots of the crisis in our common home to "an undifferentiated and one-dimensional paradigm" that exalts the human subject and uses reason instrumentally to control and possess (§106). He invites us instead to use reason sapientially with an openness to awe, wonder, and the experience of kinship and communion.

It is not Francis's position that empirical science explains all that is within its grasp and then leaves theology to fill in the gaps by attributing what cannot yet be explained to God. That approach to the relation of theology and science assumes that creation and God are like matter and dark matter, two kinds of the same thing (the stuff of the cosmos) that differ only in that one can be directly perceived through scientific instruments and the other cannot. Rather, the Catholic tradition affirms that God precisely as *God* is both intimately present to all of creation (including both those dimensions of creation known through science and those not yet scientifically understood) and at the same time transcendent to the mutable, corruptible, and contingent cosmos. God, in the classic formulation of Thomas Aquinas (1225–74), does not belong to a kind or class of beings (*ens subsistens*) as one being among others but is *ipsum esse*—the sheer act of "being itself," the mysterious "I am who I am" of Moses's quest for God's name on Mount Horeb (Exod. 3.14), a reality that flames through all the categories and classes of being that our small limited human brains can conceive.[13] This is why God cannot be directly perceived or measured through scientific means like Laser Interferometer Gravitational-Wave Observatories, no matter how powerful they are or may become. This is not a defensive position to save God from modern science but an original and fundamental metaphysical principle of Catholic theology.

How, then, you may well ask, can we know or speak of God at all? The Catholic tradition's response to this fundamental question is complex and multifaceted. I will briefly indicate several modes of approach. First, God is known indirectly and analogically through the beauty, goodness, and truth of the created cosmos in a manner comparable to the way Claude Monet or Käthe Kollwitz can be recognized as the artists of the paintings "Water Lilies" or "Woman with Dead Child." "God has written a precious book," Francis attests, citing Pope Saint John Paul II, "whose letters are the multitude of created things present in the universe" and the "contemplation of creation allows us to discover in each thing a teaching which God wishes to hand on to us, since 'for the believer, to contemplate creation is to hear a message, to listen to a paradoxical and silent voice'" (§85).[14] Each creature "reflects in its own way a ray of God's infinite wisdom and goodness" (§69).[15]

Secondly, the very process of limning the limits of reason as we probe theological questions suggests that we are pressing up against a transcendent mystery. In his famous discussion of the "five ways" that God can be known, Aquinas observes that none of the things that we can observe with our senses—an oak tree, a gray squirrel, a cardinal—is the cause of its own existence. Each is the result of what the philosopher Aristotle termed an "efficient cause," an agency that produces an effect.[16] I was begotten by my parents and they by theirs, and we could continue this causal sequence back to the dawn of life or to the beginning of the universe. Stars and galaxies were caused by the lumping of the cosmos, and the lumping of the cosmos was caused by the force of gravity, and the force of gravity was caused by the Big Bang. But the ultimate cause of creaturely existence is never really addressed if we simply continue this chain of causes within the dimensions of space-time. We are bumping up against a mystery that transcends finite and temporal forms of causation, following a trail that leads not to a first cause in a chronological sense but to a noncontingent or unoriginate cause in the ontological or metaphysical sense.

Third, God can be known to us through divine revelation. "Ever since the creation of the world," Paul wrote in his letter to the Romans, God's "invisible attributes of eternal power and divinity have been able to be understood and perceived in what he has made" (Rom. 1.20). And yet humans claiming wisdom "became fools and exchanged the glory of the immortal God for the likeness of an image of mortal man or of birds or of four-legged animals or of snakes" (Rom. 1.23). To heal our foolish disfigurement of divine glory, the Wisdom of God spoke through the prophets and assumed human flesh in the person of Jesus Christ (John 1.14). God's covenant with the Jewish people and incarnation in Christ make known truths about God that are accessible to us through creation but that we are slow to learn.[17] At the same time, they also manifest truths about the depths of God's love that we cannot know through analogical reasoning from the created order alone. In Chapter Two of *Laudato Si'*, Pope Francis contemplates the mystery of the universe illumined through the light of the revelation of God's love, and it is in this context that he invokes Dante's *Divine Comedy*.

Beholding the mystery of the universe through the light of Christian faith

As the *Divine Comedy* opens, we find ourselves with Dante in a dark wood. He is weary and disoriented and has lost his way. At the foot of a hill, he looks up and sees the rays of the sun, which begin to quiet his fears, and he steps toward the light. But his ascent is impeded by the appearance in succession of a triad of beasts: a lithe leopard, a ravenous lion and a wolf so "craving in her leanness" that the very sight of her causes Dante to abandon hope. He retreats to lower ground and there beholds the Roman poet Virgil, sent to Dante's aid by Beatrice, a maiden beloved by Dante who died young and is now in Paradise. Virgil assumes the role of spiritual guide, but rather than leading Dante past the beasts to ascend the mountain, he accompanies him down through a gate into the suffering city of eternal pain, "the way that runs among the lost."[18] In this Inferno, Dante beholds in sweat and terror the self-imposed consequences of sin. In the fourth level of Hell, for example, hoarders eternally push boulders to the center of their circle of the conical underworld, and in the seventh circle the violent swim in a boiling sea of blood. In Hell's icy lowest pit, Satan, who in pride deified himself, grinds traitors in the teeth of his trinity of heads.

Having beheld the horror of the sin that warps and disfigures the human person and grotesquely distorts human relationships and communion, Dante and we, his literary companions, begin an ascent of the terraces of the mountain of Purgatory. This journey is a climb through the levels of the seven deadly sins—pride, envy, anger, avarice, sloth, gluttony, and lust—in which figurative antidotes to sin are actions of purification. The prideful, for example, who elevated themselves in the place of God, carry boulders on their backs that press them down, and Dante recognizes himself in them and shoulders his own rock.

On the top of Mount Purgatory, Virgil presents Dante to Beatrice, who will lead him through the light of the celestial spheres. In the ninth sphere, on the cusp of Paradise, light radiates upon Beatrice's face as she speaks to Dante of the mind of God, around which the universe moves as if on a pivot.[19] Dante turns from the luminous reflection he sees in Beatrice's face toward the light itself, around which radiate circles of angelic intelligence in degrees of assimilation to God. "I saw a point that set forth so acute a light, that anyone who faced the force with which it blazed would have to shut his eyes," the poet writes.[20] "On that Point," Beatrice explains as Dante stands in perplexed suspense, "depend the heavens and the whole of nature."[21]

The pilgrimage climaxes in Paradise itself, where the mystical theologian Saint Bernard of Clairvaux entreats the Virgin Mary to clear away the obstacles from Dante's eyes so that he might behold the vision of God. Dante exclaims:

O grace abounding, through which I presumed
to set my eyes on the Eternal Light
so long that I spent all my sight on it!
In its profundity I saw—ingathered
and bound by love into one single volume –
what, in the universe, seems separate, scattered.[22]

A journey that began on Good Friday in a shadowy forest lurking with hungry beasts approaches its conclusion with the realization that all the seemingly disparate dimensions of the universe are "bound by love into one single volume."

Whosoever sees the Living Light of love that binds this book, Dante continues, will not break one's gaze, for our will is attracted to goodness. As Dante's vision grows stronger, he beholds three circles each identical but for their different colors, the second reflecting the first and the third breathed simultaneously by the first two, an allusion to the procession of the Holy Spirit from God the Father and the Son. This triune communion cannot be expressed in words: "How incomplete is speech, how weak, when set against my thought!"[23] And then, as Dante looks deeply into the second circle, he is transfixed by an image of a human form that has been taken up into the spiraling triune light, not as a piece of chaff caught in a swirling wind but like a wheel that turns of its own desire and will in harmony with *l'amor che move il sole e l'altre stelle*:

> Here force failed my high fantasy; but my
> desire and will were moved already—like
> a wheel revolving uniformly—by
> the Love that moves the sun and the other stars.[24]

The love that moves the sun and the other stars that Dante discovers on Easter Sunday in Paradise is the love that gave being to creation not from a desire to control or possess, but, as Beatrice explains, because "eternal Love opened into new loves."[25] Moreover, this is an Eternal Love that in Christ humbly assumes human nature, a love that knows in the flesh the horror of the betrayal that freezes over the lowest circle of Hell, a love more powerful than Satan's pride and stronger than the words "abandon every hope" emblazoned on Hell's gate. In the *Comedia*, both the moment of the creation of the cosmos and the moment of Christ's crucifixion are marked by the spring equinox, suggesting that creation is a cruciform act of sacrificial love from its point of inception.

Principles for understanding creation in *Laudato Si'*

Dante's vision of creation as an act in which "eternal Love opened into new loves" expresses the heart of Catholicism's theology of creation and is the basis of several fundamental principles that Pope Francis highlights in *Laudato Si'*. These include the following:

"Creation" is an intentional act of the freedom of divine love

"Creation," Francis writes, echoing Dante, "is in the order of love. God's love is the fundamental moving force in all created things" (§77). Today, however, it is one possible conclusion of scientific investigation that the cosmos is the result of blind forces known through physics and evolution's random genetic mutations. Chance, according to some physicists, can account even for the "fine tuning" of the cosmos. Fine-tuning refers to the scientific observation that the physical parameters of the universe in the immediate aftermath of the Big Bang were precisely of the necessary proportion for life as we know it with conscious moral agents (i.e., us) to evolve. For example, if the dark-energy density of the universe had been only infinitesimally larger, it would have acted as a repulsive force and space would have expanded so rapidly after the Big Bang that stars and galaxies would never have formed. If, however, the dark-energy density of the universe had been just a miniscule amount smaller, it would have had a contracting effect and the universe would have collapsed upon itself before life could have evolved. "The fine tuning for life of the dark energy," philosopher Robin Collins comments, "is estimated to be around 1 part in 10^{120}—that is, 1 part in 1 followed by 120 zeros. The precision of this is comparable to that required to hit a bull's-eye on Earth less than the size of a proton when throwing a dart from outer space."[26] Physicist Stephen Hawking is among a number of scientists who conclude from studies of fine-tuning that our universe must be just one of many universes in a vast multiverse. From this perspective, "fine tuning" is neither "tuning" by an intentional agent nor statistically improbable. If we postulate a truly enormous number of universes, a habitable one like ours becomes likely, just as your chances of pulling one blue marble from a pouch with 10^{120}–1 white ones would be assured if you could pull out 10^{120} marbles rather than just one. It is not probability theory but Christian faith in God's free loving act of creation that leads Pope Francis to exclaim, "How wonderful is the certainty that each human life is not adrift in the midst of hopeless chaos, in a world ruled by pure chance or endlessly recurring cycles! The Creator can say to each one of us: 'Before I formed you in the womb, I knew you' (Jer 1:5)" (§65).

Creation is a nonviolent act of love

The theology of creation as an act of divine love that is implicit in Genesis 1 and explicit in Dante's *Divine Comedy* and *Laudato Si'* stands in sharp contrast to the *Enuma elish*, a narrative from ancient Babylon, where Scripture scholars believe that the people of Israel were living in exile when the Genesis tradition originated. In the Babylonian epic, the god Marduk creates the world by slaying the sea dragon Tiamat, cutting her body in two, and using one half of the corpse to shape the sky and the other to form the earth. Marduk also slays Tiamat's consort Kingu and makes human beings from his blood to serve as slaves to himself. How different is the Genesis account in which God creates by the power of divine speech: "And God said, 'Let there be light!'" (Gen. 1.3) "The universe," Pope Francis emphasizes, "did not emerge as the result of arbitrary omnipotence, a show of force or a desire for self-assertion" (§77), but from the triune love that moves the sun and the stars.

"God saw everything that he had made and behold it was very good" (Gen. 1.31)

"Eternal Love opened into new loves," Beatrice tells Dante as they behold the mystery of creation's origin. God creates the cosmos not to produce slaves for himself, but to share the divine goodness. This goodness is present in a special way, Pope Francis comments, in man and woman created in the divine image and likeness (Gen. 1.26) (§65).[27] But it is also true of every single creature, who each "reflects in its own way a ray of God's infinite wisdom and goodness" (§69).[28] Everything that God has made has intrinsic worth and is not simply an object for instrumental human use: "Every creature is thus the object of the Father's tenderness, who gives it its place in the world. Even the fleeting life of the least of beings is the object of his love, and in its few seconds of existence, God enfolds it with his affection" (§77). Scripture and Catholic tradition have long affirmed the intrinsic value not only of humans but of all creatures, but Australian theologian Denis Edwards believes that the clarity with which Pope Francis emphasizes that *every* creature is a locus of divine presence and a reality illumined by divine love (§76) constitutes an important development in church teaching.[29]

Creation, a gift ex nihilo of God's goodness, exists in ontological distinction from the Creator

The fundamental ontological difference between the unoriginate Creator and the contingent creature means that nature is not divine (§78) and that "we are not God" (§67). Nor is the cosmos made from some preexistent matter. Rather, God created the cosmos ex nihilo (out of nothing) as a gift, a theology that invites us to turn from our technocratic attitudes. "Nature," Pope Francis writes, "is usually seen as a system which can be studied, understood, and controlled, whereas creation can only be understood as a gift from the outstretched hand of the Father of all, and as a reality illuminated by the love which calls us together into universal communion" (§76).

God's creative action is ongoing

The God who creates the cosmos in an act of free love sustains creation in being. The Catholic theological tradition speaks of this as *creatio continua*, or "continuous creation," and this vision is fundamentally distinct from deism, the position that God is like a clockmaker who assembles a clock, winds it up, and then leaves it to run its own course. Nor does the Catholic tradition maintain that God is a puppeteer pulling on creation's strings. The triune God of love endows creatures with their own agency and freedom, even at the risk that we may abuse these gifts and use them wrongly. "God," writes Francis, "is intimately present to each being, without impinging on the autonomy of his creature, and this gives rise to the rightful autonomy of earthly affairs" (§80).

"Then I saw a new heaven and a new earth" (Rev. 21.1)

Dante's vision in Paradise of the glory of the triune God who is the love that moves the sun and the stars is eschatological. That is to say, it is a glimpse beyond suffering and death into the new creation made possible by the resurrection of Christ and the gift of the Holy Spirit. "At the end," Pope Francis reflects, "we will find ourselves face to face with the infinite beauty of God (cf. 1 Cor 13:12), and be able to read with admiration and happiness the mystery of the universe, which with us will share in unending plentitude. Even now we are journeying toward the sabbath of eternity, the new Jerusalem, toward our common home in heaven. Jesus says: 'I make all things new' (Rev 21:5). Eternal life will be a shared experience of awe, in which each creature, resplendently transfigured, will take its rightful place" (§243). Every person and every creature, no matter how small, is encompassed by eternal love. "The ultimate purpose of other creatures," Francis emphasizes, "is not to be found in us. Rather, all creatures are moving forward with us and through us toward a common point of arrival, which is God, in that transcendent fullness where the risen Christ embraces and illumines all things" (§83).

Beauty and truth

Pope Francis's theology of creation is beautiful—but is it true? In 1990, the Hubble Telescope was deployed from the space shuttle Discovery and in the past twenty-five years the cosmic scenes it has enabled us to behold have delighted and astonished people around the world and necessitated the rewriting of astronomy text books. Hubble has brought us such iconic images as "pillars of creation" —but no photographs of the point of light Dante saw reflected in Beatrice's face nor pictures of the "Love that moves the sun and the stars." Pope Francis's encyclical does not explicitly address the challenge that twenty-first-century science poses to a Catholic theology of creation forged in the patristic and medieval eras. But his caution in *Laudato Si'* about the limits of "technoscience" gives us a clue as to how he might respond to someone who believes that modern physics, chemistry, and biology render the vision of theologians such as Origen, Aquinas, and Dante irrelevant.

One reason that empirical science has become intellectually dominant is that it has been so astonishingly effective. The knowledge that humanity has gained through application of the scientific method has enabled us to build steam engines, factories, skyscrapers, automobiles, airplanes, nuclear reactors, computers, and spaceships that can take a human being all the way to the moon and back again, and Francis is appreciative of the good that technology can enable (§103). Empirical science has borne fruit, and the technological achievements that science has made possible are powerful evidence of its truth. At our current juncture of human and planetary history, however, the limitations of technoscience are also evident. The way in which we have used the Promethean power enabled by science has carried us on a high-speed journey that has taken us to a social and ecological "breaking point" (§61). Ecological degradation is so severe, Francis lamented in his address to the United Nations, that it "could place the human species in danger of extinction."[30] Here science and religion arrive at the same concern.

The fact that our technoscientific civilization is at a breaking point can open us to another way of seeing the world. It is not that science is false nor that it is irreconcilable with theology, but rather that it is insufficient. Technoscience, Pope Francis writes, gives us the means to reshape the planet but no vision of the goal and purpose of human activity (§61). It puts no limits on human freedom (§6) and gives no direction to human desire. Francis seeks out "the best scientific research available today" and invites us to let this "touch us deeply" (§15). But science alone cannot set us on a new course.

Moreover, it is not the only form of knowledge that has proven to be fruitful. The joy of Saint Francis that inspired the rapid growth of the Franciscan order is in its own way evidence of the truth of the theology of creation of *Laudato Si'*. Franciscan spirituality is grounded in forms of knowledge that are distinct from those of mathematics, physics, and biology but that "take us to the heart of what it is to be human" (§11). The life of the man who embraced lepers and gently moved earthworms from the road to spare them from being crushed is evidence of the truth of Dante's conviction that at the foundation of the universe is indeed an affectionate and tender love that moves the sun and the stars, assumes flesh in Jesus Christ and conquers death through the wood of the cross. Moreover, as Lynn White suggested over 40 years ago in his famous critique of the role of Western European Christianity in the ecological crisis: had all Christians lived according to the exemplar of Saint Francis, we would not currently find ourselves in a state of planetary ecological emergency.[31] That Francis's theology of creation could have led to an ecologically viable human civilization is evidence of its fruitfulness and truth.

Living in the Love that moves the sun and the stars

What would it mean, in practice, to live the theology of creation of *Laudato Si'*? Other chapters in this volume will explore some of the implications of the encyclical for our households, parishes and dioceses, communities, and public policy. Here I will simply delineate briefly three principles of Christian spirituality that follow from the encyclical's theology of creation:

Conversion from anthropocentrism

Francis's theology of creation is an invitation to a conversion from our culture's common assumption that humans stand at the center of the universe and that the Earth is nothing but a disposable resource at the service of our every desire. The best way to restore ourselves to our rightful place in creation, Francis writes, is to recognize that the Earth is not raw material to which we are entitled but a common home that is a gift of a loving God (§75–76). "The misuse of creation begins," he continues, citing his predecessor Pope Benedict XVI, "when we no longer recognize any higher instance than ourselves, when we see nothing else but ourselves" (§6).[32]

Dante scholar Christian Moevs describes Dante's pilgrimage from the Earth to Paradise, from space-time to its source, as "a journey of self-crucifixion."[33] The crucifixion of the ego-self is necessary because human desires are easily prone to a self-serving misorientation. In the *Divine Comedy*, the denizens of the Inferno are not inherently evil people but persons whose desires have been warped. In Hell, for example, the good desire for love has become lust, and the divine command to love one's neighbor twisted into a grotesque cannibalism. In Dante's state of final purification and beatitude, his will and desire finally turn not in service of his own ego but "like a wheel in perfect balance" with the desire of God. This divine desire and love have the power to convert our human hearts from egoism and anthropocentrism and lead us to the joy of communion with God and all creatures. I am told by people who have met the pope in person that he radiates the joy of which he writes in both *Laudato Si'* and *Evangelii gaudium* (The Joy of the Gospel), and this gives authenticity to his words.

Living in communion with all creation

Because all creatures belong to the Lord who loves the living (Wis 11.26), Francis reflects, "All of us are linked by unseen bonds and together form a kind of universal family, a sublime communion which fills us with a sacred, affectionate and humble respect" for all of our fellow human beings and for all creatures (§89–91). Theologian and bishop Robert Barron writes in a reflection on the writings of Trappist monk Thomas Merton that in the practice of contemplative prayer one may find "the place in you where you are here and now being created by God."[34] This discovery of one's own center within the love of God, Barron explains, is at the same time the discovery of one's point of connection with everything else in the cosmos, for the same love that is here and now creating me is also here and now creating you.

This theological conviction that all creatures are linked by unseen bonds of communion finds some resonance with evolutionary science. Charles Darwin's *Origin of Species*, theologian Elizabeth Johnson reflects, is "a watershed for human awareness" that profoundly alters not only our understanding of speciation but also our sense of "our own membership in the evolving community of life."[35] Darwin, she explains, is not a threat to theology but a gift, for he enables us to see in a new way the reality that every species of life is indeed interconnected, all part of the same evolutionary family tree.

A famous sketch from Darwin's notebooks depicts species emerging from a common ancestor like branches on a tree, and biologists today have refined and enhanced this image of the evolutionary family tree of life using twenty-first-century databases and computer technology to produce interactive electronic genealogies of species.[36] To sing with Saint Francis of "brother wolf" and "sister sparrow" is not naïve romanticism but an expression of both theological and scientific truth.

Moreover, we are learning through science that the differences that distinguish us from our closest of kin on the evolutionary tree of life are, in some cases, differences of degree rather than kind. Dante describes the humans he encounters in his journey through the Inferno as "beastly" because of their failure to moderate human desires through reason and virtue. Yet today, Celia Deane-Drummond writes, scientists have found that "reason, freedom, morality and language all have their counterparts in those animals who have relevant cognitive and social abilities."[37] Scientists who study animal behavior have witnessed magpies, foxes, wolves, llamas, and gorillas mourning dead mates, kin and companions, and there is evidence that chimpanzees, dolphins, and elephants have self-awareness.[38] Some animals even exhibit what could be described as empathy and altruism. There have been witnesses, for example, of dolphins staying beside an injured or dying companion even at the risk of their own lives. Theologian Sarah Coakley concludes after years of working closely with Harvard evolutionary scientist Martin Nowak that cooperation and even self-sacrifice are just as important in the drama of evolutionary history as competition for survival.[39] In an awareness of the communion of all creatures that is informed by both scientific and theological forms of knowledge, Pope Francis exclaims, "God has joined us so closely to the world around us that we can feel the desertification of the soil almost as a physical ailment, and the extinction of a species as a painful disfigurement" (§89).

The common destination of goods

Finally, the theological principle that all creation originates in the love of God grounds the Catholic Social Tradition's principle of the common destination of goods. "The Earth is the Lord's, and the fullness thereof" (Ps. 24.1), Francis reminds us (§67). The goods of creation are ours to enjoy not as a natural right but as a gift. The Catholic ethical tradition does uphold the legitimacy of property ownership insofar as this social structure serves the common good. At the same time, the Catholic tradition emphasizes that owners of property are ethically obliged to use the goods of creation in a manner that serves God's purposes. Moreover, the right to private property is not absolute or inviolable but subordinate to the principle of the universal destination of goods. "For believers," Francis writes, "this becomes a question of fidelity to the Creator, since God created the world for everyone. Hence every ecological approach needs to incorporate a social perspective which takes into account the fundamental rights of the poor and the underprivileged" (§93). This is a well-established moral principle in Catholic social teaching. In *Laudato Si'*, Francis expands this social morality to take into account the need of all creatures for a habitat within our common home.

Praised be

We have strayed into a dark wood and are now on the cusp of a journey through a social and ecological Hell of our own making, a world of impoverished and displaced human beings and the sixth mass extinction of life in the Earth's history. Pope Francis squarely faces the scale and scope of ecological degradation and does not flinch. Instead, he calls us to behold with Dante the eschatological vision of the "Love that moves the sun and the stars" and to act in the faith and hope of the One who said "I make all things new" (Rev. 21.5). We live in anticipation of that eternal day when we will find ourselves face to face with the infinite beauty of God (1 Cor. 13.12) and, "in the meantime, we come together to take charge of this home which has been entrusted to us, knowing that all the good which exists here will be taken up into the heavenly feast. In union with all creatures, we journey through this land seeking God" (§244). Francis draws his encyclical toward conclusion with words inviting us to join the chorus of creatures in a canticle of praise: "Let us sing as we go" (§244).

Questions

1   What is Christian fundamentalism? What is scientism? How and why does the Catholic tradition differ from both of these approaches to knowledge of creation?

2   What leads Dante to exclaim that it is ultimately love that moves the sun and the stars? What does Dante's vision contribution to the theology of creation in *Laudato Si'*?

3   Identify the six principles of a theology of creation that are discussed in this chapter. Give examples of their practical application.

4   Why might someone with a twenty-first-century worldview question the validity of a Catholic theology of creation? According to the chapter, what are some signs of the truth of this theology?

Notes

1   Dante Alighieri, *Inferno*, trans. Allen Mandelbaum (New York: Bantam, 1980), I, 1–3.

2   Johan Rockström, Will Steffen, Kevin Noone, Asa Persson, Stuart F. Chapin, Eric F. Lambin, Timothy M. Lenton, Marten Scheffer, Carl Folke, Hans Joachim Schellnhuber, Björn Nykvist, Cynthia A. de Wit, Terry Hughes, Sander van der Leeuw, Henning Rodhe, Sverker Sörlin, Peter K. Snyder, Robert Costanza, Uno Svedin, Malin Falkenmark, Louise Karlberg, Robert W. Corell, Victoria J. Fabry, James Hansen, Brian Walker, Diana Liverman, Katherine Richardson, Paul Crutzen, Jonathan A. Foley, "Planetary Boundaries: Exploring a Safe Operating Space for Humanity," *Nature* 461, no. 7263 (2009): 472–75; Will Steffen, Katherine Richardson, Johan Rockström, Sarah E. Cornell, Ingo Fetzer, Elena M. Bennett, Reinette Biggs, Stephen R. Carpenter, Wim de Vries, Cynthia A. de Wit, Carl Folke, Dieter Gerten, Jens Heinke, Georgina M. Mace, Linn M. Persson, Veerabhadran Ramanathan, Belinda Reyers, and Sverker Sörlin, "Planetary Boundaries: Guiding Human Development on a Changing Planet," *Science* 347, no. 6223 (February 2015): 736 ff.

3   Dennis Alexander, "Creation and Evolution," in *The Blackwell Companion to Science and Christianity*, ed. J. B. Stump and Alan G. Padgett (Malden, MA: Blackwell, 2012), 236.

4   Richard Dawkins, *The God Delusion* (Boston: Houghton Mifflin, 2006), 70.

5   Second Vatican Council, *Dei Verbum* (Dogmatic Constitution on Divine Revelation), in *The Basic Sixteen Documents: Vatican Council II: Constitutions, Decrees, Declarations*, ed. Austin Flannery (New York: Costello Publishing Company, 1996), 3:11–13.

6   Origen, *On First Principles*, trans. G. W. Butterworth (Glouchester, MA: Peter Smith, 1973), IV.3.5 and IV.2.4.

7   John Cavadini, Origen Seminar, University of Notre Dame, Spring 1995.

8   Christopher Kaiser, "Early Christian Belief in Creation and the Beliefs Sustaining the Modern Scientific Endeavor," in *The Blackwell Companion to Science and Christianity*, ed. J. B. Stump and Alan G. Padgett (Malden, MA: Blackwell, 2012), 3.

9   Sean Salai S.J., "The Faith and Science of Georges Lemaître: 11 Questions for Dr. Karl van Bibber," *America Magazine* (May 25, 2016); http://www.americamagazine.org/content/all-things/faith-and-science-georges-lemaitre-11-questions-dr-karl-van-bibber

10   On this point, see Ruth Graham, "An F in Science: Why Should America's Crisis of Scientific Illiteracy Concern Catholics?" *U.S. Catholic* 80 (December 2015): 13–17.

11 John Paul II, "Deep Harmony Which Unites the Truths of Science with the Truths of Faith," *L'Osservatore Romano* (November 26, 1979): 9–10. See also Maurice A. Finocchiaro, "The Copernican Revolution and the Galileo Affair," in *The Blackwell Companion to Science and Christianity*, ed. J. B. Stump and Alan G. Padgett (Malden, MA: Blackwell, 2012), 14–25.

12 Theologian Ian Barbour outlines four different ways in which our culture has approached the relationship of religion and science: conflict, independence, dialogue, and integration. In the terms of this typology, Catholicism practices dialogue or integration between religious and scientific knowledge. It does not hold that these two forms of knowledge are in irreconcilable conflict, nor that they are so disparate that they can have nothing to do with one another. See Barbour, *When Science Meets Religion: Enemies, Strangers, or Partners?* (New York: HarperCollins, 2000), 7–38.

13 On these points see Kathryn Tanner, *God and Creation in Christian Theology* (Minneapolis: Fortress, 1988).

14 The reference is to John Paul II, *Catechesis* (January 26, 2000), 5: *Insegnamenti* 23, no. 1 (2000): 123.

15 Pope Francis is here citing *Catechism of the Catholic Church*, §339.

16 Thomas Aquinas, *Summa Theologiae*, I, q. 3, a. 3.

17 Although the complexities of interreligious relations are beyond the scope of this chapter, it is important to note that Islam can also mediate knowledge of the God of Abraham and Sarah, and *Laudato Si'* does include one citation from the Sufi Muslim mystic Ali al-Khawas (*LS* n. 159).

18 Dante, *Inferno*, III. 4.

19 Dante, *Paradiso*, trans. Allen Mandelbaum (New York: Bantam, 1984), XXVII, 103–18.

20 Ibid., XXVIII, 16–18.

21 Ibid., 41–42.

22 Ibid., XXXIII, 82–88.

23 Ibid., 121.

24 Ibid., 142–45.

25 Ibid., XXIX, 18.

26 Robin Collins, "The Fine-Tuning of the Cosmos: A Fresh Look at Its Implications," in *The Blackwell Companion to Science and Christianity*, ed. J. B. Stump and Alan G. Padgett (Malden, MA: Blackwell, 2012), 208.

27 On the special character of human beings, see also §81 and §90.

28 Pope Francis is here citing *Catechism of the Catholic Church*, §339.

29 Denis Edwards, "'Sublime Communion': The Theology of the Natural World in *Laudato Si'*," *Theological Studies* 77 (2016): 383.

30 Pope Francis, Address to the United Nations (25 September, 2105). http://w2.vatican.va/content/francesco/en/speeches/2015/september/documents/papa-francesco_20150925_onu-visita.html.

31 Lynn White Jr., "The Historical Roots of Our Ecologic Crisis," *Science* 155 (1967): 1203–07.

32 Benedict XVI, Address to the Clergy of the Diocese of Bolzano-Bressanone (August 6, 2008): *AAS* 100 (2008): 634.

33 Christian Moevs, *The Metaphysics of Dante's Comedy* (New York: Oxford University Press, 2005), 160.

34 Quoted in Robert Barron, *Catholicism: A Journey to the Heart of the Faith* (New York: Crown Publishing, 2011), 248.

35 Elizabeth Johnson, *Ask the Beasts: Darwin and the God of Love* (New York: Bloomsburg Continuum, 2014), 99.

36 Charles Darwin, *On the Origin of Species*, A Facsimile of the First Edition (Cambridge: Harvard University Press, 1964), pull-out insert between pages 116 and 117. Today's versions of the evolutionary tree of life include Tree of Life web project: http://tolweb.org/tree/; Open Tree of Life: http://www.opentreeoflife.org/; and OneZoom Tree of Life: http://www.onezoom.org/.

37 Celia Deane-Drummond, *The Wisdom of the Liminal: Evolution and Other Animals in Human Becoming* (Grand Rapids: Eerdmans, 2014), 302.

38 Marc Bekoff, *The Emotional Lives of Animals: A Leading Scientist Explores Animal Joy, Sorrow, and Empathy–and Why They Matter* (Novato, CA: New World Library, 2007).

39 Sarah Coakley, "Sacrifice Regained: Evolution, Cooperation, and God," The 2012 Gifford Lectures, http://www.giffordlectures.org/lectures/sacrifice-regained-evolution-cooperation-and-god; Martin A. Nowak with Roger Highfield, *SuperCooperators: Altruism, Evolution, and Why We Need Each Other to Succeed* (New York: Free Press, 2011).

5

"To praise, reverence, and serve": The theological anthropology of Pope Francis

Daniel Castillo

> ### ENCYCLICAL READING GUIDE
>
> Francis discusses his understanding of the human person throughout the encyclical:
>
> - St Francis as an exemplar of humanity, §10–12; 87
> - The human/earth relationship §66–70; 80–84;
> - The importance of Jesus Christ for anthropology §82; 96–100; 221
>
> Further suggested reading: Genesis 1-4

As [Jesus] said of the powers of his own age: "You know that the rulers of the Gentiles lord it over them, and their great men exercise authority over them. It shall not be so among you; but whoever would be great among you must be your servant." (§80)

Introduction

In this chapter, we will examine the theological anthropology of *Laudato Si'*. Theological anthropology explores who we are as human persons in relationship to God. This does not mean, however, that theological anthropology is concerned strictly with the human/God relationship. After all, the human person—as a created being within history—always exists in a complex web of social and ecological relationships. Therefore, when considering whom the human person is in relation to God, we can also take into consideration our existence within this broader web of relationships. For example, theological anthropology can ask: What type of relationships does God call us to have with other humans and with the earth? In fact, it is Pope Francis's response to this question that is at the heart of the theological anthropology of *Laudato Si'*.

In exploring the pope's vision of the human person, we will begin by considering briefly the Jesuit spiritual tradition that has shaped Francis's life. We will use the insights gained from this consideration to establish a framework in order to explore the social and ecological dimensions of the pope's theological anthropology, focusing especially on Francis's understanding of God's call to humanity.

St. Ignatius's "principle and foundation"

As many commentators have noted, Pope Francis's formation as a Jesuit priest has had a profound effect on his thought.[1] Therefore, in exploring the pope's understanding of what it means to be human, it is appropriate to turn to the views of St Ignatius—the founder of the Jesuit order—for insight into Francis's own vision of humanity. We can begin by noting that at the center of St Ignatius of Loyola's theological anthropology is his view that "human beings are created to praise, reverence, and serve God our Lord and by means of this to save their souls."[2] This is the opening line of "The Principle and Foundation" of Ignatius's *Spiritual Exercises*. From there, Ignatius continues, writing, "The other things on the face of the earth are created for human beings, to help them in working toward the end for which they were created."[3]

Here, we must immediately pause to raise a number of critical observations. For while the "Principle and Foundation" is central to an Ignatian understanding of the human person, it may appear strange to begin a chapter aimed at developing the *ecological* dimensions of Francis's theological anthropology by turning to this passage from the *Exercises*. Ignatius's language seems to present an instrumental view of creation (a view in which the created order is of value only to the degree that it can be manipulated to be of benefit to human beings). Likewise, his view that "the other things on the face of the earth are created for the human person" appears to resound with the very anthropocentrism that Lynn White Jr argued was at the root of the ecological crisis.[4] Moreover, the language of the salvation of the soul can conjure a worldview that seems to endorse escape from the created order.

In what follows, we will respond to these potential concerns by arguing that, in *Laudato Si'*, Francis develops the key terms of the "Principle and Foundation"— "praise," "reverence" and "serve"—in a manner that allows him to construct a theological anthropology deeply sensitive to contemporary ecological and social concerns. Specifically, we will observe that, for Francis, the human person's vocation to praise, reverence and serve God cannot be separated from the call to serve "the garden of the world" (§67).

"To praise and reverence": The Pope and the Saint

To begin to grasp the manner in which Pope Francis applies the language of "The Principle and Foundation" in his encyclical, it is instructive to turn to the pope's consideration of the other saint most closely associated with him—his namesake—St Francis of Assisi. In the opening chapter of *Laudato Si'*, the pope points his readers to the figure of the saint, asserting that St Francis takes "us to the heart of what it is to be human" (§11). The pope continues, writing of the saint, "Just as happens when we fall in love with someone, whenever he would gaze at the sun, the moon or the smallest of animals, he burst into song, drawing all other creatures into his praise" (§11). This description is striking. The pope observes that in falling in love with creation, St Francis does what Ignatius claims humanity has been created for: St Francis bursts into praise for God the creator and savior of the world. The saint's praise of God is his response to the goodness and fecundity of the created world. The pope makes this connection clear in the opening lines of *Laudato Si'*, when he quotes the words of the saint: "Praise be to you, my Lord, through our Sister, Mother Earth, who sustains and governs us, and who produces various fruit with colored flowers and herbs" (§1). Indeed, the title of the encyclical, *Laudato Si'*, is taken from a passage from St Francis and translates as, "praise be to you Lord."

In continuing his reflection on St Francis, the pope makes a similar observation regarding the character of the saint's reverence for God. The pope writes:

He communed with all creation, even preaching to the flowers, inviting them "to praise the Lord, just as if they were endowed with reason." His response to the world around him was so much more than intellectual appreciation or economic calculus, for to him each and every creature was a sister united to him by bonds of affection. That is why he felt called to care for all that exists. His disciple Saint Bonaventure tells us that, "from a reflection on the primary source of all things, filled with even more abundant piety, he would call creatures, no matter how small, by the name of 'brother' or 'sister'." (§11)

Here the pope underscores the manner in which St Francis's reverence of God was inextricably intertwined with his experience of communion with and his affection for creation. The saint did not worship creation as Divine. Rather, he discerned the sacramental character of the created order, an order that—to draw on the thought of Franciscan theologian Zachary Hayes—offers a "window to the Divine."[5] In so doing, the saint was "filled with abundant piety," drawn to reverence the Creator through creation.

In sum, in the pope's account we find that St Francis's praise and reverence of God is intimately bound up with his experience of the beauty and goodness of the created order. This observation is vital because the pope clearly views the saint as an exemplar of the human person. Thus, the manner in which St Francis "praises" and "reverences" God through and with creation illuminates the way in which humanity, as a whole, is called to respond to its vocation to praise and reverence God. Pope Francis captures the character of the proper human response well, writing, "When we can see God reflected in all that exists, our hearts are moved to praise the Lord for all his creatures and to worship him in union with them" (§87). Thus, the human person's praise and reverence of God is tightly interwoven with her ability to delight in the created order.

Love of neighbor and God in the Christian tradition

The question that remains, then, is: What of the call to "serve" God? What does Pope Francis's theological anthropology say about this third term in "the Principle and Foundation"? The pope's analysis of the life of St Francis does not provide a clear answer to these questions. Therefore, it is necessary to shift focus away from the figure of Saint Francis and toward the pope's interpretation of the first four chapters of the book of Genesis. There, the pope delineates the way in which the human vocation to serve God is intertwined with the work of caring for creation.

However, in order to draw out the full significance of Pope Francis's interpretation of Scripture, it will be helpful to consider first some important contours of what might be termed a traditional Roman Catholic theological anthropology. This will surface, by way of contrast, the more striking elements of Francis's understanding of the human person's call to serve God. Let us, therefore, turn briefly to the thought of three important theologians within the Catholic Christian tradition—Augustine of Hippo (354–430 AD), Thomas Aquinas (1225–74 AD) and the contemporary liberation theologian Gustavo Gutiérrez (1928–Present). We will briefly consider their understandings of the human person's relation to sin, the grace of God, and the call to love.

For Augustine, the human person is created to love and serve God and neighbor.[6] Through love and service, the human person lives in a rightly ordered state of communion with the objects of his love. Sin, however, radically distorts the way in which the human person relates. Love of God and neighbor is overthrown by a distorted version of self-love. Within the human heart, sin unleashes *libido dominandi*—lust for domination. As a result, the person no longer seeks communion with God and neighbor. Instead, the human person's desires are ordered toward an unrelenting self-aggrandizement in which he seeks to enthrone himself as God and force his neighbors to serve his own disordered desires.

In Augustine's understanding of the human person, this account of sin is answered with the story of salvation in which God graciously works in history—through the Holy Spirit—to save humanity from the power and consequences of sin. For Christian belief, God's saving work is fully realized through the person of Jesus Christ, who conquers the power of sin while also expressing most fully humanity's capacity to love and serve God and neighbor. The grace of God, then, is directed toward reestablishing and bringing to fulfillment the human person's communion with God and neighbor.

While this is an extremely generalized account of Augustine's thought, it does summarize the basic way in which Augustine has been received and interpreted within the traditions of Western Christianity. Note that missing from this account is any discussion of the manner in which sin disorders the human person's relationship to nonhuman creation. Likewise, this account does not consider how God's saving grace might heal the human/earth relationship.

To be sure, throughout his voluminous writing Augustine demonstrates a clear sense in which sin disorders both nonhuman creation and the human person's relationship to nonhuman creation.[7] Nonetheless, this element of Augustine's thought appears secondary to his analysis of the human person's relationship to God and neighbor.[8] The marginalization of the human/earth relationship from the story of salvation becomes even more pronounced in the manner in which Augustine's thought has been interpreted over the centuries in the West.[9] As a result, the human/earth relationship appears to be marginal to the drama of salvation.

Augustine is not the only significant theologian whose thought has been interpreted in a manner that diminishes the importance of the human/earth relationship for the Christian faith. Thomas Aquinas, whose theology represents a synthesis of Christian belief with Aristotelian philosophy, articulates a systematic account of the tenets of Christian faith. Aquinas integrated Aristotle's concern for the integrity of each creature's nature with the Christian understanding of grace. For Aquinas, grace not only healed sin, it also perfected nature. Grace elevates human nature to more fully serve the good in love. This respect for nature also enabled Aquinas to value nonhuman creation as a proper object of human love. Nonetheless, the Western Christian tradition has tended to receive the thought of Thomas in a manner that did not consider the human/earth relationship in relation to the central mystery of the Christian faith: salvation. Only recently have scholars begun to reflect upon this issue.[10]

The marginalization of the human/earth relationship in the drama of sin and salvation has continued within many contemporary theological projects aimed at underscoring the historical realities of sin and grace. Consider, for example, the thought of Gustavo Gutiérrez. Gutiérrez—commonly referred to as "the father of liberation theology"—draws upon the heritages of both Augustine and Aquinas in expressing his understanding of the human person. Gutiérrez's great contribution was to emphasize the manner in which the human person's love of God is intimately tied to her love of neighbor. Indeed, as Gutiérrez asserts, "Love of God is unavoidably expressed *through* love of one's neighbor."[11] (By "neighbor" it must be stressed, Gutiérrez intends especially "the ones of no account," a priority that reflects God's own preferential option for the poor and oppressed.)[12] Therefore, as Gutiérrez emphasizes, one's experience of communion with God is necessarily expressed through the move toward a deeper solidarity with one's neighbor.[13] By the same principle, sin is that reality which frustrates communion and solidarity with God and neighbor.

Here, we can note that Gutiérrez's reflections on the nature of sin and grace challenge any assumption that salvation can be reduced to an otherworldly or individual phenomenon. For Gutiérrez, the drama of salvation has profound implications for the state of this world—God's grace is at work in history for the liberation of the poor and oppressed. Nevertheless, Gutiérrez's view of the human person continues to emphasize two dimensions of human relatedness: God and neighbor. As a result, even in this theology intent upon emphasizing the historical character of salvation, the human person's relationship to the earth is left at the periphery. To serve God one must serve her neighbor, left unconsidered is the possibility of serving creation.[14]

God, neighbor, and creation: Francis's understanding of the vocation to serve

In *Laudato Si'*, Francis articulates a vision of the human person that expands the traditional Christian understanding of the person's vocation to love and serve. As we observed in the section above, reception of the Christian tradition in the West tends to present this vocation as two-dimensional—God calls the human person to love God and neighbor. In his encyclical, the pope expands this understanding of the human vocation from two dimensions to three: God calls the human person to love and serve God, neighbor, and nonhuman creation. Francis articulates this view of the human person most fully through his interpretation of the opening chapters of Genesis.

In reflecting upon the first chapters of the Bible, the pope writes,

> The creation accounts in the book of Genesis contain, in their own symbolic and narrative language, profound teachings about human existence and its historical reality. They suggest that human life is grounded in three fundamental and closely intertwined relationships: with God, with our neighbor and with the earth itself. (§66)

Here, Francis makes plain that, when exploring the relatedness of the human person, Christian theology cannot constrain its focus to the person's relationships to God and neighbor—theology must also take into account the person's relationship to the earth.

The pope's view, we can note, is consistent with much of contemporary biblical scholarship. In her book *Scripture, Culture, and Agriculture*, Ellen Davis maintains, "A fundament of biblical anthropology, as set forth in the first chapters of Genesis, is that there is a kinship between humans and the earth."[15] More recently, Davis expands upon this claim, arguing that within the worldview of the biblical prophets, "there exists an essential three-way relationship between God, humanity, and the earth."[16]

Indeed, the close connection between the person and the earth is recognized in the second chapter of Genesis, where God forms the human person out of the fertile soil of the garden, thereby emphasizing the link between the person and the earth. The author of the second chapter of Genesis underscores this connection etymologically through the name that God gives to the first human: "Adam," derives from the Hebrew word for soil *adama*. Although Francis does not elaborate upon this element of Genesis 2, he makes much the same point later in the encyclical when he writes of humanity, "God has joined us so closely to the world around us that we can feel the desertification of the soil almost as a physical ailment, and the extinction of a species as a painful disfigurement" (§89). The human person is irrevocably linked to the soil and all that comes from the soil.[17]

After underscoring the indissoluble relationship between the human person and the earth, Francis moves to explicate the character of this relationship when it is properly ordered. In this explication (and throughout *Laudato Si'*), the pope vehemently rebukes any attempt to read the Divine command in the first chapter of Genesis, "to subdue" and "have dominion" over the land (Gen. 1.29) as a license to dominate the earth. As Francis asserts, "This is not a correct interpretation of the Bible as understood by the Church. . . . We must forcefully reject the notion that our being created in God's image and given dominion over the earth justifies absolute domination over other creatures" (§67).

THE DIGNITY OF THE HUMAN PERSON

Although Francis describes the human/earth relationship in terms of "mutual responsibility," he, nevertheless, consistently stresses the unique status of the human person within the created order. Francis writes:

"Each of us (humans) has his or her own personal identity and is capable of entering into dialogue with others and with God himself. Our capacity to reason, to develop arguments, to be inventive, to interpret reality and to create art, along with other not yet discovered capacities, are signs of a uniqueness which transcends the spheres of physics and biology. The sheer novelty involved in the emergence of a personal being within a material universe presupposes a direct action of God and a particular call to life and to relationship on the part of a 'Thou' who addresses himself to another 'thou'" (§81).

Later, Francis emphasizes the "intrinsic value" of nonhuman creation, he also simultaneously affirms the "special value" of human beings (§118). Accordingly, the pope argues against a flattened ontology that would equate (for example) the value of a mouse to that of a human. "A misguided anthropocentrism" writes Francis, "need not necessarily yield to a 'biocentrism' that would entail adding yet another imbalance, failing to solve present problems and adding new ones" (§118).

Instead of a call to dominate creation, then, the pope finds that God tasks the human person with caring for the earth. The pope finds warrant for his view in the creation story in the second chapter of Genesis, in which God calls the human person to "'till and keep' the garden of the world (cf. Gen. 2:15)." As Francis observes, "'Tilling' refers to cultivating, plowing or working, while 'keeping' means caring, protecting, overseeing and preserving. This implies a relationship of mutual responsibility between human beings and nature" (§67) (see text box on Dignity of the Human Person). The human vocation, properly understood, is to actively care for "the garden of the world." Thus, the pope affirms that the human/earth relationship must be characterized by love and service.

Recall that, for St Ignatius, all things are created for the use of the human in attaining salvation. Here, Francis breaks with the view of Ignatius. As the pope asserts, the things of this world find their end not in human use but in God through the risen Christ. Francis writes:

The ultimate purpose of other creatures is not to be found in us. Rather, all creatures are moving forward with us and through us towards a common point of arrival, which is God, in that transcendent fullness where the risen Christ embraces and illumines all things. (§83)

Notably, Francis finds in the person of Jesus Christ the supreme example of how human persons are called by God to exercise their power for service and not domination. The pope argues that attempts by humanity to dominate nonhuman creation are "completely at odds with . . . the ideals of harmony, justice, fraternity and peace as proposed by Jesus." Francis continues, noting that Jesus "said of the powers of his own age: 'You know that the rulers of the Gentiles lord it over them, and their great men exercise authority over them. It shall not be so among you; but whoever would be great among you must be your servant' (Mt 20:25-26)" (§80). For Francis, then, Jesus reveals how humanity, through the work of service, is to relate properly to the earth. The objects of the human person's vocation to love and serve—as fully revealed in the person of Jesus Christ—include God, neighbor, and nonhuman creation.

Conversely, the pope also makes clear that the person's sinful lust for domination leads to a breach in communion in all three dimensions of human relatedness. As Francis writes, "According to the Bible, these three vital relationships have been broken, both outwardly and within us. This rupture is sin. The harmony between the Creator, humanity and creation as a whole was disrupted by our presuming to take the place of God and refusing to acknowledge our creaturely limitations" (§66).

In his interpretation of the biblical story of Cain and Abel, Francis elaborates upon the threefold sense in which sin distorts humanity's relatedness. Here, it is worth citing the pope at length:

> In the story of Cain and Abel, we see how envy led Cain to commit the ultimate injustice against his brother, which in turn ruptured the relationship between Cain and God, and between Cain and the earth from which he was banished. This is seen clearly in the dramatic exchange between God and Cain. God asks: "Where is Abel your brother?" Cain answers that he does not know, and God persists: "What have you done? The voice of your brother's blood is crying to me from the ground. And now you are cursed from the ground" (Gen 4:9-11). *Disregard for the duty to cultivate and maintain a proper relationship with my neighbor, for whose care and custody I am responsible, ruins my relationship with my own self, with others, with God and with the earth.* When all these relationships are neglected, when justice no longer dwells in the land, the Bible tells us that life itself is endangered. (§70, italics added)

Here, we can note that humanity's desire to dominate nonhuman creation, far from something that is pleasing to God, is, in fact, a sinful imitation of Cain.

Moreover, through this reading of the Cain and Abel narrative, the pope stresses how the loves of God, of neighbor, and of creation are tightly interwoven. Distortions of any one of these relationships unvaryingly echo through the other two. In Genesis, the cry of Abel's blood emanates from the soil itself and the very ground is cursed because of Cain's sin. The cry of the earth, then, cannot be separated from the cry of the poor. Thus, Francis indicates that the task of caring for the earth cannot be separated from the work of serving neighbor and God. As noted above, the human person is formed from the fertile soils of the garden and must continue to be understood as part of the garden. Thus, the call to care for "the garden of the world" represents an implicit call to care for one's neighbor. Francis emphasizes this point in *Laudato Si'*, noting that today the world is "faced not with two separate crises, one environmental and the other social, but rather with one complex crisis which is both social and environmental" (§139). Everything is connected.

For Francis, the contemporary global political economy is, to a great extent, reflective of the character of Cain—it demonstrates a proclivity toward domination and fails to hear and respond to the cries of the earth and poor. This is why Francis terms the global political economy "a false or superficial ecology" (§59).

Domination, however, is not the only option. Francis finds that by positively responding to God's call to serve and to care for the garden we cooperate with the work of the Creator (§80). Thus, the human person enters into the service of God precisely through serving and caring for her neighbor and the earth. Francis's understanding of the vocation of service and care, then, is one that broadens the terms of Gutiérrez's position that love of God is expressed through love of neighbor. For Francis, love of God must be expressed through love of neighbor *and love of nonhuman creation* (these are, of course, as closely linked as Adam is to *adama*). This three-dimensional response of service and love is the proper response in history to the gift of God's saving grace. Likewise, service and love best describe how the human person is to "make use" of creation while participating in the drama of salvation.

Contemplation in action

We have seen that in *Laudato Si'* Pope Francis develops the key terms from the "Principle and Foundation" of the *Spiritual Exercises* in a manner that emphasizes that the human person's "praise, reverence, and service" of God must be expressed through both love of neighbor and love of nonhuman creation. We will now consider the ways in which these key terms—praise, reverence, and service—relate to one another in Francis's theological anthropology.

To begin with, we can note that the tasks of praise and reverence are most proper to the contemplative dimension of Christian life. This is evidenced in the passages cited above regarding St Francis. It was his contemplation of creation that drew the saint to praise and reverence the Creator. (See Chapter 6 for a fuller exploration of nature and the contemplative life of the Christian.) By way of distinction, the task of service connotes action. In Pope

Francis's view, these dimensions of the Christian life—the contemplative and the active—must be held together (this, in fact, aligns with the Jesuit charism of being contemplatives in action).

It is vital that contemplation and action remain interconnected for two reasons. Recall that, for the pope, the human person is called to "cultivate and work" with creation but must refrain from dominating it. However, this raises the question: How does one distinguish between an act of cultivation and an act of domination? This is a difficult question. In *Laudato Si'*, Francis does not attempt to establish a theory of justice that might be utilized to make this distinction. Rather, he argues throughout the encyclical that the human person's proclivity to dominate creation arises, at least in part, from the person's failure to discern the goodness of creation. By failing to see and reverence this goodness, nature becomes "a problem to be solved" (§12) so as to facilitate its maximal exploitation. Thus, in order to "cultivate" creation properly, the person must also cultivate a spirituality that rejoices in and reverences the goodness of the earth. The human person must "see" the earth properly in order to act upon it properly. (See Chapter 1 on "integral ecology.")

From a different perspective, contemplation and action should not be separated in the life of Christian faith because, apart from action, contemplation can lead to an escapist spirituality that does little to address the needs of the planet. Such a spirituality, even as it contemplates the world, can fail both to confront the reality of sin in the world and to take responsibility for one's actions. As Francis makes clear throughout *Laudato Si'*, the earth is in crisis. It is not enough to simply contemplate the beauty or even the wounds of the world. God calls us to respond to these wounds so as to heal them to the best of our ability.

Conclusion: Ignatius, Pope Francis, and humanity's "special service"

We began this chapter by pointing to Ignatius's claim that the human person "is created to praise, reverence, and serve God our Lord, and by this means to save [her] soul." Subsequently, we have observed that, in *Laudato Si'*, Pope Francis presents his audience with a profound and nuanced reflection on the manner in which the human vocation to praise, reverence, and serve God must be realized through the reverence and care of both the earth and neighbor. We also have noted that for Francis the contemplative dimension of this vocation (praise and reverence) must inform its active dimension (service) so as to order rightly Christian praxis.

In this view, then, the human person cooperates with God's saving grace precisely through reverencing and serving "the garden of the world." Put another way, the human person bears witness to the salvation of her soul *through* caring for the soil and all that comes from the soil. With this in mind, it is fitting to conclude by considering an illuminating story from the life of Ignatius. The story begins with Ignatius addressing his student Diego Láinez.[18]

"Master Láinez," Ignatius asks, "if God were to say to you: If you want to die at once, I will give you eternal glory, but if you choose to live, I do not guarantee you the gift of final perseverance. If you thought that by remaining on earth, you would be able to achieve some great thing, what would your choice be?"

"To die at once, so that I would be sure," Láinez responds.

To this, Ignatius replies, "For my part, I would not. If I thought that by continuing to live I could accomplish some great work for God, I would beg Him to leave me on earth till I had done it. I would turn my eyes toward God and not toward myself. I would take no account of my danger or my security."

In commenting on this story, Gutiérrez observes that the narrative emphasizes Ignatius's "deep love for a God who acts in history and [Ignatius's] aspiration to go on collaborating with [God's] task."[19] Throughout *Laudato Si'*, Francis demonstrates that same "deep love" for a God who labors in history to care for the whole of God's creation. As Francis's encyclical makes clear, today, humanity is tasked with a "special service" that is both weighty and pressing. The human person is called to hear and respond to the cries of the earth and poor and in so doing enter into a praxis of care for our common home. In this way humanity positively responds to its vocation and in so doing bears witness to salvation.

Questions

1   How does Francis's understanding of both the human vocation to love and the effects of sin differ from the more traditional view of Western Christianity?

2   What is the relationship between contemplation and action? What are the dangers in separating the two?

3   In what ways does Francis connect his vision of the human person's vocation "to praise, reverence, and serve" the garden of the world to Jesus Christ?

4   Based on what you have read here, as well as your own experience/ understanding of Christianity, to what extent do you think Lynn White Jr's critique of Christianity is valid?

5   Does the call to "cultivate and care" for the garden of the world require an agrarian lifestyle? Could an engineer be one who cultivates and cares? Could a farmer be one who dominates creation? Explain your answers.

6   What practices might be helpful in allowing you to see the beauty and goodness of creation?

Notes

1 See, for example, Austen Ivereigh, *The Great Reformer: Francis and the Making of a Radical Pope* (New York: Henry Holt, 2014).

2 Ignatius, *Ignatius of Loyola: Spiritual Exercises and Selected Works*, ed. George E. Ganss (New York and Mahwah: Paulist, 1991), 130.

3 Ignatius, *Spiritual Exercises*, 130.

4 Lynn White, "The Historical Roots of Our Ecologic Crisis," *Science* 155, no. 3767 (March 10, 1967): 1203–7.

5 Zachary Hayes, *A Window to the Divine: Creation Theology* (Winona, MN: Anselm, 2009).

6 I draw this account of Augustine's anthropology largely from Books XI–XV of *City of God*. See Augustine, *City of God*, trans. Henry Bettenson (New York: Penguin Books, 2003).

7 On this point, see Scott A. Dunham, *The Trinity and Creation in Augustine: An Ecological Analysis* (Albany: SUNY, 2008), esp. 105–24.

8 For evidence of this, see Tarsicius J. Van Bavel, "Love," in *Augustine through the Ages: An Encyclopedia*, ed. Allan D. Fitzgerald (Grand Rapids: Eerdmans, 1999): 509–15.

9 Anne Clifford argues that in the wake of the Galileo and Darwinian controversies, Christianity neglected to develop its theology of creation. This resulted in "theological emphasis on the salvation of humans and the virtual surrender of nature—not just nonhuman earth forms but the entire cosmos—into the hands of scientists. It was less and less to the world and more and more to the human soul that believers turned to find signs of God." See Clifford, "Foundations for a Catholic Ecological Theology of God," in *And God Saw that it was Good': Catholic Theology and the Environment* (Washington, DC: US Catholic Conference, 1996), 21. This phenomenon helps to explain why early Christian thinkers were interpreted in problematically anthropocentric ways in recent centuries.

10 See for example, Willis Jenkins, *Ecologies of Grace: Environmental Ethics and Christian Theology* (New York: Oxford University Press, 2008), esp. 115–51.

11 Gustavo Gutiérrez, *A Theology of Liberation*, 15th Anniversary Edition, trans. Caridad Inda and John Eagleson (Maryknoll: Orbis, 1988), 114. Emphasis is Gutiérrez's.

12 This is why Gutiérrez argues that the preferential option for the poor is grounded in one's faith in God. On this point, see Gustavo Gutiérrez, "The Option for the Poor Arises from Faith in Christ," trans. Robert Lassalle-Klein, et al., *Theological Studies* 70 (2009): 317–26. See also Gutiérrez, "Option For the Poor," trans. Robert R. Barr in *Mysterium Liberationis: Fundamental Concepts of Liberation Theology*, ed. Ignacio Ellacuría and Jon Sobrino (Maryknoll: Orbis Books, 1993).

13 In *A Theology of Liberation*, Gutiérrez makes this point unrelentingly by tying communion with God to communion with neighbor throughout his argument. For a helpful consideration of the relationship between liberation

and communion in Gutiérrez's thought, see Joyce Murray, "Liberation for Communion in the Soteriology of Gustavo Gutiérrez," *Theological Studies* 59 (1998): 51–59.

14   In his more recent work, Gutiérrez has shifted his position, rejecting a largely instrumentalist view of nature and acknowledging the importance of caring for creation. On these points, see Gutiérrez, *The God of Life* (Maryknoll, NY: Orbis, 1991), 118; and Gutiérrez, *On Job: God-Talk and the Suffering of the Innocent* (Maryknoll, NY: Orbis, 1987), 74. In his commentary on *Rerum Novarum*, Gutiérrez also addresses the need to further theological reflection on the ecological crisis and its relationship to the crisis of material poverty ("New Things Today: A Rereading of *Rerum Novarum*," in Gustavo Gutiérrez, *The Density of the Present: Selected Writings* (Maryknoll: Orbis, 1999), 53–55.

15   Ellen Davis, *Scripture, Culture, Agriculture: An Agrarian Reading of the Bible* (Cambridge: Cambridge University Press, 2009), 29.

16   Ellen Davis, *Biblical Prophecy: Perspectives for Christian Theology, Discipleship, and Ministry* (Louisville: Westminster John Knox, 2014), 84.

17   Here we can note that God also fashions the living creatures of the land and sky from the soils of Eden (Gen. 2.19).

18   Cited in Gustavo Gutiérrez, "Friends of God, Friends of the Poor," in *The Density of the Present: Selected Writings*, trans. Margaret Wilde (Maryknoll: Orbis, 1999), 149–50.

19   Gutiérrez, "Friends of God, Friends of the Poor," 150.

6

Becoming painfully aware: Spirituality and solidarity in *Laudato Si'*

Douglas E. Christie

ENCYCLICAL READING GUIDE

- The key insight concerning awareness is found in §19
- St. Francis of Assisi, §10–12, 66, 125, 218
- A Universal Communion, §89–92
- The Gaze of Jesus, §96–100
- Ecological Conversion, §216–217

Spirituality is central to the great challenge presented to us in *Laudato Si'*. Without a profound renewal of our spiritual lives, Pope Francis suggests, we will have little hope of cultivating the kind of deep and sustained ethical response the crisis of global climate change is asking of us. We are capable of such renewal, the Pope claims, but only if we commit ourselves to a growth and deepening of our *awareness*—of our intimate relationship with God, of the deep communion we enjoy with all the living beings and of our ethical responsibility to care for the world and one another. Still, we are far from realizing this communion, something evidenced by the continued destruction of species, ecosystems, and the human communities that depend on them for their life and well-being. To understand why this is so and how we might transform both our awareness and our way of being in the world, we must be willing to engage in a kind of examination of conscience—searching out of the deep sources of our alienation from God and the living world. But this work also entails, *Laudato Si'* suggests, a gradual awakening to the beauty and wonder of the "whole" (the whole of creation, of which we are an integral part) within which we live and move and have our being. The renewal we seek is nothing less than the *metanoia* that has long occupied the very center of Christian spirituality: a transformation of awareness that enables us to recognize the kingdom of heaven unfolding in our midst and to respond to the needs of the world with wholehearted care and attention.

In what follows, I describe the character of this spiritual renewal as outlined in *Laudato Si'* in three sections. First, I consider the spiritual significance of Francis's vision of "integral ecology." Here, I also note the particular importance of contemplative thought and practice to this eco-spiritual vision, in particular in the encyclical's insistent focus on the need for a renewal of awareness. Second, I engage the question of what it might mean to rekindle an awareness of what *Laudato Si'* refers to as our "common origin" with all living beings, in light of the deep alienation and lack of awareness that characterizes so much of our relationship with the natural world in the present moment. And finally, I consider some of the key practices and attitudes that, according to *Laudato Si'*, we will need to cultivate as we struggle to develop the "loving awareness" of the world that is necessary for developing a meaningful and ethically sustainable response to the threat of global climate change.

Spirituality, contemplative practice, and ecological awareness

It is so telling that Pope Francis begins his great encyclical with the witness of his namesake from Assisi. The joyous, ecstatic response to the living world for which St Francis is renowned offers us an important model for rethinking our own relationship to the living world and for inquiring more deeply into the spiritual character of this relationship. The sense of awe and wonder that characterized the saint's attitude toward all living things—the sun, the moon, the air, fire, water, birds, wolves, the entire living cosmos—can and must also be ours, Pope Francis suggests. And it must be woven into our commitments, our way of living, especially in this moment of acute environmental crisis. This is one of the clear messages of the encyclical. But it is not the only one. Nor does it entirely capture the significance of the *poverello*—the little poor one—for the vision of spiritual life and practice the encyclical presents to us.

The joy of St Francis

St Francis is, after all, so much more than a friendly backyard saint who loved animals; he is a strange, wild figure, someone who felt the living world coursing through his veins and who understood the cost of his all-involving relationship with the living world. Yes, he saw and felt the presence of other living creatures as manifestations of God's own presence in the world. Francis dwelt in a paradisal world in which the capacity to communicate with and be touched by the presence of other living beings had been beautifully and deeply restored. Think of Giotto's great, light-infused rendering of Francis's joyful sermon to the birds. Or of the charming stories called *fioretti*—"little flowers" that depict (among other things) a man incapable of treading on "sister water" lest he bring harm to her. Or, perhaps most significantly, St Francis's own deeply lyrical *Canticle of the Creatures* in which the praise and adoration of God cannot be conceived of as arising within us in any other way but in and through the living world. Still, St Francis also knew what it meant to dwell deeply within the mystery of darkness and suffering. His is not the language of the dark night, well known to us from the writings of St John of the Cross. But from his intimate encounter with lepers early on in his life, something that utterly transformed his sense of what it meant to be a follower of Christ, to the intense physical suffering he endured late in his life (malaria, trachoma and a gastric ulcer so acute that it caused him to vomit blood), to the final harrowing experience of receiving the stigmata at La Verna, we see how far and deep into this mystery of suffering he was willing to travel.

A sense of great joy suffuses the life and writings of St Francis as it does *Laudato Si'*. We are called to behold all beings in the living world as our own brothers and sisters and to live accordingly. At the same time, we are called to reckon seriously with the reality of all that is broken, in us and in the world. We are facing a moment of crisis in our world and we must not turn away from it. It is for this reason that Pope Francis invites us to take seriously what it will mean for us to cultivate the kind of awareness that can help us learn to behold the astonishingly varied and intricate texture of the living world, to delight in its beauty and goodness and to respond by living in a way that reflects the deep value the living world has for us. Pope Francis describes this as a kind of "ecological conversion." And it "entails," he says, "a loving awareness that we are not disconnected from the rest of creatures, but joined in a splendid universal communion" (§220).

The cultivation of a "loving awareness" is critical to our capacity to renew our relationship with the created world, to rediscover our own deep communion with the world. But we are also being invited to open ourselves to the almost unimaginable loss and destruction we are visiting upon the living world and the pain and suffering embodied in this loss. It is for this reason that Pope Francis, in a statement that can be seen as a kind of axis around which the whole document turns, calls for the cultivation of a "painful awareness." "Our goal," he says, "is . . . to become painfully aware, to dare to turn what is happening to the world into our own personal suffering and thus to discover what each of us can do about it" (§19).

Becoming painfully aware

To become "painfully aware." What a beautiful and haunting idea. Also a great challenge. But what does it mean? What kind of awareness is this? What might it mean for us to cultivate such awareness in response to our contemporary experience of the living world? And how can we best understand the call to cultivate such "painful awareness" in relation to the equally urgent call, found throughout the encyclical, to open ourselves to an awareness of joy and delight and wonder—"loving awareness"—in response to the living world? And to risk being transformed by this awareness, utterly, and completely? Finally, what difference might it make—to us and to the world we inhabit—for us to open ourselves to the transforming power that such awareness promises?

To consider these questions seriously is, I believe, to risk reimagining the very character of our relationship with the living world and our entire way of life. This is very much in keeping with the fundamental approach of *Laudato Si'*, which at every turn invites an utterly wholehearted and searching response to our relationship with the creation and with one another. And it suggests the profound level to which the pope is appealing in writing this document. The word "awareness" has real weight and significance here. It points to our capacity for taking into our consciousness the full range and texture of reality and to responding to that reality from the deepest center of our being. It is no accident that the encyclical couches its understanding of "ecological conversion" in terms of the need for a transformed awareness. This is also, I believe, where the real spiritual significance of the document lay for us (§217).

It is for this reason that *Laudato Si'* can and should be understood as a call for spiritual renewal and transformation. In particular, it is a call to renew our commitment to a contemplative practice that can help us deepen our capacity to pay more careful attention to, feel more fully the presence of, and practice responsibility toward every living being. It is a holistic vision of spiritual transformation rooted in a commitment to become more fully aware—of the world itself and of our felt sense of relationship with and responsibility for the living world, in God. It can also become a means of expressing our solidarity with all living beings.

The gift of tears

Where to begin with this work of spiritual renewal? For Pope Francis, there is a clear sense that any meaningful change must begin with the work of *repentance*: "In calling to mind the figure of Saint Francis of Assisi, we come to realize that a healthy relationship with creation is one dimension of overall personal conversion, which entails the recognition of our errors, sins, faults and failures, and leads to heartfelt repentance and desire to change" (§218). Repentance is not a word that comes easily to our lips in the contemporary moment, even for many Catholics. Often it calls to mind another idea we would rather avoid: sin. The ancient monks' understanding of sin was quite different from our narrow individual conceptions. Sin for them spoke to the "tear in the fabric of the whole"—the brokenness of the world around them which was manifest in their own lives as well.[1] How then are we to orient ourselves toward the idea of repentance as central to the kind of conversion to which the Pope is calling us?

One way of approaching this question is to recall the fundamentally transformational and renewing character of repentance as it arises in the New Testament and the subsequent Christian tradition. *Metanoia*, which is at the root of the Christian idea of repentance, suggests a radical reorientation of one's entire being toward God. It means turning around and facing in a different direction, along the path of discipleship and new life. It is this kind of radical renewal of heart, mind, and sensibility for which the Pope is calling. Part of this renewal involves acknowledging our shortcomings, flaws, and, yes, sins—all the ways we have fallen short and neglected to turn our face toward God and life. But another dimension of the renewal we seek involves coming to recognize who we truly are in God, that deeply healing awareness that we are and always have been at home in God and in God's beautiful world. Still, it is not always easy to arrive at this awareness. Our hearts, to call upon that ancient biblical expression, have become hardened. We have grown distant from ourselves, from one another, from God, and from the living world.

Still, there is a tradition of spiritual practice aimed at softening our hardened hearts, something that can contribute to the kind of spiritual conversion for which we are so desperately longing. The ancient Christian monastics of the Egyptian desert called this spiritual practice "the gift of tears." In Greek, the terms used to describe this practice are *penthos* or *katanyxis*, both of which suggest a profound piercing of the heart that is the very source of the tears and deep spiritual renewal. Such tears, the monks realized, could not be manufactured or planned for; when they came, they came mysteriously, unexpectedly, as a gift. Yet, one could seek them, open oneself to them. Tears were highly valued by the early Christian monks, for they were believed to express and make possible an honest reckoning with one's life (especially one's fragility), a life-changing transformation and a reorientation to God and to the larger community.[2] There is an undeniable dimension of sadness or grief woven into this experience, for to wake up to one's moral, spiritual fragility (as well as that of others) means facing, directly and without evasion, the harsh ambiguity of existence itself, including all that is broken and in need of repair—in oneself and in the world. Tears signal a willingness to open oneself to this reality, to mourn for what has been lost or is in danger of being lost, and to open oneself to the possibility of renewal, regeneration.

And what if tears do not come, if one is not so moved? Is renewal still possible? The monks were not dogmatic about this and never went so far as to suggest that tears were absolutely necessary for spiritual transformation and renewal. But they recognized how important it was to feel grief in the face of loss and brokenness. The inability to weep was something to be taken very seriously.

I wonder if we can say the same. I am thinking here in particular of our apparent inability or unwillingness to mourn the loss of life, the rapid and pervasive diminishment of life forms on earth. The note of loss sounds throughout *Laudato Si'*—loss of plants, animals, biodiversity, and entire species; loss of a place in the world for those millions of human beings displaced due to environmental disasters; loss of cultural values, a sense of purpose in life and community living; and loss of "appreciation for the whole." But do we feel this loss? Do we mourn all we are losing? Echoing a question that the ancient desert monks asked continuously, it seems important to ask whether our capacity to mourn—to feel deep grief and sadness in the face of all that is being lost—will in some sense determine our ability and willingness to engage in sustained, meaningful work of ecological restoration? Conversely, will our inability to mourn prevent us from seeing and taking into ourselves all that is being lost and thus prevent us from honestly engaging the reality of loss, from responding and acting?

Mourning is often thought of as a fundamentally personal, even private matter, an isolating experience that closes one off from others.[3] Moreover we commonly mourn the loss of persons, not animals or species or places. Is it even meaningful, therefore, to transpose such an experience into an ecological or cosmic register? I think it *is* meaningful and necessary to think of mourning in such terms, that it can be conceived of as a collective and communal act as well as a personal one and that its moral and spiritual range should be understood to include the entire living world. In calling us to the work of repentance, *Laudato Si'* invites us to reconsider the particular role tears and grief and mourning can play in kindling a deep and lasting moral engagement with the living world.

A story told about one of the early Christian monks, Abba Arsenius, relates that "he had a hollow in his chest channeled out by the tears which fell from his eyes all his life while he sat at his manual work."[4] Perhaps we have now arrived at a moment where such tears can again begin to flow from us, reawakening us to our capacity to face and name and mourn what is being lost. Real and sustainable ecological restoration may well depend on it.

Learning to see

At the heart of the Christian contemplative tradition is the challenge of learning to see: to see more deeply and capaciously and to live out of that deep seeing. This is also one of the primary concerns of *Laudato Si'*. In the traditions of contemplative thought and practice that arose in the ancient desert monastic communities of Egypt, Asia Minor and the Judean desert, and which flourished in a variety of settings in the subsequent Christian tradition, this seeing refers primarily to the challenge of learning to live more deeply into the awareness of God at the center of our lives. It is sometimes understood as the discovery or rediscovery of our fundamental identity—as beings created in the image and likeness of God—other times as an awakening to the ground or the spark of the soul: God alive at the heart of our being.[5] It is a fundamentally relational awareness, born of a recognition that the rediscovery of our deepest identity in God connects us to the whole of reality, including the suffering and bereft in our midst, and every creature in the living world. We undertake the work cultivating this awareness for our own sake, to discover the deep source of our freedom in God. But we also do it for the sake of learning how to stand with others in solidarity and contribute to the healing work that is at the very heart of our faith.

This, I would suggest, is the power of the contemplative gaze and of our rich spiritual traditions of contemplative thought and practice. It is no accident that Pope Francis invokes the witness not only of Francis of Assisi, but also of St Bonaventure, St John of the Cross, St Therese of Lisieux, and others. As *Laudato Si'* makes clear, the writings of these saints and mystics remind us continuously that the contemplative gaze reveals the deeply sacramental character of the world. Francis honors the fact that these traditions are cultivated outside of Christianity by citing the Muslim Sufi writer Ali al-Khawas: "The universe unfolds in God, who fills it completely. Hence, there is mystical meaning to be found in a leaf, in a mountain trail, in a dewdrop, in a poor person's face." From the Christian tradition, St Bonaventure offers this reminder of what looking long and carefully at the world can help us realize: "Contemplation deepens the more we feel the working of God's grace within our hearts, and the better we learn to encounter God's creatures outside ourselves" (§233). Here we catch a glimpse of the profoundly holistic character of *Laudato Si'*s spiritual vision. To come to awareness in the way that the saints and mystics have always understood this work is to see and notice and feel the presence of *everything*. It is to see deeply into the sacramental beauty of all that exists and celebrate joyfully the gift that this beauty gives to us. Such contemplative practice helps us cultivate an attitude of simple appreciation and gratitude for all that we have been given and to respond wholeheartedly. We must learn, suggests Pope Francis, how to gaze upon the world as a "joyful mystery to be contemplated with gladness and praise" (§12).

Still, we miss so much. And our awareness is so often small and poor, leaving us unable to take in or appreciate the beauty and depth of the living world. Or care for it. This diminished capacity to behold has many sources— the speed of contemporary life, the seductive power of consumerism, the dream of continuous progress, an inability or unwillingness to value the common good. But at the root of things, suggests *Laudato Si'*, and coursing through all of these disparate realities, is a deep spiritual alienation. Which is why any meaningful response to the current ecological crisis must also address this spiritual crisis, in particular our deep-seated habits of inattention and carelessness. Our lack of awareness.

Obstacles to awareness

In *Laudato Si'*, the question of awareness is approached both negatively and positively. Or, perhaps it is better to say there is a serious analysis of its deep ambiguity. On the one hand, there is a serious and searching critique of the spiritual, cultural, political, and economic habits and sensibilities that are preventing us from engaging seriously the challenges before us. Not least among the difficulties here is our chronic inability or unwillingness to pay attention to the deeper values that can and ought to shape our lives and to the world itself. For many in the global north, this alienation takes the form of a deepening sense of fragmentation and loneliness brought on by excessive dependence on the digital world and social media. We are increasingly living within what *Laudato Si'* calls "a culture of recklessness" and experiencing the proliferation of what Adolfo Nicholas, SJ has described as "the globalization of superficiality."[6] This phenomenon has personal meaning, certainly, something that is especially evident in individual experiences of alienation and loneliness that so often accompany prolonged immersion in the digital world; but it also has social and political meaning, often undermining the capacity of individuals to interact with one another and with the larger culture of which they are a part.[7] It is within this larger context of personal and social fragmentation and alienation that Francis notes the significance of our inattention to the poor and marginalized, who inevitably suffer the most from environmental degradation. Here, *Laudato Si'* makes the case for a moral-spiritual web of concern, borne of our willingness and capacity to pay attention to one another and the world we share. This web is fraying and we are increasingly paying the price.

On the other hand, the encyclical returns again and again to the possibility of a renewal of our capacity to see and care for the world. Digging deeply into biblical stories and images as well as the teachings of mystics, poets, and contemplatives, *Laudato Si'* invites us to reimagine a way of being in the world that values profoundly the presence of other living beings and considers our capacity for gazing upon the beauty of these creatures to be one of God's great gifts to us. Nor does *Laudato Si'* consider this simple gaze as somehow separate from our ethical obligation to love and care for these beings or for one another. Our capacity to see and cherish the world for what it is, whole and unbroken and holy, enables us to respond to it more thoughtfully and carefully.

Rekindling an awareness of our common origin

Throughout *Laudato Si'*, Pope Francis calls attention to a fundamental tension in our attitudes and relationship with the created world: on the one hand, we lack the awareness we need to live attentively and responsibly in relationship to the created world; on the other hand, it is also true that we already possess, by virtue of our faith, the awareness we need to participate in the healing of the created world. One of the signs of the great moral honesty of this document is that it does not attempt to diminish the force of this apparent contradiction; rather, it seeks to engage it and ask what we can learn from it. First, the Pope suggests that something crucial is missing in the way we think about and respond to the created world: "We lack an awareness of our common origin, of our mutual belonging, and a future to be shared with everyone. This basic awareness would enable the development of new convictions, attitudes and forms of life. A great cultural, spiritual and educational challenge stands before us" (§202). Yes, we lack this fundamental awareness of who we are in the universe and in God. And this lack undermines any serious effort to respond to the unfolding crisis. But it is also true to say that we already possess the awareness we so desperately need: "The awareness that each creature reflects something of God and has a message to convey to us, and the security that Christ has taken unto himself this material world and now, risen, is intimately present to each being, surrounding it with affection and penetrating it with his light" (§221). Here, we are reminded of one of the great gifts of faith: the sure knowledge of who we are in God and the meaning this can have for deepening our response to the created world.

This fundamental tension runs throughout the encyclical and helps to account for its spiritual depth and reach. Francis does not minimize the seriousness of the problems we face or the harm we are doing to the world and to one another. Nor does he suggest that the predicament we have landed ourselves in has any simple or easily achievable resolutions. We are moving through a deep darkness, and the way forward is uncertain. Still, paradoxically, in faith, we already possess the knowledge (and the light) we seek: "the awareness that each creature reflects something of God and has a message to convey to us."

Shallow culture, shallow ecology

Still, why do we see so little? Why is our capacity to gaze upon and love the world so underdeveloped? Pope Francis confronts these questions early on in *Laudato Si'*, declaring, "We still lack the culture needed to confront this crisis" (§53). This is an important reminder that the idea of transformation that Pope Francis has in mind touches into the very depths of what we understand to constitute us as a people: our culture. That is, our values and norms, our linguistic habits, our ritual practices, our understanding of what it means to live in community, our capacity for awe. *Laudato Si'* is engaged in what we might refer to as an exercise of "cultural critique," calling into question many of our most cherished (and destructive) cultural and political assumptions. This is why the encyclical gives such careful attention to critical elements of contemporary culture such as our attachment to the ideal of progress, the often-unquestioned value we place upon technology, and our inability, under the pressing speed of existence, to cultivate the kind of attention that would allow us to make the crucial decisions regarding our shared future.

Underlying and often driving these cultural realities, *Laudato Si* suggests, is something even more insidious: "the rise of a false or superficial ecology which bolsters complacency and cheerful recklessness" (§59). This particular reference to ecology is telling. Pope Francis is speaking here of an attitude toward the environmental crisis that is, by any reasonable standard, utterly inadequate. The "false or superficial ecology" to which he refers suggests the lack of depth (moral, spiritual, and political) inherent in our responses. A profound inattention to the "whole." There are so many examples of this: long-standing habits of clear-cutting, strip mining and overfishing, driven by the short-term demands of the bottom line, which leave whole parts of the created world utterly and sometimes permanently degraded; inattention to food production and food safety with its devastating effects on both public health and the environment; and uncritical acceptance of the ethos of consumerism and capitalism.[8] All of which lead to an impoverishment of the created world and a sense of fragmentation in own social, political, and spiritual lives: a diminished awareness that we are part of a whole and responsible for tending and caring for it.

A sense of the whole

Still, *Laudato Si'* expresses a sense of hope that we might yet recover and rekindle a "sense of the whole," something that is critical to both ecology and spirituality. Such a rekindling must begin, Francis suggests, with a recovery of our capacity for relationship and reciprocity with all other living beings: "Because all creatures are connected, each must be cherished with love and respect, for all of us as living creatures are dependent on one another" (§42). There is an echo here of the great environmental thinker Aldo Leopold. "We can be ethical," Leopold said, "only in relation to something we can see, feel, understand, love, or otherwise have faith in."[9] It is not easy to say precisely what love means in these statements. The call to love the world is striking and encouraging. It suggests an engagement with the natural world that runs far deeper than a political or environmental position or a theological doctrine: a regard for the other so strong and deep that it opens up within us an unexpected and much-needed capacity for vulnerability and reciprocity in relation to other living beings.

Yet, such an attitude, the encyclical notes, is sadly missing from much of our current thinking about who we are in the world; it is also missing from our ways of living. Our inattention to the whole, our inability to exchange love with other living beings, reverberates through so many dimensions of our shared life: certainly in relation to our feeling for the natural world, which has been profoundly undermined by our long-standing habit of thinking of it as our own possession.

A lack of encounter

This "false or superficial ecology" reflects not only our own alienation from the world; it also helps to account for our inability or unwillingness to see the environmental crisis as deeply connected to the broader social crisis unfolding in our midst: "There is little in the way of clear awareness of problems which especially affect the excluded" (§49). No small part of this problem, the Pope suggests, arises from "the lack of physical contact and encounter." Many of us have no direct experience of the dismal reality of those living on the margins, or those, like the victims of the environmental catastrophes at Chernobyl, Bhopal, and Flint, who suffer, often without voice or hope, from what Rob Nixon describes as "slow violence" of chronic environmental degradation.[10] The suffering of the poor becomes an abstraction, or worse, invisible.

This insistence on the significance of the social and political dimensions of environmental degradation is one of the most significant contributions of *Laudato Si'*. It touches directly on the question of what it means to cultivate an authentic spiritual practice. Here is another critical expression of what it means to become "painfully aware": "Today . . . we have to realize that a true ecological approach *always* becomes a social approach; it must integrate questions of justice in debates on the environment, so as to hear *both the cry of the earth and the cry of the poor*" (§49). Francis insists that we must begin to reckon more seriously and concretely with the intimate relationship between environmental degradation and poverty, with the great human cost of our inattention to the created world.

Why are we not already doing this? And what, if anything, will motivate us to take the challenge of such a reckoning seriously? In response to the first question, *Laudato Si'* suggests that it has to do with the habit of "evasiveness" that has now become too much the norm in our dealings with the world. In one of the most powerful descriptions of this culture of evasion, something that can be understood as yet another expression of the "false or superficial ecology" within which we are living, Pope Francis states: "Such evasiveness serves as a license for carrying on with our present lifestyles and models of production and consumption. This is the way human beings contrive to feed their self-destructive vices: trying not to see them, trying not to acknowledge them, delaying important decisions and pretending that nothing will happen" (§59). Here we encounter one of the encyclical's most trenchant and insightful critiques of our alienated spiritual condition: we have fallen into a habit of not seeing certain things, *trying* not to acknowledge them or allow them to affect us. So pervasive has our habit of evasiveness become, Pope Francis suggests, that our very capacity to see— ourselves, the world around us and God—has become utterly compromised.

A slow, loving gaze

The contemplative gaze, that long, slow, loving way of regarding the deepest realities—our own identity as created in the image and likeness of God and the created world as God's sacramental gift to us—is increasingly being supplanted by a quick, superficial, and evasive glance that leaves us unable to see and respond to the things that matter most to us with real thoughtfulness or feeling. It is in this sense that the Pope is suggesting to us that the environmental crisis unfolding in our midst reflects a spiritual crisis, a kind of moral-spiritual blindness that impacts every dimension of the life in the world. So too any meaningful response to this crisis will require a profound spiritual renewal. What would it mean for us to examine seriously the habits of thought and practice that have contributed so much to the ongoing destruction of the environment? What would it mean for us to rekindle the sense of what poet Denise Levertov describes simply as "primary wonder," an openhearted response to all living beings rooted in respect and reverence?[11] Or what Francis describes as "loving awareness?" How might the cultivation of such an awareness help us renew our spiritual identity and practice, our social and political life and the life of the world?

Cultivating loving awareness: Rekindling a sense of the whole

The honesty and severity with which *Laudato Si'* lays bare our spiritual alienation is balanced by a tone of hopefulness and even joy that runs throughout the encyclical. One of the truly remarkable things about *Laudato Si'* is that, in spite of so many reasons to feel pessimistic about our prospects, the note of hope is so strong. The particular note of hope arising from the encyclical gains strength and force, I would suggest, from its profound realism regarding our current predicament. There is no false hope here, no wishful thinking. But there is a deep conviction that we retain a capacity to regard the world with love and awe and that we can learn to live out of this habit of regard and set a different course for our future than the one that has brought us to this current moment of environmental crisis.

But how to do this? How to overcome our profound alienation from the living world? How can we rekindle our feeling for other living beings, our sense of being part of a vibrant, encompassing community? To consider these questions seriously is to arrive very close to the heart of *Laudato Si*'s vision of ecological conversion. Two ideas have particular importance here. The first is that the depth of change we need will require us, personally and communally, to undergo an experience of what the Christian spiritual tradition refers to as "metanoia," a profound conversion in our thought and affections. "If we want to bring about deep change," Pope Francis reminds us, "we need to realize that certain mindsets really do influence our behavior" (§215). Such change requires an uncommon level of personal and moral honesty, an openness to facing and engaging the sources of spiritual emptiness that so often fuel consumerist habits and that also undermine, directly or indirectly, our capacity to care for the common good (§203, 204). The second idea is intimately related to the first, but is more positive in character. With disarming simplicity, the Pope reminds us that we need not succumb to the "mindsets" that contribute so much to our alienation and proposes his own sense of what is possible (and necessary) for us: "It [ecological conversion] entails a loving awareness that we are not disconnected from the rest of creatures, but joined in a splendid universal communion" (§220).

Everything must flow from this "loving awareness." Without it, the encyclical insists, we will have little hope of arriving at a true understanding of who we are in the world or what it means for us to care for it. Pope Francis is so clear on the deep connection that exists between a renewed spiritual awareness and the capacity for the kind of sustained ethical practice that into which we are being called in the present moment:

> More than ideas or concepts as such, I am interested in how such an [ecological] spirituality can motivate us to a more passionate concern for the protection of the world. A commitment this lofty cannot be sustained by doctrine alone, without a spirituality capable of inspiring us, without an "interior impulse which encourages, motivates, nourishes and gives meaning to our individual and communal activity." (§216)

Still, given our impaired condition, we must learn to see again and differently than we have become accustomed to seeing. One of the real contributions of the encyclical is its practical and imaginative instruction on how to do this, how to cultivate the kind of loving awareness that will energize and sustain the strong sense of ecological responsibility we so desperately need in the present moment.

A prophetic and contemplative spirituality

Pope Francis does not shy away from calling attention to the distinctive and deeply subversive character of the Christian spiritual tradition and how its values can help us rethink our prospects in the present moment: "Christian spirituality proposes an alternative understanding of the quality of life," he says, "and encourages a prophetic and contemplative lifestyle, one capable of deep enjoyment free of the obsession with consumption" (§222). This is an important reminder of how the lived reality of faith can alter one's entire perception of and approach to life. Central to this statement is the refreshing, unexpected, and deeply countercultural call to adopt a lifestyle that enhances our capacity to live with "deep enjoyment free of the obsession with consumption." This way of life is, the Pope notes, "prophetic and contemplative" in character. But it might be truer to the spirit of the encyclical to say that it is prophetic precisely in and through its abiding commitment to a contemplative vision of life.

This is not a vision of life reserved for a select few. Nor does it refer only to that part of life that we associate with prayer and meditation. It is all-encompassing and holistic touching potentially on every aspect of our life in the world. To live contemplatively is to open oneself to an abiding commitment to see and respond to every living being with care and attention. It is to ask how we might practice such awareness in every facet of our lives.

A slow revolution

One way of realizing this vision, according to the *Laudato Si'*, is to rethink our relationship to time. Early on in the encyclical, the Pope calls attention to "the continued acceleration of changes affecting humanity and the planet" and its connection to "a more intensified place and life and work" (§18). He dubs this large-scale phenomenon "rapidification." And in one of the more poignant and thought-provoking observations in the entire encyclical, he remarks: "The speed with which human activity has developed contrasts with the naturally slow pace of biological evolution" (§18). It may seem an obvious and simple thing to note how far out of step we are with the slow-moving biological processes which sustain the living world. And how much harm comes from this chronic "rapidification." But in truth it is hardly obvious to us. Nor do we pay much attention to it. The Pope addresses this question directly much later in the encyclical: "We do need to slow down and look at reality in a different way . . . to recover values and the great goals swept away by our unrestrained delusions of grandeur" (§114).

In its concern with the pernicious effects of speed upon our lives and upon the world, *Laudato Si'* can be seen as reflecting on and contributing its own voice with a larger social-cultural movement concerned with calling into question the cult of speed and with articulating the outlines of a "slower" approach to life and thought. There has been growing attention in recent years to the need for a strong critique of our addiction to speed, for "slow living," "slow food," "slow thinking" among others.[12] What "slowness" connotes in almost all these contexts is a commitment to a more careful, attentive, responsible relationship to the crucial realities of our lives, a commitment to something very close to what Pope Francis in this encyclical calls "loving awareness."

On the face of it, such a commitment might well appear too small and humble to register in any significant way amid the larger concerns we face in relation to the current ecological crisis. Thus, we might deem it to be not practical enough to command our attention and respect. But is this really true? Among the most powerful and compelling aspects of *Laudato Si'* is the uncanny way it balances attention to the largest, most pressing and most practical concerns arising from the ecological crisis with a searching inquiry into the root causes of the crisis, often found in our habits and values and manifested in the most ordinary dimensions of everyday life. It is here that the apparently humble and small-scale concerns of the encyclical gain their power and meaning.

Serenely present

A statement toward the end of the *Laudato Si'* captures this idea beautifully. It can be seen as a kind of summing up of the teaching of the entire encyclical. Francis observes, "To be serenely present to each reality, however small it may be, opens us to much greater horizons of understanding and personal fulfillment." Here, we encounter the simple beauty of *Laudato Si's* deeply incarnational spirituality. Everything that exists is sustained and gives life, meaning, and sacred value by having been brought into being through Christ the Logos (Jn 1.1). "Each reality, however small," is worthy of our attention and care. But there is more. "Christian spirituality," Pope Francis continues, "proposes a growth marked by moderation and the capacity to be happy with little. It is return to that simplicity which allows us to stop and appreciate the small things, to be grateful for the opportunities that life affords us, to be spiritually detached from what we possess, and not to succumb to sadness for what we lack" (§222). There is a sense of modesty, humility, and simplicity woven into the very heart of this spiritual vision. And, again, a call to be "serenely present" and grateful in response to all that we have been given.

This call is breathtaking in its simplicity and its richness. It addresses one of the primary expressions of cultural and spiritual malaise that affects so many contemporary persons: the sense that what we have in our lives is never enough and will never be enough. The call to be "serenely present" and appreciative of all that we have serves as an important counterpoint to this feeling. "It is not a lesser life or one lived with less intensity," Francis notes. "On the contrary, it is a way of living life to the full. In reality, those who enjoy more and live better each moment are those who have given up dipping here and there, always on the look-out for what they do not have. They experience what it means to appreciate each person and each thing, learning familiarity with the simplest things and how to enjoy them"

(§223). Here again, we encounter the call to resist the temptation to live superficially or, as the encyclical notes elsewhere, with "complacency and cheerful recklessness"(§59). Instead there is an invitation to take the time to go deeper, to cultivate a sense of appreciation and familiarity with the intricate beauty of the living world. Once again, we hear the note of enjoyment. All those other living beings amid whom you yourself live and move? Learn to *enjoy* them, says the Pope. Open yourself to "a loving awareness that [you] are not disconnected from the rest of creatures" (§220). Yes, enjoy them.

Conclusion

Is this enough? Is it enough to enter into deep enjoyment of every living being? To cultivate sense of "loving awareness" that we are deeply bound to, dependent upon, and responsible for all of creation? It can be and will be enough, *Laudato Si'* suggests, if we allow this awareness to penetrate into the depths of our being and transform both our awareness of who we are in the world and how we act and live in the world. It becomes more and more clear that the commitment to cultivate such awareness will not allow us to stand aloof from any other living being—not from our brothers and sisters on the margins who suffer most grievously from our ecological recklessness, nor from all those luminous beings threatened with extinction. To practice "loving awareness," we begin to realize, also means opening ourselves to the kind of "painful awareness" to which Pope Francis calls us at the outset of *Laudato Si'*. It means becoming vulnerable to all that we behold—the intricate beauty of the living world and the awful degradation we are visiting upon it—and allowing ourselves to be moved and changed by our vulnerability.

We must learn how to bring this awareness into every facet of our existence so that it can inform our personal identity, our cultural understanding, our politics, our relationship with other living beings. The "integral ecology" to which *Laudato Si'* calls us compels us to take this transformation of spiritual awareness seriously. Which means ensuring that it is integrated into what Michel de Certeau has felicitously described as "the practice of everyday life"; Or as Pope Francis says, it must be "made up of simple daily gestures which break with the logic of violence, exploitation and selfishness" (§230). Here is where our transformed spiritual awareness becomes concrete and particular—incarnate in the world.

Questions

1   What is the significance of Pope Francis's invitation to become "painfully aware?" Of what is he calling us to be aware? And why?

2   What might it mean for us to read *Laudato Si'* as a call for us to renew our spiritual practice, in particular to deepen our capacity for contemplative spiritual practice in relation to the natural world?

3   What does it mean to see? And why do we so often see so little? What is the significance of seeing in *Laudato Si'*? What prevents us from seeing?

4   How does *Laudato Si'* understand the challenge of practicing solidarity? With whom does the encyclical invite us to be in solidarity?

5   What is the significance of the idea of "ecological conversion" in *Laudato Si'*? What does it entail? What practical steps can we take to answer this call?

6   What does *Laudato Si'* mean by its invitation for us to "be serenely present to each reality?"

Notes

1   See the fuller discussion of "Penthos" in Douglas E. Christie, *The Blue Sapphire of the Mind: Notes for a Contemplative Ecology* (Oxford: Oxford University Press, 2013), 70–101, quote at 76.

2   The classic study of this phenomenon in early Christian spirituality is Irénée Hausherr, *Penthos: The Doctrine of Compunction in the Christian East.* trans. Anselm Hufstader, OSB (Kalamazoo, MI: Cistercian Publications, 1982).

3   On the isolating power of mourning, see Anthony Storr, *Solitude: A Return to the Self* (New York: Ballantine, 1988), esp. 29–41.

4   Arsenius 41. In *The Desert Christian: Sayings of the Desert Fathers. The Alphabetical Collection* (New York: Macmillan, 1975), 18.

5   For a thoughtful introduction to Christian contemplative thought and practice, see Martin Laird, *Into the Silent Land: A Guide to the Christian Practice of Contemplation* (New York: Oxford University Press, 2006).

6   Adolfo Nicholás, SJ. "Depth, Universality, and Learned Ministry: Challenges to Jesuit Higher Education Today," Remarks for "Networking Jesuit Higher Education: Shaping the Future of a Humane, Just, Sustainable Globe." Mexico City, April 23, 2010, 3.

7   See Sherry Turkle, *Alone Together: Why We Expect More from Social Media and Less from Each Other* (New York: Basic Books, 2011).

8   Claude Martin, On the Edge: *The State and Fate of the World's Tropical Rainforests* (Vancouver, BC: Greystone, 2015); Carlo Petrini, *Slow Food Nation: Why Our Food Should be Good, Clean and Fair* (New York: Rizzoli, 2007); Vincent Miller, *Consuming Religion: Christian Faith and Practice in a Consumer Culture* (New York: Continuum, 2003); Daniel M. Bell, Jr. *The Economy of Desire: Christianity and Capitalism in a Postmodern World* (Grand Rapids, MI: Baker, 2012).

9   Aldo Leopold, *A Sand County Almanac* (New York: Oxford University Press, 1989), 214.

10 Rob Nixon, *Slow Violence and the Environmentalism of the Poor* (Cambridge, MA: Harvard University Press, 2011).

11 Denise Levertov, *Sands of the Well* (New York: New Directions, 1998), 129.

12 Mark C. Taylor, *Speed Limits: Where Time Went and Why We Have So Little Left* (New Haven: Yale University Press, 2014). See also Jonathan Crary, *24/7: Late Capitalism and the Ends of Sleep* (London: Verso, 2014); Carlo Petrini, *Slow Food Nation: Why Our Food Should Be Good, Clean and Fair* (New York: Rizzoli, 2007). Carl Honoré, *In Praise of Slowness: Challenging the Cult of Speed* (New York: HarperOne, 2005); Douglas E. Christie, "The Eternal Present: Slow Knowledge and the Renewal of Time," *Buddhist Christian Studies* 33 (2013): 13–21; David Orr, *The Nature of Design: Ecology, Culture and Human Intention* (New York: Oxford University Press, 2002), 35–42.

7

Liturgy: The exaltation of creation

Sandra Yocum

ENCYCLICAL READING GUIDE

- Water, §30
- The Gospel of Creation, Esp. §66, 76, 83, 85, 87, 89, 99
- Ecological Conversion, §216–217
- Sacramental Signs and the Celebration of Rest, §235–237
- The Trinity and the Relationship Between Creatures, §239–240

The sacramental life of the church exists within, depends upon, and draws deeply from the web of life, which Pope Francis affectionately calls "our common home." And at the same time, Francis invites us to consider how our "common home" exists within, depends upon, and draws deeply from God's very life, a life which the sacraments make manifest. Orthodox Christians call the sacraments "holy mysteries," an evocative phrase that suggests a depth to the sacraments which their familiarity and seeming ordinariness can mask. Sacraments, after all, rely on the tangible, the visible, and the familiar to communicate mystery, whose deepest realities remain hidden from our sight and elude our complete comprehension. The tangible, however, is not some poor substitute for God's real revelation. Olivier Clément in his beautiful work, *The Roots of Christian Mysticism*, reminds his readers that "the true way to approach the mystery is in the first place, celebration, celebration by the whole cosmos. . . . The universe is the first Bible."[1] Pope Francis, in a similar vein, describes the sacraments as "a privileged way in which nature is taken up by God to become a means of mediating supernatural life" (§235). In the liturgy, Christians celebrate the sacraments in, with, and through the cosmos.

Laudato Si' casts a unique light on liturgy, a reflection of Pope Francis's deep formation in the church's sacramental life as source and inspiration for the integral ecology which he envisions. As he notes, "Through our worship of God, we are invited to embrace the world on a different plane" (§235). This chapter explores how the church accepts that invitation "to embrace the world on a different plane" in every liturgical celebration. The exploration begins with a brief explanation of "liturgy" and, in the encyclical's light, considers how liturgy forms participants in a kind of "deep ecology" of God's Kingdom. Then it focuses on the centrality of the Eucharistic liturgy as "cosmic act of love" (§236). The remainder of the chapter offers an extended reflection on the Easter Triduum, a three-day liturgical enactment of the mysteries central to the Christian faith: Jesus's self-gift in bread and wine at his last supper with his disciples (Holy Thursday), his passion and death on the cross (Good Friday) and his resurrection (Holy Saturday night into Easter Sunday). The Triduum liturgy provides one of the most powerful distillations of the "privileged way in which nature is taken up by God" in the church's sacramental life (§235).

Liturgy: Formation in the deep ecology of God's kingdom

The term "liturgy" refers to those rites and practices which gather Christians as a community to participate in the sacramental life, the holy mysteries revealed in Christ. The word "liturgy" combines two Greek words, "leitos," having to do with "people," in the sense of their being a social or public body; and "ergon," referring to work. So liturgy involves the work of a people, but, more than that, liturgy presumes personal participation in common work that benefits more than the individual participant. Liturgy creates a communal space in which Christians gather to do the work of their common life as the body of Christ, to enact their gradual formation located within a kind of deep ecology of the Kingdom of God.

Can Christians legitimately claim any such deep ecology? Among environmental philosophers, "deep ecology" refers to a radical reorientation in understanding humans' place within the ecosystem, stripping them of any privileged place as a species.[2] Such a vision of deep ecology seems difficult to reconcile with a Christian vision formed by the all-too-familiar Genesis passage where God grants humans, created in God's image, dominion over the rest of creation (Gen. 1.28). Francis places the verse in its broader biblical and ecclesial context to emphasize "that human life is grounded in three fundamental and closely intertwined relationships: with God, with our neighbor and with the earth itself" (§66). (See Chapter 5.) Francis's choice of "intertwined" to characterize these three fundamental relationships highlights humans as created for lives of interdependence. Here is a starting point for claiming a deep ecology of the Kingdom of God.

Jesus Christ, in his words and actions, makes this Kingdom present. He described the Kingdom using parables that involve natural processes often stressing interdependence. The Kingdom of God is like the planted mustard seed, a tiny powerhouse transforming soil and sun into branches to welcome birds, or the leaven that meets flour, water, and a woman's kneading skills to become bread. The inhabitants of this Kingdom are called the light, which enables sight, or salt, which enhances flavor and is a preservative (Mt. 13. 31-33). Disciples are to take instructions from birds, who know exactly what "God will provide" means. Their fashion sense comes not from Solomon's stylist but from fields clothed in wild flowers (cf. Mt. 6.25-34). The Kingdom is also like a hidden treasure and a pearl of great price but requires giving up everything rather than accumulating more (Matthew 13).

Jesus's actions, like his words, display the power of nonviolence to heal ruptures in those fundamental relationships—with God, neighbors, and the earth. Yet, Jesus's challenging words coupled with his gracious works of just mercy brought him to an ignominious end: death on a cross. The violent powers of human domination enjoyed a stunning victory, only to be thwarted by God's creative and healing power of love that transformed Jesus's self-giving death into a new and more powerful life, now present not as an idea but a reality in every time and place. When Pope Francis calls Christians to "an ecological spirituality grounded in the convictions of our faith," he has in mind this person, Jesus, whose life, death, and resurrection reveals God's steadfast love of this world in all its beauty and horror. Thus, Francis can insist that this "life of the spirit is not dissociated from the body or from nature or from worldly realities, but lived in and with them, in communion with all that surrounds us" (§216). Not unlike proponents of the deep ecology movement, he understands that "the ecological crisis is also a summons to a profound interior conversion" (§217) as well as a "community conversion" (§219). Where he differs, and it is a significant difference, is the source. Conversion comes in an "encounter with Jesus Christ." Its "effects . . . become evident in their [the converts'] relationship with the world around them" (§217). In the church, "the life of the spirit is not dissociated from the body or from nature or from worldly realities, but lived in and with them, in communion with all that surrounds us" (§217). Participation in the church's sacramental life through the liturgy offers ongoing opportunities for this personal and communal encounter with Jesus Christ which like so many natural processes of change work their effects only gradually, almost imperceptibly.

To dwell in the sacramental life is to dwell in Christ Jesus, to learn how to recognize his face in our neighbor and the earth itself and how it feels to be Christ's body in our place and time, caring for our common home and all who share it. Sacramental liturgies distill these realities into concentrated moments. They exist within, depend upon, and draw deeply from the bare necessities which sustain the pleasure of day-to-day living—water, light, air, bread—as well as extravagances which compound the joy of day-to-day living—fragrant oils and wine, which are made sweeter when accompanied by story and song. The liturgical context reveals these staples' deepest identity as gifts to be shared among neighbors in gratitude to the One from whom all good things come. Participation in Christian liturgy is work necessary for sustaining the common life as a people called to repentance and reconciliation for the sake of those "three fundamental and closely intertwined relationships: with God, with our neighbor and with the earth itself" constitutive of the deep ecology of God's Kingdom.

The Eucharist: "Act of cosmic love"

Among Roman Catholics, the term "liturgy" is often used interchangeably with Eucharist or Mass. To be clear, many other Catholic rites and communal prayer practices are quite appropriately called "liturgy," for example, baptisms or reconciliation rites. The recitation of psalms, prescribed in the Rule of St. Benedict, bears the name "Liturgy of the Hours" to describe the monastic communal prayer which sanctifies the natural rhythms of daily life as night becomes day and returns to night. For most Catholics, or at least those with access to a parish with a priest, the Mass remains their most frequent liturgical encounter with Christ.[3]

Francis employs some of his most extravagant language to convey the Eucharist's significance within an ecological spirituality, as in this passage where he quotes his predecessor, Benedict XVI:

> In the Eucharist, fullness is already achieved: it is the living center of the universe, the overflowing core of love and of inexhaustible life. Joined to the incarnate Son, present in the Eucharist, the whole cosmos gives thanks. Indeed, the Eucharist is itself an act of cosmic love: "Yes cosmic! Because even when it is celebrated on the humble altar of a country church, the Eucharist is always in some way celebrated on the altar of the world." (§236)

In naming the world as "the altar" of this act of cosmic love, Pope Benedict XVI radically reorients any understanding of Eucharist as somehow separate or removed from the world in which Christ poured out God's creative, redemptive, and sanctifying love.

Many Catholic parishes celebrate Eucharist daily, but, as Francis notes, Sunday's celebration "has special importance. Sunday, like the Jewish Sabbath, is meant to be a day which heals our relationships with God, with ourselves, with others and with the world" (§237). Sunday to Sunday, Jesus "gathers a people" to himself to form them as his body unified across a truly marvelous diversity of cultures, languages, music, and sacred images, expressed in a panoply of colors, dress, architecture, and landscape. Across the globe, "from the rising of the sun to its setting," the faithful work on their common life: listening to the same Scripture passages and partaking in the one bread and cup, the body and blood of the Lord (Cf. Eucharist Prayer III). Over a year's time, these liturgical celebrations take this people on an annual pilgrimage, accompanying Jesus from his birth to baptism and ministry, following him into his passion and death, and rejoicing in his resurrection.

The Easter Triduum

The liturgy invites these pilgrims to participate in a living faith as it unfolds in the changing seasons, Advent into Christmas, Lent into Easter, interspersed with ordinary time. Yet of all the liturgies that Christians celebrate each year, none is more central to entering into God's act of cosmic love than the Easter "Triduum," a Latin word, which means "three days." This liturgy occurs over the course of three days, beginning the evening of Holy Thursday and concluding on Easter Sunday with evening prayer. Those who participate in this liturgical work, celebrating the sacraments of Christian initiation (Baptism, Confirmation, and Eucharist), enter into the central reality of Christian life, the Paschal Mystery, Christ's passing over from death into the new life of resurrection.

Holy Thursday: "Small gestures of mutual care" and "a fragment of matter"

Triduum begins on Holy Thursday, a participation in Jesus's last supper with his disciples, where water, bread, wine become sacramental signs of Jesus's gift of self-emptying love. Heeding the Lord's command, contemporary disciples wash feet, enacting Jesus's command to follow his example of humble service. One might recall Pope Francis washing and kissing the feet of inmates from a Roman prison in 2015 and, in 2016, Muslim, Hindu, and Christian refugees. This liturgical act deeply resonates with Francis's words in *Laudato Si*. "Love, overflowing with small gestures of mutual care, is also civic and political, and it makes itself felt in every action that seeks to build a better world" (§231). Liturgy truly demands hard work from those people who enact their identity as the body of Christ even to the point of risking taking the liturgy beyond the church's threshold into prisons and refugee camps.

Holy Thursday liturgy then gathers participants around a table-become-altar where Jesus, on the night before his death, transforms simple fare, unleavened bread and a cup of wine, with his words: "This is my body that is for you." "This cup is the new covenant in my blood" (1 Cor. 11. 25, 26). The next day Jesus reveals the deeper reality of these words on the cross. Pope Francis describes this gift of self-emptying love in all its wonder. "Grace, which tends to manifest itself tangibly, found unsurpassable expression when God himself became man and gave himself as food for his creatures. The Lord, in the culmination of the mystery of the Incarnation, chose to reach our intimate depths through a fragment of matter" (§236). The Eucharist enacts in a startling way the deeply intertwined relationships among God, humans, and the earth itself.

The intertwined relationships are clearly present in the liturgical actions which precede the saying of Jesus's words over the bread and wine. The priest descends from the altar to receive bread and wine from the hands of the assembly's representatives. Every Eucharistic liturgy, including that of Holy Thursday, the celebrant places them on the altar and then lifts up each element, echoing the ancient Jewish blessing, Berakah: "Blessed are you, Lord God of all creation," whose "goodness" is evident in this simple fare present in the assembly. The bread, "the fruit of earth and work of human hands . . . will become for us the bread of life," and, the wine, "the fruit of the vine and work of human hands . . . will become our spiritual drink."[4] The prayer illuminates the collaborative work of a generous Creator, fruitful earth, and inventive humans that makes possible even this fleeting liturgical moment, aptly named "preparation of the gifts." Pope Francis has performed this gesture with the accompanying prayer hundreds of times since his 1969 ordination. These liturgical actions give credence to his inclusive vision of creation at worship. "The Eucharist joins heaven and earth; it embraces and penetrates all creation. The world which came forth from God's hands returns to him in blessed and undivided adoration" (§236). With thousands upon thousands of daily celebrations of Mass, creation's work of adoration through the Eucharist traverses the globe in all of its glorious biodiversity.

As Pope Francis notes in *Evangelii Gaudium*, "Realities are greater than ideas" (§201). The Holy Thursday liturgy celebrates the reality of Jesus's self-gift first in a "small gesture of mutual care," washing feet, and then more mysteriously glorious, in "a fragment of matter" (§231, 236). Participants enter into the mystery, the sacrament of Incarnation, when God came as servant and then "gave himself as food" on a particular time, the night before Jesus died, and in a particular place, at table with his disciples (§236).

Good Friday: "Even to the cross"

Holy Thursday liturgy concludes in dramatic fashion. The celebrant processes with the consecrated hosts (the Eucharistic bread) from the main altar to place them in a temporary dwelling on an altar of repose. A few prepare the church's worship space for Good Friday. They strip the altar of all coverings and leave the tabernacle door open to reveal its empty interior. Many remain to pray at that altar of repose, an ironic name, given that their prayer enacts Jesus's request to remain with him as he undergoes his agony in the Garden of Gethsemane. Participants depart Holy Thursday liturgy in silence and begin their great fast.

Every aspect of the rite's conclusion communicates the gravity of the evening's events to follow—Jesus arrested, abandoned, abused and tortured, condemned to death and, in less than 24 hours, dead by crucifixion. This second day of the Triduum demarcates Good Friday with an absence. No Mass is celebrated on this day. Catholics and other Christians enter into Jesus's passion through its dramatic proclamation in John's Gospel, prayers of intercessions for the flourishing of peoples of deep faith (and not just Christians) as well as those of no faith, a simple gesture of veneration—a bow, a kiss, an embrace—of a physical form of the cross, often made of rough wood, and reception of communion, using hosts consecrated the prior evening and reserved on the altar of repose. The stark reality of Jesus's crucifixion requires little liturgical embellishment. "One Person of the Trinity entered into the created cosmos, throwing his lot with it, even to the cross" (§99). Participants depart again in silence, continuing their great fast, which serves to heighten awareness of the great Christian mystery unfolding among them.

Easter Vigil: "Night of grace"

The following day, Holy Saturday, Christians make their final preparations for Easter, a 50-day celebration, inaugurated with the Easter Vigil liturgy, the Triduum's most magnificent liturgical celebration. The Easter Vigil liturgy offers a panoramic view of just how deep the ecology of God's Kingdom is. It is no exaggeration to say that all other Christian liturgies take their inspiration from Easter Vigil liturgy. For those unfamiliar with the liturgical celebration, a brief overview is in order. The rituals trace their origins to the early church's Easter celebrations. Liturgy begins with the blessing of a fire which will light the evening's candles, then an extended Liturgy of the Word tracing God's redemptive work, and culminates in the initiation of new members into the faith community through celebrations of the sacraments of Baptism, Confirmation, and Eucharist.[5] Each part provides a deepening awareness of the intertwined relationships between God, neighbor, and the earth itself.

"Vigil" shares the same etymological root as vigilant and more distantly "watch" and "wake." Every Holy Saturday, as the sun sets, Christians gather to keep their annual Vigil, as they both remember and anticipate Easter morning, rejoicing in their ever-dawning new life in Christ. Those gathered in watchful awareness enact their ongoing formation in the life of Christ through stories, songs, prayers, and sacramental actions. Some are there to enter more fully in this formative way of life, as their months of preparation as catechumens culminate in initiation into the church. Every participant is invited to encounter church at its most profound, as "the sacrament of the Risen One who imparts his resurrection to us."[6]

Lighting the Paschal Candle: Keeping company with Brother Fire and Mother Bees

The contemporary Easter Vigil takes its cue from the ancient church's celebration. The early Christians reveled in Jesus Christ through whom heaven and earth embraced so that even the most ordinary stuff of life reveals something of God's glory in the risen Lord. Easter Vigil begins in darkness to recall the in-between time from Good Friday to Easter Sunday. This darkness heightens anticipation of light by its absence. Very soon the night is made a little brighter with the lighting of a new fire, which is then blessed. This holy fire becomes the flame for a single candle, the Paschal Candle, which signifies the light of Christ, the light through whom Christians see all that exists. From that single flame, many flames appear as participants light the candles that they hold—the one and the many sharing the same light source.

It seems worthwhile to pause for a moment to consider how proclaiming "Christ as the light of the world" (cf. John 8.12) resonated with all those Christians who depended not on the power grid and a light switch but the sun by day and fire by night. St Francis of Assisi gives voice to light's wondrous existence in the opening verse of his hymn, *Laudato Si'*. "Praised be you, my Lord, with all your creatures/especially through Sir Brother Sun,/ who is the day; and through whom you give us light./And he is beautiful and radiant with great splendor;/and bears a likeness of you, Most High" (§87). Truly sunlight is a precious commodity that enables the flourishing of life in a multitude of ways. As human activity changes the atmosphere, our relationship to "Sir Brother Sun" has become more evident. The sun's constancy in simply being day requires nothing from us; its intensity in radiant splendor demands greater respect and evokes awe. Human eyes depend on the sun's light to see, and yet no human eye can withstand direct observation of the light.

Perhaps this inability to gaze directly at "Sir Brother Son" offers some explanation as to why the light to signify Christ, the face of God's mercy, comes as flames of fire in darkness rather than the full sun. St Francis also assists our consideration of the wonder of this other source of light as he gives praise to God "through Brother Fire,/through whom you light the night,/ and he is beautiful and playful and robust and strong" (§87). Christians take a new fire's blessed flame, "beautiful and playful and robust and strong," and light the Pascal Candle so that all might praise the wondrous light of Christ, constant and intense. Around this single Paschal Candle, the people gather to engage once more in their liturgical work, which, at that moment, involves holding candles lit from the single flame and listening to the celebrant sing the ancient Easter Proclamation, the "Exsultet."[7] The name comes from the opening word, "Exult!" which literally means to leap up or out, to dance with joy. The song opens with a call to all creation, "the hosts of heaven" and "all corners of the earth," to "exult," to join this dance of joy. The celebrant exhorts those gathered: "Let this holy building shake with joy,/filled with the mighty voices of the peoples." These instructions, always given though seldom achieved, seem more than appropriate on such a wondrous night of remembering and anticipation.

The candle itself presents the joint efforts among God's creatures to praise the Creator on "this night" filled with the "dazzling" light of God's redemptive love and mercy. The celebrant prayerfully sings: "On this, your night of grace, O holy Father, accept this candle, a solemn offering, the work of bees and of your servants' hands"—an echo of the prayer preparing the gifts of bread and wine. Now at its liturgical work as light-bearer, the candle enacts the wonder of "a fire into many flames divided, yet never dimmed by sharing its light, for it is fed by melting wax, drawn out by mother bees to build a torch so precious." The wax from "mother bees" offers even more than fuel for the fire. The celebrant continues to sing: "Receive its pleasing fragrance, and let it [the fragrance] mingle with the lights of heaven." The air feeding the flame also receives a gift, the sweet scent of beeswax, which it carries to envelop the stars. The celebrant concludes: "May this flame be found still burning by the Morning Star: who never sets, Christ your Son, who, coming back from death's domain, has shed his peaceful light on humanity, and lives and reigns for ever and ever." And the people sing, "Amen!" "So be it."[8]

The Paschal Candle, whose flame comes from "the work of bees and your servants' hands," sheds some light on Pope Francis's proclamation of the Gospel of Creation: "The ultimate purpose of other creatures is not to be found in us. Rather, all creatures are moving forward with us and through us towards a common point of arrival, which is God, in that transcendent fullness where the risen Christ embraces and illumines all things" (§83). Busy bees, fragrant wax, servants' hands, fire, air, heavenly lights, Morning Star, and voices in song participate in the sacramental life of this single Paschal Candle. All witness and offer praise of Christ, who gives light to the world.

Then they remembered . . . listening to the story of God creator and liberator

What follows in the Easter Vigil is story and song, an extended form of the Liturgy of the Word. All nine of the possible readings are taken from Christian Scripture, the church's "first sacrament":[9] seven from the Hebrew Scripture and the final two from the New Testament. In extolling "the Wisdom of the Biblical Accounts," in his account of the "Gospel of Creation," Pope Francis provides a useful summary of the overall effect of the Easter Vigil's readings. "In the Bible, the God who liberates and saves is the same God who created the universe, and these two divine ways of acting are intimately and inseparably connected" (§73). On this "night of grace," Christians listen to these readings as touchstones in the single story of God's creative love and just mercy, which in turn helps them read the deepest truths of the world.

The first reading, Genesis's poetic rendering of God's creative work, begins the evening's lessons concerning the deep ecology of God's Kingdom within a liturgy celebrating God's love and care for all creatures. As each creative moment unfolds in the first Genesis creation story, God pauses to hold creation in a contemplative gaze and pronounces in that moment each and every creature as "good," that it is of value in and of itself as it exists. On the sixth day, God surveys all creation as a whole and judges it to be "*very* good."

God then completes the creative work with rest, a creative act in itself since it makes the day "holy." Perhaps these contemplative moments provide another hermeneutical key for interpreting this story in light of the deep ecology of God's Kingdom. "We tend to demean contemplative rest as something unproductive and unnecessary, but this is to do away with the very thing which is most important about work: its meaning. We are called to include in our work a dimension of receptivity and gratuity, which is quite different from mere inactivity" (§237). If God's work culminates in rest which makes holiness, then what ought to be the end of the work of those made in God's image and likeness? And what does that daily work have to do with the work which is liturgy?

The Easter Vigil's Liturgy of the Word has only begun. The community responds to the first reading, singing portions of a psalm. Six more readings from the Old Testament may be read, though usually not all are. Each is followed by a responsorial psalm, usually sung. Most participants would probably admit that these readings are too many from the vantage point of human patience and the powers of concentration, and, at the same time, amazingly few from the vantage point of telling the story of God's creative and saving work that began nearly 14 billion years ago. Clearly, the people's liturgical work involves attentive listening and heartfelt singing.

Those participants who stick to this liturgical work soon discover just how frequently Scripture's revelatory power draws from experiences in the natural world: God's first "precious book, 'whose letters are the multitude of created things present in the universe'" (§85). God's creative and liberative work truly finds a myriad of expressions. Through Moses's trust in God's commands, the Red Sea becomes a pathway to Hebrew freedom and the enslavers' destruction. The Prophet Isaiah announces to a people under duress that God's love endures even if "mountains fall away and the hills be shaken" (Isa. 54.10). In a subsequent Isaiah reading, the prophet proclaims God's assurance of the divine word's effectiveness like rain and snow soaking the earth to produce seed, which in turn provides food to eat. The sixth reading from the Prophet Baruch urges the people to follow the "light" of Lady Wisdom, sent from God to illumine nature's deeper realities as creation, or in Pope Francis's words, "as a gift from the outstretched hands of the Father of all, and as a reality illuminated by the love which calls us together into universal communion" (§76). In the final Old Testament reading, the Prophet Ezekiel communicates God's promise to transform a wayward people through actions, both simple and dramatic. "I will sprinkle clean water over you to make you clean. . . . I will give you a new heart, and a new spirit I will put within you. I will remove the heart of stone from your flesh and give you a heart of flesh" (Ezek. 36.25-26). No deluge required as in Noah's time, just a sprinkling of clean water and a much-needed heart transplant, enlivened with a new spirit, like a breath of fresh air.

Two more readings, both from the New Testament, complete the Easter Vigil's Liturgy of the Word. Before hearing those proclaimed, the people pause to express an overwhelming joy in a God whose "divine ways" are ever creating, ever liberating. Together they sing: "Glory to God in the highest, and on earth peace to people of good will." This opening verse expresses the glory of those "three fundamental and closely intertwined relationships: with God, with our neighbor and with the earth itself" (§66). Since receiving their Wednesday ashes to begin Lent, the people have sung about this glorious reality only once at liturgy, on Holy Thursday. Now they resume this effusive recitation of praise and thanksgiving spoken directly to the triune God. "We praise you . . . have mercy . . . receive our prayer. . . . You alone are the Holy One . . . . Jesus Christ/with the Holy Spirit,/ in the glory of God the Father."[10] Every Sunday liturgy, except during the Advent and Lenten liturgical fast, the people's work of glorifying God expresses succinctly what Francis identifies as "that Trinitarian dynamism which God imprinted on them when they were created." This almost-every-Sunday, too-familiar prayer seems like the liturgical preparation for meeting St Bonaventure's "challenge of trying to read reality in a Trinitarian key" (§239). Glorifying God immediately evokes a greeting of peace to all people of goodwill. "Everything is interconnected, and this invites us to develop a spirituality of that global solidarity which flows from the mystery of the Trinity" (§240). Such a liturgical moment becomes more than an abstract idea, if, following the lead of Pope Francis, Christians make every effort "to enter into dialogue with all people about our common home" (§3). Such efforts seem like a natural extension of the liturgical work of giving glory to God in the highest.

The remainder of the Easter Vigil Liturgy of the Word ends surprisingly quickly with a brief reading from St Paul's Letter to the Romans and a Gospel account of courageous women who come to anoint Jesus's lifeless body only to find an empty tomb. Given that it is the Easter Vigil, the brevity of the readings that focus directly on the risen Christ may seem puzzling, even disappointing. Yet, like all the other readings, these two prepare the people for the liturgical work that follows: participation in the very life of the risen Lord through the sacramental liturgies. In the passage from Romans, St Paul speaks directly to this participation beginning with a question startling to ancient and contemporary Christians alike. "Or are you unaware that we who were baptized into Christ Jesus were baptized into his death?" (Rom. 6.3). He responds as one, deeply immersed in the sacramental life of the Paschal Mystery. "We were indeed buried with him through baptism into death, so that, just as Christ was raised from the dead by the glory of the Father, we too might live in newness of life" (Rom. 6.4). Those who die with Christ pass over into new life, to participate more fully in the deep ecology of God's Kingdom.

The Easter proclamation in the four Gospels share much in common. The selection from the Gospel of Luke will be the focus here. Curiously enough, the portion of Luke read at Easter Vigil features no appearance from the risen Lord. The story begins at daybreak, signaling to those at Vigil, their night watch is ending—Easter is at hand. A few women, among Jesus's most faithful disciples, approach his tomb to perform a final loving act, to anoint his lifeless, crucified body with fragrant oils. Confusion ensues as they find the tomb empty and encounter "two men in dazzling clothes." These two mysterious figures ask the most basic question of the Christian faith: "Why do you look for the living among the dead?" They respond almost matter-of-factly: "He is not here, but has risen." They then advise the perplexed women: "Remember how he told you . . ." of his death and resurrection. The Gospel continues, "Then they remembered his words." Those at Easter Vigil have followed this same advice about remembering beginning with their gathering for the lighting of the new fire. When the women inform the others of the empty tomb, all of them, even the 11, thought it "an idle tale, and they did not believe them." Impetuous Peter "ran to the tomb, stooping and looking in, he saw the linen cloths by themselves; then he went home, amazed at what had happened" (Lk. 24.5-12). Thus ends "The Gospel of the Lord," leaving those at Easter Vigil to ask, "Why do you seek the living one among the dead?" Their response comes in celebrating the sacraments of Baptism, Confirmation, and Eucharist. These sacraments, the holy mysteries, proclaim: "He is here among us, the living; He has indeed been raised!" Olivier Clément reveals the cosmic implications of faith in the risen Christ. "The whole of the Church's life should be a 'laboratory for the resurrection' (Dumitru Staniloae); it ought to vibrate with a mighty resurrectional upsurge embracing all humanity and the whole universe."[11] Here, in dramatic fashion, Clément reiterates that invitation "to embrace the world on a different plane" through worship of a God whose love for the world is revealed in the crucified Christ now risen (§235).

Immersion in Christ's life: The precious gift of Sister Water

Christian life begins with baptism, and so it begins immersed in light and water—basic elements that bring forth life on earth. As the Easter Vigil's previous readings make very clear, water's power threatens and invites, brings destruction as well as refreshment, the end of life as well as its beginning. The liturgy which celebrates baptism draws deeply from the wide range of water's properties. From what we know of the earliest Christian celebrations, baptism came after a long period of instruction to prepare the person to enter into Christ's death to pass over into new life, the Paschal Mystery. Some of the earliest baptismal fonts required one to descend into a cross-shaped opening dug into the ground filled with water, as if to respond in earth and stone to Paul's question. "Or are you unaware that we who were baptized into Christ Jesus were baptized into his death?" Awareness grew with each step deeper into the font.

Paul uses "we" not "I" in his question because baptism is not a private affair but deeply personal and therefore communal. Becoming a person requires being grounded in those three fundamental relationships: God, neighbors, and the earth itself. The celebrant assigns the first liturgical task to those who will witness the baptisms.[12] After greeting the "dearly beloved," he asks them to pray "with one heart and one soul," as a single body. Here those already dwelling in the body of Christ come to the aid of "our brothers and sisters" who "approach the font of rebirth." Then the celebrant again addresses the "dearly beloved" asking them to "humbly invoke upon this font the grace of God." The relationship between God and neighbor clearly intertwines in the work of rebirth.

Then before proceeding any further with the baptismal preparations, those gathered enlist the aid of saints, neighbors of a different order, hidden from sight but present in the risen Christ. The litany of saints begins and ends with prayers asking Christ directly for mercy and deliverance to leave no doubt the ultimate source of sanctity. Usually less than 30 specific saints receive mention, but many more are invoked with the final appeal to "All holy men and women,/Saints of God," to "pray for us." To these holy men and women, Easter Vigil participants owe a debt. These saints, the unnamed as much the named, show what intergenerational solidarity looks like. Their fidelity helps to sustain the deep ecology of God's Kingdom for subsequent generations up to and including present-day celebrations of new life in Christ. They offer guidance in living out an "integral ecology" in which "we realize that the world is a gift which we have freely received and must share with others" (§159). The sacrament of baptism itself offers a powerful witness to this gift.

After gathering a multitude of members in the body of Christ through prayer, the people with the celebrant turn to the third partner in that relationship, the earth, who graciously grants the means to complete the work of the baptismal liturgy. Fire and water become indispensable participants in the sacrament. The Paschal Candle, thanks to those "mother bees" and their fragrant wax, still bears the flame of the new fire. The celebrant plunges the lit candle into the waters of the baptismal font, enacting the power of the Holy Spirit to transform this watery tomb into a womb. Many note the erotic dimensions of the symbolic action. There is an earthiness to the Creator's love for creatures. With candlelight hovering over the waters, the blessing remembers other sacred stories of water—wind over waters, flood, Red Sea, River Jordan, and water mixed with blood. As the celebrant lifts the candle out of the water, the people proclaim: "Springs of water, bless the Lord;/praise and exalt him above all forever." Living water now blessed joins in the prayers of praise.

Again it seems worthwhile to pause for a moment to consider the significance of water. Saint Francis praises God "through Sister Water who is very useful and humble and precious and chaste" (§87). The people who gave us these sacred tales of water knew desert and the desperate need for a reliable source of water. Many biblical romances, like that of Jacob and Rachel (Genesis 29), begin when boy meets girl at well. Even Jesus meets the Samaritan woman at Jacob's well not exactly for romance but certainly for a relationship that offers her new life through Jesus, source of living water. Early Christians puzzled over Jesus's baptism in the River Jordan since he had no need for John's baptism of repentance. After long reflection, they came to see in Christ's baptism a truly cosmic event. Here is an example: "Jacob of Serugh is explicit in saying that by stepping down into the Jordan, Jesus consecrated all waters: 'The entire nature of the waters perceived that you [Jesus] had visited them—seas, deeps, rivers, springs and pools all thronged together to receive the blessing of your footsteps.'"[13] What is especially delightful in Jacob's praise of Jesus is the life within the waters themselves who sensed something different and gathered to receive this blessing.

This spread of sanctification through the cosmos stands in sharp contrast to the human-created pollutants that contaminate not only water but also air and soil. Perhaps the waters feel this degradation as much as they felt Jesus's foot. Pope Francis calls us to consider our own feel for the earth. "Here I would reiterate that 'God has joined us so closely to the world around us that we can feel the desertification of the soil almost as a physical ailment, and the extinction of a species as a painful disfigurement'" (§89). Christ's entrance into the Jordan's flowing waters offers the opposite, sanctification, even purification. The baptismal waters blessed at the Easter Vigil flow into holy water fonts which invite fingers to take a dip and bless their bodies with the sign of the cross each time they enter and leave the worship space. These waters testify to God's open invitation: "Come to the waters!" That testament poses a challenge to those who treat water "as a commodity subject to the laws of the market. Yet *access to safe drinkable water is a basic and universal human right, since it is essential to human survival and, as such, is a condition for the exercise of other human rights*" (§30). Water is sacred in itself, "essential to human survival." Saint Francis finds the perfect adjective for water—precious. How precious water is! It seems so fitting that Jesus begins his earthly ministry of bringing life in abundance rising out of the flowing waters of the River Jordan. He in turn becomes the font of new life, signified in the waters of baptism, accessible to all who desire to follow in the way of Christ crucified and risen.

With the baptismal waters blessed, the Paschal Candle burning brightly, the candidates for baptism come forward. The celebrant addresses a few final questions about renouncing sin and professing the church's faith in the triune God to those seeking baptism or to parents and godparents. The candidate or parents usually respond to each question with a resounding "I do!" Each adult or child then comes forward to the baptismal font where the life-giving waters cover her or him three times either through pouring or immersion as the celebrant proclaims: "I baptize you in the name of the Father, and of the Son, and of the Holy Spirit." The newly baptized emerges from the water for anointing with chrism, olive oil fragrant with botanical oils, the local community's share of the holy oils blessed by the local bishop on Tuesday of Holy Week. "[God] now anoints you with the chrism of salvation, so that . . . you may remain for ever a member of Christ who is Priest, Prophet, and King." The oil soaks into the skin and the fragrance accompanies the new member through the night, natural signs of the Spirit's effects. The baptized then receives a white garment, signifying to all who see them that they "have become a new creation and have clothed [themselves] in Christ." Finally, each receives a candle lit from the Paschal Candle, "the light of Christ," the spark of this new creation. After the baptisms are complete, those who have prepared also receive the sacrament of confirmation, signified by the laying on of hands on their heads, calling upon the Holy Spirit "to be their helper and guide" by bestowing a multitude of gifts: wisdom, understanding, right judgment, courage, knowledge, reverence and, finally, "wonder and awe in your presence." This action is followed by a second anointing with chrism accompanied by the acclamation: "Be sealed with the Gift of the Holy Spirit."[14] The Spirit's gifts never diminish but grow in their use—reassuring to all those who depend on them in pursuit of an integral ecology.

Taken together these actions probably take less than 15 minutes for each person, a few fleeting liturgical moments in which "nature is taken up by God to become a means of mediating supernatural life" (§235). Ordinary stuff of life serves as signs and witnesses of life as gift from a triune God ever manifest in creating, redeeming, and sanctifying. "Encountering God does not mean fleeing from this world or turning our back on nature. This is especially clear in the Christian East. 'Beauty, which in the East is one of the best loved names expressing the divine harmony and the model of humanity transfigured, appears everywhere: in the shape of a church [or baptismal font], in the sounds, in the colors, in the lights, in the scents'" (§235). In the sacraments of Baptism and Confirmation, fire and water, fragrant oil, and a new garment convey something of the breadth and depth of God's love, cosmic, and personal—a love whose beauty becomes manifest in drawing all creation into the work of praise and thanksgiving.

Go in peace in the company of Jesus

This beauty which is love finds expression in the Easter Vigil's final action, the liturgy of the Eucharist. The remainder of the liturgy varies little from that celebrated on Holy Thursday, that first evening of Triduum, or from any other Mass, for that matter. Yet, in the context of Easter Vigil, especially in the company of the newly baptized, with the sweet smell of holy oils lingering, and the Paschal Candle still flickering, Pope Francis's claim that the Eucharist becomes the site where "all that has been created finds its greatest exaltation" comes into clearer focus. God provides the stuff of creation which humans transform and return as a truly humble offering. And what does God do? God immediately returns the gifts of bread and wine now transformed into God's very self as revealed in Jesus Christ. Humans are invited to take this heavenly food and to become what they eat—to become the body of Christ. Those who come forward accept God's offer "to reach our intimate depths through a fragment of matter" (§236). Easter Vigil liturgy ends as all others do with a blessing in the name of the triune God, Father, Son, and Holy Spirit. Consider how many times Francis has performed this gesture and then consider his words in *Laudato Si'*. "The hand that blesses is an instrument of God's love and a reflection of the closeness of Jesus Christ, who came to accompany us on the journey of life" (§235). Companions, of course, are those who break bread together. God, neighbor, and the earth itself are companions of those who go forth with their final liturgical assignment still ringing in their ears: "Go in peace, Alleluia! And the people respond, 'Thanks be to God, Alleluia!' 'Thanks be to God' for the gifts that allow the work enacted at each Eucharist to continue as members of Christ's Body go forth to live the Gospel of Creation and care for our "common home."

Conclusion

Participation in the "holy mysteries," or the sacraments, plays a crucial role in developing those "new convictions, attitudes and forms of life" (§202) which an integral ecology demands. As the work of the people called to be the body of Christ, liturgy gradually forms its participants in the deep ecology of the Kingdom of God, "grounded in three fundamental and closely intertwined relationships: with God, with our neighbor and with the earth itself" (§66). From an ordinary daily or Sunday Mass or the elaborate rites of the Triduum, Christian worship invites participants "to embrace the world on a different plane" (§235). For in every liturgy, Christians celebrate all of creation's exaltation in Christ, the Word Incarnate, who embraced the cosmos in his death to transfigure it into the new life of his resurrection.

Questions

1   What is the basis in *Laudato Si'* and other Christian sources for claiming the existence of a "deep ecology of the Kingdom of God"? What is the relationship between this "deep ecology" and the church's sacramental life?

2   Why does Pope Francis grant a unique place to participation in the Eucharist celebration in his discussion of an ecological spirituality?

3   What are the specific examples from the Triduum that illustrate the exaltation of creation within the three-day liturgical celebrations?

4   Why does Pope Francis place in one chapter "Ecological Education and Spirituality"?

5   This essay claims that "liturgy gradually forms its participants in the deep ecology of the Kingdom of God." How does that claim resonate with your experience of liturgy? What are the challenges to such a claim?

Notes

1   Olivier Clément, *The Roots of Christian Mysticism* (New City Press, 1995, 2008, 9th printing), 27.

2   See, for example, the "Introduction" to Eric Katz, Andrew Light, and David Rosthenberg (eds), *Beneath the Surface: Critical Essays in the Philosophy of Deep Ecology* (Cambridge, MA: The MIT Press, 2000), 1.

3   Those unfamiliar with the Catholic Mass can find an outline of the basic structure at the U.S. Conference of Catholic Bishops website under "Prayer and Worship, the Mass." http://www.usccb.org/prayer-and-worship/the-mass/order-of-mass/index.cfm.

4   The *Roman Missal,* English translation according to the third typical edition (Washington, DC: United States Conference of Catholic Bishops, 2011), 529.

5   The chapter website offers a more detailed explanation of the Easter Vigil rites under worship/liturgical year/Triduum. http://www.usccb.org/prayer-and-worship/liturgical-year/triduum/roman-missal-and-the-easter-vigil.cfm.

6   Clément, *The Roots of Christian Mysticism,* 95.

7   All Exsultet quotes are taken from *the Roman Missal,* 353–56.

8   The *Roman Missal,* 356.

9   Clément, *The Roots of Christian Mysticism,* 97.

10   The *Roman Missal,* 522.

11   Clément, *The Roots of Christian Mysticism,* 82.

12   The prayers which follow are taken from the *Roman Missal,* rubrics §37–58, 369–84.

13 Quoted in Kilian McDonnell, *The Baptism of Jesus in the Jordan: The Trinitarian and Cosmic Order of Salvation* (Collegeville, MN: The Liturgical Press, 1996), 61.

14 The texts of the sacramental rites are taken from *The Rites of the Catholic Church, Volume One, Study Edition* prepared by the International Commission on English in the Liturgy, a Joint Commission of Catholic Bishops' Conferences, approved for use in the Dioceses of the United States of America by the National Conference of Catholic Bishops and confirmed by the Apostolic See (Collegeville, MN: A Pueblo Book, Liturgical Press, 1990), 157–64.

8

The option for the poor in *Laudato Si'*: Connecting care of creation with care for the poor

María Teresa Dávila

ENCYCLICAL READING GUIDE

- Global Inequality, § 48-52
- The Principle of the Common Good, §156-158
- Justice Between the Generations, §158-162
- Dialogue On the Environment in the International Community, §170, 172, 175
- The terms "poor" and "solidarity" are so important that they appear throughout the encyclical.

Is everything connected?

In *Laudato Si'* the phrase "everything is connected" suggests that the Christian life demands a holistic approach to care for the earth that looks critically at the complicated systems that impact our relationship with each other, the poor, and the earth. One of the deepest connections made in *Laudato Si'* is how care for creation directly impacts real human beings, real communities, and entire societies, especially the poor and racially marginalized. In other words, care for the environment is a matter of "environmental justice," a term that brings together care of nature and care for the poor as interrelated and interdependent practices in Christian ethics. Francis states that "the deterioration of the environment and of societies affects the most vulnerable people on the planet: 'Both everyday experience and scientific research show that the gravest effect of all attacks on the environment are suffered by the poorest'" (§48).[1]

One need only look at the examples of the recent water crisis in Flint, Michigan; the collapse of an industrial dam which spilled tons of toxic mud in the state of Minas Gerais, north Brazil, last November; and the chemical poisoning of the Elk River in West Virginia, in January 2014, as a result of a break in tanks holding a chemical used in coal production to understand the connections between care for the environment and care for the poor that are at the heart of *Laudato Si'*.[2] These examples highlight that access to safe drinking water, safe air to breathe, and safe dirt to use for growing food is increasingly denied to lower class, working class, and communities of color. These rights are in danger of becoming privileges. *Everything is Connected.*

This chapter will highlight the importance of the preferential option for the poor within *Laudato Si'*. Pope Francis insists that the ecological suffering of the poorest and most marginalized communities is an essential criterion for judging the success or failure of our environmental efforts. Reading the encyclical through the lens of the option for the poor brings together social justice and earth justice as intimately connected requirements of the Christian life. This requires reading *Laudato Si'* in tandem with Pope Francis's earlier apostolic exhortation *Evangelii Gaudium (EG)*, where the term "option for the poor" appears seven times (while appearing five times in *Laudato Si'*).[3] Both have been referred to as part of Francis's theology of "encounter,"[4] his emphasis on the globalization of indifference[5] and his special attention to mercy as a central attribute of divine life and identity.[6] But our reading of both documents, and of *Laudato Si'* specifically, suffers if we fail to pay attention to Francis's appreciation of the central insight of liberation theology and key element of Catholic social teaching: the preferential option for the poor, as key to understanding Francis's ethics for the human community and for the earth.[7]

This chapter will also identify the way that an integrated vision of the option for the poor as essential to Francis's social teaching raises the issue of conflict. Conflict arises when the best of intentions, in this case to "save the planet," run into our inability to overcome the racism, xenophobia, and classism that mark human interactions in this country and globally. And yet, embedded in *Laudato Si'* we also find potential ways of integrating social justice and ecological concern in ways that make it possible to unite action to address the environmental crises, with work for justice on behalf of the poorest who bear the initial and most significant brunt of these crises.

The preferential option for the poor

The option for the poor in church teaching

Official Church teaching stresses the importance of moral concern for the poor with the doctrine of the "preferential option" or "love for the poor." Quoting Pope John Paul II, the *Catechism of the Catholic Church* states: "'The Church's love for the poor . . . is a part of her constant tradition.' This love is inspired by the Gospel of the Beatitudes, of the poverty of Jesus, and of his concern for the poor."[8]

The *Catechism* teaches that life in community must be centered on the building and sustaining of the common good and insuring the flourishing and participation of all.[9] In addressing the command of love of neighbor, the *Catechism* teaches that the goods of God's creation are meant to be shared by all (the so-called "universal destination of goods").[10] It specifically names the poor as recipients of the church's active attention as a task of discipleship, as a biblical call to faithfulness and as an act of love of Jesus. "I was hungry and you gave me food, I was thirsty and you gave me drink, a stranger and you welcomed me" (Mt. 25.35-37).[11]

The *Catechism* discusses the seventh commandment, "You shall not steal," in a way that applies it to caring for the material well-being of the human family at the communal, social, national, and international level. Theft here means much more than directly taking something from another person. The *Catechism* broadens theft to encompass our participation in unjust systems that produce inequality and poverty. It cites St John Chrysostom (349–407): "Not to enable the poor to share in our goods is to steal from them and deprive them of life. The goods we possess are not ours, but theirs."[12]

Likewise, the *Compendium of the Social Doctrine of the Church* clearly relates the universal destination of goods and the option for the poor: "The principle of the universal destination of goods requires that the poor, the marginalized and in all cases those whose living conditions interfere with their proper growth should be the focus of particular concern. To this end, the preferential option for the poor should be reaffirmed in all its force."[13] Alternatively, fighting poverty as a sign of solidarity—standing together with and working with the oppressed—is also a key element in social doctrine. The suffering of poverty calls Christians to individual and communal acts of solidarity that directly impact the life of the poor but also through work to address the structural dimensions of injustice.[14]

The documentary history of Catholic social thought presents different challenges to concretely live out this call for solidarity attentive to the suffering of the world. While rooted in Scripture and Tradition, the contemporary concept of the preferential option emerged from the 1968 and 1979 meetings of the bishops of Latin America who gathered to apply the teachings of the Second Vatican Council (1962–65) to the situation in Latin America.[15]

Laudato Si', as the most recent addition to the church's social teaching, expresses it thusly: "This sister [Earth] now cries out to us because of the harm we have inflicted on her by our irresponsible use and abuse of the goods with which God has endowed her" (§2). Compare this language with that of the Medellín (1968) document on poverty of the church: "A deafening cry pours from the throats of millions of men [and women], asking their pastors for a liberation that reaches them from nowhere else."[16] Francis's image of the earth as another one of the poor who cries out for justice should also bring to mind Leonardo Boff's important work *Cry of the Earth/Cry of the Poor*, a phrase that appears in *Laudato Si'* as well.[17]

The option for the poor in Pope Francis's teaching

In both *Evangelii Gaudium* and *Laudato Si'*, Francis uses the preferential option for the poor as the hermeneutical key for understanding and applying the social teaching of the church. Through its threefold understanding of poverty as (1) the lack of material and social goods needed for human life to be sustained and to thrive, (2) radical openness to the will of God, and (3) solidarity with the poor and marginalized as we work together in the struggle against injustice and oppression, the option for the poor offers a comprehensive vision of what Christian discipleship ought to look like in historical circumstances marked by radical differences and human suffering as a result of the sin of the world. As such, it calls the faithful to make the destiny of others who suffer and are poor in some way their own.

Francis cemented the place of the option for the poor in his social teaching in his first major document: *Evangelii Gaudium*—"*The Joy of the Gospel.*" In a section on "The Inclusion of the Poor in Society," Francis states: "Each individual Christian and every community is called to be an instrument of God for the liberation and promotion of the poor, and for enabling them to be fully a part of society." Francis intimately links the fate of the poor to the fate of all who call themselves Christian (and to all humanity) and who are therefore mandated to attentively listen to their cry for justice in solidarity (that third notion of "poverty" in the option for the poor). "This demands that we be docile and attentive to the cry of the poor and to come to their aid."[18] To not do so is the sin of indifference. This call for solidarity includes personal and social transformation. "It means working to eliminate the structural causes of poverty and to promote the integral development of the poor, as well as small daily acts of solidarity in meeting the real needs which we encounter."[19] Conversely, "None of us can think that we are exempt from concern for the poor and for social justice."[20] Attentiveness to the cry of the poor—developing an ability to listen to the vulnerable and oppressed—is a responsibility of every Christian and every community, and a necessary first step to true solidarity. Therefore Francis includes a section on particular voices of the poor: women, trafficked peoples, migrants, the unborn and, at the end of this list, "other weak and defenseless beings who are frequently at the mercy of economic interests or indiscriminate exploitation."[21] Francis is "speaking of creation as a whole," and proposes that we "not leave in our wake a swath of destruction and death which will affect our own lives and those of future generations."[22] Here we glimpse Francis expanding the preferential option for the poor in a way that will develop into a central theme of *Laudato Si'*; bringing together the life of all Christians with that of the poor and suffering, and that of the land, the waters, and the air in a common journey of solidary love and struggle for justice.

In *Laudato Si'*, the "excluded," the "vulnerable," or the "poor" are mentioned over 65 times throughout the document, almost as many times as the word "creation" (which appears 66 times)! Francis's environmental encyclical offers little distinction between justice for the poor and vulnerable and care of creation. The two are intimately linked throughout in ways that challenge previous notions of complicity and economic and social conflict in Catholic social teaching.

The option for the poor and conflict

The encyclical presents humanity's destructive impact on the environment as violence: violence that is in our hearts and that our sin has occasioned against the earth and against the poor (§2). Attending to the link between the ecological crises and the suffering of the poor opens our eyes to many hidden conflicts that are no less violent in their outcomes despite the covert nature. Environmental crises driven by climate change fuel military conflicts around the world. Resource scarcity, especially water for consumption and agriculture, visits grueling deprivations on affected populations, and the hidden ecological destruction that is part and parcel of globalized consumer production despoils the environment and deprives the poor around the world. This violence is often hidden within our daily consumption choices.

Environmental crises and military conflict

Ravages to the environment are linked to the destiny of marginalized communities nationally and internationally through the direct and immediate impact of having to migrate to avoid natural disasters and in response to lack of resources. Often conflict and violence erupt as a result. On the level of overt military conflict, climate change is already playing an important, but ignored, role in the events that dominate today's headlines. The civil war in Syria and the resulting rise of ISIS/Daesh emerged in the aftermath of a year-long drought and water shortage in the Tigris-Euphrates Basin. This drove millions of people off of parched farmland into urban centers seeking sustenance. These massive population shifts brought tensions to Syria's biggest cities, tensions that contributed to the outbreak of civil war.[23] *Laudato Si'* notes that wars themselves also bring profound environmental harm (§57).

Water shortages and pollution as a denial of human rights

"The issue of water" goes far beyond massive droughts. The conflict water shortages unleash are often far less visible than overt war. "Fresh drinking water is an issue of primary importance, since it is indispensable for human life and for supporting terrestrial and aquatic ecosystems." Increasingly, in many places, "demand exceeds the sustainable supply, with dramatic consequences in the short and long term" (§28). Francis employs the term "water poverty" to name the particular impact of such shortages on the poor: lack of water for drinking and agriculture and the health effects of polluted and diseased water sources (§29). Many scientific projections warn of immanent water shortages in many parts of the world—affecting both rich and poor alike.[24] "The environmental repercussions could affect billions of people; it is also conceivable that the control of water by large multinational businesses may become a major source of conflict in this century" (§31).

Francis names "access to safe drinkable water" as "a basic and universal human right, since it is essential to human survival and, as such, is a condition for the exercise of other human rights."[25] As such, "Our world has a grave social debt towards the poor who lack access to drinking water, because they are denied the right to a life consistent with their inalienable dignity" (§30).

The violence hidden behind consumer goods

The relationship between environmental justice and justice for the poor reveals the too-often hidden conflict in contemporary social and economic dynamics. More than other documents in the Catholic social tradition, *Laudato Si'* acknowledges that seeking environmental justice and justice for the poor requires a challenge to the workings of contemporary global capitalism.

"Cheap fashion" is an example of the hidden exploitation and violence that *takes place every day* as market values clash with care for the environment and concern for the poor.[26] In a class I taught on the Occupy Movement, one student group chose to analyze ethical questions around the fashion and garment industries. This group exposed the class to the true cost of cheap fashion, very much showing that *everything is connected*.

The process of producing cheap clothing demands large quantities of raw materials as well as massive toxic pollution of water in the process of using and dumping tannins, dyes and other chemicals post production (§29). These chemicals can be found miles from the factories that produce the fabrics that then go into the bright, colorful $5 shirts we buy without a second thought at popular fashion chains in the developed world. Consider your clothes closet. How many of the labels say "Made in Bangladesh" or other low-wage, poorly regulated countries?

The people involved in the production of cheap clothing are often exposed to harsh chemicals and unsafe conditions such as crumbling buildings, overcrowded facilities, and little ventilation; often receiving poor pay for long hours and no overtime pay. Recall the collapse of the Rana Plaza building in Bangladesh in 2013, which produced clothing for brands that are household names in the United States.[27] Over 1,100 workers died in that building collapse.[28]

On the consumer side, people purchasing cheap clothing end up disposing them when they rip or tear—perhaps not used to mending clothes. This disposal, whether in trash or donation, is also a problem. While donations might give an item of clothing a longer life, they often end up in bales of clothes being shipped to a number of African countries for sale or donations, where they disrupt domestic clothing production and, in the end, are incinerated or dumped in trash heaps in the receiving country.

Cheap clothing, a key product of global market exchanges, has a high cost to our environment, our workers, and communities. The land and the human family suffer directly and indirectly from our unfettered desire to buy one more piece of clothing, one more pair of shoes. In addition to the damage done to the environment and workers, old and often wise ways are left behind. Local industries, particularly farming and local ecologies, are devastated by the move to commercial production of clothing, centuries-old strategies for relating to the land and to the animals that provide for wool and other fabrics are left behind in the quest for increased production and economic growth.

Laudato Si' acknowledges the damage done by unfettered consumption on local ways of life, the life of workers, and the environment (§51, 55, 143, 154, 161–62). But in addition it acknowledges the ways these conflicts also continue to fuel a very distorted view of the human person who begins to see personal worth in terms of its consuming power alone (§203).

These various critiques of the hidden violence and conflict combine to describe the profound global inequality of the current global economic order. For Francis, this has both a systemic and a personal dimension. The two are interconnected.

On the systemic level, Francis calls for restitution for the ecological damage and oppression that began with natural resource extraction by colonial powers from colonized peoples and continues in the current global order. Francis argues that there is a "true ecological debt" between the global north and the south "connected to commercial imbalances with effects on the environment, and the disproportionate use of natural resources by certain countries over long periods of time" (§51). Reflecting on relationships of inequality with respect to care for the earth, Francis again warns that there are different levels of responsibility that powerful nations, with industries that dominate the laws of global markets and the use of natural resources, owe to poorer nations who have historically been on the receiving end of unjust economic relations.

Francis notes how often even so-called international efforts to address climate change obey the dynamics of political and economic power by being housed in the centers of commerce, privileging the voices of powerful players and decision-makers, and where the last thing that gets addressed is the fate of the most vulnerable. The poor remain at the bottom of considerations for environmental sustainability in these conversations because

> many professionals, opinion makers, communications media and centres of power, being located in affluent urban areas, are far removed from the poor, with little direct contact with their problems. They live and reason from the comfortable position of a high level of development and a quality of life well beyond the reach of the majority of the world's population. This lack of physical contact and encounter, encouraged at times by the disintegration of our cities, can lead to a numbing of conscience and to tendentious analysis which neglect parts of reality. (§49)

On the personal level, our interaction with these global dynamisms takes place through our participation in consumer-oriented global capitalism. As Chapter 1 noted, consumer goods are presented to us in a way that fundamentally hides their origins and impacts. Consumer culture is a training in imagination that deprives us of the ability to see that everything is connected. Francis argues that this anthropological failure of the consumer era shapes indifference to human suffering and vulnerability. Most especially it prevents us from understanding where these might be, and indeed are *shared* vulnerabilities, not just those of the poor. Lack of an understanding of shared vulnerability leads to myopia of how to really address the problem and perpetuates efforts based on the lie that the earth's resources are unlimited if we can only advance our technologies enough to overcome perceived scarcity. The interrelationship of the personal and systemic is evident throughout Francis's constructive proposals, to which we now turn.

Option for the poor, environmental justice, and recognition of the other

Laudato Si''s proposals for addressing environmental justice recall the tradition of Catholic social teaching and its emphasis on "conversion of heart" as the way to transform institutions and restore right relationship with creation and the human family. The sixth chapter of the encyclical, dedicated to "Ecological Education and Spirituality," emphasizes the reeducation of our economic habits away from overconsumption and for the development of economic virtues that train our impulses to consume (§203). Francis describes how the human spirit has become sick with desire for new things and is unable to set limits for the good of the earth, human relations, and our own spiritual health (§211). Francis's notion of "ecological conversion" (§216–221) combines the task of personal education and "interior conversion" with a social spirituality that seeks to establish relationships that support a comprehensive vision of the person and the community, including the environment. 'The ecological conversion needed to bring about lasting change is also a community conversion'" (§219).

This social dimension of conversion includes not simply concern for the poor, but conversion *toward the poor*. If the option for the poor is the hermeneutical key to reading *Laudato Si'*, as I argued, then their fate should be not just an illustration of the sin of the world, but also the rubric by which authentic conversion for environmental justice is measured. More specifically, the preferential option for the poor is more than a moral principle about who we should help; it is an incarnational principle of divine love.[29] The God of the Bible, and indeed Jesus's very life, witness to a divine love that enters human history in the journey of salvation. Not only is this God *with us*, but also is with us *in our deepest suffering and vulnerability*, that of historical death. Therefore, imitating Christ as part of Christian discipleship means entering the suffering of others. Faithful solutions toward environmental justice and sustainability demand that we personally share the vulnerability of the poor that Francis mentions so often throughout the document. Solutions grounded on conversion that do not involve becoming incarnate in the *cotidiano*—the everydayness—of those suffering the impact of environmental violence, human and other creatures, inevitably do not interrupt the very structures of power and violence grounded on an anthropology of ravenous acquisitive consumption that got us here in the first place. As Francis states, "Lack of physical contact and encounter, encouraged sometimes by the disintegration of our cities, can lead to a numbing of conscience and to tendentious analyses which neglect parts of reality" (§49).

Acknowledgment of the other—the racial, religious, ethnic, political, and economic other—and their experience must be a central dimension of a response to environmental justice grounded on the preferential option for the poor. As the last element of the term "poor" in the option for the poor reminds us, solidarity with the poor in their struggle for justice is a key element in any effort at social transformation. The Medellín document from the Latin American Bishops remind us that "all members of the church are called to live in evangelical poverty, but not all in the same way, as there are diverse vocations to this poverty, that tolerate diverse styles of life and various modes of acting."[30] In *Evangelii Gaudium*, Francis relates the option for the poor to being attentive to the suffering and needs of others.[31] In *Laudato Si'* we are called to be particularly attentive to the suffering produced by ecological damage.

Concretely, *Laudato Si'* makes specific suggestions with regard to policies and market practices that transform the focus of our economic practices from profit and unfettered growth to sustainability and positively impacting communities and those on the margins. *Laudato Si'* invites the faithful and the global community as a whole to understand the breadth of possibilities available for personally and corporately impacting global climate. It points to specific policies and actions: the search for short- and long-term alternatives to fossil fuels; the implementation and oversight of international agreements; the regulation of carbon credits, governance, cooperation, and oversight at the local and regional levels; the centrality of community impact in considering new ventures, consumer movements (including boycotting products) directly impacting businesses' decisions; the Earth Charter as a global voice for environmental consciousness, environmental education, and the building of a civilization of love that will impact macro and political dimensions of life in community.[32]

The moral and spiritual teachings of the document require us to go beyond its inevitably limited concrete analyses and proposals. First, in acknowledging that the environmental crisis creates multiple forms of conflict—such as wars and material hardship—conversion toward the victim of such effects of environmental damage call us to be particularly attentive to the plight of the migrant and the refugee at our steps at the same time that we acknowledge how our lifestyle has contributed to this plight. The plight of migrants and refugees is ever present in Francis's work,[33] as is his analysis of the ways in which the global economy directly impacts communities' lives and destinies, specifically as it relates to creating dynamics of inequality that lead to violence.[34] Diverse churches and other religious groups attempt to attend to the plight of economic and environmental migrants and refugees in a variety of ways. In the short time since the encyclical's release, the issue of refugees (which we have seen is tied to climate change) has grown increasingly demanding and contentious. We have a public responsibility to advocate for a different political reading of the migrant as ecological refugee. In Francis's words, environmental refugees "are not recognized by international conventions as refugees; they bear the loss of the lives they have left behind, without enjoying any legal protection whatsoever. Sadly, there is widespread indifference to such suffering, which is even now taking place throughout our world" (§25).

Second, attentiveness to the disproportionate impact of environmental destruction on the poor also requires us to note what is often termed "environmental racism"—the even more disproportionate impact on minority communities and communities of color. *Laudato Si'* doesn't quite address the concept of environmental racism, though its discussion of North/South and colonial dynamics of abuses in resource extraction and dumping of toxic and other waste could be construed as acknowledging environmental racism at a global level (§51).

Since the 1980s numerous studies have recorded the increased exposure to toxic environmental conditions to communities of color and low socioeconomic status. A 2007 study found that "communities near commercial hazardous-waste facilities consisted mainly of people of color."[35] In 1987 this phenomenon brought the United Church of Christ's Commission on Racial Justice to lift up the term "environmental justice," noting that care for the earth must go hand in hand with attention to unjust conditions for marginalized, oppressed, and excluded groups, locally and globally.[36] These statistics confirm that racial demographics are a determinant of higher toxicity suffered by black and brown communities and speak to the ways our consumption of energy and other goods impact poor and nonwhite communities around us, and also those farthest away, such as garment workers in Bangladesh and poor communities around the Amazon basin.

Attentiveness to the poor in a way that becomes incarnate in the world of the poor—witnessing to the contact and presence that Francis advocates for in both *Evangelium Gaudium* and *Laudato Si'*—means that we become present in communities sometimes not our own in order to advocate for environmental justice with them. The example of the Flint water crisis highlights how race, nationality, religion, geographical distance, and other categories prevent some of us with more power to acknowledge these particular kinds of suffering. Solidarity shaped by the option for the poor and Francis's theology of encounter and presence would demand that we make these particular, sometimes quite removed, but sometimes nearby, forms of suffering our own, by understanding the links between our practices and our policies and others' inabilities to enjoy the right to safe drinking water, good soil for planting, and safe working conditions. Indeed, Francis's push for a conversion through reeducation of our consumerist habits can be inclusive of solidarity in occasions of environmental racism. For centuries powerful groups have understood and portrayed consumption, resource extraction, and dumping of waste products as having little or no consequence because we had become accustomed to treat others as nonexistent or disposable.

Francis's message to indigenous communities during his visit to Mexico and to popular movements (many representing marginalized groups) in Bolivia acknowledged the other's struggle, often considered nonpersons. To the gathering of popular movements Francis declared that

> this rootedness in the barrio, the land, the office, this ability to see yourselves in the faces of others, this daily proximity to their share of troubles . . . and their little acts of heroism: this is what enables you to practice the commandment of love, not on the basis of ideas or concepts, but rather on the basis of genuine interpersonal encounter.[37]

Conclusion

In *Laudato Si'*, Pope Francis clearly and profoundly links environmental ethics and care for the poor in his contribution to Catholic social doctrine. *Laudato Si'* demands that we be attentive to the ways in which everything *is* connected. Environmental harm and ecological crises directly impact the life of the poor. We are bound to this destruction and exploitation through a web of production and consumption that is environmentally unsustainable and spiritually toxic. Specifically, the encyclical refocuses our gaze to be attentive to the ways in which the poor suffer the impact of environmental crises first, their ways of life impacted and ability to use the earth diminished, condemning many to the fate of being environmental refugees.

Laudato Si' alerts us to the ways that environmental harm contributes to conflict, deepening the suffering of vulnerable communities and increasing the possibilities for regional violence and war. The concept of environmental racism helps us understand where this might be the case in communities closer to us than we previously thought. Therefore, immediate responses such as governance and oversight, regional cooperation, local participation in policy and decision-making, and consumer advocacy play an important role in addressing ongoing environmental deterioration and potential conflict.

Through the option for the poor, deeply embedded in Catholic tradition, *Laudato Si'* calls all Christians and people of good faith globally to a transformation of heart that pierces through all dimensions of life in community, but particularly our cycles of production and consumption. It calls us not only to be mindful of the needs of the poor, but to stand with them in solidarity. It calls us to link personal transformation with collective action to uphold the dignity of the most vulnerable. Ultimately it is a challenge to proceed boldly in efforts toward the personal and corporate changes that need to happen to address these issues, but which must be grounded on the encounter with the suffering of the poor and their hopes for a different world.

Questions

1   What are the Biblical foundations of the option for the poor? In what context does the *Catechism of the Catholic Church* discuss the preferential option for the poor?

2   Where are the poor most prominently featured in *Laudato Si'*?

3   How do environmental degradation and the ecological crisis affect the poor directly?

4   What are five ways in which *Laudato Si'* suggests that solidarity with the poor can be expressed through care of the environment?

5   How does *Laudato Si'* help us consider the question of environmental racism?

6   Name a situation of environmental racism within 50 miles from your community. What are key factors in the environmental problem? In what ways do these intersect with questions of racial justice?

Notes

1 Quote from the Bolivian Bishops Conference, Pastoral Letter on the Environment and Human Development in Bolivia, "El Universo, Don de Dios para la vida" (March 23, 2012), 17.

2 Brian Clark Howard, "What's the Chemical Behind West Virginia's Chemical Spill?," *National Geographic* (January 11, 2014), http://news. nationalgeographic.com/news/2014/01/140110-4-methylcyclohexane-methanol-chemical-spill-west-virginia-science/, Dom Phillips, "Brazil's Mining Tragedy: Was it a Preventable Disaster?" *The Guardian* (November 25, 2015), http://www.theguardian.com/sustainable-business/2015/nov/25/brazils-mining-tragedy-dam-preventable-disaster-samarco-vale-bhp-billiton; Ashley Southall, "State of Emergency Declared of Man-made Water Disaster in Michigan City," *The New York Times* (January 17, 2016), http://www.nytimes. com/2016/01/18/us/obama-flint-michigan-water-fema-emergency-disaster.html.

3 Pope Francis, *Evangelii gaudium* (November 24, 2013), https://w2.vatican. va/content/francesco/en/apost_exhortations/documents/papa-francesco_esortazione-ap_20131124_evangelii-gaudium.html, §§ 195, 198, 199, and 200.

4 Mike Jordan Laskey, "It's Time for a Theology of Encounter," *The National Catholic Reporter* (June 4, 2015), http://ncronline.org/blogs/young-voices/its-time-theology-encounter.

5 *Evangelii gaudium*, 54.

6 Pope Francis and Andrea Tornielli, *The Name of God is Mercy (A Conversation with Andrea Tornielli)*, trans. Oonagh Stransky (New York: Random House, 2016).

7 From his election as Pope, Francis's relationship and appreciation for liberation theology and its insights have been widely discussed from a range of perspectives. While it is uncontested that he favors the option for the poor as a key lens through which to engage theological and ethical questions, perspectives include Ambrose Evans-Pritchard, "Liberation Theology Is Back as Pope Francis Holds Capitalism to Account," *The Telegraph* (January 8, 2014), http://www.telegraph.co.uk/finance/comment/ambroseevans_pritchard/10559802/Liberation-Theology-is-back-as-Pope-Francis-holds-capitalism-to-account.html; Steven S. Hayward, "How Is Liberation Theology Still a Thing?," *Forbes* (May 10, 2015), http://www. forbes.com/sites/stevenhayward/2015/05/10/how-is-liberation-theology-still-a-thing/#1cb1f35213ab; Daniel P. Horan, "Living la Vida Justicia: Pope Francis and 'Liberation Theology'," *American Magazine* (March 17, 2013), http://americamagazine.org/content/all-things/living-la-vida-justicia-pope-francis-and-liberation-theology; Inés San Martín, "Liberation Theology Founder Praises 'New Atmosphere' Under Pope Francis," *Crux* (May 12, 2015), http://www.cruxnow.com/church/2015/05/12/liberation-theology-founder-praises-new-atmosphere-under-pope-francis/

8 *Catechism of the Catholic Church* (Libreria Editrice Vaticana, 1993), §2444. http://www.vatican.va/archive/ENG0015/_INDEX.HTM.

9   *Catechism of the Catholic Church*, "The Common Good," §1905–1910 (2003).

10 *Catechism of the Catholic Church*, "The Universal Destination and Private Ownership of Goods," §2402–2406.

11 *Catechism of the Catholic Church*, "Love for the Poor," §2443–2449.

12 *Catechism of the Catholic Church*, §2446.

13 Pontifical Council for Justice and Peace, *Compendium of the Social Doctrine of the Church* (2004), "The Universal Destination of Goods and the Preferential Option for the Poor," §182 (2005), http://www.vatican.va/roman_curia/pontifical_councils/justpeace/documents/rc_pc_justpeace_doc_20060526_compendio-dott-soc_en.html. The universal destination of goods and the preferential option for the poor.

14 *Compendium of the Social Doctrine of the Church*, "The fight against poverty," §448–449.

15 The literal term "preferential option for the poor" appeared for the first time in the subsequent CELAM meeting in Puebla in 1979. See "Evangelization in Latin America's Present and Future: Final Document of the Third General Conference of the Latin American Episcopate," Pt. 4, Chap. 1., in *Puebla and Beyond: Documentation and Commentary,* ed. John Eagleson and Philip Scharper (Maryknoll, NY: Orbis, 1979), 264ff.

16 CELAM, "Medellín (Poverty of the Church)" (1968), http://theolibrary.shc.edu/resources/medpov.htm, §2.

17 Leonardo Boff, *Cry of the Earth, Cry of the Poor* (Maryknoll, NY: Orbis Books, 1997). Sustainability and post-growth philosopher Barbara Muraca (Oregon State University) talks about the bibliography implicit in *Laudato Si'*, much of it coming from post-growth and sustainability schools in Europe, but unknown to an American readership. (Barbara Muraca, presentation to a joint session of the Ecclesiological Investigations and other groups at the American Academy of Religion Meeting in Atlanta, GA, November 22, 2015. Personal notes.) The phrase appears in *Laudato Si'*, §49.

18 *Evangelii gaudium*, §187.

19 Ibid., §188.

20 Ibid., §201.

21 Ibid., §215.

22 Ibid., §215.

23 Joshua Hammer, "Is a Lack of Water to Blame for the Conflict in Syria?," *Smithsonian Magazine* (June 2013), http://www.smithsonianmag.com/innovation/is-a-lack-of-water-to-blame-for-the-conflict-in-syria-72513729/?no-ist; and Brad Plummer, "Drought Helped Cause Syria's War. Will Climate Change Bring More Like It?," *Washington Post* (September 10, 2013), https://www.washingtonpost.com/news/wonk/wp/2013/09/10/drought-helped-caused-syrias-war-will-climate-change-bring-more-like-it/.

24 See "A Primer on the Global Fresh Water Crisis," in *Just Water: Theology, Ethics, and the Global Water Crises*, ed. Christiana Peppard (Maryknoll, NY: Orbis Books, 2014), 19–35.

25 On the issue of whether access to clean water is a human right, please see United Nations, "International Decade for Action: Water for Life 2005-2015," http://www.un.org/waterforlifedecade/human_right_to_water.shtml; "Trickle Down: Is Access to Clean Water a Human Right?," *Scientific American* (6 April 2011), http://www.scientificamerican.com/article/the-right-clean-fresh-water/; Eve Warburton, "A Right, a Need, or an Economic Good? Debating our Relationship to Water," State of the Planet, Earth Institute—Columbia University (June 6, 2011), http://blogs.ei.columbia.edu/2011/06/06/a-right-a-need-or-an-economic-good-debating-our-relationship-to-water/; Peppard, *Just Water.*

26 Elizabeth Cline, *Overdressed: The Shockingly High Cost of Cheap Fashion* (New York: Penguin Group, 2012).

27 Clare O'Connor, "These Retailers Involved in Bangladesh Factory Disaster Have Yet to Compensate Victims," *Forbes* (26 April 2014), http://www.forbes.com/sites/clareoconnor/2014/04/26/these-retailers-involved-in-bangladesh-factory-disaster-have-yet-to-compensate-victims/#240688fa57c5.

28 Shashank Bengali and Mohiuddin Kader, "Bangladesh Faculty Owner, 40 Others Charged with Murder in 1,100 Deaths," *LA Times* (June 1, 2013), http://www.latimes.com/world/asia/la-fg-bangladesh-factory-charges-20150601-story.html.

29 María Teresa Dávila, "The Role of the Social Sciences in Catholic Social Thought: The Incarnational Principle of the Preferential Option for the Poor and Being Able to 'See' in the Rubric 'See, Judge, Act'," *Journal of Catholic Social Thought* 9, no. 2 (Summer 2012): 229–44.

30 "Medellín," §6.

31 See *Evangelii gaudium* (§187 and 282).

32 See *Laudato si'* (§165, 167, 171, 183, 206, 207, 210, 231.)

33 See, for example, his "Message for the World Day of Migrants and Refugees 2016," (January 17, 2016), https://w2.vatican.va/content/francesco/en/messages/migration/documents/papa-francesco_20150912_world-migrants-day-2016.html; and "Pope Calls for Solidarity Ahead of UN World Refugee Day," *Vatican Radio* (June 19, 2016), http://en.radiovaticana.va/news/2016/06/19/pope_calls_for_solidarity_ahead_of_un_world_refugee_day/1238424.

34 *Evangelii gaudium,* §59, 62.

35 Bryce Covert, "Race Best Predicts Whether You Live Near Pollution: Environmental Racism Extends Far Beyond Flint," *The Nation* (February 18, 2016), https://www.thenation.com/article/race-best-predicts-whether-you-live-near-pollution/.

36 Dwight Hopkins, "Holistic Health and Healing: Environmental Racism and Ecological Justice," *Currents in Theology and Mission* 36, no. 1 (February 2009): 8.

37 Pope Francis, "Address of the Holy Father to the World Meeting of Popular Movements" (July 9, 2015), http://w2.vatican.va/content/francesco/en/speeches/2015/july/documents/papa-francesco_20150709_bolivia-movimenti-popolari.html, §2.

9

The economic vision of Pope Francis

Anthony Annett

ENCYCLICAL READING GUIDE

- Global Inequality, §48–52
- The Common Destination of Goods, §93–95
- Modern Anthropocentrism, §115–121
- The Principle of the Common Good, §156–158
- Justice Between the Generations, §158–162
- Politics and Economy in Dialogue, §189–198

The economic vision of Pope Francis is a human vision. In full accord with the tradition of Catholic social teaching, it insists that all people should be able to contribute to, and benefit from, humanity's collective economic endeavors. Yet it is also an expansive vision that appreciates the relationship between human flourishing and the health of the earth—both because creation has value in its own right and because a degraded environment hurts the poor, the excluded, and those not yet born.

This chapter begins by situating *Laudato Si'* within the tradition of Catholic social teaching.[1] A main theme of Pope Francis is that the world is facing interlinked economic, social, and environmental crises, and these crises have the same source—a disordered anthropocentrism that has proven incapable of escaping the narrow confines of immediate self-interest. Following this, the chapter explores the basis of this mindset by contrasting the assumptions of neoclassical economics—which underpin the free-market ideology of neoliberalism—with the assumptions of Catholic social teaching. It argues that the latter offers a more realistic and healthy foundation for economic relations, which can explain why extreme market ideology lies behind the dysfunctions diagnosed by Pope Francis. The next section describes Pope Francis's solution, which is integral and sustainable human development—an economic vision of the common good for the twenty-first century.

The interlinked social and environmental crises

The analysis of *Laudato Si'*

Laudato Si' is the latest in a long sequence of papal social encyclicals that began with *Rerum Novarum* in 1891. In that seminal document, Pope Leo XIII offered a moral response to the massive social and economic upheavals and inequities brought about by the industrial revolution. *Rerum Novarum* set the stage for modern Catholic social teaching, built on such principles as justice, solidarity, concern for the poor and the worker, and the participation of all in development. In the years that followed, successive popes—including Pius XI, St John XXIII, Paul VI, St John Paul II, and Benedict XVI—updated these principles and applied them to the particular circumstances of their times.

Pope Francis is following in footsteps of popes before him in *Laudato Si'* by applying and updating the principles of Catholic social teaching to new circumstances. Yet *Laudato Si'* occupies a unique position in the corpus, and it can be seen as the twenty-first century's *Rerum Novarum*. While *Rerum Novarum* responded to the moral challenges of the early industrial economy, *Laudato Si'* is responding to the moral challenges of advanced capitalism. When *Rerum Novarum* was written, the great economic liftoff brought about by technological innovation was still in its infancy. But today, world output is now over 200 times larger than at the outset of the industrial revolution, with most of that expansion taking place after the Second World War.

This gives rise to a major theme of *Laudato Si'*: the scale of economic activity is putting unprecedented pressure on the earth and its inhabitants, especially the poor. "Never have we so hurt and mistreated our common home as we have in the last two hundred years," says Pope Francis (§53). Scientists tell us that, because of this, we are bumping up against some vital planetary boundaries.[2] (See the discussion in Chapter 3.) Just as we are living in a globalized economy, we are now living in the globalized phase of environmental change—whereby human activity is disrupting the earth's core cycles of biology, chemistry, and geology. In the words of Pope Francis, our earth is facing a future of "debris, desolation and filth" (§161).

The expansion of economic activity that puts such pressure on the planet shows no sign of slowing down. By mid-century, the size of the global economy could increase threefold.[3] Without a serious change in our pattern of carbon-fueled economic growth, we are, to put it bluntly, on a path of increasing peril.

Alongside this grave environmental crisis, the world is also facing a social crisis—immense poverty, social exclusion, and attacks on human dignity in a world of great plenty and promise. For Pope Francis, these are all related. Indeed, a key mantra of *Laudato Si'* is that "everything is connected"—so much so that "we are faced not with two separate crises, one environmental and the other social, but rather with one complex crisis which is both social and environmental" (§139).

This reflects the core theological idea of integral ecology—the notion that relationships between human beings and the natural world are inseparable and tied to a larger whole. We are asked to listen and respond to "both the cry of the earth and the cry of the poor," as they are really different aspects of the same cry (§49).

The diagnosis of *Laudato Si'*

Having identified the problem, let us now turn to the underlying causes. Pope Francis is claiming that the desolation of the earth and the degradation of human dignity spring from the same flawed mindset, a mindset that seeks conquest over care, competition over cooperation, and selfishness over solidarity. This mindset turns people into "masters, consumers, ruthless exploiters, unable to set limits on their immediate needs" (§11), which in turn leads to a "might is right" or a "winner takes all" mentality (§82).

Laudato Si' speaks of a "modern anthropocentrism," which really has two pillars—and these pillars align with the worldview that comes down to us from the Enlightenment. The first lies in the turn away from the community and the common good and toward the sovereign individual. The second lies in the emphasis on using science to gain knowledge and control over the natural world—and, in doing so, to attain progress and better the lives of people.

Both pillars are criticized in *Laudato Si'*. The denunciation of individualism has a long history in Catholic social teaching—it harks back to *Rerum Novarum*, and Pope Pius XI famously railed against the "twin rocks of shipwreck," collectivism and individualism, back in 1931.[4] In *Laudato Si'*, Pope Francis singles out "rampant individualism" connected to a "self-centered culture of instant gratification" (§162). This repudiates the broader responsibilities of integral ecology—to God, to our fellow human beings, and to creation itself. It reflects a blinkered attitude that puts narrow self-interest above common responsibility and elevates short-term financial reward over longer-term cultivation and stewardship.

The criticism of the second pillar of modern anthropocentrism—the use of human ingenuity to master nature—is a fairly new departure for Catholic social teaching. This is because the challenge is new—in the early phases of the industrial revolution, environmental damage was far more limited and localized.

In this diagnosis, Pope Francis lays a lot of the blame on how we view and use technology. He is not completely opposed to technology, and he lauds the improvements in human well-being that have come from technological progress. (§102) But he is concerned that technology bestows power, and that humanity tends not to use that power well. "Immense technological development has not been accompanied by a development in human responsibility, values and conscience," he says (§105). If the mentality is "might is right," then the "might" is coming from technological dominance.

But the problem runs deeper still. The real issue is the dominance of what Pope Francis calls the "technocratic paradigm." This is an all-encompassing mindset of extraction in the service of self-interest. It regards creation as an external object to be manipulated, mastered, and controlled, with no concern for its inherent value or limits. In economics, this mentality is manifested through a purely utilitarian approach to intervening in nature, "in which efficiency and productivity are entirely geared to our individual benefit" (§159). In turn, this gives rise to the idea of "infinite or unlimited growth . . . based on the lie that there is an infinite supply of the earth's goods" (§106).

The combination of the cult of individualism with the technocratic paradigm can have pernicious consequences. It can lead people to take advantage of others and the bounty of nature, treating everybody and everything as mere means to their own personal ends. As Pope Francis puts it, "When human beings place themselves at the center, they give absolute priority to immediate convenience and all else becomes relative"—everything is "irrelevant unless it serves one's own immediate interests" (§122).

This is also related to what Pope Francis calls the "throwaway culture" (§§16, 22, 43), which he sees as the driving force behind an economy of exclusion: "Those excluded are no longer society's underside or its fringes or its disenfranchised—they are no longer even a part of it. The excluded are not the 'exploited' but the outcast, the 'leftovers'."[5]

The assumptions of Catholic social teaching and neoclassical economics

To fully appreciate *Laudato Si's* criticism of individualism and the technocratic paradigm as it pertains to economics, it helps to understand the profound differences between the dominant economic paradigm and Catholic social teaching. Most economists today are trained in the neoclassical tradition, which stems from very different assumptions from Catholic social teaching (see Table 9.1).

Table 9.1 The differing assumptions of neoclassical economics and catholic social teaching

	Neoclassical economics	Catholic social teaching
Understanding of the person	Autonomous individuals	Beings-in-relation
Motivating virtue	Self-interest	Solidarity
The good of the individual	Satisfaction of subjective material preferences	Integral human development
The good of society	Aggregation of subjective material preference satisfaction	The common good
Standard of judgment	Pareto efficiency	Universal destination of goods
Norms of justice	Commutative	Commutative, distributive, social

These differences start at the most basic level—the understanding of the human person. The neoclassical economic paradigm is founded on the Enlightenment-era assumption of individual autonomy. For many economists, the idea of individual autonomy is also appealing because it allows them to treat individuals in the same way that physicists treat atoms and electrons—to adopt a scientific veneer when it comes to studying human behavior.

What motivates these autonomous individuals? The answer, according to neoclassical economics, is self-interest—not altruism, compassion, empathy, generosity, or other pro-social inclinations. It is further assumed that this self-interest is directed toward material gain—more precisely, toward the maximization of subjective material preferences. This is "material" in the sense that satisfaction comes from the consumption of goods and services that can be bought and sold on the market. And it is "subjective" in the sense that these preferences are not to be questioned—there is no judgment regarding their value or worth, and no role whatsoever for self-improvement and ethical formation.

These are the building blocks of what is called "homo economicus," the view of human beings as autonomous self-interested individuals motivated to maximize utility and profit. In a world inhabited by people like this, radically disconnected from each other, the good of society comes from simply adding up the good of each individual.

On this basis, how can we maximize the satisfaction of these subjective preferences? The answer, according to neoclassical economics, is through free-market transactions. This is often traced to Adam Smith's insight that an "invisible hand" guides the economy toward the best possible outcome. Neoclassical economics sets the standard as "Pareto efficiency," a point when all voluntary trades that can satisfy individual preferences have been made—in other words, a point from which it would no longer be possible to make somebody better off without making another person worse off. Against this standard, it could be shown that unfettered and competitive markets with complete information lead to efficient outcomes. While these stringent conditions almost never hold in practice, the free market is nonetheless held up as the ideal without a serious examination of the real world consequences—this is the basis of the "neoliberal" ideology.

Neoliberals and neoclassical economists do, however, recognize that market transactions need to be embedded in certain norms of justice, because markets cannot function with trust. Free-market ideology therefore upholds "commutative justice," which is the justice between individuals that forms the basis of contracts and agreements. And the main role of government is to act as this kind of neutral referee.

These are the basic assumptions behind neoclassical economics. The assumptions behind Catholic social teaching are entirely different, from top to bottom.

As a starting point, Catholic social teaching emphasizes interdependence over autonomy. It regards people less as atomistic individuals and more as "beings-in-relation," finding meaning and purpose through encounter with others. Instead of living on metaphorical islands, human beings are called upon to mirror the communion of persons in the Trinity.

With such an emphasis on relationality, it follows that the virtue motivating human interaction is less self-interest than solidarity. In Catholic social teaching, solidarity is defined as "a firm and persevering determination to commit oneself to the common good; that is to say to the good of all and of each individual, because we are all really responsible for all."[6] Solidarity with the poor and the excluded are especially important: in the words of Pope Francis, "Solidarity must be lived as the decision to restore to the poor what belongs to them."[7] *Laudato Si'* argues that solidarity between generations is also critical: "Intergenerational solidarity is not optional, but rather a basic question of justice," says Pope Francis (§159). Since the earth is a common inheritance, it should be seen not only as a legacy from those who came before us, but a loan from those who will come after us. This deepened sense of solidarity also extends to all creation, as each creature has its own value and significance. In other words, solidarity is the correct response to the cry of the earth and the cry of the poor.

What about the good of the individual? Instead of material preference satisfaction, Catholic social teaching points toward integral human development—the development of the whole person and all people. This is neither individualistic nor materialistic. It offers an expansive vision of human flourishing in which people seek what is intrinsically worthwhile, especially in and through relationship with others. As Pope Francis puts it, people are called upon to "find meaning, a destiny, and to live with dignity, to 'live well'."[8]

It follows, then, that a "good society" is one in which everyone can flourish without exception or exclusion. Pope Francis refers to this idea of the common good—defined as the "sum of those conditions of social life which allow social groups and their individual members relatively thorough and ready access to their own fulfillment"[9] —as the central and unifying principle of social ethics (§156). Unlike in the neoclassical system, the common good cannot be reduced to the mere aggregation of individual goods. The flourishing of the individual and the community are inseparable, and they actively reinforce each other.

It follows that the standard of judgment for the economic system cannot be Pareto efficiency. Pareto efficiency is compatible with large-scale inequality and exclusion. As Amartya Sen, Nobel laureate in economics, put it: "A society or an economy can be Pareto optimal and still be perfectly disgusting."[10] For Catholic social teaching, the economy is judged on whether it achieves the universal destination of goods—the notion that the fruits of the earth are meant for everyone. This is regarded by Pope Francis as "a golden rule of social conduct" (§93). As he puts it:

> Working for a just distribution of the fruits of the earth and human labor is not mere philanthropy. It is a moral obligation. For Christians, the responsibility is even greater: it is a commandment. It is about giving to the poor and to peoples what is theirs by right.[11]

A key implication of this is that the right to private property, the bedrock of the market system, is always conditional on meeting the needs of all. In St John Paul II's words, private property "is under a social mortgage."[12]

This also implies that the norms of justice will be different. For neoclassical economics, the sole standard of justice is the commutative justice of the marketplace. Catholic social teaching certainly endorses commutative justice, but it also goes well beyond it. It endorses a more expansive notion of justice—incorporating what the community owes each individual (distributive justice) and the institutional framework by which all can participate in the common good and share in its benefits (social justice). This is justice in the service of the common good.

Laudato Si' and free-market ideology: The evidence

The economic vision of Pope Francis is frequently criticized for its lack of appreciation for the functioning of modern market economies. Yet this claim is superficial and fails to appreciate the layered differences between the neoliberal and Catholic worldviews. From this deeper perspective, Pope Francis has the better argument. The economic vision encapsulated by

Catholic social teaching is superior, in terms of both its assumptions about human nature and its consequences for human well-being.

Human nature

Starting with human nature, the evidence suggests that the Catholic conception of human nature is more in accord with reality than its neoliberal counterpart.[13] It suggests that human beings are cooperative creatures, inclined to pro-social behavior and strongly motivated by altruistic instincts. Experiments show that they value fairness and reciprocity, and are willing to forego the maximal benefit to themselves to help others, and also to punish those who violate pro-social norms, even if this is personally costly. This has often been traced to evolutionary forces, as this kind of altruism proved useful throughout the development of the human species. The psychological literature also shows that authentic flourishing is related to factors like relationships, meaning and purpose in life, engagement, accomplishment, and achievement.

Not surprisingly, therefore, the evidence shows that money does not buy happiness, at least once a basic income threshold has been met. According to the *World Happiness Report*, the differences in happiness across countries boil down to six key factors: GDP per capita, healthy years of life expectancy, social support, generosity, perceived freedom to make life decisions and freedom from corruption.[14] In other words, while money matters to some extent, it is ultimately a minor part of the story. What matters more are relationship, meaning, purpose, and fulfillment. This accords with the vision of human nature endorsed by Catholic social teaching. Homo economicus is a fictitious creature.

There is an added wrinkle to all of this. While homo economicus might be a fiction, it is nonetheless a dangerous fiction. The reason is that human beings are highly susceptible to being influenced adversely by market values. These market values can actually crowd out social norms based on civic virtue.[15] Sociological studies show that economists and students of economics are more selfish and less pro-social.[16] Another study shows that richer people tend to behave less generously, display less empathy, and are more likely to lie or cheat—because the prevailing ideology tells them that such behavior is acceptable.[17] As another example, when bankers think of themselves as bankers instead of inhabiting other social roles, they are more likely to act dishonestly.[18] So while homo economicus might be alien to human nature, its true believers often act parasitically upon society.

Consequences for human well-being

Before going any further, it is important to recognize that Catholic social teaching has never rejected market economics per se. It recognizes the value of market mechanisms within their proper economic sphere and delimited by moral boundaries. And it defines strict limits to what markets can accomplish. In the words of Pope St John Paul II:

> Certainly the mechanisms of the market offer secure advantages: they help to utilize resources better; they promote the exchange of products; above all they give central place to the person's desires and preferences, which, in a contract, meet the desires and preferences of another person.[19]

The real problem arises when market mechanisms are proposed as the sole answer to economic, social and environmental problems, and when homo economicus is held up as the normative standard for all human activity. This runs up against a warning from Pope St John Paul II:

> Nevertheless, these mechanisms carry the risk of an "idolatry" of the market, an idolatry which ignores the existence of goods which by their nature are not and cannot be mere commodities.[20]

Pope Francis's critique of the global economic system must be seen within this context. It is not a blanket critique of markets—it is a specific critique of the ideology behind these markets. Reduced to its essence, the market is nothing more than an encounter between people to exchange for mutual benefit. But as we have seen, the ideology of the modern market economy adds many layers to this encounter—self-interest, materialism, hedonism, and value-free preferences. This ideology of neoliberalism assumes that society can be made better off by internalizing these assumptions and unleashing the power of unfettered markets.

Along these lines, Pope Francis is not condemning the market as much as a "deified market" (§56) or the "magical conception of the market" (§190). For him, the claim that market-led economic growth benefits all reflects a "crude and naïve trust in the goodness of those wielding economic power and in the sacralized workings of the prevailing economic system."[21]

The logic is straightforward: if the assumptions behind market ideology are wrong, then the conclusions are probably wrong too. Establishing economic structures and policies predicated on a false notion of the human person is bound to cause social problems. For Pope Francis, this market ideology fertilizes a "seedbed for collective selfishness" (§204), which in turn gives rise to exclusion, inequality, environmental devastation, and the throwaway culture. This is what lies behind his most forceful condemnation of the modern global economy: "That economy kills. That economy excludes. That economy destroys Mother Earth."[22]

And the facts do indeed point to a global economy of exclusion.[23] Nearly a billion people still live in extreme poverty. According to Oxfam, the world's richest 1 percent own more than all the rest, and a mere 62 people now own as much as half of the world's population.[24] Close to a billion people go hungry each day, and another billion lack vital micronutrients, in a world where a third of all food is wasted. About 1.3 billion people still lack electricity. People in the richest countries live on average 20 years longer than people in the poorest countries.

Neoliberals often respond to these facts by arguing that the solution is more market, not less. They point to the gains of the past few decades—to the fact that hundreds of millions of people have risen out of poverty in places like China following market reforms. This is true, but it reflects a shift away from a harsh form of collectivism for a more moderate system. Both rocks of shipwreck—collectivism *and* individualism—are detrimental to human flourishing. The solution is not to abolish the market but to humanize it and tame its excesses.

We can also see this over the past decade or so in Africa, where the combination of debt relief and the implementation of the Millennium Development Goals brought about major improvements in human well-being, especially in the area of health. For example, the number of people living in extreme poverty and the proportion of undernourished people halved between 1990 and 2015. So did child mortality and maternal mortality. And between 2000 and 2015, active health interventions prevented over 6 million deaths from malaria and 37 million deaths from tuberculosis.[25] This is something that the magic of the market alone simply could not accomplish.

Even in the richer countries, the limits of this market ideology are evident. The Northern European countries—accurately (if sometimes dismissively) called democratic socialist societies—not only top the world in happiness rankings, but they also show that high economic growth is fully compatible with equity and social solidarity. This is also a key lesson of the postwar era in both the United States and Europe—thanks to a strong sense of shared purpose and social solidarity, partly a residue from war and economic calamity, this was an era of broad-based prosperity on both sides of the Atlantic. In both cases, governments relied on a market economy but nonetheless intervened to limit inequality, subject business to appropriate regulation, guarantee worker's rights, and protect people against the vagaries of economic fortune that are part and parcel of a free-market system. This nexus of policies yoked the power of the market to the common good through the political oversight of government.

In recent decades, we saw the problems that can arise when this falls apart. The results of the neoliberal revolution that began in the Reagan and Thatcher era are not pretty. The idea was to spur economic growth by cutting taxes, deregulating large swaths of the economy, curbing union power, and cutting back on social safety nets. Despite the bold claims of supply-side economics, productivity—the main driver of long-term economic growth—stagnated.[26] Instead, inequality rose dramatically and trust and social capital fell precipitously. In fact, the global evidence suggests that—in direct opposition to neoliberalism—inequality undermines economic growth. According to a recent IMF study, the best way to achieve both a stronger economy and a fairer society is "trickle up" rather than "trickle down."[27] This bears out Pope Francis's intuition.

Pope Francis is also on point when he talks about the problems that arise when "finance overwhelms the real economy" (§109). In 2008, thanks to a decades-long process of financial sector deregulation and hands-off oversight, the global economy suffered the worst economic crisis since the Great Depression. This did not take place in a vacuum. It arose from the amoral market values and the policies they inspired that came to the fore in the 1980s—a perfect example of homo economicus cannibalizing social norms. Evidence shows that a large financial sector is bad for the economy—because it makes the system more unstable and prone to crises and because it diverts talent from productive to "socially destructive" activity.[28] Pope Francis is correct to note that finance should serve, not rule, the real economy.[29]

On top of all this, market ideology is a driving force behind the environmental crisis—including pollution, climate change, water stress, and loss of biodiversity. As *Laudato Si'* makes clear, a blinkered focus on profit maximization discounts the harm done to the environment, the rhythms of nature, and biodiversity and ecosystems. It leads business to ignore the effects of their actions on the earth and future generations, because they do not pay the full costs of using up shared environmental resources—only when they do so, says Pope Francis, can their actions be deemed ethical (§195). And it causes multinationals to treat their poorer host countries in ways they would never treat their richer homes—leaving legacies of pollution, depleted natural resources, impoverished agriculture, deforestation, unemployment, and abandoned towns. All of this reenacts the exploitative relationships established in the colonial era. *Laudato Si'* claims that such behavior means that the rich countries owe an "ecological debt" to their poorer neighbors (§51). Yet this debt is invisible in the neoliberal paradigm.

Laudato Si' and sustainable development

Given this strong criticism of the prevailing economic model, what exactly is *Laudato Si'* calling for? The answer is integral and sustainable human development. We have already noted the importance of integral human development—the development of the whole person and every person, giving all people the opportunity to flourish, to live fulfilling and dignified lives.

Pope Francis is calling explicitly for "an integrated approach to combating poverty, restoring dignity to the excluded, and at the same time protecting nature" (§139). This is consistent with the idea of sustainable development, which rests on the three pillars of economic development, social inclusion, and environmental stewardship. While integral human development is a broader and deeper concept, sustainable development is nonetheless nested within this encompassing framework. And indeed, the path to the common good in the twenty-first-century global economy runs through sustainable development.

As we have seen, the market economy is incapable of bringing about sustainable development. It can perhaps deliver economic growth, but even this is jeopardized by the excess it spawns. And yet economic growth alone can go so far but no further. It does not necessarily deliver social inclusion and environmental sustainability.

A key implication of the sustainable development agenda is the dethroning of economic growth as the sole goal of economic life. *Laudato Si'* does support higher growth in some countries—developing countries in particular need to grow faster to converge with their richer neighbors. But Pope Francis suggests that richer countries might need to get used to lower growth, which should be based less on consumption—what he calls a "whirlwind of needless buying and spending"—and more on investment in people and in sustainable development (§203).

For *Laudato Si'*, employment is more important than growth. This is because work is regarded as not just a source of income, but a vital component of integral human development— "a necessity, part of the meaning of life on this earth, a path to growth, human development and personal fulfillment" (§128). It follows that unemployment is corrosive to human flourishing.

Shifting to a new model of progress has implications for everyone. To succeed, sustainable development requires a partnership between countries, between public and private sectors, and between the different sectors of the economy. It cannot be achieved by the atomistic, uncoordinated, competition of the marketplace.

It will require, in the first instance, a global cooperative response. As *Laudato Si'* says, "Interdependence obliges us to think of *one world with a common plan*" (§164)—this includes strong international agreements to govern all aspects of the global commons (§174). The nations of the world have already taken the first steps. In September 2015, they adopted 17 Sustainable Development Goals at the United Nations. Pope Francis addressed the United Nations on the day they were adopted.[30] Two months later, they adopted the Paris Agreement on climate change, which commits countries to shift toward renewable sources of energy, with the goal of net-zero carbon emissions by the second half of the century. This is the context in which *Laudato Si'* was released, and it was timed to influence this agenda.

When it comes to implementation, much of the action will take place at the national and local levels. Governments are called upon to embrace a farsighted agenda that gets past short-term political constraints and stands up to vested interests. This will require a visible as well as an invisible hand—a strong complementary role of government directed toward the common good. As Pope Francis puts it, "Restraints occasionally have to be imposed on those possessing greater resources and financial power" (§129).

Business too has a key role to play. Pope Francis says that business can and should be a "noble vocation," but first it needs to orient its activities toward the common good (§129). Profit, especially short-term profit, cannot be its only goal. *Laudato Si'* gives two practical examples on how corporations can support the common good. First, they should prioritize employment over profits—for business "to stop investing in people, in order to gain greater short-term financial gain, is bad business for society" (§128). Second, they should invest in sustainable development solutions—as "more diversified and innovative forms of production which impact less on the environment can prove very profitable" (§191). These solutions need the resources and expertise at the disposal of the private sector, which needs to embrace a great sense of social purpose.

Conclusion

In *Laudato Si'*, Pope Francis is launching a radical criticism against what he calls the myths of modernity—individualism, unlimited progress, competition, consumerism, a market without rules. These are the values that animate neoliberalism, and they are an inadequate basis for genuine human progress.

But Pope Francis is not asking us to reject technology and return to the Stone Age either. Instead, he is asking us to frame the economic discussion around the basic question of all: "What kind of world do we want to leave to those who come after us, to children who are now growing up?" (§160).

The answer is a world of integral and sustainable human development. Ultimately, *Laudato Si'* is calling for a more holistic and ethical view of progress, one that gets beyond the technocratic paradigm and the cult of individualism. Pope Francis is asking us to better align economic progress with moral progress and put technology in the service of a better kind of development—one that is healthier, more human, more social and more integral (§112). And *Laudato Si'* is a moral charter for this new economic vision.

Questions

1   In what ways can *Laudato Si'* be regarded as the twenty-first-century version of *Rerum Novarum*?

2   According to *Laudato Si'*, how are individualism and the technocratic paradigm responsible for the social and environmental crises?

3   What are the main differences between neoclassical economics and Catholic social teaching?

4   Is Pope Francis's criticism of the market economy fair?

5   Pope Francis calls for integral and sustainable development. How hard would that be to attain? What kind of changes would it require at the level of governments, business, and individuals?

Notes

1   While this chapter focuses primarily on *Laudato Si'*, it will also touch upon what Pope Francis has to say about the economy in *Evangelii gaudium*—his apostolic exhortation from 2013—and his address at the World Meeting of Popular Movements in Bolivia, on July 9, 2015. For a consideration of these themes in the thought of John Paul II, see "The Social Ethics of Pope John Paul II: A Critique of Neoconservative Interpretations," *Horizons: Journal of the College Theology Society* 33, no. 1 (Spring 2006): 7–32.

2   Johan Rockström and others, "A Safe Operating Space for Humanity," *Nature* 461 (1999): 472–75.

3   Jeffrey Sachs, *The Age of Sustainable Development* (New York: Columbia University Press, 2015).

4   Pius XI, *Quadragesimo anno* [Encyclical On the Reconstruction of the Social Order], 1931, §46.

5   Francis, *Evangelii gaudium* [Apostolic Exhortation on the Proclamation of the Gospel in the Modern World], 2013, §53.

6   John Paul II, *Sollicitudo rei socialis* [Encyclical Letter on Social Concern], 1987, §38.

7   Francis, *Evangelii gaudium,* §189.

8   Francis, Speech at World Meeting of Popular Movements, Santa Cruz de la Sierra, Bolivia, July 9, 2015, §2.

9   Second Vatican Council, *Gaudium et spes* [Pastoral Constitution on the Church in the Modern World], 1965, §26.

10   Amartya Sen, *Collective Choice and Social Welfare* (San Francisco: Holden-Day, 1970), 22.

11   Francis, Speech at World Meeting of Popular Movements, §3.

12   John Paul II, *Sollicitudo rei socialis* (1987), §42.

13   For a review of this literature, see Anthony Annett, "Human Flourishing, the Common Good, and Catholic Social Teaching," in *World Happiness Report 2016: Special Rome Edition (Vol. II)*, ed. Jeffrey Sachs, Leonardo Becchetti and Anthony Annett (New York: UN Sustainable Development Solutions Network, 2016), 38–65.

14   John Helliwell, Haifang Huang and Shun Wang, "The Distribution of World Happiness," in *World Happiness Report 2016 Update (Vol. I)*, ed. John Helliwell, Richard Layard and Jeffrey Sachs (New York: UN Sustainable Development Solutions Network, 2016), 8–48.

15   Michael Sandel, *What Money Can't Buy: The Moral Limits of Markets* (New York: Farrar, Straus and Giroux, 2013); Samuel Bowles, *The Moral Economy: Why Good Incentives are no Substitute for Good Citizens* (New Haven: Yale University Press, 2016).

16   Amitai Etzioni, "The Moral Effects of Economic Teaching," *Sociological Forum* 30, no. 1 (2015): 228–33.

17 Paul Piff and other, "Higher Social Class Predicts Increased Unethical Behavior" *Proceedings of the National Academy of Sciences of the United States of America* 109, no. 11 (2012): 4086–91.

18 Alain Cohn, Ernst Fehr, and Michel Andre Marechal, "Business Culture and Dishonesty in the Banking Industry," *Nature* 516 (2014): 86–89.

19 John Paul II, *Centesimus annus* [Encyclical Letter On The Hundredth Anniversary Of Rerum Novarum] (1991), §40.

20 John Paul II, *Centesiumus annus*, §40.

21 Francis, *Evangelii gaudium* §54.

22 Francis, Speech at World Meeting of Popular Movements, §3.1.

23 See Sachs, *The Age of Sustainable Development*, 45–70.

24 Oxfam, "An Economy for the One Percent", *Oxfam Briefing Paper* 210 (2016): 2.

25 United Nations, *The Millennial Development Goals Report, 2015*.

26 From the detailed analysis of economist Robert Gordon, total factor productivity grew at an average 1.89 percent a year from 1920 to 1970. This fell to 0.57 percent from 1970 to 1994, rising a bit to 1.03 percent from 1994 to 2004, and falling again to 0.4 percent from 2004 to 2014. See Robert Gordon, *The Rise and Fall of American Growth* (Princeton: Princeton University Press, 2016).

27 Era Dabla Norris, Kalpana Kochhar, Nujin Suphaphiphat, Frantisek Ricka, and Evridiki Tsounta, "Causes and Consequences of Income Inequality: a Global Perspective," *IMF Staff Discussion Note* 15, no. 13 (2015): 1–39.

28 Stephen Cecchetti and Enisse Kharroubi, "Reassessing the Impact of Finance on Growth," *BIS Working Papers* no. 381 (2012): 1–17.

29 Francis, *Evangelii gaudium* §57–58.

30 Francis, "Address to the Members of the General Assembly of the United Nations Organization," *New York*, September 25, 2015.

PART THREE

Responding in care for our common home

10

Laudato Si': Concern for our global commons

Ottmar Edenhofer and Christian Flachsland

ENCYCLICAL READING GUIDE

- Climate as a Common Good, §23
- The Common Destination of Goods, §93–95
- The Principle of the Common Good, §156–158, 169
- Dialogue for New National and Local Policies, §176–181
- Dialogue and Transparency in Decision-Making, §182–188

Pope Francis's long-awaited encyclical *Laudato Si'* is much more than an "environmental" or "climate" document. In fact, it discusses key ethical challenges of the twenty-first century: climate change, poverty, and inequality. Climate change hits the poor the hardest and exacerbates inequality within global society. If "global commons" such as the atmosphere, the forests, the global water cycle, and the oceans are not protected, there will be no just global economic order.[1]

The encyclical was anticipated with both high expectations and great fears—expectations on the part of those seeking support from the pope for a more just globalization and fears among those concerned that the pope might side with ambitious climate and environmental policies. Indeed, even the timing of the release of the encyclical—in June 2015—was a political statement and reminded the world community of its responsibility. It was published after the G7 Summit that took place at Schloss Elmau in Bavaria in early June 2015, where the decision was taken to decarbonize the global economy, and prior to two United Nations summits (New York in September and Paris in December), where sustainable development goals and an international climate agreement were adopted.

According to *Laudato Si'*, the current generation risks going down as the most irresponsible in the history of humankind. Yet, if it chooses to, it could also be remembered for having courageously lived up to its responsibilities (§165). In saying this, Pope Francis is building on the 1963 encyclical *Pacem in Terris*, in which John XXIII made an appeal for peace to "all people of good will" at a time when the world was on the brink of nuclear war. Today, Pope Francis sees in climate change, global poverty, and deepening inequality a comparable planetary challenge. As such, he addresses his encyclical as an invitation to "every person living on this planet" to engage in dialogue (§3).

Laudato Si' has triggered a worldwide debate. The weeks after its release were marked by predictable reactions: approval from the environmental movement, rejection from conservative media, and a deafening silence from the so-called climate skeptics.

Far more interesting were the reactions from the scientific community. It is unprecedented in the history of Catholic social teaching for renowned scientific journals such as *Nature* and *Science* to publish favorable editorials before and after the publication of an encyclical.[2] These journals commended in particular the pope's desire for dialogue with the scientific community, such as that which took place at a conference organized by the Pontifical Academy of Sciences in the spring of 2014.[3] With a view to climate science, many scientists have confirmed that *Laudato Si'* accurately summarizes the state of knowledge on the climate problem as assessed by the Intergovernmental Panel on Climate Change (IPCC), whose reports reflect the current state of scientific knowledge.[4]

Climate change and the Catholic Church

The clarity and decisiveness with which *Laudato Si'* acknowledges the ethical challenges of climate change, poverty, and inequality can only be appreciated fully when one considers the Vatican's hesitation to address the topic of climate change in the past. No previous papal encyclical has dealt with climate change in a systematic manner. It has been addressed primarily by national conferences of bishops, to which the pope pays tribute with no fewer than eighteen citations in his encyclical.

Three reasons may explain the Vatican's previous difficulties with the issue of climate change.[5] First, it may not have wanted to express an opinion about the cause of climate change as long as there was no consensus in the scientific community. Again and again, interested parties tried to discourage the Vatican from taking a stand by highlighting any outstanding scientific uncertainties and disagreements. Without clarification, it was argued, it would be impossible for the church to take a position without risking damage to its moral authority.

Secondly, the Vatican may have feared that the difficult issue of population policy could resurface in the context of climate change. If the burning of coal, oil, and gas, as well as deforestation, are causing an increase in the global mean temperature, then it must be acknowledged that population growth is, alongside economic growth, a driver of climate change. Yet this raises questions for the church's moral views on population policy.

The third—and presumably main—reason for the Vatican's hesitant approach to climate change thus far is a concern for the power dynamics in play. While both Pope John Paul II and Pope Benedict XVI offered trenchant critiques of the global economic system, Pope Francis has shown a greater ability to communicate this challenge clearly and forcefully. For him, climate change, global poverty, and inequality are threatening the foundation of our "common home."

With *Laudato Si'*, the church's response to the environmental crisis has now been given. The clear style of the encyclical is a strong indication that *Laudato Si'* was not drafted by ghostwriters from academia or politics but by Pope Francis himself. In unusually sharp terms, he attacks the denial of climate change as an expression of veiled power interests— "veiled" because such endeavors are not a quest for scientific truth but efforts to protect private interests against those of the common good (§54, 135, 188).⁶ Francis emphasizes that the analysis of and response to the climate problem should not be determined by the interests of the powerful but rather by the demand for global justice.

In principle, the encyclical is structured according to the three steps of *see—judge—act*. The global environmental problems identified by science are outlined in Chapter I and are then interpreted in light of the biblical message (Chapter II) and explained in the broader context of the papal understanding of globalization and modernization (Chapter III). In Chapter IV, *Laudato Si'* then discusses ethical orientations, while chapters V and VI discuss the motives and approaches to action.

Here, we will examine key issues of the encyclical: the relationship between climate change, poverty, and inequality, and the concern for the global commons; the need to tackle poverty reduction and climate protection simultaneously; practical recommendations of the encyclical; the responsibility of humankind in dealing with the power of technology at the "end of the modern world"; and the future challenges resulting from *Laudato Si'* for the churches.

Climate change, poverty, and inequality

The starting point of the encyclical is the scientific knowledge, as summarized in the reports of the IPCC, that climate change is caused by humankind through the burning of coal, oil, and gas, through deforestation and through the emissions of other greenhouse gases. That said, the encyclical cannot, understandably, offer as systematic and comprehensive a description of the impacts of climate change as, for example, the Working Group II contribution to the IPCC's Fifth Assessment Report into the current state of climate change knowledge.[7] The encyclical emphasizes above all the consequences of climate change for the poor. It points out that the poor are affected first and hardest by climate change because, more than other segments of the population, they depend on agriculture, fisheries, and other ecosystem resources for their livelihood, and because they are not in the position to protect themselves effectively against increasing extreme weather events and water scarcity (§25). Moreover, the lack of access to clean water, loss of biodiversity and air pollution, and their adverse effects on health, are concerns for the pope. He fears that the negative effects of global environmental change and resource use could lead to migration movements or even wars in the future (§57).

The carrying capacity of the planet is already being exceeded without the problem of poverty having been solved. Yet it is important to note that the pope does not see population growth as the main culprit. It is not the number of people but the inequitable use of existing natural resources that is the problem. Rich countries consume too much, without adequately sharing with the poor.

Apparently, the pope regards the mitigation of climate change as a prerequisite for an effective fight against poverty, as it threatens to offset the medium- to long-term successes in the fight against poverty and to exacerbate global inequality. The encyclical proposes no specific targets for climate protection; the international community, however, has already set the goal of limiting global warming to 2°C above preindustrial levels. This target has far-reaching consequences as it limits the amount of carbon dioxide (CO_2) that may yet be deposited in the atmosphere. The atmosphere is still, and primarily, used as a carbon sink by rich countries. The present lack of regulation of carbon emissions serves the interests of powerful, wealthy nations at the expense of poor nations.

The struggle over the global commons

Therefore, the pope declares the climate to be a common good "belonging to all and meant for all" (§23). The oceans and the whole range of "so-called 'global commons'" should be protected by an appropriate system of governance (§174).[8] For the first time in the history of the social doctrine of the church, *Laudato Si'* applies the principle of the "universal destination of the goods of creation" to the global carbon sinks of the atmosphere, oceans, and forests. In order to protect the poorest and to avoid dangerous climate change, these sinks must be prevented from overuse.[9]

These global carbon sinks of the atmosphere, ocean, and forests are what economists refer to as "common pool resources." These are a category of good that requires special treatment because they are both finite (if very large) and difficult to exclude people from using. Fossil fuels burned anywhere cause ongoing deposition of residues of this combustion in the atmosphere, contributing to global warming everywhere. This cost is born not by the user, but by the entire world. Common pool resources differ from traditional market goods in that they are essentially shared. The atmosphere can only be parceled out to individual owners or nation states for management if there is global agreement on a respective sharing scheme. Thus, responsible governance of global commons requires carefully coordinated shared action on a global scale. It is common to speak of the so-called "Tragedy of the Commons" when discussing common pool resources. Elinor Ostrom was awarded the Nobel Memorial Prize in Economics for her work on how local common pool resources have been and can be managed in a sustainable manner as "commons."[10] On the global level such resources require international governmental cooperation. In using the language of the "global commons," Pope Francis is pointing to the need for such cooperative management of this shared resource.

As shown in the last IPCC report, compliance with the 2°C target requires that the remaining cumulative CO_2 emissions stay below about 1,000 gigatons (Gt). (More recent estimates place the total nearer 800 Gt.) As a measure of comparison, annual CO_2 emissions in 2013 were at 35 Gt, with an upward trend. Furthermore, an estimated 15,000 Gt of CO_2 are still present in the ground in the form of fossil fuels. The majority of these must therefore remain in the ground to avoid the CO_2 deposits and climate change that would result from their being burned and released into the atmosphere. Rather than a business-as-usual-scenario—in other words, a scenario without any global climate policy—meeting the 2°C objective requires that some 80 percent of the world's coal, and 40 percent each of gas and oil, be left in the ground. Finally, if CO_2 cannot be captured during combustion and stored geologically, even less fossil resources can be used.[11] However, if the great part of the world's fossil fuel reserves must remain in the ground, the assets of the owners of fossil fuel resources are devalued. This raises the question of whether a climate policy that intervenes in the property rights of owners of coal, oil, and gas can be justified.[12] But, if the climate is a global commons worth protecting, then private property rights to coal, oil, and gas must be designed so that they meet the demands of serving the common good.

With this clear positioning, *Laudato Si'* is contributing to the development of the notion of property within Catholic social teaching. Historically, the Catholic doctrine of property (especially as it is expressed in the 1891 encyclical *Rerum Novarum*) was influenced, in part, by the classical liberal tradition founded by John Locke, according to which private property rights to natural resources can be legitimized on the basis of their having been appropriated through settlement or conquest and enhanced by human labor. The discovery of America and the colonization of the "empty continent" by the Europeans (through the decimation and displacement of the indigenous population) solidified this practice of the appropriation of natural resources. Land, and later fossil resources such as oil, then belonged to those who were the first to cultivate it or use it. Yet even so, Locke had already formulated an important condition for legitimate land acquisition: the appropriation may take place only if enough resources of equal quality are available to use for others (known as the "Lockean proviso").[13] Thus, even the classical free-market concept of ownership does not allow for an unconditional right of appropriation of scarce natural resources.

Catholic social teaching reinforces this moral limit on the use of private property with the principle of the "universal destination of the world's goods."[14] *Laudato Si'* refines this principle by recognizing the overexploitation of global CO_2 sinks as an instance in which the right to private property may be justifiably restricted (§23, and especially §93–95).

> The Christian tradition has never recognized the right to private property as absolute or inviolable, and has stressed the social purpose of all forms of private property. Saint John Paul II forcefully reaffirmed this teaching, stating that "God gave the earth to the whole human race for the sustenance of all its members, without excluding or favoring anyone." (§93)

In this way, the current use of the atmosphere that serves the powerful at the expense of the poorest is delegitimized.

The recognition of the atmosphere and the climate as a shared good of the global commons could possibly have international legal consequences. For example, an obligation to protect could be invoked should the atmosphere be threatened. Some parties to the UN Framework Convention on Climate appeared to fear exactly that, given that they were reluctant to designate climate change as a global commons problem in the Fifth Assessment Report of the IPCC. In fact, in a footnote on the topic, the report states that the term "global commons," as a characterization of the climate problem, has no implications for an international agreement or for criteria of international effort—sharing when it comes to climate protection.[15] With *Laudato Si'*, however, the pope had the courage to place the status of the atmosphere as a global commons at the forefront of the collective consciousness of humanity.

Climate protection and poverty reduction—Are they mutually exclusive?

The issue of the institutional design of how access to the atmosphere could be restricted, and thus the poorest protected against climate change, is not addressed by the encyclical. From an economic point of view, the pricing of CO_2 emissions, through taxes or emissions trading systems, is the most effective means to achieve this objective. The encyclical rightly points to the economic principle that market prices should adequately reflect all social costs (§195).

> The principle of the maximization of profits, frequently isolated from other considerations, reflects a misunderstanding of the very concept of the economy. . . . only when "the economic and social costs of using up shared environmental resources are recognized with transparency and fully borne by those who incur them, not by other peoples or future generations" can those actions be considered ethical. (§195)

Yet presently, considering the shortage of usable atmospheric CO_2 disposal capacity, current market prices for carbon fuels fail to do this. If CO_2 taxes or emissions trading systems are introduced, these shortages, as well as the cost of overusing the atmosphere, are signaled to the markets. This, in turn, will induce a shift in investment and purchasing practices at both the public and private levels. Essentially, these measures translate the scarcity of the shared good of the atmosphere as a CO_2 disposal sink into the "hard" language of the profit-oriented markets and thereby facilitate a market solution that addresses this ethical problem.

Moreover, limiting the amount of carbon that is stored in the atmosphere by means of CO_2 pricing will not only protect the climate, and thus the poorest affected by climate change, but will also provide a new source of income in the form of tax revenues or auctioned emissions permits. The atmosphere being a global commons, these revenues in principle belong to all people, and their distribution should be done in compliance with the principles of justice.

Thus, the revenue from CO_2 pricing could be used to provide the poorest with access to basic goods. Such a CO_2 tax reform could be carried out by national governments who coordinate internationally.[16] For example, were the government of India to charge $10 for every ton of CO_2 emitted, it could provide electricity, clean water, sanitation, and telecommunications for more than 60 million people every year. The same applies to China or Mexico. CO_2 pricing could therefore be used to combat poverty.[17] A first step in this direction would be to abolish subsidies for fossil fuels—that alone would free up at least $550 billion for investments to help the poor.

Indeed, these measures would meet one of the key demands of the pope, namely to fight climate change and poverty together, at the same time. However, from the perspective of the encyclical, not all forms of CO_2 pricing are unobjectionable. In this regard, the pope is not afraid to venture into the more complex aspects of environmental economics.

A papal engagement with practical policy debates

When it comes to practical recommendations, papal teaching makes prudential arguments, not infallible definitions. The pope is against emissions trading, or at least he expresses serious concerns about the use of this tool (§171). He fears an ensuing speculation on the carbon markets, which would then undermine the effectiveness of this method. His assessment has been met with opposition by experts. What is truly noteworthy, however, is that a pope is even reflecting on a specific instrument of environmental policy in such detail. Indeed, unlike almost all other Catholic social teaching documents, *Laudato Si'* has not resisted the temptation to engage in the discussion of specific reform proposals. In this way, the encyclical is raising the suspicion that the pope is claiming authority on scientific matters. However, Pope Francis is not claiming a doctrinal authority in resolving policy disputes or other conflicts of interest. Rather, it is understood that the pope, when considering specific recommendations for actions, is not claiming doctrinal authority for the underlying factual judgments.[18] The statements of the encyclical on emissions trading should therefore be understood as an invitation to the experts to engage in a dialogue and to take the pope's concerns about the effectiveness of this method seriously, or to prove them groundless.

With his criticism of economic growth, the pope is not likely to attract approval from economists either. *Laudato Si'* §193 reads: "That is why the time has come to accept decreased growth in some parts of the world, in order to provide resources for other places to experience healthy growth." However, the latest IPCC report showed that, and how, economic growth and emissions growth can be decoupled through technological progress. "Degrowth," as a strategy in climate policy, is a very costly option under which the poor would likely suffer the most. Other measures, such as increasing energy efficiency, use of renewable energies, and a structural shift toward less resource-intensive lifestyles, are less costly and allow for growth that is environmentally and socially compatible.[19]

Politically, the encyclical sees the solution to the global crisis in the interplay of international cooperation, national politics, municipal engagement, and the power of an emerging diverse civil society. Some concerned commentators even wondered whether the pope is proposing in *Laudato Si'* a "world political authority" (§175). Here Pope Francis was quoting approvingly his predecessor Benedict XVI. Yet, what the pope means is not a world government but the need for international cooperation and coordination among nation states in order to manage and channel the dynamics of globalization. The encyclical draws on ideas similar to those developed by Elinor Ostrom, who proposed that a polycentric governance of global public goods could, among other benefits, allow civil society actors to play an important role alongside government institutions.[20] The encyclical regards civil society movements as a means by which to put pressure on national-level policymaking. For the pope, such movements are not limited to political protest but include empowered consumers and investors who could and should exert pressure on markets through boycotts and opposition (§206). Individual virtue ethics and collective social reform are not mutually exclusive but rather the church views them as mutually dependent.

Technology and the "end of the modern world"

The increase in human power, made possible through modern technology, requires heightened individual moral awareness and new forms of institutional responsibility. According to Pope Francis, the roots of the ecological crisis lie in the ambivalence of modernity. With repeated references, in Chapter III, to *The End of Modern World* by Romano Guardini,[21] the encyclical holds that modernity is creating, through technology, new possibilities to control nature. *Laudato Si'* essentially sees technology and its possibilities as positive (§102). Yet, from the perspective of Guardini, the problem of modernity is that humankind is in denial about these expanded opportunities for power, and so it denies its responsibility. This often tacit refusal means that technology is not consciously created and morally designed, but only executed, in a technocratic fashion with a sole focus on economic growth and profitability. The result is organized irresponsibility.[22]

The encyclical emphasizes, in contrast, that the increased opportunities for control and power allow for more freedom in decision-making; which requires ethical judgment. It is against this background that the reflections of the pope on technology should be understood, such as when he calls for greater energy efficiency and the development of renewable energies (§26) or when he expresses concerns about nuclear energy (§104, 184). *Laudato Si'* is not technology hostile but calls for a responsible approach and an ethical design of the new possibilities offered by technology. Technological progress is not a juggernaut to which people should be sacrificed; instead, it can help to solve the problems of climate change, poverty, and inequality.

A challenge to the churches

In his analysis of modernity, the pope points to the great biblical stories of creation, fall, redemption, and salvation. When applied to today's world, these stories teach us that a disfigured earth is not just an expression of a disturbed relationship between God and humankind, but also an expression of violence among people.

> Disregard for the duty to cultivate and maintain a proper relationship with my neighbor, for whose care and custody I am responsible, ruins my relationship with my own self, with others, with God and with the earth. When all these relationships are neglected, when justice no longer dwells in the land, the Bible tells us that life itself is endangered. (§70)

The biblical stories should remind people that humanity awaits fulfillment by God and that it is not doomed to tragic failure. However, averting tragedy will require humankind to face reality and to change its course. In this sense, the encyclical argues not only from a philosophical or natural law perspective but offers a new theological view of the planetary crisis. *Laudato Si'* is thereby challenging not only politics but, above all, the Christian churches. This creates opportunities for action by the churches in the following areas.

Giving the poor a voice

Already today, church aid agencies, such as Caritas Internationalis, Misereor, and Catholic Relief Services, are making outstanding contributions to combating climate change, poverty, and inequality. They should continue the dialogue with the poor and other stakeholders on climate and development policy, and one hopes that they will be able to do so even more forcefully in the future thanks to the support of the pope. The voice of the Vatican in the international climate negotiations of the United Nations could become more audible. The Holy See could become the voice within the circle of the powerful that points again and again to the requirements of the common good, without which the pursuit of national interests is at risk of degenerating to mere power politics.

A global initiative by the Church's educational institutions

The problems of climate change, poverty, and inequality call for an interdisciplinary education encompassing the natural, social, and economic sciences, together forming the basis for engaging in an ethical and theological reflection. The Catholic Church has a global education system that includes, in addition to universities, nearly all types of schools. To carry out such an educational initiative would be an important task and opportunity for religious institutions (§209–215).

Further development of the social teaching of the Catholic Church

The church's view on population policy is too often reduced to a debate about the morality of artificial contraception. Population is also a matter of social ethics. The implications of a growing, declining, or stationary population require ethical reflection in a world facing numerous ecological and environmental crises. In addition, how to ensure a fair globalization is one of the key questions raised by the encyclical. Unfortunately, the argumentation in this regard is often too simplistic. For example, it proposes that we depart from an uncritical or exaggerated reliance on the market, yet does not propose the measures required to realize such reforms. It would be good to examine which social and economic reforms might help gradually to overcome the most pressing injustices. It could also make concrete proposals for action, as it has successfully done in the past, for example for the construction of the German welfare state.[23]

Reforming how economic decisions are made in the world and the Church

In most national governments, the ministers of the environment are responsible for the climate problem, and they usually have less power than the ministers of finance and the economy. Yet the latter ministers in particular should concern themselves with the climate issue. After all, if not they, who is to introduce CO_2 pricing, abolish subsidies for fossil fuels, and make public investments in infrastructure to reduce emissions and improve the plight of the poor? The church is in a similar situation: the environmental officers in the dioceses have less power and influence than the vicars general and asset managers, who make decisions about the procurement of goods and services and the investment strategy in the capital markets (§206). Although the churches are already playing an important role in ethical investment, they could be more active and have a stronger media presence on these matters.

Continue this dialogue between the Church and science

The encyclical shows that the dialogue between religion and science is not only bringing ethical challenges to the fore, but that it can also help identifying ways to overcome them. "The gravity of the ecological crisis demands that we all look to the common good, embarking on a path of dialogue which demands patience, self-discipline and generosity, always keeping in mind that 'realities are greater than ideas'" (§201).

The pope sees history not as tragedy but as drama. And in this drama of salvation, humankind is not doomed to failure. Pope Francis reminds his readers that God wants to perfect humanity and that modern reason must engage in a holistic understanding of reality if it wishes to solve its problems. Freedom can only emerge by interweaving science with world interpretation—without this, justice cannot be attained.

A dialogue between unusual partners

Until now, the church and its social teaching appeared to be merely reacting to the challenges of modernity, and sometimes to be barely capable of meeting them. By contrast, with *Laudato Si'* the church is now challenging the world. This encyclical has initiated a dialogue with partners who are unusual for the church: scientists, diplomats, activists, politicians, and those affected. While the pope acknowledges the various contributions of these parties, he also propels and encourages them to take further steps. In the weeks after the release of *Laudato Si'*, the two authors of this chapter were impressed to see that, worldwide, scientists (even those who consider themselves to be atheists or agnostics), political conservatives who are skeptical of climate policy and activists who have long since written off the church were talking about Pope Francis and his encyclical. However, they are not just talking *about* him but also *with* him, because his concern for the "common home" is also their concern.

Questions

1   What are the characteristics of a "common pool resource"? How are they different from goods that can be treated as private property? Why is the atmosphere a common pool resource? What does this have to do with responding to climate change?

2   What does the term "global commons" mean?

3   How does *Laudato Si'* represent a development in the church's understanding of private property?

4   Under what conditions has the church traditionally understood that the right to private property can be restricted?

5   How does a system of carbon pricing or taxation represent a market-based solution to the problem of CO_2 emissions?

Notes

1 This essay originally appeared as Ottmar Edenhofer and Christian Flachsland, "Laudato Si': Die Sorge um die globalen Gemeinschaftsgüter," in *Stimmen der Zeit 9* (September 2015): 579–91. It was published in English translation as "Laudato Si': Concern for Our Global Commons," in *Thinking Faith*, the online journal of the Jesuits in Britain, http://www.thinkingfaith.org/articles/laudato-si'-concern-our-global-commons. The essay and translation have been revised for this chapter. Used with permission of *Stimmen der Zeit* and *Thinking Faith*.

2 See editorials: "Hope from the Pope," *Nature* 522, no. 7557 (June 25, 2015): 391; Marcia McNutt, "The Pope Tackles Sustainability," *Science* 345, no. 6203 (September 19, 2014): 1429; and Marcia McNutt, "The Beyond-Two-Degree Inferno," *Science* 349, no. 6243 (July 3, 2015): 7. In the latter editorial, the editor of *Science*, Marcia McNutt writes: "I applaud the forthright climate statement of Pope Francis [in *Laudato Si'*], currently our most visible champion for mitigating climate change."

3 See the following conference report published by the Pontifical Academy of Sciences: *Sustainable Humanity, Sustainable Nature: Our Responsibility* (Vatican City, 2015). Available at: www.casinapioiv.va/content/accademia/en/publications/extraseries/sustainable.html.

4 Ottmar Edenhofer, Christian Flachsland, and Brigitte Knopf, "Science and Religion in Dialogue Over the Global Commons," *Nature Climate Change* 5 (2015): 907–9.

5 These positions were clearly manifested in discussions which Ottmar Edenhofer had in 2008 with the then representatives of the Pontifical Council for Justice and Peace.

6 On the position of the so-called climate skeptics, see also Naomi Oreskes and Erik Conway, *Merchants of Doubt. How a Handful of Scientists Obscured the Truth on Issues from Tobacco Smoke to Global Warming* (New York: Bloomsbury, 2010).

7 IPCC, *Climate Change 2014: Impacts, Adaptation, and Vulnerability. Part A: Global and Sectoral Aspects. Contribution of Working Group II to the Fifth Assessment Report of the Intergovernmental Panel on Climate Change*, ed. C. B. Field, V. R. Barros, D. J. Dokken, K. J. Mach, M. D. Mastrandrea, T. E. Bilir, M. Chatterjee, K. L. Ebi, Y. O. Estrada, R. C. Genova, B. Girma, E. S. Kissel, A. N. Levy, S. MacCracken, P. R. Mastrandrea and L. L. White (Cambridge, UK, and New York, USA: Cambridge University Press, 2014); http://ipcc.ch/report/ar5/wg2.

8 Editor's note: The language in *Laudato Si'* is ambiguous. The Latin text and English translation use the term "common good" here. The common good refers primarily to a principle of social ethics. The authors are quoting the German translation of *Laudato Si'*, which does not use the equivalent technical term for a principle of social ethics *Gemeinwohl*, but a more refined term— "*Gemeinschaftsgut*" which suggests a communally shared good; a part of the global commons. In a note in the German original of this essay, the authors

note that the Latin and English text uses the term in this sense in §174, but criticize the German translation for reducing it to *Gemeinwohl*.

9   Edenhofer et al., "Science and Religion in Dialogue Over the Global Commons," 907–9.

10   See Elinor Ostrom, *Governing the Commons. The Evolution of Institutions for Collective Action* (Cambridge: Cambridge University Press, 1980); https://en.wikipedia.org/wiki/Global_commons; http://www.unep.org/delc/GlobalCommons/tabid/54404/. See also International Union for Conservation of Nature and Natural Resources, "World Conservation Strategy: Living Resource Conservation for Sustainable Development," https://portals.iucn.org/library/efiles/documents/WCS-004.pdf, #18.8.

11   Ottmar Edenhofer, Christian Flachsland, Michael Jakob, and Jérôme Hilaire, "*Den Klimawandel stoppen. Es gibt nicht zu wenig, sondern zu viel fossile Ressourcen – sie müssen in der Erde bleiben*," *Le Monde diplomatique: Atlas der Globalisierung: Weniger wird mehr* (2015).

12   See Ottmar Edenhofer, Christian Flachsland, Kai Lessmann, and Michael Jakob, "The Atmosphere as a Global Commons—Challenges for International Cooperation and Governance," in *The Handbook on the Macroeconomics of Climate Change*, ed. Willi Semmler and Lucas Bernard (Oxford: Oxford University Press, 2015), 260–96.

13   John Locke, *Two Treatises on Government and A Letter Concerning Toleration* (New Haven, CT: Yale University Press, 2003).

14   The position of Catholic social teaching on these questions is articulated in Pontifical Council for Justice and Peace, *Compendium on the Social Doctrine of the Church*, §141–170. http://www.vatican.va/roman_curia/pontifical_councils/justpeace/documents/rc_pc_justpeace_doc_20060526_compendio-dott-soc_en.html.

15   The exact wording of the footnote is "In the social sciences this [the climate problem] is referred to as a 'global commons problem'. As this expression is used in the social sciences, it has no specific implications for legal arrangements or for particular criteria regarding effort sharing." See IPCC, "Summary for Policymakers," *Climate Change 2014: Mitigation of Climate Change. Contribution of Working Group III to the Fifth Assessment Report of the Intergovernmental Panel on Climate Change*, ed. O. Edenhofer, R. Pichs-Madruga, Y. Sokona, E. Farahani, S. Kadner, K. Seyboth, A. Adler, I. Baum, S. Brunner, P. Eickemeier, B. Kriemann, J. Savolainen, S. Schlömer, C. von Stechow, T. Zwickel, and J. C. Minx (Cambridge, UK, and New York, USA: Cambridge University Press, 2014).

16   On the challenges and opportunities of a global CO_2 pricing scheme, see Ottmar Edenhofer, Michael Jakob, Felix Creutzig, Christian Flachsland, Sabine Fuss, Martin Kowarsch, Kai Lessmann, Linus Mattauch, Jan Siegmeier, and Jan Christoph Steckel, "Closing the Emission Price Gap," *Global Environmental Change* 31 (2015): 132–43.

17   Michael Jakob, Claudine Chen, Sabine Fuss, Annika Marxen, Narashima D. Rao, and Ottmar Edenhofer, "Using Carbon Pricing Revenues to Finance Infrastructure Access." Presentation at the 21st Annual Conference of the

European Association of Environmental and Resource Economists (2015). Manuscript, www.webmeets.com/eaere/2015/m/viewpaper.asp?pid=504.

18   Unlike factual statements, ethical standards require a doctrinal authorization, which is applied according to their degree of generality. However, in the scope of this chapter, we cannot address the dogmatic and ecclesiological question of what degree of doctrinal authority is to be applied to ethical standards (e.g., the polluter-pays principle as opposed to the double commandment of love God and thy neighbor), the documents of the church's social teaching in general and in *Laudato Si'* in particular. See Richard R. Gaillardetz, "The Ecclesiological Foundation of Modern Social Teaching," in *Modern Social Teaching: Commentaries and Interpretations*, ed. Kenneth R. Himes (Washington, DC: Georgetown University Press, 2005), 89 ff.; see also Oswald v. Nell-Breuning, *Soziallehre der Kirche* (Vienna: Europa Verlag, 1977), 28–31.

19   See also Michael Jakob and Ottmar Edenhofer, "Green Growth, Degrowth, and the Commons," *Oxford Review of Economic Policy* 30 (2014): 447–68.

20   Elinor Ostrom, "Nested Externalities and Polycentric Institutions: Must we Wait for Global Solutions to Climate Change before Taking Actions at other Scales?" *Economic Theory* 49 (2012): 353–69.

21   Romano Guardini, *The End of the Modern World: A Search for* Orientation (London: Sheed and Ward, 1957).

22   See Franz-Xaver Kaufmann, *Der Ruf nach Verantwortung. Risiko und Ethik in einer unüberschaubaren Welt* (Freiburg: Herder, 1992).

23   See Oswald v. Nell-Breuning, *Soziale Sicherheit* (Freiburg, 1979); Franz-Xaver Kaufmann, *European Foundations of the Welfare State* (New York: Berghahn Books, 2012).

11

What is to be done? Climate change mitigation strategies for the next generation

Robert Brecha

ENCYCLICAL READING GUIDE

- Weak Responses, §53–59
- Dialogue On the Environment in the International Community, §164–175

The science is clear: burning fossil fuels adds carbon dioxide (CO_2) to the atmosphere and oceans, warms the planet, and dramatically and rapidly changes conditions on earth under which civilizations have developed. In the end, the answer to the question posed by the title of this chapter is also clear, given what we know: the world must stop adding greenhouse gases to the atmosphere. The goal of this chapter is to provide an overview of climate change mitigation through a description of how scientists and economists think about the energy-economy-climate system. In the course of the chapter different pathways toward minimizing the effects of climate change will be presented. Although personal actions are important for the future, most carbon emissions today are embedded in a system that lies beyond the direct reach of individuals. It is important to see in a clear and unbiased way what the various options will be for climate change.

Climate change and the carbon budget

Chapter 2 looked at uncertainty in future carbon emissions pathways, one of the largest of which is knowing how societies will develop and what choices will be made in energy systems. In this section we begin by describing targets for climate change mitigation and some pathways toward reaching those targets.

We first recall that there is a relatively simple relationship between global average surface temperature increase of the earth and the total cumulative amount of fossil fuels combusted over time, as shown in Figure 2.7 in Chapter 2. Uncertainties are involved, but we can make statements such as the following: "To have at least a two-thirds likelihood of keeping global average temperature change to below 2°C, no more than a total of about 3000 Gigatons (Gt) of CO_2 can be released. That is the equivalent result of burning 820 Gt of carbon."[1] We have already burned 550 Gt of carbon, and thus emitted 2000 Gt of CO_2. Quick math tells us we have about 270 Gt of carbon left to burn. Current world emissions are the equivalent of about 10 GtC each year. There are not many years left at the current rate before we have burned through our budget.

Reaching these goals will require changes to our energy system that dramatically reduce emissions. This must be undertaken at a relatively fast pace to ensure that the current CO_2 concentration in the atmosphere of 400 parts per million volume (ppmv) (already an increase of 120 ppmv over the preindustrial level of 280 ppmv) does not rise to more than about 450 ppmv. Therefore, we are faced with reducing yearly carbon emissions by at least 50 percent worldwide by the middle of the century and to zero by the last quarter of this century.

In Figure 11.1 we show examples of possible emissions pathways, or Representative Concentration Pathways (RCP) as they are called.[2] The RCP8.5 scenario is what we might refer to as "business-as-usual, plus," and the RCP2.6 scenario is the stringent climate change mitigation scenario corresponding to a global average temperature change of no more than 2°C. These, as well as any possible pathway in between, are the choices we as societies make—which path do we want to follow?

The 2°C target requires that net CO_2 emissions be reduced to zero or below by the end of the century. This already implies a historically unprecedented energy system transformation. In the past two centuries, energy sources (mostly fossil based) have been discovered and exploited, and technological innovations and inventions have progressed in lock-step with the energy sources. This trajectory was, however, "accidental" in that no long-term planning of alternative pathways was done, mainly because possible negative effects were not taken into account. By the 1960s and 1970s, as air and water pollution were becoming problematic in industrialized countries, solutions were found in terms of regulating the harmful side outputs of energy production such as sulfur and mercury from coal-fired electric plants

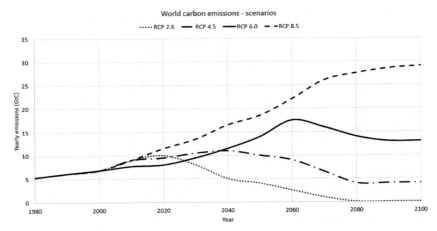

FIGURE 11. 1 *Illustration of different possible pathways for future carbon emissions, referred to as Representative Concentration Pathways. After van Vuuren et al. (2011.)*

or nitrous oxide from motor vehicles. These could be removed by installing scrubbers on smoke stacks or catalytic converters on engine exhaust systems. With CO_2 emissions, we face a fundamentally different problem. CO_2 is not a side effect. It is the primary product of the chemical reaction that produces energy when we burn carbon fuels. Thus, we face the new and much greater problem of completely changing the energy system toward sources that do not burn carbon fuels.

Although we speak here to the urgency of mitigating the most serious effects of climate change and of starting to do so as soon as possible, the scale of the challenge should not be underestimated. A few relative numbers may illustrate this point. Use of fossil fuels began in earnest in the late eighteenth century, but the rapid growth in the second half of the twentieth century is such that over 85 percent of fossil-fuel consumption has occurred in that short period and 40 percent of all fossil-fuel use has been during the lifetime of current college students. That energy use has been rapidly growing mainly in wealthy countries, however, with northern Europeans or US Americans using 10 to 20 times more energy (150–300 GJ per person per year) than citizens of Latin American countries or most of Africa (20–40 GJ per person per year).[3]

Any plan to reduce CO_2 emissions entails moral value decisions that are different from neutral scientific observation of natural phenomena. Science can describe the problems we face. Moral decisions are required to decide how we should respond. In *Laudato Si'*, Pope Francis begins by accepting the scientific foundations for understanding the climate system but sets the challenge of climate change mitigation in a larger framework of Catholic social teaching. He calls for us to pay more attention to the damage being done to the natural world, to the plight of the relatively impoverished majority of humankind and warns about the dangers of allowing a purely technocratic and market economic view of human development to continue being the driving force behind approaches to development.

Energy and development

In the previous section we emphasized the imperative that a dramatic shift in the pattern of increasing consumption of fossil fuels will be necessary in the future if the worst impacts of climate change are to be avoided. Here we consider energy use from a different point of view, one that is implicit in *Laudato Si'*, namely the positive and even crucial role that has been played by the availability of modern energy technologies and sources in enabling human development. The encyclical notes this connection in the history of the so-called "developed" nations. But it is especially concerned about the sustainable development of the majority of the world that is currently impoverished. The main point of this section is to establish an explicit link between energy consumption and human well-being at the level of individual countries. In subsequent sections, possible pathways toward resolving the tension between the need for energy access on the one hand and the necessity to reduce CO_2 emissions on the other will be discussed.

Prior to the nineteenth century, access to energy was limited to the products of solar input to the earth in the form of direct heat, indirectly through wind and water power, or, more importantly, the conversion of solar energy through photosynthesis into food and fuel energy from crops, pastures, and forests. Coal and other fossil fuels are stored forms of solar energy, having been created over millions of years (and millions of years ago) by the decay, burial, compression, and heating of plant-based life. These deposits naturally sequester carbon and hydrocarbons from the earth system, enabling the temperature to stabilize to the range in which the human species evolved. Mining of coal (and later, extraction of oil and natural gas) both began to release these deposits into the atmosphere and initiated a virtuous cycle for development starting in England and spreading around the world to those countries fortunate enough to have abundant fossil fuel resources. Production of steel, the invention and improvement of steam and internal combustion engines, railways and automobiles, as well as the beginning of electrification—all are the result of readily available fossil-fuel energy. This cycle of development is acknowledged as being important in *Laudato Si'*: "Technoscience, when well directed, can produce important means of improving the quality of human life, from useful domestic appliances to great transportation systems, bridges, buildings and public spaces" (§103).

What we must now do as a next stage of development is to recognize and accept the negative consequences of the carbon-based energy system that has powered industrialization and then redirect our capacity for invention

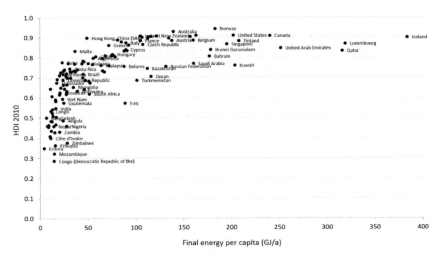

FIGURE 11.2 *Plot of data for Human Development Index as a function of final energy used per person per year (GJ/a). Data are from the United Nations Development Program (UNDP) and the International Energy Agency (IEA).*

toward new sources of energy that may satisfy future needs for both wealthier and poorer countries.

One measure of average quality of life for a country is the Human Development Index (HDI), created by the United Nations. The HDI, which is expressed in a scale between 0 and 1, is a composite index of economic wealth, education, and health indicators. In Figure 11.2 we show a plot of HDI values versus energy consumption per person.[4] The diamonds represent a snapshot of HDI values in the year 2010 for most countries. There is a noticeable trend toward higher levels of HDI with greater energy consumption. Just as noticeable, however, is that human development beyond a certain level (greater than an HDI of about 0.8) does not correlate very well with energy consumption. Human development "saturates," or, put another way, it is possible to be at a high level of human development with either large energy consumption or relatively low levels of consumption.

The other end of the scale is more crucial, however. There is essentially no country at a "very high" level of HDI (above 0.8) that does not have an availability of energy of at least 40–50 GJ per person per year. (In the United States, energy consumption is five to six times this amount.) If we were to look more closely at these data over time, we would also see that most countries follow a path that moves through stages represented by this snapshot, tracking from the lower left toward the upper right of the plot. Thus, we see both that achieving at least minimal amounts of energy availability (>40 GJ per person per year) is correlated with higher levels of human development and that individual countries appear to follow similar paths in the process of development.

To summarize these data and their relevance for a discussion about climate change mitigation strategies we can say that (1) enabling human development for all will require access to modern energy technologies, (2) past human development was enabled by fossil fuels, whose consumption must now be curtailed, and, therefore, (3) new zero-carbon technologies must be introduced over the next few decades, both in the industrialized countries and in those countries still on the path of development.

Scenarios and pathways to a zero-carbon energy system

The carbon budget implies that, by the latter half of this century, carbon emissions must approach zero if a temperature goal of 2°C is to be achieved. If the target is to not exceed a temperature change of 1.5°C, the requirements are even more stringent. In the next section several technologies will be discussed that could allow a transition to a low-carbon energy system. In this section the focus will be on frameworks used to make decisions about which pathways are most promising to follow.

There are essentially two broad ways of thinking about sustainability in general, and these map fairly directly onto technical and economic approaches to thinking about the mitigation of climate change. A first view, perhaps most commonly considered, is that of the "triple bottom line," that is, to take into account people, planet, and prosperity.[5] In this view, all spheres of action are of roughly equal importance and the goal is to strike a balance between them. Conceptually, as shown in Figure 11.3, the area of successful overlap is the sustainable solution. With regard to climate change mitigation, this might correspond to a cost-benefit analysis such as those required of federal agencies when proposing new regulations. Many of the most widely cited economic and energy system models of climate change mitigation, including those currently used by the Environmental Protection Agency (EPA) to estimate the costs to society of CO_2 emissions, are based on this approach.[6] Yet another way of phrasing this version of evaluating economic and policy options is that we can always find trade-offs between elements of the three circles. That is, for example, if we run into scarcity of one form of natural capital, we can find replacements in the form of human-made capital or simply other substitutes, mainly dictated by economic forces such as prices and supply and demand.

To bring back the connection to *Laudato Si'*, it is to this overly rationalistic, technocratic approach to dealing with climate change and human development that Pope Francis objects.

The basic problem goes even deeper: it is the way that humanity has taken up technology and its development according to an undifferentiated and

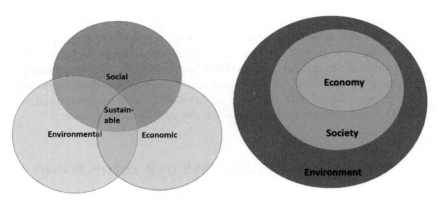

FIGURE 11.3 *Illustration of weak vs. strong sustainability concepts. The former strives for a sufficient overlap of three domains and, in economic terms, implies the ability to substitute human-made capital for natural capital, as long as the functions are the same. Strong sustainability considers our society and economy to be fundamentally embedded within the natural environment and, implicitly, that there are natural ecosystem services that cannot be replaced with human-made capital.*

one-dimensional paradigm. . . . The idea of promoting a different cultural paradigm and employing technology as a mere instrument is nowadays inconceivable. The technological paradigm has become so dominant that it would be difficult to do without its resources and even more difficult to utilize them without being dominated by their internal logic. (§106, 108)

These criticisms of attitudes toward the use of technology are not the same as being critical of the use of those same technologies properly embedded in a larger ethical framework. Any decision about alternative investments in energy systems depends on a whole suite of assumptions that are often hidden or at the very least not well publicized. For example, decisions about required rates of return on investment that vary by only a few percent can tip a cost-benefit analysis in one direction or another. Or, as is usually the case, by *not* considering the negative external costs of fossil-fuel technologies (e.g., asthma cases from particulate emissions from coal power plants or diesel automobiles) an important factor is left out, thereby effectively expressing an implicit set of values that are generally not made explicit. Pope Francis is certainly not alone in expressing these concerns; they are also frequently expressed by economists and environmental experts.[7]

One way to read *Laudato Si'* is to view the encyclical as an expression of a second "strong" conception of sustainability that takes as a starting point the view that natural systems and resources are fundamentally limited and at some point exhibit inflexibility with respect to substitutions and replacements. On this view, there are limits to human societal activities (and the economic activities that we create within our societies) that are set by nature, as illustrated in the right-hand side of Figure 11.3. Attempting to go beyond those limits can only be at the risk of significant and unknown damage both for natural systems and potentially for human society itself. In the language of the models used by scientists (and much of the work that goes into the reports on mitigation by the IPCC), this view leads to the use of a "cost-effectiveness" approach to evaluating future pathways. Simply put, the starting assumption is that scientists studying natural systems are correct in the general statement that there are temperature change limits we should not go beyond, such as 2°C or 1.5°C (the boundary of the natural system) and that this target places limits on human activities. The role of the economist and policymaker then becomes to figure out how to achieve that target in the most efficient manner. Our thinking about the economy must be bounded by a deep respect both for the societal constructs within which economic life takes place and for the natural resources we obtain from nature and the potentially grave impacts our activities can have on our surroundings.

It is within this context that many of the political and policy debates about mitigating climate change are carried out. A great deal of effort over the past few decades has gone into making model projections for the costs of mitigation more comprehensive. These models are extremely complex, and the final messages on mitigation costs do, unfortunately, often depend on input assumptions. However, in the tradition of scientific inquiry, as more research groups have become involved in these efforts, an overall movement toward consensus can be found. As summarized by the IPCC AR5 report achieving even relatively stringent climate protection goals, such as the 2°C target might result in decreases of available world economic output of a small fraction of a percent per year throughout the century.[8] These results are fairly robust across modeling groups and assumptions about input parameters, future growth rates in population and the economy, and technology options.

There are several important points to keep in mind when thinking about these techno-economic analyses of climate change mitigation. The first is that the manner in which costs are reported matters greatly. We sometimes hear in political discussions in the United States that climate change policy would be a choice to unwittingly destroy the economy and that mitigation efforts could cost trillions of dollars. This absolute number may be true, but compared to total world economic output over the course of a century, it turns out to be a small percentage of the total, and thus, a relatively small amount.

A second caution is that, by definition, framing climate change mitigation in terms of cost-effectiveness analysis, that is, taking the target as given and then working with technology and economics to calculate possible solutions, means that the potential damages due to climate change are being left out of the calculus. This is not the result of an impulse to hide something, but rather because of the practical decision that calculating specific damages is so inherently difficult that we should not be making decisions based on that level of uncertain inputs for the distant future. However, this means that the "costs" for climate change mitigation that are reported by the IPCC and modeling research groups, even though minimal, do not include the profound benefit of avoiding potentially devastating future costs to human civilization.[9]

The true price of carbon fuels: Addressing the problem of external costs

The focus here is on climate change mitigation policies, but it must also be borne in mind that the current world energy system based on fossil fuels carries with it many "negative externalities" or "external costs," that is, real costs to society in the form of disease from pollution and so on that are not covered by what we pay for energy. These external costs are paid indirectly through health care, lost work days, and more. Making a transition to a less-polluting energy system would have benefits beyond those associated with avoiding climate change. This is especially true in developing countries where highly polluting cooking facilities take a large toll on women's health. These costs, as well as those in industrialized and threshold countries (e.g., China) due to pollution from coal-fired power plants, for example, are estimated to be as much as a few percent of GDP, ten times or more higher than the projected costs of climate change mitigation.[10]

How can we take into account costs that are currently external to our energy system? Economists agree that if there is a public harm being done by the practice of dumping excess CO_2 into the atmosphere and oceans, those costs should be included in the price of fossil-fuel services so that the market system can function properly. Therefore, a critical step is to set a cost for carbon emissions.

One way to do this would be to tax all CO_2 emissions at a certain number of dollars per ton, thereby affecting the price of gasoline and electricity. Alternatively, a limit could be set on total emissions, and then permits for those emissions could be traded in a market. Industries that could figure out how to inexpensively avoid emissions would do so and then sell permits to those that could not reduce their own emissions. A similar system has long been in place in the United States for reducing sulfur emissions from power plants, established by the 1990 Clean Air Act. Since the goal is to reduce emissions, either the tax would increase over time or the cap would decrease.

According to economists, the two plans should be equivalent, but it is not easy to know how to set the level of a tax to achieve CO_2 reduction goals. Some variant of a so-called cap and trade system starts with the scientific question of how much CO_2 can be released before causing an intolerable risk of damages, and the markets would then help decide how to allocate the atmospheric capacity to best achieve that goal. It is important to note that revenues from carbon taxes or permits do not have to be additional income to governments. They can replace other taxes, for example. The point is not to raise extra money but to balance out real costs to society, either now or in the future. Effectively, we could start to tax "bads," that is, things that harm us, instead of "goods," the things we want to encourage. The income from taxes or permits could potentially be returned to households as a kind of dividend. Finding a way to properly price the destructive effects of CO_2 emissions into the economy is certainly a policy that fulfills Francis's desire for long-term economic thinking rather than focusing on immediate profits and short-term economic growth (§178, 181). Pope Francis does express skepticism about the use of "carbon credits," as potentially being a "new form of speculation" that may "simply become a ploy which permits maintaining the excessive consumption of some countries and sectors" (§171). As with most economic market constructs, however, it is up to civil society to set the ground rules for how markets are to function. The text of the encyclical does not explicitly oppose all such mechanisms.

Technological means of mitigating climate change

As we saw in Chapter 1, *Laudato Si'* is deeply critical of the "technocratic paradigm" which works by the techniques of "possession, mastery and transformation"; treating the world as an object of human domination (§106). He warns, "Merely technical solutions run the risk of addressing symptoms and not the more serious underlying problems" (§144). For that reason, a discussion of large-scale technological means of mitigating climate change may seem to be out of keeping with the moral judgments of the encyclical. But it is clear that Francis envisions using technology in a manner that does not succumb to the technocratic paradigm.

> We are the beneficiaries of two centuries of enormous waves of change: steam engines, railways, the telegraph, electricity, automobiles, aeroplanes, chemical industries, modern medicine, information technology and, more recently, the digital revolution, robotics, biotechnologies and nanotechnologies. It is right to rejoice in these advances and to be excited by the immense possibilities which they continue to open up before us, for "science and technology are wonderful products of a God-given human creativity." (§102)

Francis is not opposed to technology *per se*, but forms and uses of it that refuse to place it under moral guidance and limits. Such uses of technology often hide immoral decisions under the guise of "purely instrumental" decisions. The encyclical specifically calls for a transition from carbon energy technologies to renewable energy technologies. "Technology based on the use of highly polluting fossil fuels—especially coal, but also oil and, to a lesser degree, gas—needs to be progressively replaced without delay. Until greater progress is made in developing widely accessible sources of renewable energy, it is legitimate to choose the less harmful alternative or to find short-term solutions" (§165).

As we have seen, our current carbon-based energy system is both integral to our current level of development and deeply disruptive to the planetary climate and ecological systems. It is important to realize the scale of this disruption as we consider potential technological solutions—some of which have serious potential risks. Scientifically, we know that continuing with business as usual is not merely risky but certain to produce catastrophic outcomes.

There are many potential pathways toward deep reductions in CO_2 emissions, both within the energy system and through more direct alterations to the earth system. Here we will survey these possibilities. References provide resources for more in-depth investigation of these topics. We first look at some renewable energy technologies, then discuss nuclear power as a low-carbon option and, finally, turn to what are often referred to as geoengineering solutions to climate change.

Looking back at the discussion of energy use and human development, it was clear that after having reached a relatively high level of HDI, there was little correlation between further increases in well-being and energy use. A corollary to this observation is that countries that have high-energy use could likely find ways to become more efficient without significantly reducing their HDI.

Before discussing various technologies, it is worthwhile to consider a snapshot of current world energy consumption patterns. We have been saying that fossil fuels are an important part of the current energy system,

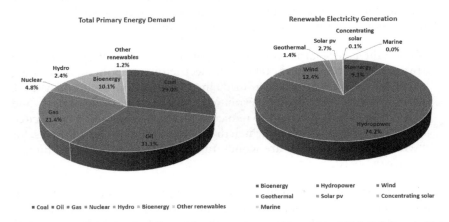

FIGURE 11.4 *Shares of total world primary energy demand in 2013 (left-hand side) and shares of world renewable electricity generation in the same year (right-hand side). Data from the International Energy Agency, World Energy Outlook 2015.*

and Figure 11.4 illustrates just how large the shares really are. The left-hand side shows that 80 percent of all the primary energy consumed in the world in 2013 was from fossil fuels.[11] As was pointed out above, the category of "bioenergy" is currently mostly made up of traditional fuels used for cooking in the poorest of countries. On the right-hand side of Figure 11.4 the shares of different technologies within the category of renewable electricity generation are shown; a relatively old technology, hydropower, makes up the largest fraction by far. One very positive sign for the transformation of the energy system is the extreme rapidity with which sources such as wind power and solar photovoltaics are growing—25 percent to 30 percent or more per year.

Renewable and low-carbon energy technologies

The list of available renewable energy technologies is long and varied, so only a few will be discussed here. All of these technologies result in very low emissions of CO_2, even when taking into account the lifecycle energy inputs needed for manufacturing. We can begin by remarking that, especially in the case of solar energy, the potentially available resources are far larger than what might be needed to power human societies. Having said that, it is important to consider carefully how renewable energy infrastructure is expanded in the future so that negative impacts, such as those on ecosystems, are avoided as much as possible. A thorough summary of many technologies, of the economics of renewable energy, and how renewable energy fits more broadly into climate change mitigation and sustainable energy needs can be found in the IPCC Special Report on Renewable Energy Sources.[12]

Hydropower

Hydroelectric power is still the renewable energy technology that plays the largest role in many countries, although this is beginning to change. There are two main types of hydroelectric power, one based on the construction of large dams and reservoirs, accompanied by diversion of water through turbines to convert the energy of flowing water to electricity. In the United States and other countries, large hydroelectric power plants were a feature of increasing electrification in the early and mid-twentieth century. Many industrializing countries are still following this pathway due to the availability of water resources (although this can also be problematic) and because hydroelectric power is easily controllable to match demand for electricity. A further advantage of some power plants is that they can essentially be run in reverse, that is, water can be pumped up into a reservoir at times of low demand and then made available in the form of electricity when demand increases. Thus, hydropower has the potential to be incorporated as part of an energy system with intermittent renewable technologies such as wind and solar energy, acting as a storage technology.

The second type of hydropower, less invasive in terms of impact on ecosystems, is "run of the river" systems. Here as well, water is diverted from a river through generating turbines, and the water is returned to the river. Run of the river hydropower does not require building large dams or reservoirs, relying instead on height differences as the river flows, as well as the volume of water flowing. These plants are typically very much smaller than hydroelectric dams, and the resource, while not yet exhausted in the United States or worldwide, is somewhat limited. On the other hand, run of the river hydropower is also controllable and therefore compatible with fluctuating renewable energy sources.

Wind power

Wind energy production has been growing steadily at about 25 percent per year worldwide over the past two decades, although growth has showed signs of slowing more recently. Overall, wind power makes up about 12 percent of total electricity worldwide, and the total generation has increased by a factor of 200 in the last couple of decades. Along with the rapid growth in wind power capacity has come a steady decrease in costs of wind power such that in many areas the cheapest available source of power for a utility to invest in is wind. Currently the cost of new wind power generating capacity is competitive with that of fossil-fuel sources, even without taking into consideration any available subsidies for wind power or negative external costs, including CO_2 emissions, of fossil-fuel electricity. Such statements must be made carefully, because at low penetrations in the electricity grid this may be true, but as presently structured, there is plenty of additional capacity to make up for times when wind power is not available.

For this reason of backup capacity, it was once assumed that increasing the amount of wind or solar energy in the electricity-generating mix beyond about 20 percent would be impossible due to increased instability in power production. Thus far, this has not been the case, even though some countries have much higher percentages of wind power (Denmark is at 40 percent or more averaged over the year). It appears that, thus far, engineers have been able to adapt to fluctuating renewable sources, given flexible options for regulating other generators, importing and exporting electricity across political boundaries and, increasingly, taking advantage of storage technologies.

Solar power

Ultimately, solar energy is the source upon which we rely for nearly everything, including the fundamental energy balance that keeps the earth habitable. The amount of sunlight incident on the earth, even counting only the land area, is about 300 times more than the total energy used by the world currently. Even if that direct solar energy can only be captured with an efficiency of 1 percent, there is in principle plenty to go around.

Solar energy conversion comes in at least three different forms, in addition to the obvious passive use of the sun's energy for heating buildings. First, solar energy can be used to heat water; in its simplest form, in warm-climate countries, one can often find black containers on a roof that absorb solar energy and provide hot water for domestic use. Active solar hot water systems are more common in industrialized countries and, combined with energy efficiency measures, can provide a significant fraction of yearly water needs for a family in temperate climates. Currently this technology is economically viable but has struggled to gain as much acceptance as had been anticipated a few decades ago.

The second way to convert solar energy to a more useful form is that of concentrating solar power (CSP), which in turn has several different technologies that can be used. The basic idea is to focus the rays of direct sunlight onto a fluid, thereby directly or indirectly creating steam that can be used to drive a turbine and generate electricity. Conceptually, one can imagine replacing a boiler fired by coal or natural gas with a solar heated front end (although it is not as technically simple as that). Coupled with possibilities of storage of some of the generated heat, which can later be released to generate electricity when the sun is no longer present, CSP represents a flexible power source. The drawback to CSP is that it only works in direct sunlight and is most economical with very large arrays of concentrating collectors, meaning that current systems are located only in very sunny, often desert-like, environments and take up a large tracts of land.

The solar technology receiving the most attention now is that of photovoltaic (pv) solar panels. Although known in some form for many decades, growth in installations in the last 20 years, and especially in the past decade, has been explosive—a factor of 100 in 10 years.[13] This growth, encouraged by various government policies around the world but especially in Germany, followed by Spain and Italy, and later the United States and China, has also led to a dramatic decrease in the cost of electricity generated by solar panels. Solar pv electricity is a fairly simple process: sunlight impinges on panels made of materials like silicon and the sunlight directly causes electrons to become freed within the material and move as electrical current to help us run appliances in our homes. There are no moving parts, no turbines, no emissions, and no noise from solar pv power. Furthermore, solar pv panels can be installed on existing roofs, as canopies for parking lots, and even as a direct replacement for shingles on roofs.

The drawback of solar pv is, of course, that the sun is only shining a portion of the time, so solar pv must be supplemented with other sources, or with storage options that effectively increase the cost of a system that is heavily based on solar energy. It is important to consider these extra costs when making claims about the comparatively low cost of solar electricity, but at the same time, full fairness would require always considering the external costs of fossil-fuel electricity sources as well.

Bioenergy

The use of so-called modern bioenergy is an important future technology in nearly all integrated assessments of climate change mitigation. The adjective "modern" is important because currently about 10 percent of world energy consumption is in the form of biomass—wood and dung, for example.[14] These are used in many of the poorest countries in the world and represent the choice for the 40 percent of the world's population without access to clean and healthy cooking technology. Modern bioenergy, in contrast, would be sustainably harvested wood, crops grown for energy needs without competing with food needs and without compromising ecosystem services, fuels made from algae, and others. In other words, the aim is ideally to move from unsustainable, but currently necessary, practices and to enable access to cleaner, more efficient, renewable energy sources. Bioenergy for the future comes in two forms— for combustion, to generate electricity (and perhaps heat), and for liquid fuels.

Estimates for future bioenergy needs vary widely, depending on assumptions that are made as to other sustainability factors. In fact, there is a growing concern and active amount of research about the linkages between food, water, and energy systems. In the past, one could fairly safely look at each of these subsystems in isolation; today, we realize that carelessly made policies to encourage the use of biofuels in the United States or Europe, for example, can have impacts on rainforest ecosystems in Indonesia (when palm plantations for oil replace forests). Ripple effects from mandates to use corn to create ethanol can mean increasing food prices in other parts of the world or result in the clearing of land that had been absorbing CO_2 for additional planting of corn or soybeans. As agriculture spreads (and this depends highly on the exact region), more irrigation may be necessary, which can increase stress on water resources that are already scarce in some areas. Finally, demands for higher crop yields, both to feed a growing population and for energy needs, can lead to greater use of fertilizers, with concomitant increases in nutrient runoff to rivers making its way to larger bodies of water and creating hypoxia (low-oxygen) zones and algal blooms.

On the positive side, there are significant amounts of available biomass from crop residues, animal waste, landfills, and forestry, and these sources of biomass could become an important part of regional and local energy systems, tailored to specific conditions. With more localized generation of electricity from biomass, for example, the potential exists for building more efficient systems that take advantage of the "waste" heat inherent in generating electricity and use that heat for local industrial processes or domestic heating and hot water, so-called combined heat and power systems. Especially in the case of residues and other material that would otherwise decay and emit either CO_2 or methane to the air, use of these sources of material can actually result in "negative emissions" of CO_2 while providing energy efficiently.

Finally, the case of bioenergy is interesting because it calls our attention to the fact that a large fraction of crops in many wealthy countries, and some less-wealthy ones, is currently being used as feed for animals that are then consumed by humans. The energy and greenhouse gas consequences of eating higher on the food chain will become an increasingly large fraction of total emissions as emissions from other sectors decrease; as this happens, we will have to make difficult (for some) decisions about trade-offs between bioenergy for food, for feed and for energy, not to mention the basic nutrition requirements for citizens in poorer countries around the world.

We now turn to a current technology that is neither carbon emitting nor renewable, and that is in widespread use today: nuclear power.

Nuclear power

After a boom in construction starting in the 1970s, nuclear power accounts for about 10 percent of worldwide electricity generation, with much higher percentages in the United States (20 %), Europe (20 %), and specifically in France (75 %).[15] Nuclear power represents an interesting case study in attitudes toward environmental issues. Dating back to the 1960s, it was nuclear power along with air and water pollution in industrialized Western countries that was a trigger for the creation of the environmental movement. Nuclear power is a (very nearly) CO_2-free source of electricity. Even considering the entire life cycle of fuel production and construction, it is on par with solar and wind energy.[16] A growing number of scientists and citizens are weighing the pros and cons of a technology that has some known threats against the uncertainty and potentially disastrous, long-term impacts of climate change. Here we briefly consider a few of the points that are often raised, including safety and newer technologies, waste disposal, proliferation, and other security dangers, costs, and compatibility with renewable sources.

The seemingly uncontrollable nature and long-term consequences of (even infrequent) nuclear accidents is one of the subjectively most worrisome aspects of this technology. Statistically, far more people die (hundreds of thousands per year worldwide[17]) from the effects of coal-fired electricity than have ever been killed in nuclear accidents. However, the scale and immediacy of nuclear accidents and the repeated inability or unwillingness of those in charge of nuclear facilities to provide accurate information when there is an accident has helped undermine the industry.

The most commonly cited issue with regard to nuclear power is that of waste disposal. Given the large amount of commentary available on that topic, we mention here only that the long-term storage issues have still not been solved satisfactorily. Even if the engineering solutions suggested thus far are viable, societies have not accepted those proposals.

Nuclear power has an advantage over some fossil-fuel technologies in that most of the costs of generation come at the construction and planning stages. Fuel costs for nuclear power are relatively minor compared to capital costs, and, therefore, once a plant is built there is a degree of certainty with regard to the cost of electricity for the future. In contrast, coal and natural gas power are always subject to the uncertainties in changing costs of fuel over time. On the other hand, over time the upfront capital costs of nuclear power plant construction have increased in real terms (accounting for inflation), a tendency that is very different from that of other technologies, which usually become cheaper with gained experience.[18] There is some controversy as to why this is the case with nuclear power, with some blaming overzealous environmental regulation and others claiming that experience shows a need for ever-increasing safeguards to prevent accidents. A final economic uncertainty with nuclear technology costs is that of de-commissioning or deconstruction of power plants at the end of their life span. Operators of nuclear power plants are required to set aside funds for this purpose, but it is not yet clear (due to lack of experience) whether those funds are sufficient.

An important factor to consider with nuclear power is the integration of various technologies in a coherent system for the future. Presumably it would be possible for a country to construct a carbon-free electricity system based on nuclear power entirely, with small amounts of renewable energy. Many countries appear to be moving in the other direction, with renewables playing a key role; in that case, nuclear power can become problematic due to its relative lack of flexibility. Since solar pv and wind power are intermittent in supplying electricity, the remainder of the electricity system must be able to make up for times when these sources are not available. Nuclear power plants can be ramped up and down but only within limits. As the penetration, or percentage, of fluctuating renewables increases, nuclear power may become less compatible with these other sources. Thus, in a long-term view a country or region must likely choose well in advance the general characteristics of the electricity system they wish to achieve so that incompatibilities may be avoided.

Geoengineering or "climate intervention"

Although much of this chapter has focused on reducing carbon emissions, there are other potential solutions to the challenge of climate change in the form of engineering that would allow us to continue burning fossil fuels (or to reduce the consequences if we fail to reduce carbon emission soon enough) while altering other parts of the earth and energy systems, often referred to collectively as "geoengineering" or "climate intervention." The National Research Council prefers the latter term "because the term 'engineering' implies a more precisely tailored and controllable process than might be the case for these climate interventions."[19] These proposals rely heavily on technologies whose regional and long-term consequences are not well defined, and they tend to address one part of the climate change issue without necessarily taking into account multiple interactions. It is against such approaches that Pope Francis warns:

> Ecological culture cannot be reduced to a series of urgent and partial responses to the immediate problems of pollution, environmental decay and the depletion of natural resources. There needs to be a distinctive way of looking at things, a way of thinking, policies, an educational programme, a lifestyle and a spirituality which together generate resistance to the assault of the technocratic paradigm. Otherwise, even the best ecological initiatives can find themselves caught up in the same globalized logic. To seek only a technical remedy to each environmental problem which comes up is to separate what is in reality interconnected and to mask the true and deepest problems of the global system. (LS §111)

Many scientists would agree with this assessment of the potential dangers of attempting to geoengineer the climate. However, the debate about doing research on different types of geoengineering has arisen precisely because many of these same scientists are so concerned about the dangers of uncontrolled emissions and the resulting consequences of climate change that they feel society must be prepared with as many tools as possible, even if some would only be used as a last resort. That some of these are being considered at all should be read as an indicator of the seriousness of the problems we face.

Carbon capture and sequestration

A broad category of geoengineering is that of carbon capture and sequestration (CCS). In essence, we would keep burning fossil fuels but use technologies to capture the CO_2 at a power plant, for example, before it can escape to the atmosphere. After being captured, the CO_2 must be transported to a location where it can be compressed and then injected into a storage site. A great deal of research has gone into CCS technology, particularly in the electric power sector (it would be much more difficult to capture CO_2 from mobile sources such as automobiles). Aside from the obvious motivation to develop CCS, because successful implementation of this technology would require only minor adjustments to the current energy system as a whole, integrated models of the energy system, economy, and climate change mitigation seem to indicate that at some point in the future, achieving a 2°C temperature (or less) increase target will require having some possibilities for negative net emissions—taking more CO_2 out of the atmosphere than we input through combustion.[20]

In spite of efforts to develop CCS technology, success in implementation has been mixed at best thus far.[21] Several challenges arise in furthering CCS. Retrofitting existing power plants is an expensive proposition with little current motivation for doing so. Worldwide, a series of new CCS-equipped power plants has been either planned or partially completed but with little indication that the technology is ready to become standard practice. The cost of building a power plant with CCS is estimated to be 50 percent to 100 percent higher than the same plant without CCS.[22] In addition, enough energy is needed for the capture, compression, transport, and storage processes that a power plant needs to consume from 15 to 25 percent more fossil fuels for the same amount of electricity output.[23] Since there is currently no price charged for carbon emissions, the incentive to invest in CCS power plants is very limited, given the increased capital and operating costs. This disadvantage could be removed if a price were to be placed on carbon emissions in the future.

CCS technologies raise concerns about the efficacy with which CO_2 remains in the ground for what will necessarily be many centuries, if not millennia. In principle, geologists can be reasonably certain of the characteristics of storage sites and thus minimize risk. On the other hand, some of the most attractive sites suggested to date are former wells used to extract fossil fuels, which are by definition compromised with respect to the original state that allowed fossil fuels to form in the first place. Even if geologists and engineers can guarantee with a high level of certainty that the CO_2 will remain underground, many citizens and property owners have been reluctant to have storage sites located near where they live.[24]

Direct-air carbon dioxide capture

A variation of this method is direct-air capture of CO_2.[25] This aims to remove already-emitted CO_2 from the atmosphere. Technologies under current development make use of large physical structures that capture CO_2 from the ambient air for storage as above, or that use chemical reactions to transform the CO_2 to benign compounds, or even to materials that can be used in industrial processes such as construction. Although some laboratory-scale projects have shown that direct-air capture of CO_2 can work, the larger question is one of scale and cost, as well as that of imagining a landscape dotted with structures hundreds of feet tall, being used not to generate energy (like wind turbines) but simply to act as high-tech vacuum cleaners to clean up the by-products of fossil-fuel combustion. It may be that direct-air capture will be a necessary part of climate change mitigation strategies in the future.

Albedo modification: Using chemicals to increase atmospheric reflection of sunlight

A more radical technology proposed for managing earth's energy balance takes its inspiration from the observation that volcanic eruptions can emit large quantities of tiny particles (aerosols) into the atmosphere with a resulting decrease in sunlight reaching the earth.[26] In 1815 the eruption of the Indonesian volcano Tambora was followed in 1816 by the "year without summer" in many parts of the world that were far from the volcano itself. In a modern version of anthropogenically induced reflection (albedo) of sunlight by aerosols, airplanes, or tethered balloons would be used to disperse particulate matter into the stratosphere in controlled quantities.[27] There are several reasons why this technique might be advantageous—and several notes of caution as well.

In principle, relatively fine control can be exercised over the amounts of aerosols to be released into the atmosphere. The lifetime of aerosols in the atmosphere is short—on the order of a year or two—so that the ability to make corrections exists as well. Finally, initial estimates of the cost of aerosol injection indicate that this form of geoengineering would be relatively inexpensive compared to many renewable energy technologies and surface-based management of CO_2 emissions. Deploying aircraft-delivered sulfate aerosols might cost only a small fraction of the estimated costs due to climate change itself on the timescale of a few decades.[28]

There are several issues to consider with regard to aerosol albedo modification. We have seen that increasing surface temperatures are not the only effect that is caused by additional greenhouse gases in the atmosphere. Ocean acidification would continue as long as emissions increase, thereby leading to negative impacts on marine life, and thus to the important fisheries crucial for many coastal populations. One of the commonly proposed chemicals, sulfur dioxide, is itself a pollutant that causes acid rain. Furthermore, negative impacts on one element of an ecosystem will undoubtedly have ripple effects, as discussed in the chapter on ecology in this book. Since it does not change the level of greenhouse gases and can even mask the consequences of their continued emission, Albedo modification carries the risk of very rapid warming should it ever be stopped.

Finally, there are a whole host of international governance questions that would be raised by such a program: there are risks that this technology could have vastly uneven geographic effects, causing disruption in some regional climates. Who decides when, where, and how much to inject? Who pays? Who chooses when to stop the program? How are unintended consequences dealt with? Fossil-fuel-induced climate change can be viewed as an unintended example of geoengineering, but the countries of the world have not been able to agree in three decades of negotiations on a robust strategy of mitigation; there is little reason to believe that agreement on future levels of geoengineering efforts would be any easier to negotiate.[29]

All of the geoengineering solutions presented here, as well as others, could potentially satisfy the goal of mitigating the worst effects of climate change, or even help reduce greenhouse gas levels in the future. Each of these solutions raises questions that must be answered by societies around the world based on levels of risk and willingness to pay the costs of development and deployment of these technologies. The latter point is especially crucial, since at the level of economic considerations, mitigating climate change will always be a question of costs versus benefits and of making trade-offs between possible future pathways. And of course, we should always be cognizant of the potential pitfalls that come with trying to implementing these technological fixes on what would necessarily be a very large scale. Again citing from *Laudato Si'*, "Merely technical solutions run the risk of addressing symptoms and not the more serious underlying problems" (§144).

Conclusion

Laudato Si' is an exhortation to consider the connectedness of all of earth's systems, both the natural and physical systems being altered by our human activity and our socially constructed systems. In the end, protection of creation is necessary for human flourishing, but a strong argument can also be made for the intrinsic value of intact ecosystems. As humans gain an ever-deeper understanding of the workings of the natural world, we realize how delicately balanced the earth system really is. Along with the knowledge gained from the pursuit of science and the wisdom gained through reflection on that knowledge, as well as through our own human creations in technology and the arts, it can be hoped that we are able to avoid negative impacts that we do have the ability to foresee.

The challenge of mitigating climate change and transitioning to sustainable energy and ecological systems may seem daunting. However, in spite of the relatively short time over which serious efforts have been made to address these challenges, there are a number of successful examples that can serve as models for the future and no shortage of plans for how to achieve these ambitious goals. Germany has increased renewable energy generation from electricity from 3 percent to 30 percent in the past 25 years and has set a target of reducing greenhouse gas emissions by at least 80 percent by 2050, and previous targets have always been met ahead of schedule.[30] Costa Rica has garnered headlines in the past two years by running for months at a time on 100 percent renewable electricity, and has a goal of become completely carbon neutral by 2021.[31] In the United States, California researchers have also published a plan for carbon neutrality in their state by 2050,[32] the National Renewable Energy Laboratory (NREL) has examined how the United States could generate 80 percent of all electricity from renewables by 2050,[33] and many states and cities are moving forward with ambitious proposals to dramatically reduce CO_2 emissions. The technology, although there are still challenges to overcome, is already in existence. The will to make changes has thus far been lacking, together with sufficient incentives to overcome the inertia of the current system of energy production and to reevaluate our relationship to the natural world.

One of the strongest messages of *Laudato Si'* is that we must not allow ourselves to become beholden to a false view of the economic system as being the driving force behind human pursuits. Our societies have created a wide variety of economic systems that can serve different purposes. Given the picture of nested rings of sustainability presented in this chapter, it is useful to always remember that the natural climate and ecological systems described in Chapters 2 and 3 also represent our recognition of limits to human action. The social systems discussed elsewhere in this text operate within those natural and ecological boundaries. Economics is one tool that we can use to help guide some types of decisions about how to move forward, but economics must take its cues from nature and society.

Questions

1   Is mitigation of climate change a technical issue in your opinion? Why or why not? If so, which are the main barriers to overcome? If not, what are the necessary tools for addressing climate change?

2   Economics plays a big role in many different decisions we make in society, and, effectively, economics is the study of how best to allocate scarce resources. Is mitigation of climate change, in the end, just a question of balancing costs and benefits of various actions we choose to take in the next few years?

3   Sustainable development and mitigating climate change could be seen to be at odds with one another, since every industrialized country has used fossil fuels to enable development. Describe in detail scenarios that would allow climate change mitigation and sustainable development for the poorest countries of the world.

4   Explain the differences between strong and weak sustainability and how these two concepts might lead to very different kinds of policies if taken as guidelines decision-making.

5   The carbon budget concept was introduced in this chapter and discussed as well in Chapter 2. Defend, or contradict, the following proposal: the rights to burn the remaining fossil fuels that can be consumed (which is much less than what is in the ground) within the budget should be equally divided among all people in the world. Those who feel they need to consume more than their share would then pay into an international fund which would then be used to help poorer countries (who are currently consuming much less than their allotment) create energy infrastructure that is renewable and sustainable.

Notes

1   Each carbon fuel has a different proportion of energy derived from carbon—coal the highest, petroleum, and natural gas less.

2   Detlef P. van Vuuren, Jae Edmonds, Mikiko Kainuma, et al., "The Representative Concentration Pathways: An Overview," *Climatic Change* 109 (2011): 5–31, doi:10.1007/s10584-011-0148-z.

3   The standard metric unit for energy is a Joule; a Gigajoule, or GJ, is one billion Joules. To put it in terms that appear on your electricity bill, one GJ is equal to about 278 Kilowatt hours. The energy use numbers cited include all energy used, not just electric bills. Representative data can be found at https://en.wikipedia.org/wiki/List_of_countries_by_energy_consumption_per_capita based on data from the World Bank.

4   http://hdr.undp.org/en/content/human-development-index-hdi and http://www.iea.org/media/statistics/IEA_HeadlineEnergyData_2016.xlsx.

5   See, for example, Paul Hawken, Amory B. Lovins, and L. Hunter Lovins, *Natural Capitalism: Creating the next Industrial Revolution* (New York: Little, Brown and Co, 2000).

6   See, for example, William Nordhaus, *The Climate Casino: Risk, Uncertainty, and Economics for a Warming World* (New Haven, CT: Yale University Press, 2013).

7   See, for example, Michael Grubb, Jean Charles Hourcade, and Karsten Neuhoff, *Planetary Economics: Energy, Climate Change and the Three Domains of Sustainable Development* (New York: Routledge, 2013).

8   See, for example, Table SPM.2 in *Climate Change 2014: Mitigation of Climate Change. Contribution of Working Group III to the Fifth Assessment Report of the Intergovernmental Panel on Climate Change*, ed. Ottmar Edenhofer, Ramón Pichs-Madruga, Youba Sokona, et. al. (Cambridge, UK, and New York, USA: Cambridge University Press, 2014); http://www.ipcc.ch/report/ar5/wg3/.

9   Estimating damages is a difficult task. IPCC Working Group III concludes that their methods systematically understate potential damages: "Our general conclusion is that the reliability of damage functions in current IAMs [Integrated Assessment Models] is low. Users should be cautious in relying on them for policy analysis: some damages are omitted, and some estimates may not reflect the most recent information on physical impacts; the empirical basis of estimates is sparse and not necessarily up-to-date; and adaptation is difficult to properly represent. Furthermore, the literature on economic impacts has been growing rapidly and is often not fully represented in damage functions used in IAMs." *Climate Change 2014: Mitigation of Climate Change*, 247.

10   *Climate Change 2014: Mitigation of Climate Change*, 15 and Global Commission on the Economy and Climate, *Better Growth, Better Climate: The Synthesis Report*, http://www.newclimateeconomy.report (2014), 21.

11   *World Energy Outlook 2015* (Paris, France: International Energy Agency, 2015).

12   *IPCC Special Report on Renewable Energy Sources and Climate Change Mitigation*, ed. Edenhofer, et al. (Cambridge: Cambridge University Press, 2011).

13   BP, *Statistical Review of World Energy 2015, Data Workbook*, http://www.bp.com/en/global/corporate/energy-economics/statistical-review-of-world-energy/downloads.html.

14   https://www.iea.org/statistics/.

15   BP, *Statistical Review of World Energy 2015*.

16 *IPCC Special Report on Renewable Energy Sources and Climate Change Mitigation*, 19.

17 *World Energy Outlook Special Report 2016: Energy and Air Pollution* (Paris: International Energy Agency, 2016), 35, https://www.iea.org/publications/freepublications/publication/weo-2016-special-report-energy-and-air-pollution.html.

18 Arnulf Grubler, "The Costs of the French Nuclear Scale-up: A Case of Negative Learning by Doing," *Energy Policy* 38, no. 9 (2010): 5174–88, doi:10.1016/j.enpol.2010.05.003.

19 Committee on Geoengineering Climate: Technical Evaluation and Discussion of Impacts, Board on Atmospheric Sciences and Climate, Ocean Studies Board, Division on Earth and Life Studies, National Research Council, *Climate Intervention: Reflecting Sunlight to Cool Earth* (Washington, DC: National Academies Press, 2015), 1.

20 International Energy Agency (IEA), *Technology Roadmap: Carbon Capture and Storage* (Paris: IEA, 2013); Committee on Geoengineering Climate: Technical Evaluation and Discussion of Impacts, Board on Atmospheric Sciences and Climate, Ocean Studies Board, Division on Earth and Life Studies, National Research Council, *Climate Intervention: Carbon Dioxide Removal and Reliable Sequestration* (Washington, DC: National Academies Press, 2015), http://www.nap.edu/catalog/18805/climate-intervention-carbon-dioxide-removal-and-reliable-sequestration; *Climate Change 2014: Mitigation of Climate Change : Working Group III Contribution to the Fifth Assessment Report of the Intergovernmental Panel on Climate Change*, Ottmar Edenhofer, Ramón Pichs-Madruga, Youba Sokona, et. al. (Cambridge: Cambridge University Press, 2014), http://dx.doi.org/10.1017/CBO9781107415416.

21 Christian von Hirschhausen, Johannes Herold, and Pao-Yu Oei, "How a 'Low Carbon' Innovation Can Fail—Tales from a 'Lost Decade' for Carbon Capture, Transport, and Sequestration (CCTS)," *Economics of Energy & Environmental Policy* 1, no. 2 (2012), doi:10.5547/2160-5890.1.2.8.

22 Energy Information Administration (EIA), *Updated Capital Cost Estimates for Utility Scale Electricity Plants* (Washington, DC: U.S. Dept. of Energy, 2013), https://www.eia.gov/forecasts/capitalcost/

23 EIA, Updated Capital Cost Estimates for Utility Scale Electricity Plants.

24 R. M. Krause, S. R. Carley, D. C. Warren, J. A. Rupp, and J. D. Graham, "'Not in (or Under) My Backyard': Geographic Proximity and Public Acceptance of Carbon Capture and Storage Facilities," *Risk Analysis* 34, no. 529–40 (2014). doi:10.1111/risa.12119; Reiner, David, et al., "An International Comparison of Public Attitudes Towards Carbon Capture and Storage Technologies," *NTNU* (2006), http://www.ukccsc.co.uk/Publications/Reiner1.pdf.

25 National Research Council, *Climate Intervention: Carbon Dioxide Removal and Reliable Sequestration*; Klaus S. Lackner, Sarah Brennan, Jürg M. Matter, A.-H. Alissa Park, Allen Wright, and Bob van der Zwaan, "The Urgency of the Development of CO2 Capture from Ambient Air," *Proceedings of the National Academy of Sciences* 109, no. 33 (2012): 13156–62, doi:10.1073/pnas.1108765109.

26 National Research Council, *Climate Intervention: Reflecting Sunlight to Cool Earth*, 5.

27 Ibid., 29.

28 Justin McClellan, David W Keith, and Jay Apt, "Cost Analysis of Stratospheric Albedo Modification Delivery Systems," *Environmental Research Letters* 7, no. 3 (2012), doi:10.1088/1748-9326/7/3/034019.

29 National Research Council, *Climate Intervention: Reflecting Sunlight to Cool Earth*, 121.

30 https://en.wikipedia.org/wiki/Renewable_energy_in_Germany.

31 https://en.wikipedia.org/wiki/Renewable_energy_in_Costa_Rica.

32 Veerabhadran Ramanathan, Juliann E. Allison, Maximilian Aufhammer, David Auston, et al., Executive Summary of the Report, *Bending the Curve: 10 Scalable Solutions for Carbon Neutrality and Climate Stability* (Berkeley: University of California, 2015), http://uc-carbonneutralitysummit2015.ucsd.edu/_files/Bending-the-Curve.pdf.

33 http://www.nrel.gov/analysis/re_futures/.

12

Creation care through consumption and life choices

Daniel R. DiLeo

ENCYCLICAL READING GUIDE

- Lifestyles: §203–208
- Individual Actions: §211, 216–220
- Consumerism: §32, 50, 184, 203, 209–210, 215, 219, 232
- Throwaway Culture: §16, 22, 43
- Virtue: §88, 211, 217, 224

Pope Francis's *Laudato Si'* is a groundbreaking encyclical that addresses the causes, effects, and potential responses to ecological degradation. On a practical level, Pope Francis seeks to help protect our common home by encouraging people to take sustainable individual actions and pursue ecologically sensitive structural reforms—two levels and sorts of activity sometimes respectively described in Catholic social teaching as charity and justice.[1]

In the face of modern global ecological problems like climate change, individual actions might seem inconsequential. To paraphrase Derrick Jensen's trenchant critique of proposing personal solutions to environmental destruction, "We aren't going to save the world by taking shorter showers."[2] Certainly, solutions to global ecological challenges will require coordinated local, national, and international efforts institutionalized in policies and laws. These are the subjects of the next chapter. Personal actions, perhaps even shorter showers, nevertheless, remain important for several reasons. First, personal consumption and lifestyle choices have discernible ecological impacts that cannot be ignored: in 2014, for example, each American emitted an average of 16.50 tons of carbon dioxide (CO_2)—more than the citizens of all but 11 other countries in the world.[3] Next, individual choices and actions are theologically significant in the Christian tradition. Our choices and actions bear upon our salvation and determine what sort of people we become through the cultivation of virtue, and Christians believe that God calls each person to "cultivate and care for" creation (Gen. 2.15). Our personal choices are an important realization of the "profound interior conversion" to which we are called (§217). Finally, and most simply, societal structures require the participation of individual persons, and thus, transformation of structural systems requires individual action as well.

Given the importance of individual consumption and lifestyle choices for ecological sustainability, this chapter considers how individuals can practically respond to *Laudato Si'*. First, the chapter briefly outlines the contemporary ecological crisis and highlights the significance of individual actions. Next, the chapter reviews Pope Francis's recommendations in *Laudato Si'* for how individuals can better care for our common home. Finally, the chapter considers additional personal consumption and lifestyle choices by which individuals can care for creation and cultivate virtue in the areas of consumption, disposal, and transportation.

"What is happening to our common home?"

Through this provocative question that titles Chapter One of *Laudato Si'*, Pope Francis sets the stage upon which we might, as Douglas Christie writes in Chapter 6, "become painfully aware" of the present ecological crisis and so respond appropriately. In particular, Francis recognizes that the contemporary world is faced with challenges related to pollution, climate change, water, biodiversity, "quality of human life," the stability of society, and "global inequality" (§20–52). Additionally, the pope highlights the reality that ecological degradation harms human persons and communities—often especially the poor and vulnerable who often do least to harm creation (e.g., §20, 51, 52).

Pope Francis proposes a response to these problems that engages both their structural and individual dimensions. On the one hand, he recognizes that global challenges such as these emanate from unjust systems, structures, and institutions. For example, the pope recognizes that human-forced climate change is driven "by a model of development based on the intensive use of fossil fuels, which is at the heart of the worldwide energy system" (§23). In the United States, for example, 30 percent of 2014 domestic carbon emissions came from the electricity sector.[4] As such, and since humans are part of creation, Francis emphasizes that social and ecological problems are intrinsically connected and thus require "comprehensive solutions which consider the interactions within natural systems themselves and with social systems" (§139).

At the same time that he advocates for the reform of systems, structures, and institutions on behalf of our common home, Pope Francis also calls on the other hand for people to take individual actions that will preserve the integrity of creation. A survey of *Laudato Si'* reveals several reasons for this focus on the individual: the impact of individual choices within a "consumerist" economy, the importance of individual will within the Christian understanding of the human person, and the cultivation of "sound virtues" which are necessary in order for "people to make a selfless ecological commitment" (§211). Pope Francis explicitly says that individual activities are important because "they benefit society, often unbeknown to us, for they call forth a goodness which, albeit unseen, inevitably tends to spread. Furthermore, such actions can restore our sense of self-esteem; they can enable us to live more fully and to feel that life on earth is worthwhile" (§212).

The importance of individual actions

Individual actions matter for four reasons: the impact of our personal choices within an economy focused on the desires of First World consumers, the Christian focus on the significance of individual moral choices, the Christian notion of the development of moral virtue—which connects our individual life choices with the development of the moral strength to face difficult issues—and, finally, the links between individual moral development and broader social change.

First, our individual decisions have profound ecological consequences. Each person in the United States through her or his actions emitted an average of 16.50 metric tons of climate-changing CO_2 in 2014. That same year, each American also produced an average of 4.40 pounds of waste *every day*.[5] Americans came in last place on the 2014 Greendex global survey of consumer sustainability, and by some estimates it would take four planets for everyone in the world to consume as those in the United States.[6]

Since carbon emissions and waste production can contribute to environmental degradation, we can reasonably infer that individual acts are significant insofar as they harm creation. Additionally, and since the consequences of ecological harm can injure human persons—especially the poor and marginalized—we can also recognize that personal consumption and lifestyle choices are theologically significant insofar as they compromise core principles of Catholic social teaching (e.g., human life, dignity, and the preferential option for the poor and vulnerable).[7]

Second, in addition to the material impacts of our choices, the Christian tradition places great emphasis on the importance of individual choice. Christianity properly understood is not a religion of individual salvation but of communal salvation within the church. Nevertheless, Christianity still holds that the choices of individual persons have salvific consequences. We have the power to accept or reject God's offer of salvation, and our response is expressed through our myriad of daily moral decisions to act for or against the good. In particular, Jesus teaches that salvation depends on the discrete actions that we take and which impact others (Mt. 25.31-46). The Catholic tradition reinforces the theological importance of individual actions by naming as sin any action that does not express love for God or another person.[8] Moreover, *Laudato Si'* extends the scope of relationships in which we are called to lovingly live by echoing Ecumenical Patriarch Bartholomew that failure to "cultivate and care for" creation (Gen. 2.15) is a sin (§8).[9]

Third, individual actions of all kinds matter ecologically and theologically because our choices and actions determine what sort of persons we become. This interaction between action and moral character is called virtue. Francis names virtue as an essential part of our response to the ecological crisis: "Only by cultivating sound virtues will people be able to make a selfless ecological commitment" (§211).

The ancient Greek philosopher Aristotle (384–522 BCE) taught that repeated actions guided by reason shape the innate human passions into virtues and vices, that is, habits that incline a person to respectively act in accord with or against ultimate goodness.[10] St Thomas Aquinas (1225–74) united Aristotle's philosophy with biblical insights to construct a system of theological ethics attentive to the role that virtues and vices play in inclining a person to do good or evil in accord with God.[11] For Aquinas, a virtue is "a good quality of the mind, by which we live righteously, of which no one can make bad use."[12] Virtues are strengthened by repeated use and weakened by refusal to do what is right.

In particular, Aquinas identifies four "cardinal virtues" that are cultivated through repeated acts and enable persons to enjoy temporal happiness. First, prudence enables us to "discern our true good in every circumstance and to choose the right means of achieving it."[13] Toward this end, prudence directs the other three cardinal virtues to attain their respective means (since virtues always seek the mean "between excess and deficiency," I-II, q. 64, a. 1).[14] Next, justice enables a person to habitually give what is "due to God and neighbor" and so protects human rights, equality, and the common good.[15] Third, fortitude cultivates habitual courage and resolve that enables a person to "resist temptations and to overcome obstacles in the moral life."[16] Finally, temperance "moderates the attraction of pleasures and provides balance in the use of created goods."[17]

Nancy Rourke has applied this traditional framework to contemporary ecological ethics.[18] First, prudence can help people recognize the interconnectedness of all creation and correctly apply pertinent details to realize justice, fortitude, and temperance amid ecological challenges. Next, justice can inspire sustainable action which ensures that all persons are able to flourish and can show the respect owed to nonhuman creature invested by God with intrinsic goodness. Third, fortitude can enable persons to fight through present obstacles to ecological sustainability and embolden them to relinquish ecologically harmful attitudes. Finally, temperance can moderate consumeristic tendencies and enable individuals to enjoy material goods in the balanced ways that bring authentic happiness.

Miller's discussion of "integral ecology" in Chapter 1 illustrates the connection between the central theme of the encyclical and the notion of moral virtue. Integral ecology is an awareness and way of acting based on the truth of our ecological interconnections with the rest of creation. While we may know the fact of this interconnection from theology and science, we must develop our awareness in order to see it in our lives. This way of seeing is a skill, a power, that we can develop through attentiveness to our relationships with the world around us. This ability to see is a necessary step toward action; and it is deepened by action. By striving to act in harmony with the rest of creation, we become more adept at noting our relationships and acting to respect them. For that reason, our individual responses to the ecological crises we face often involve taking time and effort to find out the connections between our everyday actions and the world around us.

Fourth, individual actions matter ecologically and theologically because they perpetuate or challenge harmful systems, structures, and institutions.[19] By seeking to act in harmony with the rest of creation and by developing moral virtue, we can contribute to reorienting systems, structures, and institutions toward ecological sustainability, justice, and human flourishing. In Pope Francis's words, "The resolve to live differently should affect our various contributions to shaping the culture and society in which we live."[20]

Let us return to the example of taking a shorter shower and consider it on these four levels. On the level of environmental impact, long showers consume energy and resources to treat, deliver, and heat the water I use. If, as is usually the case, that energy is derived from fossil fuels, a longer shower will thus produce more greenhouse gas emissions. Multiply that by 365 days a year and the environmental impact starts to be significant. On the level of choice, these environmental impacts mean that the decision to take a longer shower can be seen as a rejection of God's call to live in the goodness of right relationship with God, others, and creation. On the level of virtue and vice, taking a long shower is a small but significant action in which I develop the habit of ignoring the ecological consequences of my actions. On the level of social structures and institutions, this decision accepts and perpetuates the "throwaway culture" that Pope Francis identifies as damaging creation (§16, 22, 43). Conversely, my decision to sacrifice and take a shorter shower arguably better cares for creation directly and represents a choice to accept God's call to goodness. This small practice of self-denial helps develop virtue. It takes significant temperance to end a warm shower on a cold, or even not so cold, winter morning. Finally, the more attentive I become to the impact of my everyday actions upon the world around, the more I challenge the "throwaway culture" within myself and in society. We develop such virtue in every act of self-denial or mindful consumption choice aimed at lessening our destruction of creation.

In his address for the 2016 World Day of Prayer Care for Creation, Pope Francis described our response to the ecological crises we face in terms of sin, examination of conscience, and repentance.

> Turning to this bountiful and merciful Father . . . we can acknowledge our sins against creation, the poor and future generations. "'Inasmuch as we all generate small ecological damage,' we are called to acknowledge our contribution, smaller or greater, to the disfigurement and destruction of creation." This is the first step on the path of conversion.[21]

St Ignatius of Loyola, founder of the Jesuits, developed the *Examination of Conscience* (or *Examen*) into a daily spiritual practice. In the *Examen*, a person reflects on her day in order to recognize where God was especially present, where she either responded to or resisted God's love, and how she might respond better tomorrow. Different versions of the *Examen* have been developed to meet various needs, and in light of contemporary ecological challenges, Joseph Carver, SJ has written the *Ecological Examen* with which persons can systematically discern how they might be personally called to better care for creation through specific actions.[22]

Ecological Examen
Joseph Carver, SJ

All creation reflects the beauty and blessing of God's image. Where was I most aware of this today?

Can I identify and pin-point how I made a conscious effort to care for God's creation during this day?

What challenges or joys do I experience as I recall my care for creation?

How can I repair breaks in my relationship with creation, in my unspoken sense of superiority?

As I imagine tomorrow, I ask for the grace to see the Incarnate Christ in the dynamic interconnections of all Creation.

Conclude with the prayer of Jesus:
"I have given them the glory you gave me, so that they may be one, as we are one, I in them and you in me, that they may be brought to perfection as one, that the world may know that you sent me, and that you loved them even as you loved me" (John 17:22-24).

Francis notes that a sincere examination of conscience should lead to a desire to repent from the evil we have done, manifest in what is traditionally called "a firm purpose of amendment." That is, a sincere commitment to change our actions. He writes, "This in turn must translate into concrete ways of thinking and acting that are more respectful of creation."[23] In addition, he underscores in this address the connection between action and mercy—a move that unites the teaching of Laudato Si' with the Jubilee of Mercy and proposes an addition to the traditional spiritual and corporal works of mercy:

> As a spiritual work of mercy, care for our common home calls for a "grateful contemplation of God's world" which "allows us to discover in each thing a teaching which God wishes to hand on to us." As a corporal work of mercy, care for our common home requires "simple daily gestures which break with the logic of violence, exploitation and selfishness" and "makes itself felt in every action that seeks to build a better world."[24]

Significant actions

Given the importance of individual actions to Christian life, Pope Francis proposes several discrete ways that individuals can better care for God's good gift of creation. First, the pope suggests that persons eschew "compulsive consumerism" and the "consumerist lifestyle" that is constantly offered to us in order to avoid getting "caught up in a whirlwind of needless buying and spending" that exhaust and degrade creation (§203–204). Additionally, Francis links the cultivation of virtue to practical steps that individuals can take to better care for our common home:

> Only by cultivating sound virtues will people be able to make a selfless ecological commitment. A person who could afford to spend and consume more but regularly uses less heating and wears warmer clothes, shows the kind of convictions and attitudes which help to protect the environment. . . . [This can also be achieved by] avoiding the use of plastic and paper, reducing water consumption, separating refuse, cooking only what can reasonably be consumed, showing care for other living beings, using public transport or car-pooling, planting trees, turning off unnecessary lights, or any number of other practices. (§211)

Here we will supplement Pope Francis's reflections with a more systematic and comprehensive consideration of how individuals can virtuously care for creation. We will consider our consumer decisions in terms of decisions about our consumption of consumer goods, energy, food, water, and health care. Miller noted in his discussion of integral ecology in Chapter 1 that the problems of economic externalities and the technocratic paradigm cause a profound lack of knowledge about the consequences of our consumption decisions. For that reason, our discussion of practices will address the use of various "footprint calculators" to enable us to better understand the impact of our consumption decisions. These can help us better understand the interconnections between our consumption choices and our impact on the rest of creation.

The consumption of consumer products

Building on Pope Francis's aforementioned comments about consumerism, the consumption and disposal of products are activities that impact the integrity of human and nonhuman creation. Products require resource extraction, transportation, and storage, and all of these activities can degrade the environment and, in turn, harm human persons. Similarly, product disposal—even recycling—entails transportation and material breakdown that can similarly harm all of creation: both planet and people.

Take, for example, a typical smartphone.[25] Its production likely requires the mining of minerals and drilling of oil and gas for plastics—activities that can both scar local ecology and release hazardous toxins into nearby communities. Moreover, smartphone production also entails assembly at an energy-intensive facility, shipment via fossil-fuel-powered means and temperature-controlled storage via carbon-emitting electricity—actions that all drive climate change. If the phone is then recycled, it must again be transported, worked on, and stored in the above-mentioned ways. If the phone is discarded into a landfill—many of which are located in or near poor and marginalized communities—it may leach toxic chemicals into the local ecology.

Given that the economic models which underpin and pervade many societies—especially the wealthiest—presume the constant consumption and disposal of consumer products, it should not be surprising that modern lifestyles are devouring and disposing of creation at a rate which is both unsustainable for the planet and harmful for persons. For example, although the United States—which arguably represents the apex of consumerism—accounts for about 5 percent of global population, Americans produce half of the world's solid waste and use roughly one-third of the paper, 20 percent of the copper, and one-fourth of the oil, coal, and aluminum consumed around the world.[26] As noted above, the United States came in last in the Greendex survey of global sustainability.

Responsible consumption is profoundly limited by the lack of information we are given about the things we consume. In order to care for creation and live virtuously amid a consumer society, we can start by gathering information about the ecological impact of our consumption patterns using the Personal Footprint Calculator from the Global Footprint Network.[27] Informed by this data, we can take a number of actions to develop temperate consumption habits and so better care for creation. First, and in light of the fact that a large amount of product consumption and disposal is driven by artificially induced *wants* rather than *needs*, we can commit to reduce extraneous, luxury purchases. Then we can work on a process of discernment of our true needs. After this step, we can take several actions when we consume and dispose of products in accord with more basic needs. For example, repair things currently owned, buy used items, and share products (especially "big ticket" items) to avoid the ecological footprint associated with the production of new goods. Additionally, we can purchase products made with nontoxic chemicals and materials that are recycled, recyclable, and biodegradable.

Energy consumption

"Energy decisions are ethical decisions."[28] This is due to the fact that energy production, by-products, and policies can enable or prevent the flourishing of human and nonhuman creation. The use of solar and wind energy can catalyze carbon-neutral integral human development, while continued consumption of coal drives climate change and often depends upon socio-ecologically deleterious mountaintop removal and toxin runoff into the communities of local power plants. Given that the residential sector accounted for more than 20 percent of the energy consumed by the United States in 2015, individuals thus have an opportunity to impact an energy-intensive segment of society through consumption choices and lifestyles.[29]

In order to care for creation and develop prudent energy habits, we can use the Household Carbon Footprint Calculator from Carbon Footprint to obtain insights about our current energy consumption level, fuel mix, and associated carbon footprint.[30] Guided by this information, we can then take informed decisions that cultivate justice and temperance with respect to the types and quantities of energy consumed.

Energy types

Clean or renewable energy technologies are those that do not emit climate-changing greenhouse gases and/or cause other forms of harmful pollution. With respect to individuals' most immediate spaces (residences, businesses, etc.), these generally include wind, solar, hydro, and geothermal. In order to consume more of these energy types, a person might install localized clean energy systems—for example solar panels, which can often be leased in order to avoid upfront purchasing costs—onto existing structures/grounds.[31] Additionally, many customers can purchase Renewable Energy Certificates (RECs) and so have their utility add renewable energy to the grid from which they draw power.[32]

Energy quantities

In addition to addressing the sources of our energy, we can also work to reduce the amount of energy we consume. Toward this end, it is important to first assess the details of how energy is used in a particular space. Households can most easily do this by conducting an energy audit offered by the local utility company (often for free), and businesses can use both utility company audits and ENERGY STAR benchmarking tools.[33]

Once we know the details of our energy consumption patterns, we can take several steps to increase energy efficiency and lower our overall energy consumption. Possibilities include changing particular habits (e.g., turning off lights when leaving a room), choosing more energy-efficient products like electronics and home appliances, and reducing home energy use through improved insulation, automated thermostats, and energy-efficient windows. Such approaches often lead to reduced energy bills and there are often tax credits and rebates available to help alleviate upfront purchasing costs.[34]

Carbon offsets

Carbon offsets are, in theory, a way for individuals and institutions to exercise justice through the regular compensation for their carbon footprint.[35] In general, carbon offsets are financial instruments, the sale of which fund projects that reduce, avoid, or remove carbon emissions at another site. As such, individuals and institutions might nurture justice by regularly offsetting the amount of carbon they emit through the purchase of carbon offsets to support projects that will reduce, avoid, or remove the same amount of carbon that would have otherwise been emitted or in existence somewhere else—for less than it would cost to effect the changes oneself or at a local institution.

On the one hand, carbon offsets provide a way to make up for and theoretically neutralize our carbon footprint. Additionally, the sale of offsets can provide important funding for sustainability projects in communities that might not otherwise be able to afford them. On the other hand, however, it is not entirely clear that the use of offsets is a prudential activity. George Monbiot warns that offsets cannot substitute for real changes in immediate consumer behavior and, among other things, notes that purported carbon reductions/avoidances can be difficult to verify.[36] Although some organizations work to independently verify their offset projects, verification uncertainty remains a concern regarding the general model of carbon offsets.[37]

The consumption and disposal of food

The human and nonhuman elements of the environment are impacted for better or worse by the types and quantities of food consumed, as well as the ways food waste is handled. Julie Hanlon Rubio highlights several ways in which this is so.[38] First, the model of contemporary agribusiness—which relies heavily on petro-chemicals, the practice of mono-cropping and the export of luxury foodstuffs, primarily via fossil fuel-based transport from the Global South to the Global North—can contribute to environmental degradation from soil erosion to climate change. This is especially the case for the "cold chain" supply routes which are necessary to bring us fresh fruit and vegetables from across the country and, indeed, from other continents. These require constant refrigeration or freeze in the processing plants, trucks, planes, and ships that bring our food. For that reason, there is often a much larger carbon footprint for vegetables brought from afar than those grown locally. Additionally, factory farming—which often warehouses animals indoors in cramped, disease-prone conditions—can cause God's creatures to suffer. Moreover, meat production contributes significantly to climate change through deforestation for grazing and methane emission from manure. Livestock supply chains produce 14.5 percent of global greenhouse gas emissions, and cattle account for 65 percent of livestock emissions.[39] Finally, food processing and packaging can degrade the environment through inordinate amounts of energy inputs and the excessive use of nonrecyclable/nonbiodegradable materials. To Rubio's list, I would add that food waste—the largest element of municipal landfill input in the United States—results in overproduction and a significant amount of greenhouse gas emissions.[40]

In response to the recognition that individual food choices impact creation, we can use online emission calculators to analyze the sustainability of individual diets such as FoodEmissions.com. For example, a weekly diet that consists of 3 servings of beef, 3 servings of chicken, 2 servings of pork, 14 cups of milk or yogurt, 6 servings of hard cheese, and 7 eggs requires 1.3 acres of grain and grass needed for animal feed, uses 46.1 pounds of fertilizer to grow animal feed, and creates 8,347 pounds of animal manure.[41] Given the US Department of Agriculture estimates that food waste accounts for between 30 and 40 percent of food supply in the United States, Americans especially would do well to track their amount of discarded food. Informed by this data, people can then take several of the steps recommended by Rubio to increase the ecological sustainability of their food choices: consume more foods that are unprocessed and self-prepared, "less meat and fewer animal products," more organically produced goods and "more local, seasonal produce."[42]

In addition to these recommendations, we can work to grow our own food by cultivating a garden. This not only reduces our environmental impact, it also can serve as a practice that attunes us to the ecological connections that sustain us: our dependence on soil and sun, the fact that our lives require the flourishing of other creatures (and indeed, competition with them for food). We can expand this ecological awareness to include human community by participating in community gardens.[43] Moreover, when food scraps or spoilage must be disposed of, I think it important for individuals to consider composting organic matter to create nutrient-rich humus that can be used to build better garden soil. This helps us "close the loop" and participate consciously in the nutrient cycles upon which all life depends.

The consumption and disposal of water

As with products, energy, and food, the ways we interact with water—both directly and indirectly—can uphold or injure the dignity of human and nonhuman creation. Directly, people consume and dispose of water for cooking, cleaning, landscaping, etc. Indirectly, people consume and pollute water through the purchase of products that entail industrial and commercial water use at the production points of resource extraction, manufacturing, transportation, and storage. Thus, while real GDP per capita has risen in many places since 1900 and enabled citizens to purchase more goods and services, it is unsurprising that "water use has been growing at more than twice the rate of population increase in the last century."[44] Thus, as Christiana Z. Peppard observes, many places are faced with freshwater scarcity and pollution that risk denying persons and communities their intrinsic right to water—and, by extension, to life and dignity—which is affirmed by both the United Nations and Catholic Church.[45] In addition to Peppard's insights, I also think it is important to recognize that human actions which harm the world's oceans wound the intrinsic dignity of nonhuman creation and further harm human persons. For example, CO_2 emissions from fossil fuel use are damaging marine life and fishing capacities by acidifying the water of the oceans.[46]

In order to make more sustainable use of water, we can first assess our own water footprint using calculators from Water Footprint Network and GRACE Communications Foundation.[47] Additionally, we can use resources from the Virtual Water Project to consider how much water is used to produce everyday foodstuffs.[48] With that knowledge, we can commit to reducing the "virtual water" content of their food choices. To give but one example, the Virtual Water Project calculates that it takes 1230 gallons (4,650 liters) of virtual water to produce 10 ounces (300 grams) of beef— the size of a typical steak!

We can reduce their point-of-consumption water use by turning off idle taps (e.g., while brushing teeth or applying soap in the shower), taking shorter showers, and making use of "low-flow" fixtures. We can employ rain barrels for landscaping and plant terrains that do not require inordinate amounts of water. Moreover, people can abstain from bottled water to avoid the pollution and waste associated with its production, transportation, and disposal.

Health care consumption

The connection between ecology and health care illustrates well Pope Francis's insight in *Laudato Si'* that "everything is connected" (§91). Although these areas may seem separate from each other, the modern provision of health care consumes a tremendous amount of resources and produces a large volume of waste. For example, inpatient health care facilities in the United States are the second-highest commercial consumers of energy nationally.[49] Additionally, the health care sector produces around 8 percent of America's greenhouse gas emissions.[50] Moreover, health care facilities produce an average of 25 pounds of "biohazardous, solid, recyclable and hazardous waste" per bed per day. Finally, "wrap around" health care services like those in hospital cafeterias respectively consume and produce additional resources and waste.

In response to the connections between ecology and health care, individuals can care for creation by taking actions that promote healthy living and thereby decrease the requirement of health care services which may unjustly harm nonhuman and human creation.[51] For example, exercising and eating a healthy, balanced diet can help individuals avoid the need for curative health care and associated ecological footprints from the use of energy, medical supplies, and so on. Similarly, breaking unhealthy habits like smoking can further reduce the amount of health care consumed and corresponding ecological footprint. In other words, healthy people can help foster a healthy planet and so care for other people.

Transportation

In the United States, hydrocarbons provide the majority of transportation fuel. In 2014, for example, the US transportation sector—which accounts for 28 percent of American energy use—derived 56 percent of its fuel from gasoline (petroleum), 22 percent from diesel (petroleum), 11 percent from jet fuel (petroleum), 5 percent from biofuels, 3 percent from natural gas, and 3 percent from other sources.[52] In that same year, the US transportation sector accounted for 26 percent of all US greenhouse gas emissions.[53] Given how transportation choices can thus contribute to or avoid climate change, individual choices in this area are important with respect to the care of creation and promotion of human flourishing.

In order to reduce the ecological impact of their personal transportation choices—both the immediate effects and those related to fuel extraction, refining, and transportation—we can use calculators, such as those from the American Public Transportation Association and Clear Offset, to compute the carbon footprint of their driving or commuting patterns.[54] Based on this information, individuals can adopt any of the transportation actions recommended by the US Environmental Protection Agency.[55] One of the most impactful decisions we make is where to live in relationship to work. We can make carbon emissions part of this decision. In addition to that, we can work to reduce the distances and/or frequency of travel. When we must travel, we can look to use lower-carbon fuel sources, take fuel-efficient vehicles, carpool, and ride public transit. Moreover, we can commit to walking and/or biking as much as possible and resist the temptation to take less physically taxing means of transportation.

Connecting individual consumption with the globe

Becoming aware of such a broad range of our impacts on the environment can be overwhelming, even though it brings with it an equally broad range of potential actions we can undertake to lessen our impact to live in greater harmony with creation. Still, where do we begin? And how can we access our progress? In Chapter 2, Brecha introduced the concept of the planetary carbon budget. Given what we know about the current amount of CO_2 in the atmosphere, and the temperature rise we cannot safely exceed, we can calculate the remaining total carbon fuels that we can burn in order to stay within the 2°C goal. We can also make these calculations for the more ambitious 1.5°C goal to which the Paris Agreement aspires and for which Catholic bishops from every continent have called.[56]

We can use the global carbon budget as a model for our own decisions by developing a personal carbon budget to track how well we are doing our own part of the global goal. Beginning with an estimate of our current carbon footprint (discussed above) we can then plan reductions in the next years and decades that enable us to contribute to the reductions required to meet global emissions reductions. The website ShrinkThatFootprint. com has an extended discussion of this method. A web search for "personal carbon budget" provides many other resources.

A personal carbon budget helps us prioritize our consumption changes. Air travel and red meat have a huge impact, investing in a backpack made of recycled fibers much less. It also provides a way to imagine the connection between our personal consumption and collective action to avert climate change and ecological destruction—the topic of the next chapter.

Conclusion

This chapter began by addressing the concern that individual consumption and lifestyle choices are inconsequential in the face of contemporary ecological challenges. In response, this chapter worked to show both the ecological and theological significance of individual activities. We saw that our personal decisions impact not only the world around us but also our moral character. They are also a key way in which we either reinforce or challenge unjust structures. The chapter then explored a range of ecological and climate impacts on individual and household consumption and suggested resources for lessening that impact.

Questions

1   What are the four reasons for which the author says that individual actions matter to the care of creation?

2   How does St Thomas Aquinas define virtue?

3   Why does the author argue that, as Catholic energy ethics for the twenty-first century puts it, "Energy decisions are ethical decisions"?

4   The author suggests that virtue ethics can be a source of wisdom with which individuals might better *care for our common home*. Are you moved by this proposal? Why or why not?

5   This chapter identifies several areas in which individuals could take more ecologically sustainable actions. Which area do you find to be the most challenging area and why?

Notes

1   U.S. Conference of Catholic Bishops, "Two Feet of Love in Action," http://www.usccb.org/beliefs-and-teachings/what-we-believe/catholic-social-teaching/two-feet-of-love-in-action.cfm.

2   Derrick Jensen, "Forget Shorter Showers," *Orion Magazine,* https://orionmagazine.org/article/forget-shorter-showers/.

3   European Union- European Commission- Joint Research Commission, "CO2 Time Series 1990-2014 Per Capita for World Countries," http://edgar.jrc.ec.europa.eu/overview.php?v=CO2ts_pc1990-2014&sort=des9.

4   U.S. Environmental Protection Agency, "Sources of Greenhouse Gas Emissions," https://www3.epa.gov/climatechange/ghgemissions/sources/electricity.html.

5   European Union-European Commission-Joint Research Commission, "CO2 Time Series 1990-2013 Per Capita for World Countries," http://edgar.jrc.ec.europa.eu/overview.php?v=CO2ts_pc1990-2013; U.S. Environmental Protection Agency, *Advancing Sustainable Materials Management: 2013 Fact Sheet* (Washington, DC: U.S. Environmental Protection Agency, 2015).

6   National Geographic. "Greendex-Americans," http://images.nationalgeographic.com/wpf/media-live/file/Greendex-Americans_FINAL-cb1409253792.pdf; The British Broadcasting Corporation, "How Many Earths do we Need?" http://www.bbc.com/news/magazine-33133712.

7   William J. Byron, "Ten Building Blocks of Catholic Social Teaching," *America Magazine,* http://americamagazine.org/issue/100/ten-building-blocks-catholic-social-teaching.

8   Libreria Editrice Vaticana, *Catechism of the Catholic Church* (Vatican: Libreria Editrice Vaticana, 1993), §1849.

9   Ecumenical Patriarch Bartholomew, *Address at the Environmental Symposium, Saint Barbara Greek Orthodox Church, Santa Barbara, California* (Istanbul, Turkey: The Ecumenical Patriarchate of Constantinople, 1997).

10 Aristotle (ed.), *Aristotle's Nicomachean Ethics: A New Translation*, trans. Robert C. Bartlett and Susan D. Collins (Chicago, IL: University of Chicago Press, 2011), Esp. books I–II.

11 Thomas Aquinas, *Summa Theologica*, trans. Fathers of the English Dominican Province, Second and Revised edn (London: Burns, Oats & Washburne Ltd., 1920), I–II, qq. 49–50, 55–56, 71.

12 Thomas Aquinas, *Summa Theologica,* I–II, q. 55, a. 4.

13 *Catechism of the Catholic Church*, §1806.

14 Aquinas, *Summa Theologiae*, I–II, q. 66, a. 3, ad. 3; II–II, 47, aa. 6–7.

15 *Catechism of the Catholic Church*, §1807.

16 Ibid., §1808.

17 Ibid., §1809.

18 Nancy M. Rourke, "The Environment Within," in *Green Discipleship: Catholic Theological Ethics and the Environment*, ed. Tobias Winright (Winona, MN: Anselm Academic, 2011), 175.

19 *Catechism of the Catholic Church*, §1869.

20 Francis, "Show Mercy to our Common Home," Message for the Celebration of the World Day for the Care of Creation, September 1, 2016, §4.

21 Francis, "Show Mercy to our Common Home," §3. Quoting the Orthodox Leader, the Archbishop of Constantinople, Bartholomew I," Message for the Day of Prayer for the Protection of Creation," September 1, 2012.

22 Joseph Carver, S.J., "Ecological Examen," http://www.sjweb.info/documents/sjs/docs/EcologicalExamen_ENG.pdf. Used with permission.

23 "Show Mercy to Our Common Home," §4.

24 Ibid., §5. Citing *Laudato Si'* §230.

25 This example is inspired by the example of a radio discussed in Annie Leonard, "The Story of Stuff: Referenced and Annotated Script," http://storyofstuff.org/wp-content/uploads/movies/scripts/Story%20of%20Stuff.pdf. For an extended analysis of how smartphones impact the environment, see James Suckling and Jacquetta Lee, "Redefining Scope: The True Environmental Impact of Smartphones?" *The International Journal of Life Cycle Assessment* 20, no. 4 (2015): 1181–96.

26 Roddy Scheer and Doug Moss, "Use it and Lose it: The Outsize Effect of U.S. Consumption on the Environment," *Scientific American*, http://www.scientificamerican.com/article/american-consumption-habits/.

27 Global Footprint Network, "Personal Footprint," Last modified November 20, 2015, http://www.footprintnetwork.org/pt/index.php/GFN/page/personal_footprint/.

28 Catholic Energy Ethics for the twenty-first century, "Executive Summary: 'Catholic Moral Traditions and Energy Ethics for the Twenty-First Century,'" https://catholicenergyethics21century.wordpress.com/2015/06/08/hello-world.

29 U.S. Energy Information Administration, "Energy Consumption by Sector," http://www.eia.gov/beta/MER/?tbl=T02.01#/?f=A&start=1949&end=2015&charted=3-6-9-12.

30 Carbon Footprint, "Household Carbon Footprint Calculator," http://calculator.
    carbonfootprint.com/calculator.aspx?tab=2.

31 U.S. Department of Energy, "Solar, Wind, Hydropower: Home Renewable
    Energy Installations," http://energy.gov/articles/solar-wind-hydropower-home-
    renewable-energy-installations.

32 For more on RECs, see U.S. Environmental Protection Agency, "Renewable
    Energy Certificates (RECs)," https://www.epa.gov/greenpower/renewable-
    energy-certificates-recs#how.

33 U.S. Environmental Protection Agency & U.S. Department of Energy,
    "Benchmark Energy Use," https://www.energystar.gov/buildings/about-us/how-
    can-we-help-you/benchmark-energy-use.

34 E.g., U.S. Department of Energy, "Tax Credits, Rebates & Savings," http://
    energy.gov/savings.

35 Cf. *The Guardian*, "A Complete Guide to Carbon Offsetting," http://www.
    theguardian.com/environment/2011/sep/16/carbon-offset-projects-carbon-
    emissions.

36 Ibid.

37 E.g., Native Energy, "Certifications," http://www.nativeenergy.com/
    certifications.html.

38 Julie Hanlon Rubio, "Toward a just Way of Eating," in *Green Discipleship:
    Catholic Theological Ethics and the Environment*, ed. Tobias Winright
    (Winona, MN: Anselm Academic, 2011), 360–78.

39 P. J. Gerber, et al., *Tackling Climate Change through Livestock: A Global
    Assessment of Emissions and Mitigation Opportunities* (Rome: Food and
    Agriculture Organization of the United Nations (FAO), 2013), 15.

40 U.S. Department of Agriculture, "Frequently Asked Questions," http://www.
    usda.gov/oce/foodwaste/faqs.htm.

41 Center for Science in the Public Interest, "Eating Green Calculator," https://
    foodday.org/EatingGreen/calculator.html (accessed July 6, 2016).

42 Rubio, "Toward a just Way of Eating," 370–76.

43 I am grateful to Elizabeth Groppe for this suggestion.

44 Max Roser, "GDP Growth Over the Last Centuries," https://ourworldindata.
    org/gdp-growth-over-the-last-centuries; United Nations, "Water Scarcity,"
    http://www.un.org/waterforlifedecade/scarcity.shtml.

45 Christiana Z. Peppard, *Just Water: Theology, Ethics, and the Global Water
    Crisis* (Maryknoll, NY: Orbis Books, 2014).

46 Intergovernmental Panel on Climate Change, *Climate Change 2014 Synthesis
    Report: Contribution of Working Groups I, II and III to the Fifth Assessment
    Report of the Intergovernmental Panel on Climate Change* (Geneva,
    Switzerland: IPCC, [2014]).

47 Water Footprint Network, "Personal Water Footprint Calculator," http://
    waterfootprint.org/en/resources/interactive-tools/personal-water-footprint-
    calculator/; GRACE Communications Foundation, "Water Calculator," http://
    www.watercalculator.org/.

48 The Virtual Water Project, "The Virtual Water Project," http://virtualwater.eu/.

49 "Leaner Energy," https://practicegreenhealth.org/topics/leaner-energy.

50 "Leaner Energy."

51 For this insight, I am grateful to Judith A. Vessey, Ph.D., R.N., DPNP, M.B.A., FAAN, Leila Holden Carroll Professor in Nursing at Boston College.

52 U.S. Energy Information Administration, http://www.eia.gov/Energyexplained/?page=us_energy_transportation.

53 U.S. Environmental Protection Agency, "Transportation Sector Emissions," https://www3.epa.gov/climatechange/ghgemissions/sources/transportation.html.

54 American Public Transportation Association, "Carbon Savings Calculator," http://www.publictransportation.org/tools/carbonsavings/Pages/default.aspx; Clear Offset, "Calculate Your Carbon Footprint," https://clear-offset.com/carbon-footprint-calculator-commute.php.

55 U.S. Environmental Protection Agency, "Transportation Sector Emissions."

56 United Nations, *Paris Agreement* (New York: United Nations, 2015), Article 2.1(a); CIDSE, "Catholic Bishops' statement in Lima on the road to Paris," http://www.cidse.org/articles/item/675-catholic-bishops-statement-in-lima-on-the-road-to-paris.html (accessed September 20, 2016).

13

Working together to address the climate crisis

Erin Lothes Biviano

ENCYCLICAL READING GUIDE

- Dialogue and Transparency in Decision-Making, §182–188
- Civic and Political Love, §231–232

The last chapter explored the importance of personal consumption and lifestyle decisions for caring for creation and forestalling climate change. It argued that such decisions would never, on their own, be enough. We won't end climate change by recycling or taking shorter showers. But our consumption decisions nevertheless do have a significant impact. Equally importantly, it argued that personal decisions are also important because they form us in virtue. In this chapter we turn to collective action for structural change. As we will see, here as well, these larger, systemic actions are not just solutions to a problem. They too have a theological dimension. They are expressions of love: social love.

In *Laudato Si'*, Pope Francis sets forth a detailed definition of social love. "Love, overflowing with small gestures of mutual care, is also civic and political, and it makes itself felt in every action that seeks to build a better world." He goes on to say, "Love for society and commitment to the common good are outstanding expressions of a charity which affects not only relationships between individuals but also 'macro-relationships, social, economic and political ones'" (§231). Here Pope Francis cites

Pope Benedict XVI, "Charity is at the heart of the Church's social doctrine," as the principle pervading personal and social relationships.[1]

"Macro-relationships" indicate the relationships that are part of the larger circles of community, city, country, and planet, transcending the individual relationships of sister, brother, parent, and friend. The social love that binds these larger circles of relationships is a love that matters tremendously. In fact, as Pope Francis observes, with a reference to the *Compendium of the Social Doctrine of the Church*, "Social love is the key to authentic development," which should be the guiding norm of all activity, making society "more worthy of the human person" (§231).

Social love points to the community aspect of the ecological conversion to which we are called. "Social problems must be addressed by community networks and not simply by the sum of individual good deeds. . . . The ecological conversion needed to bring about lasting change is also a community conversion (§219)." Love and conversion have a social dimension.

Putting social love into action is the theme of this chapter. The social dimensions of love, and its orientation toward the common good, will be considered first, including how social love necessarily engages multiple levels of society, including international law and local communities. Second, I will consider *how* communities are effectively inspired and engaged for this action and will note the critical importance of effective communication, given the complexity of climate change. Third, I will consider ways that faith congregations can work together for the common good, putting social love into action. The fourth section focuses on particular policies that merit attention and advocacy, for it is through advocacy that meaningful structural change can occur at the larger levels of society.

The social dimensions of love

We could also call social love "collective action for social change." It is key to Catholic social thought. Social love is inseparable from our relationship with God and with our own selves. *Laudato Si'* continuously emphasizes that "human life is grounded in three fundamental and closely intertwined relationships: with God, with our neighbour and with the earth itself" (§66). "Everything is interconnected," and so "genuine care for our own lives and our relationships with nature is inseparable from fraternity, justice and faithfulness to others" (§70). Thus, neglect, inequality, or violence in any one of these relationships reverberates through the interconnections.

Furthermore, these interconnected relationships mean that the impacts of any action are intensified in a globalized world whose cultural, ecological, political, and chemical linkages are increasingly evident. Ethics expands beyond how one treats the local neighbor we can see to how our actions ripple throughout "macro-relationships, social, economic, and political." In short, love, justice, and faithfulness are enacted on a global stage.

Policy, law, and international treaties

On this global stage, significant, large-scale solutions to climate change require systemic change. Responsible citizens must make ethical judgments that entail advocacy for fair policies at all levels of society: personal, community, regional, and national. Otherwise, society's political, economic, and social structures often function by default in perhaps unintended but negative ways. Actions for systemic change are therefore necessary, effective, and inspiring examples of social love: actions that are neither optional nor secondary.

Laudato Si' emphasizes that constructive solutions require global cooperation, a dialogue that takes the counsel of all nations, and a mindset centered on humanity as "one people living in a common home" (§164). While Pope Francis refers to a common plan, he does not recommend a hegemonic world government. In fact, his specific references to international laws seem to point to their limitations, to situations where international accords, such as those of the 1992 Rio Earth Summit, failed to be fully implemented. However, these limitations point precisely to what is needed for global cooperation: attention to the needs of all nations, not simply the powerful few, and the protective enforcement that local authorities cannot provide (§167, 173). Thus, *Laudato Si'* was aimed, in part, to encourage the international community to pass a courageous and effective agreement at the Paris Climate Conference, which the Vatican has since commended and supports.

Francis's understanding of the importance of international structures was evident in his address to the United Nations during his visit to the United States in the Fall of 2015.

The praiseworthy international juridical framework of the United Nations Organization and of all its activities, like any other human endeavor, can be improved, yet it remains necessary; at the same time it can be the pledge of a secure and happy future for future generations. And so it will, if the representatives of the states can set aside partisan and ideological interests, and sincerely strive to serve the common good.[2]

International law remains a necessary complement to the ecological, theological conversion summoned by *Laudato Si'*. There is a converging attention to justice, prudence, and the common good between international law and the Catholic social tradition.[3] The state's responsibility for the common good is presumed by traditional Catholic social teaching: "Society as a whole, and the state in particular, are obliged to defend and promote the common good" (§157). Though a traditional affirmation of the common good, Pope Francis's summons to "solidarity and a preferential option for the poorest" occurs in the new context of climate change. This paradoxical mix of the old and new requires astute evangelization that recognizes the challenges of communicating the "gospel of creation."

Inspiring personal and communal energy ethics

Climate change and energy as a faith issue?

Why is this issue so urgent as a matter of faith? Climate change is already a reality many people confront, and the most vulnerable suffer the greatest impacts. As previous chapters have made clear, for Christians who praise God as the Creator, the Incarnate Savior who took on earthly form, and the Spirit who renews creation, it is a matter of reverence and gratitude to care for creation as the primordial gift of the loving God, who provides abundantly for our needs. Yet, the painful truth is that simply highlighting Catholic values and the clear teachings about care for creation, the revelation of God in the beauties of creation, and the preferential option for the poor too often fails to inspire action. This oversimplified catechetical approach overlooks the reality that core faith values are often eclipsed by more operative cultural values. Wise and pragmatic communication is needed to connect core faith values with practices that engage people's hearts and minds, challenge operative cultural values, and foster faith-based responses to climate change as a form of social love.

The witness of social love in faith-based environmentalism

For example, members of faith congregations have been committed environmental advocates for many years. Young people often connect through online campaigns such as the Catholic Climate Covenant (http:// www.catholicclimatecovenant.org) and the Global Catholic Climate Movement (https://catholicclimatemovement.global). Their faith-based environmentalism is sparked by the illuminating fusion of climate literacy, a sincere concern for social justice, and awareness of global interdependence such that people understand how their energy decisions impact others.[4]

But taking action is not easy even for the most committed, ethical, and inspired environmentalists. As Pope Francis observes, we are very good at pretending that what is hard to do is unclear. There are multiple ways we can fool ourselves into thinking the situation is vague and ambiguous.

The barriers to facing these problems include the knowledge, caring, and action gaps. Without understanding the real long-term impacts, people don't act, and in fact it would be unreasonable to expect people to address a problem they don't understand or accept. Thus, awareness is a critical first step.[5]

Furthermore, climate change is complicated and it requires revisions to long-held beliefs and worldviews. Without open discussion, these tough concepts remain in a tightening ball of unexamined concerns about the environment. Simply creating opportunities for conversation allows people to unpack the difficult and painful realities of climate change, relate them to their own spirituality, and find ways to work together for solutions.[6] As people learn more about the solutions, recognizing that in fact a clean energy revolution is already taking place, there is enormous reason for optimism and hope.

Then there's the caring gap, in which our ability to truly care about the climate crisis is overcome by the anxieties of everyday life, the pressures of consumerism, a desire to keep in step with "Progress," the relentless distractions of our society and just plain indifference. Take a deep breath. Climate change can be an overwhelming problem. But like a toothache, the problem gets worse if it's untreated, and the anxiety remains even if it's ignored. There is a redemptive power in allowing ourselves to become "painfully aware" (§19) and to hear the "cry of the earth and the cry of the poor" (§49) as a revelation of the love of God that calls us powerfully to conversion. There is peace of mind in accepting this conversion, in taking action.

Finally, there is the action gap, in which distraction, busyness, convenience, and even addiction to our habits of consumption prevent lifestyle changes.[7] In all our efforts to overcome the knowledge, caring, and action gaps, it is essential to be both profoundly faithful and relentless pragmatic. Profoundly faithful means that we must honor the cumulative message of Catholic teaching on the environment that care of creation is an issue of faith—it is *not* a political issue in the sense of divisive and ideological partisan debate. Climate change is a scientific fact and a reality causing suffering that requires a faith response. Nonetheless, solving the crisis requires policy actions. This chapter focuses on energy, as energy use contributes directly to the cause of climate change, and because energy policy offers many opportunities for effective advocacy and change.

The justice dimension of energy policy

Within an emerging paradigm of Catholic energy ethics, energy is now recognized as a factor in solidarity and integral ecology, part of the consistent and cumulative message of Catholic social teaching. Love of neighbor today requires we critically examine our actions and inactions with regard to energy.

Energy decisions are ethical decisions, because how we use energy impacts people and all life. As *Laudato Si'* states directly: "The problem is aggravated by a model of development based on the intensive use of fossil fuels, which is at the heart of the worldwide energy system" (§23). Therefore, "technology based on the use of highly polluting fossil fuels—especially coal, but also oil and, to a lesser degree, gas—needs to be progressively replaced without delay" (§165).

Nobody knew that the accumulated impacts would be so devastating when coal was first used to create steam, power manufacturing, and lift standards of living. The historical causes of climate change are not a reason to feel guilty. Still, with our current knowledge, it's foolish at best, and ecocidal at worst, to ignore the scientific consensus that the impacts are under way due to human influences.[8]

Globally, fossil fuels are terrifically unhealthy, often deadly. Lacking clean energy, three billion people globally resort to deforestation and smoky indoor fuels. The black carbon pollution from the cooking stoves of the poor makes a significant contribution to global warming.[9] Building a clean energy system for the poor not only creates clean energy access and reduces energy poverty, but will also dramatically reduce the air pollution which every year costs seven million lives and destroys tens of millions of tons of crops.[10] Developing nations suffer the impacts of climate change the most, despite contributing the least to its causes [see Fig. 13.1]

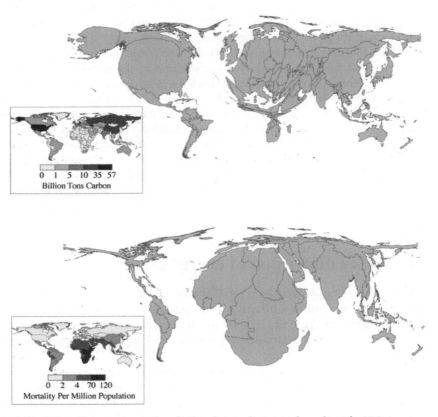

FIGURE 13.1 *Comparison of undepleted cumulative carbon dioxide (CO_2) emissions (by country) for 1950 to 2000 versus the regional distribution of four climate-sensitive health effects (malaria, malnutrition, diarrhea, and inland flood-related fatalities). From Jonathan A. Patz, Holly K. Gibbs, Jonathan A. Foley, Jamesine V. Rogers, and Kirk R. Smith, "Climate Change and Global Health: Quantifying a Growing Ethical Crisis," EcoHealth 4 (2007): 397–405. © Ecohealth Journal Consortium 2007. Used with permission of Springer.*

Therefore, today, a key site of ethical action is advocacy for the essential energy revolution that will keep global temperature increase to below 2° or even 1.5°C. This is the ambitious and necessary target set by the Paris Accord. To have a reasonable chance of meeting these targets, the current fossil fuel-based energy sector has to fundamentally change with the aim of reaching decarbonization by 2050.[11]

This will not be easy, given the deep entrenchment of fossil fuels in virtually all aspects of modern living. "Progressively replacing fossil fuels without delay" means tackling global problem with implications for almost all dimensions of social and political life. But faith communities and individuals can and have been a great force for change, through awareness, advocacy, and action. Every generation has a great opportunity to remake the world, and this is ours.

The Pontifical Council for Justice and Peace states that energy should "primarily solve the shortages of the most vulnerable and poorest populations, and, only subsequently, ensure greater consumption for those who already have plenty of energy." Advanced countries have "the moral duty of developing the use of the most complex and capital-intensive energy technologies, in order to allow poor countries to feed their development, resorting to simpler and less expensive energy technologies."[12] What this is saying is that wealthy nations should stop using simpler and less expensive energy technologies—fossil fuels—and start buying, developing, and sharing renewable energy technologies!

The priorities of Catholic energy ethics

Concretely, this means that to accomplish the essential and accelerated shift to renewable energy, society must end the use and development of coal, oil, shale gas, and tar sands. Natural gas can be a transitional fuel that builds a clean economy if the tax revenues and increased economic activity it creates are used to reform fossil fuel subsidies and construct renewable energy infrastructure.[13] Though natural gas has had many significant and often beneficial impacts upon the global economy, fracking comes with potentially grave risks to the climate and all living communities in groundwater pollution and the release of methane into the atmosphere (natural gas is a potent greenhouse gas). Policy leaders must establish correct incentives with monitored timelines to ensure that transition—and citizens must advocate for them.[14]

According to Bloomberg News, in 2013, "The race for renewable energy has passed a turning point, and there's no going back. The world is now adding more capacity for renewable power each year than coal, natural gas, and oil combined."[15] The energy revolution is already underway; this is good news. But we must accelerate the pace of change. Global society has a decade to accelerate this revolution; we have a decade to accelerate this revolution; you have a decade to accelerate this revolution.

The chain of action

How can we accelerate the revolution? Imagine a chain with three links: "unpaying," rebuilding, and choosing. Accelerating this revolution is like pulling on the chain, with each link of action connected to the ones before. First, we must recognize the hidden costs of fossil fuel energy for which we are paying knowingly or unknowingly, and "unpay" for it, ending the subsidies and other practices whereby society collectively supports dirty energy. Second, we must work collectively, through practices, purchases, and policies, to build clean energy alternatives. The third link is the personal lifestyle conversion and personal actions that further inspire acts of social love.

Indeed, this love inspires the most powerful link between ourselves and others: the tug of personal and social love that energizes us to pull on that chain of action, to dismantle, rebuild, and choose sustainable and life-giving changes, against the inertia of effort and resistance, in our collective action and personal lives.

We in what Pope John Paul II would call "superdeveloped" societies belong to the world's top 1.1 billion, who have unlimited access to energy and thus disproportionate power over the lives and futures of the planet.[16] To recognize this power, precisely as disruptive and destructive, is painful. Yet to face it squarely can be a grace and a source of empowerment. There is grace in accepting the disquieting truth of our destructive power, enduring the discomfiting prod to change, and the grace of feeling a deeper love for the earth and all who live on it. There is grace in allowing that love to move us into action that defends the vulnerable, the future, our own home.

Particular policies for awareness and advocacy

"In this framework, along with the importance of little everyday gestures, social love moves us to devise larger strategies to halt environmental degradation and to encourage a 'culture of care' which permeates all of society" (§231).

So let's get back to recycling plastic and taking shorter showers. Most of us recognize the demoralizing limitations of "little everyday gestures" that rehabilitate only one's own, private lifestyle. However, paradoxically, by taking personal action, people report feeling empowered to do more.

While advocating for global energy policies seems beyond the sphere of influence of the private citizen, in fact we are public citizens who may and should voice and vote our values in each community to which we belong according to the principle of subsidiarity. None of these are easy one-step actions. Collective action is a series of many steps, precisely because the system itself is made of up of many policies, purchases, and practices, many of them invisible. In the section that follows, I'll discuss key actions on the personal, community, and federal levels.

Personal actions

Personal action can effect large-scale, systemic change, especially when leveraged within a group. Within your own communities, your voice matters. Will this take time? Yes. How much time is up to you, but everyone must juggle competing priorities and often sacrifice lesser priorities to make space for more important ones. We do this in every part of our lives, if we are honest about choosing what is healthy, fair, and wise in the long run.

Electrifying your transportation

Society needs to electrify rapidly as much as possible, to take advantage of electricity powered by renewable energy, and the transportation sector offers a major opportunity. Even electric vehicles powered by coal are more efficient than the most efficient gas-powered engines.[17] One of the most effective actions you can take is to prioritize saving for a hybrid or electric vehicle, or finding ways to reduce your commute. In fact, college students who prioritize finding a job near their home can avoid the stress, cost, time, and carbon footprint of a commute in the first place. As a local citizen, urge your public agencies to shift city fleets to electric vehicles now.[18] This can have a major impact: New York City is transitioning half of their city staff vehicles by 2025.

Choosing renewable energy

A beautiful insight of *Laudato Si'* is that economics and technology, like art, music, or relationships, should have direction, goals, and meaning (§109). This applies to home economics! The first-time homeowner can opt for efficient appliances. If you have a 403b plan at work, stop personally investing in fossil fuels and choose socially responsible funds. If your company does not offer a fund with low-carbon options, ask for one. Choose renewable energy in your own apartment: one's utility bill can be an expression of meaning and solidarity.

Contributing to clean energy globally as a charitable act

If the top one billion causing climate change contributed $150 each to organizations that provide solar lamps and cookstoves to families in developing nations, that would be enough to cover clean solar energy for the bottom three billion who have no or only intermittent electricity.[19]

Community actions

Advocate locally for renewable energy

State representatives, municipal directors, and mayors, who are often more accessible than national Congresspeople and less mired in national politics, often have control over contracts with utilities. Through an invitation for coffee and conversation, local citizens can advocate for reducing the carbon intensity of our community's electricity and pressure utilities to increase renewable energy sources toward a target date for decarbonization. As Marie Venner, a renewable energy consultant, states, the message is that we want clean energy and we expect to have clean energy (not just renewable energy credits) and our utility to be decarbonized by a certain date. For example, 50,000 evangelicals organized by Rev Mitch Hescox have asked Texas to decarbonize by 2030.[20]

Understand legal frameworks and insist on utility policies that move toward sustainability

Utility policies that have a huge impact on the profitability and success of rooftop solar are being debated in state legislatures right now. It's important to understand these issues, communicate with your representatives about the policies you support, and then vote. Young people have a great deal of power, but if they do not vote, the power is concentrated in those blocs that do vote—and they will.

For example, "feed-in tariffs" are rates offered by a utility to purchase locally produced renewable energy. These rates encourage renewable energy developers and create jobs. However, in some states the feed-in rates have been eliminated, or low caps set on the amount of renewable energy that the utility will purchase.[21] "Net metering" allows residential or commercial customers with solar power to sell unused energy they generate back into the grid. Net metering allows customers to generate clean energy and save money, and their extra energy can moderate utilities' peak loads and reduce distribution loss from long-distance transmission, as well as create jobs in the solar industry.

Different pricing systems make a huge difference in the profitability for individual solar owners—and there are important political battles being fought far from the public eye to advance or roll back policies that support domestic solar and wind.[22] A comparison of how the same solar installation and usage would fare under different state regulations shows that in Massachusetts, a homeowner would see a profit in the first year; in Nevada, where utilities pay wholesale rather than retail price for the energy returned to the grid, the homeowner doesn't profit until year 13.

These policies influence affordability and profitability for individuals and, thus, influence the progress of the American renewable revolution. Rooftop solar is only part of the burgeoning solar scene. Take the example of New York State, which is committed to 50 percent renewable energy by 2030, which builds on industrial-scale solar and other modernizations. These goals are critical for remaining within the global budget for the remaining emissions that the atmosphere can tolerate. There is a short timeline for decarbonization. Continuing to develop fossil fuel infrastructure risks exceeding the 2°C target. Citizens must strongly advocate for a rapid shift away from fossil fuels and reject the building of new fossil fuel infrastructure.[23]

Thus, be aware of expansions of natural gas drilling in your state and its health impacts. Write to your governor and state legislators. Work with the state Catholic conferences to support renewable energy infrastructure. Take hope from the New York State ban on fracking, despite sitting on the Marcellus Shale, one of the largest natural gas deposits in the United States. If fracking exists in your state, insist on the highest standards for monitoring natural gas leaks. If leaks exceed 2 percent, the climate benefit of natural gas is lost.[24]

Federal advocacy

End subsidies for fossil fuels

A low-carbon world requires both disinvestments in fossil energy infrastructure and increased investments in solar and wind power.[25] Simply put, this means ending subsidies that perpetuate the fossil fuel infrastructure. Direct subsidies for fossil energy and fossil electricity totaled at least $480 billion globally in 2011, a sum that is six times the subsidies for renewables in 2011.[26] Post-tax subsidies that incorporate the externalities of environmental damage of energy consumption and ordinary consumption taxes are even higher. According to the International Money Fund global post-tax subsidies were $4.9 trillion in 2013, much higher than previous estimates, and are projected to reach $5.3 trillion in 2015.

Energy subsidy reform would have tremendous effects on fiscal, environmental, and physical well-being. Eliminating post-tax subsidies will raise government revenues, slash global CO_2 emissions, and reduce premature deaths from air pollution.[27] As the *Economist* reported, "The plunging price of oil, coupled with advances in clean energy and conservation, offers politicians around the world the chance to rationalize energy policy. They can get rid of billions of dollars of distorting subsidies, especially for dirty fuels, whilst shifting taxes towards carbon use. A cheaper, greener, and more reliable energy future could be within reach."[28]

These subsidies for fossil fuel exploration and development are politically entrenched and tightly lodged in the US tax code. Collective action to restructure them are not easy one-step actions. Yet there is power in traditional, old fashioned, political advocacy like personal letter writing. Though online petitions swamp our email boxes, writing a personal message to congressional leaders remains more effective. I've written to my own senator and received a letter stating she would share my support for a carbon price at committee discussions.

Other ways to leverage your voice include learning about the fossil fuel investment policies of any group you belong to and advocating for divestment and reinvestment. When grounded in a comprehensive advocacy platform including a call for a carbon price, divestment sends a significant moral message.[29]

Having tackled the first link, "unpaying" for dirty energy, how should we pay for clean energy instead? I'll discuss two important issues: carbon pricing and the Green Climate Fund.

A realistic carbon price

Collectively, society ignores the true costs of fossil fuels not only by subsidies, but by externalizing the costs of pollution. Cheap fossil fuels are really not cheap—it's just that the true costs of pollution have been shifted somewhere else, and the public is paying them another way. This is called "externalizing costs." The costs might be shifted to the disaster relief budget line, as with Hurricanes Sandy and Katrina. As retired Navy admiral and climate security expert David Titley says, by paying the costs of disaster relief and storm cleanup, we are paying a climate tax for which no one voted. Or, costs are piled onto the health care budget line, for those suffering from asthma, cancer, malnutrition, or even increasing tropical diseases such as Zika.[30]

A carbon price identifies the true costs of pollution and incorporates these costs into products made with fossil fuels. This allows market mechanisms to properly process the full costs of carbon energy. This discourages buying products that are carbon intensive and incentivizes investments into clean energy. Carbon-free technology becomes more reasonable and attractive. Furthermore, a carbon fee creates revenues that may be used to reduce taxes or build infrastructure, such as sanitation and telecommunications or even clean energy production and modernized electrical grids.

While estimates for the social cost of carbon range from $7 to $85 per ton and up, a recent White House report calculates the social cost of carbon at $38 per ton.[31] One conservative policy suggests a revenue-neutral carbon tax—that is, it returns the funds collected through tax reductions to corporations and individuals, compensates individuals for any increased energy costs, and would increase economic growth, jobs and competition, and avoids new spending by government.[32] Other policies advocate returning a dividend to consumers alone. Multiple policy paths have been devised by many of the world's leading economists, among whom there is significant consensus that a carbon price is one of the most effective ways to simplify, equalize, and incentivize clean energy use.[33] However structured, the price must be high enough to drive down CO_2 emissions, incentivize conservation, and spur the development of alternative energy sources.[34]

Global justice: Addressing ecological debt

A second mechanism for building a renewable system is the Green Climate Fund, an international fund which recognizes the obligations of ecological debt. "As the bishops of Bolivia have stated, 'the countries which have benefited from a high degree of industrialization, at the cost of enormous emissions of greenhouse gases, have a greater responsibility for providing a solution to the problems they have caused'" (§170). Researchers correctly calculate that "The cost for providing this access can be as high as \$90 billion per year . . . but it pales compared with the \$1100 billion cost . . . for decarbonizing . . . sufficiently to mitigate 13 billion tons/year of CO_2 emission by 2030."[35] The pope reminds us, "these are primarily ethical decisions, rooted in solidarity between all peoples" (§172).

Paying into the climate fund assures that renewable energy technologies are made available to developing nations. Developing nations also have a responsibility to develop cleaner energy, but they may require technological transfer, technological assistance, and funding for infrastructure, enabling the developing nations to climb the clean renewable ladder. It will benefit no one if developing nations use fossil fuels and climb this dirty and dangerous ladder out of poverty. And in fact developing nations are leapfrogging conventional technologies in many parts of the world.[36] Thus, building a clean energy ladder for the 1.1 billion without power is not only essential, it is possible.[37] This is a policy plank on which the US bishops have taken a stand, and Catholics can support their advocacy.

Conclusion

Our direct and indirect actions as members of society have profound ethical meaning. Bishop McElroy explains powerfully why addressing social sin is "neither optional nor secondary." He writes:

> Poverty . . . is the result of countless specific human actions with varying degrees of responsibility that give rise to social structure and practices imbued with selfishness and evil. The category of intrinsic evil cannot capture the type of entrenched evil inherent in poverty. Yet Francis clearly teaches that alleviating the grave evil of poverty must be at the very heart of the church's mission. It is neither optional nor secondary.[38]

The insistent call to counteract poverty applies to care of creation as well, as the cry of the poor joins the cry of the earth. We are our brothers' and sisters' keepers, whether on the distant shores where salty water encroaching on islands are driving waves of climate refugees, to polluted areas in our own cities.

The path to a green future that expresses our faith and environmental concern with integrity is indeed taken with the two steps of charity and justice and actions that transform one's personal and community life. Collective actions are made personally meaningful by the integrity of one's ongoing lifestyle conversion to a low-carbon and sustainable lifestyle. And engaging our vocation as Christians in the public square calls for new attention to energy ethics that acknowledge the real impact of structures that shape the "macro-relationships, social, economic, and political."

It is essential to remember that with all the technicalities about greenhouse gas emissions in parts per million, megawatts of electricity, and financial investment mechanisms, climate change is not merely an economic issue, a technological problem, or a partisan, political spat to be conducted in the trenches of the culture wars. It is a human issue, and most profoundly of all, it is a summons to faith.

> Any technical solution which science claims to offer will be powerless to solve the serious problems of our world if humanity loses its compass, if we lose sight of the great motivations which make it possible for us to live in harmony, to make sacrifices and to treat others well. Believers themselves must constantly feel challenged to live in a way consonant with their faith and not to contradict it by their actions. They need to be encouraged to be ever open to God's grace and to draw constantly from their deepest convictions about love, justice and peace. (§200)

Responding to the challenge of climate change through social love puts that faith into action. "When we feel that God is calling us to intervene with others in these social dynamics, we should realize that this too is part of our spirituality, which is an exercise of charity and, as such, matures and sanctifies us" (§231). Through *Laudato Si'*, Pope Francis sends a personal invitation. Renewing our common home begins with you . . . and it ends with us.

Questions

1   How does the teaching regarding "social love" transform your view of personal and communal ethical responsibilities?

2   In what way does responding climate change represent an expression of Catholic faith?

3   How do the claims of energy ethics for personal conversion and behavioral change differ from the claims of other kinds of ethical questions?

4   Given the challenges to creating systemic change, what gives you the most hope?

5   What kinds of action for meaningful and large-scale change express your own identity and values?

Notes

1 Pope Benedict XVI, *Caritas in veritate* [Encyclical: On Integral Human Development in Charity and Truth] (2009), §2.

2 Francis, Address to General Assembly of the United Nations, September 25, 2015, http://w2.vatican.va/content/francesco/en/speeches/2015/september/documents/papa-francesco_20150925_onu-visita.html.

3 See William P. George, "Catholic Theology, International Law, and the Global Climate Crisis," in *Confronting the Climate Crisis: Catholic Theological Perspectives*, ed. Jame Schaefer (Milwaukee: Marquette University Press, 2011), 177–98.

4 Erin Lothes Biviano, "Worldviews on Fire: Understanding the Inspiration for Congregational Religious Environmentalism," *CrossCurrents* 62, no. 4 (2012): 495–511.

5 Creating awareness and overcoming the knowledge gap requires addressing the four dimensions of the knowledge gap. These are literacy limits, cognitive limits, personal interests, and willed ignorance. See Erin Lothes Biviano, *Inspired Sustainability: Planting Seeds for Action* (Maryknoll, NY: Orbis Books, 2016), 61–84.

6 Erin Lothes Biviano, "Come with Me into the Fields: Inspiring Creation Ministry among Faith Communities," *New Theology Review* 26, no. 2. (2014): 33–42.

7 Lothes, *Inspired Sustainability*, 94–110.

8 http://climate.nasa.gov/scientific-consensus/; IPCC: *Climate Change 2014: Synthesis Report. Contribution of Working Groups I, II and III to the Fifth Assessment Report of the Intergovernmental Panel on Climate Change*, ed. R. K. Pachauri and L. A. Meyer (Geneva, Switzerland: IPCC, 2014), 151.

9 Veerabhadran Ramanathan and Gregory Carmichael, "Global and Regional Climate Changes Due to Black Carbon," *Nature Geoscience* 1, no. 4 (2008): 221–27.

10 Veerabhadran Ramanathan, "The Two Worlds Approach for Mitigating Air Pollution and Climate Change," in *Sustainable Humanity, Sustainable Nature, Our Responsibility, Pontificiae Academiae Scientiarum Extra Series 41/Pontificiae Academiae Scientiarum Socialium Acta* 19, ed. Partha S. Dasgupta, Veerabhadran Ramanathan, and Marcelo Sánchez Sorondo (Vatican City: Pontifical Academy of Sciences, 2015), 285–300.

11 To achieve a 100 percent renewable energy sector by 2050, 42 percent renewable energy is needed by 2030, with increasingly accelerated expansion of renewable energy from 2030 to 2050. Sarah Wykes, et al., "Energy in the Post-2015 Development Framework," *Catholic Agency for Overseas Development (CAFOD)* (2014): 6 note 24. http://pubs.iied.org/pdfs/G03811.pdf.

12 Pontifical Council for Justice and Peace, *Energy, Justice and Peace: A Reflection on Energy in the Current Context of Development and Environmental Protection* (Citta del Vaticano: Libreria Editrice Vaticana, 2014).

13   Jason Bordoff, "Why the Shale Revolution is More Boon than Bane," *Financial Times* (June 8, 2014), https://www.ft.com/content/fcea14a2-e66d-11e3-bbf5-00144feabdc0.

14   Erin Lothes Biviano, David Cloutier, Elaine Padilla, Christiana Z. Peppard, and Jame Schaefer, "Catholic Moral Traditions and Energy Ethics for the Twenty-First Century," *Journal of Moral Theology* 5, no. 2 (2016): 1–36.

15   Tom Randall, "Fossil Fuels Just Lost the Race Against Renewables," *Bloomberg Business* (April 14, 2015), www.bloomberg.com/news/articles/2015-04-14/fossil-fuels-just-lost-the-race-against-renewables.

16   John Paul II, *Sollicitudo rei socialis* [Encyclical: On Social Concern] (1987), §28.

17   Marie Venner, Chair, Climate Change, Energy, and Sustainability and Environmental Maintenance Special Task force of the Transportation Research Board, personal communication, June 2016.

18   Liam Dillon and Chris Megerian, "California Lawmakers Unplug the State's Electric Car Program," *Los Angeles Times*, June 24, 2016, http://www.latimes.com/politics/la-pol-ca-clean-vehicle-rebate-project-no-money-20160616-snap-story.html.

19   Marie Venner, personal communication.

20   Ibid.

21   Policy Matters Ohio, "Feed-in Rates at Electric Utilities," http://www.policymattersohio.org/feed-in-rates-nov2012.

22   Solar Energy Industries Association, "Issues and Policies: Net Metering," http://www.seia.org/policy/distributed-solar/net-metering. Scott Clavenna, "What If Nevada's Solar Regulators Came to Massachusetts?," http://www.greentechmedia.com/articles/read/What-if-Nevadas-Solar-Regulators-Came-to-Massachusetts.

23   Marie Venner, personal communication.

24   A study from the National Center for Atmospheric Research concluded that unless leaks can be kept below 2 percent, gas lacks any climate advantage over coal. Tom M. L. Wigley, "Coal to Gas: The Influence of Methane Leakage," *Climatic Change* 108, no. 3 (2011): 606.

25   Mark A. Delucchi and Mark Z. Jacobson, "Providing All Global Energy with Wind, Water, and Solar Power, Part I: Technologies, Energy Resources, Quantities and Areas of Infrastructure, and Materials," *Energy Policy* 39, no. 3 (2011): 21.

26   David McCollum, et al., "Energy Investments Under Climate Policy: A Comparison of Global Models," *Climate Change Economics*, LIMITS Special Issue (2014): 20.

27   David Coady, et al., "How Large Are Global Energy Subsidies?," http://www.imf.org/external/pubs/ft/wp/2015/wp15105.pdf., 5,6. Energy subsidies are a highly inefficient way to provide support to low-income households since most of the benefits from energy subsidies are typically captured by rich households.

28   "Seize the Day: The Fall in the Price of Oil and Gas Provides a Once-in-a-Generation Opportunity to Fix Bad Energy Policies," *The Economist*, January 17, 2015.

29 See Erin Lothes, "The Catholic Case for Divestment," http://catholicclimatemovement.global/catholic-case-for-fossil-fuel-divestment/

30 http://www.climatecentral.org/news/zika-virus-climate-change-19970.

31 United States Government Interagency Working Group on Social Cost of Carbon, "Technical Update of the Social Cost of Carbon for Regulatory Impact Analysis under Executive Order 12866" (Washington, DC, 2013).

32 See Partnership for Responsible Growth, http://www.partnershipforresponsiblegrowth.org/team/.

33 Peter Cramton, David J. C. MacKay, Axel Ockenfels, and Steven Stoft, "Global Carbon Pricing We Will If You Will," December 2015; http://carbon-price.com/wp-content/uploads/Global-Carbon-Pricing-cramton-mackay-okenfels-stoft.pdf and http://carbon-price.com/faq. See also Daniel R. DiLeo, "Faithful Citizenship in the age of Climate Change: Why U.S. Catholics Should Advocate for a National Carbon Tax," *Journal of Catholic Social Thought* 11, no. 2 (2014): 431–64.

34 Michael J Graetz, "Energy Policy: Past or Prologue?" *Daedalus, the Journal of the American Academy of Arts & Sciences* 141, no. 2 (2012): 39.

35 Ramanathan, "The Two Worlds Approach for Mitigating Air Pollution and Climate Change," 294.

36 "According to a worldwide analysis by Bloomberg New Energy Finance (BNEF), developing countries' renewable energy capacity grew 143 percent between 2008 and 2013, while OECD nations saw only 84 percent growth." Jeff Spross, "How Renewables in Developing Countries Are Leapfrogging Traditional Power," (November 4, 2014). https://thinkprogress.org/how-renewables-in-developing-countries-are-leapfrogging-traditional-power-337766c13f3a#.8871y3qvc.

37 "Power to the Powerless," *The Economist*, 418, no. 8978 (February 27, 2016): 49–50, http://www.economist.com/news/international/21693581-new-electricity-system-emerging-bring-light-worlds-poorest-key.

38 Bishop Robert W. McElroy, "A Church for the Poor," *America Magazine* 209, no. 11 (October 21, 2013): 15.

SELECTED BIBLIOGRAPHY

Alighieri, Dante. *Inferno*. Translated by Allen Mandelbaum. New York: Bantam, 1980.

Alighieri, Dante. *Paradiso*. Translated by Allen Mandelbaum. New York: Bantam, 1984.

Annett, Anthony. 'Human Flourishing, the Common Good, and Catholic Social Teaching'. In *World Happiness Report 2016: Special Rome Edition (Vol. II)*. Edited by Jeffrey Sachs, Leonardo Becchetti and Anthony Annett, 38–65. New York: UN Sustainable Development Solutions Network, 2016.

Aquinas, Thomas. *Summa Theologica*. Translated by Fathers of the English Dominican Province. 2nd and Revised ed. London: Burns, Oats & Washburne Ltd., 1920.

Aristotle. *Aristotle's Nicomachean Ethics: A New Translation*. Translated by Robert C. Bartlett and Susan D. Collins. Chicago, IL: University of Chicago Press, 2011.

Augustine. *City of God*. Translated by Henry Bettenson. New York: Penguin Books, 2003.

Barbour, Ian. *When Science Meets Religion: Enemies, Strangers, or Partners?* New York: HarperCollins, 2000.

Barnosky, Anthony, Nicholas Matzke, Susumu Tomiya, Guinevere O. U. Wogan, Brian Swartz, Tiago B. Quental, Charles Marshall, Jenny L. McGuire, Emily L. Lindsey, Kaitlin C. Maguire, Ben Mersey and Elizabeth A. Ferrer. 'Has the Earth's Sixth Mass Extinction Already Arrived?' *Nature* 471 (2011): 51–7.

Barron, Robert. *Catholicism: A Journey to the Heart of the Faith*. New York: Crown Publishing, 2011.

Bartholomew, Ecumenical Patriarch. Address at the Environmental Symposium, Saint Barbara Greek Orthodox Church, Santa Barbara, California. Istanbul, Turkey: The Ecumenical Patriarchate of Constantinople, 1997.

Beck, K. George, Kenneth Zimmerman, Jeffrey D. Schardt, Jeffrey Stone, Ronald R. Lukens, Sarah Reichard, John Randall, Allegra A. Cangelosi, Diane Cooper and John Peter Thompson. 'Invasive Species Defined in a Policy Context: Recommendations from the Federal Invasive Species Advisory Committee'. *Invasive Plant Science and Management* 1 (2008): 414–21.

Bekoff, Marc. *The Emotional Lives of Animals: A Leading Scientist Explores Animal Joy, Sorrow, and Empathy – and Why They Matter*. Novato, CA: New World Library, 2007.

Bell, Daniel M., Jr. *The Economy of Desire: Christianity and Capitalism in a Postmodern World*. Grand Rapids, MI: Baker, 2012.

Benedict XVI. Address to the Clergy of the Diocese of Bolzano-Bressanone, 6 August 2008.

Benedict XVI. *Caritas in veritate* [Encyclical On Integral Human Development in Charity and Truth], 29 June 2009.

Benedict XVI. Meeting of the Holy Father Benedict XVI with the Clergy of the Dioceses of Belluno-Feltre and Treviso, 24 July 2007.

Biviano, Erin Lothes. 'The Catholic Case for Divestment'. Available online: http://catholicclimatemovement.global/catholic-case-for-fossil-fuel-divestment/.

Biviano, Erin Lothes. 'Come with Me into the Fields: Inspiring Creation Ministry among Faith Communities'. *New Theology Review* 26, no. 2. (2014): 33–42.

Biviano, Erin Lothes. *Inspired Sustainability: Planting Seeds for Action*. Maryknoll, New York: Orbis Books, 2016.

Biviano, Erin Lothes. 'Worldviews on Fire: Understanding the Inspiration for Congregational Religious Environmentalism'. *CrossCurrents* 62, no. 4 (2012): 495–511.

Biviano, Erin Lothes, David Cloutier, Elaine Padilla, Christiana Z. Peppard and Jame Schaefer. 'Catholic Moral Traditions and Energy Ethics for the Twenty-First Century'. *Journal of Moral Theology* 5, no. 2 (2016): 1–36.

Bolivian Bishops Conference. 'El Universo, Don de Dios para la vida [Pastoral Letter on the Environment and Human Development in Bolivia]'. 23 March 2012. Available online: http://www.iglesiasantacruz.org/wp-content/uploads/2012/03/el_universo_don_de_dios_para_la_vida.pdf.

Boff, Leonardo. *Cry of the Earth, Cry of the Poor*. Maryknoll, NY: Orbis Books, 1997.

Bowles, Samuel. *The Moral Economy: Why Good Incentives are no Substitute for Good Citizens*. New Haven: Yale University Press, 2016.

BP. *Statistical Review of World Energy 2015. Data Workbook*. Available online: http://www.bp.com/en/global/corporate/energy-economics/statistical-review-of-world-energy/downloads.html.

British Broadcasting Corporation. 'How Many Earths Do We Need?' Available online: http://www.bbc.com/news/magazine-33133712.

Bullerjahn, George, Robert M. McKay, Timothy W. Davis, David B. Baker, Gregory L. Boyer, Lesley V. D'Anglada, Gregory J. Doucette, Jeff C. Ho, Elena G. Irwin, Catherine L. Kling, Raphael M. Kudela, Rainer Kurmayer, Anna M. Michalak, Joseph D. Ortizm, Timothy G. Otten, Hans W. Paerl, Boqiang Qin, Brent L. Sohngen, Richard P. Stumpf, Petra M. Visser and Steven W. Wilhelm. 'Global Solutions to Regional Problems: Collecting Global Expertise to Address the Problem of Harmful Cyanobacterial Blooms. A Lake Erie Case Study'. *Harmful Algae* 54 (2016): 223–38.

Byron, William J. 'Ten Building Blocks of Catholic Social Teaching'. *America Magazine*, 31 October 1998. Available online: http://americamagazine.org/issue/100/ten-building-blocks-catholic-social-teaching.

Campbell, Neil A. *Biology: Third Edition*. San Francisco: Benjamin-Cummings Pub Co, 1993.

Cardille, Jeffrey and Marie Lambois. 'From the Redwood Forest to the Gulf Stream Waters: Human Signature Nearly Ubiquitous in Representative US Landscapes'. *Frontiers in Ecology and the Environment* 8 (2010): 130–4.

Carlo Petrini. *Slow Food Nation: Why Our Food Should be Good, Clean and Fair*. New York: Rizzoli, 2007.

Catechism of the Catholic Church. Citta del Vaticano: Libreria Editrice Vaticana, 1993.

Cecchetti, Stephen and Enisse Kharroubi. 'Reassessing the Impact of Finance on Growth'. *BIS Working Papers* 381 (2012): 1–17.

Christie, Douglas E. *The Blue Sapphire of the Mind: Notes for a Contemplative Ecology*. Oxford: Oxford University Press, 2013.

Christie, Douglas E. 'The Eternal Present: Slow Knowledge and the Renewal of Time'. *Buddhist Christian Studies* 33 (2013): 13–21.

CIDSE. 'Catholic Bishops' statement in Lima on the road to Paris'. Available online: http://www.cidse.org/articles/item/675-catholic-bishops-statement-in-lima-on-the-road-to-paris.html.

Clark, Duncan. 'A Complete Guide to Carbon Offsetting'. *The Guardian*, 16 September 2011. Available online: http://www.theguardian.com/environment/2011/sep/16/carbon-offset-projects-carbon-emissions.

Clavenna, Scott. 'What If Nevada's Solar Regulators Came to Massachusetts?' Available online: http://www.greentechmedia.com/articles/read/What-if-Nevadas-Solar-Regulators-Came-to-Massachusetts.

Clément, Olivier. *The Roots of Christian Mysticism*. New York: New City Press, 2008.

Clifford, Anne M. 'Foundations for a Catholic Ecological Theology of God'. In *And God Saw that it was Good': Catholic Theology and the Environment*. Edited by Drew Christiansen and Walter Grazer, 19–46. Washington, DC: US Catholic Conference, 1996.

Cline, Elizabeth. *Overdressed: The Shockingly High Cost of Cheap Fashion*. New York: Penguin Group, 2012.

Coady, David, Ian Parry, Louis Sears and Baoping Shang. 'How Large Are Global Energy Subsidies?' Available online: http://www.imf.org/external/pubs/ft/wp/2015/wp15105.pdf.

Coakley, Sarah. 'Sacrifice Regained: Evolution, Cooperation, and God'. Gifford Lectures, 2012. Available online: http://www.giffordlectures.org/lectures/sacrifice-regained-evolution-cooperation-and-god.

Cohn, Alain, Ernst Fehr and Michel Andre Marechal. 'Business Culture and Dishonesty in the Banking Industry'. *Nature* 516 (2014): 86–9.

Collins, Robin. 'The Fine-Tuning of the Cosmos: A Fresh Look at Its Implications'. In *The Blackwell Companion to Science and Christianity*. Edited by J. B. Stump and Alan G. Padgett, 207–19. Malden, MA: Blackwell, 2012.

Committee on Geoengineering Climate: Technical Evaluation and Discussion of Impacts, Board on Atmospheric Sciences and Climate, Ocean Studies Board, Division on Earth and Life Studies, National Research Council. *Climate Intervention: Carbon Dioxide Removal and Reliable Sequestration*. Washington DC: National Academies Press, 2015.

Committee on Geoengineering Climate: Technical Evaluation and Discussion of Impacts, Board on Atmospheric Sciences and Climate, Ocean Studies Board, Division on Earth and Life Studies, National Research Council. *Climate Intervention: Reflecting Sunlight to Cool Earth*. Washington, DC: National Academies Press, 2015.

Consejo Episcopal Latinamericano (CELAM). 'Evangelization in Latin America's Present and Future: Final Document of the Third General Conference of the Latin American Episcopate'. In *Puebla and Beyond: Documentation and Commentary*. Edited by John Eagleson and Philip Scharper, 264–6. Maryknoll, NY: Orbis, 1979.

Consejo Episcopal Latinamericano (CELAM). 'Medellín (Poverty of the Church)', 1968. Available online: http://theolibrary.shc.edu/resources/medpov.htm.

Covert, Brad. 'Race Best Predicts Whether You Live Near Pollution: Environmental Racism Extends Far Beyond Flint'. *The Nation*, 18 February 2016. Available online: http://www.thenation.com/article/race-best-predicts-whether-you-live-near-pollution/.

Cramton, Peter, David J. C. MacKay, Axel Ockenfels and Steven Stoft. 'Global Carbon Pricing We Will If You Will'. December 2015. Available online: http://carbon-price.com/wp-content/uploads/Global-Carbon-Pricing-cramton-mackay-okenfels-stoft.pdf.

Crary, Jonathan. *24/7: Late Capitalism and the Ends of Sleep*. London: Verso, 2014.

Dainat, Benjamin, Jay D. Evans, Yan Ping Chen, Laurent Gauthier and Peter Neumann. 'Predictive Markers of Honey Bee Colony Collapse'. *PLoS* 7 (2012): e32151: 1–9.

Darwin, Charles. *On the Origin of Species: A Facsimile of the First Edition*. Cambridge, MA: Harvard University Press, 1964.

Daughton, C. G. and T. A. Ternes. 'Pharmaceuticals and Personal Care Products in the Environment: Agents of Subtle Change?' *Environmental Health Perspectives*, 107 Supplement 6 (1999): 907–38.

Dávila, María Teresa. 'The Role of the Social Sciences in Catholic Social Thought: The Incarnational Principle of the Preferential Option for the Poor and Being Able to "See" in the Rubric "See, Judge, Act"'. *Journal of Catholic Social Thought* 9, no. 2 (Summer 2012): 229–44.

Davis, Ellen. *Biblical Prophecy: Perspectives for Christian Theology, Discipleship, and Ministry*. Louisville: Westminster John Knox, 2014.

Davis, Ellen. *Scripture, Culture, Agriculture: An Agrarian Reading of the Bible*. Cambridge: Cambridge University Press, 2009.

Dawkins, Richard. *The God Delusion*. Boston: Houghton Mifflin, 2006.

Deane-Drummond, Celia. *The Wisdom of the Liminal: Evolution and Other Animals in Human Becoming*. Grand Rapids: Eerdmans, 2014.

Delucchi, Mark A. and Mark Z. Jacobson. 'Providing All Global Energy with Wind, Water, and Solar Power, Part I: Technologies, Energy Resources, Quantities and Areas of Infrastructure, and Materials'. *Energy Policy* 39, no. 3 (2011): 1154–69.

Dennis, Alexander. 'Creation and Evolution'. In *The Blackwell Companion to Science and Christianity*. Edited by J. B. Stump and Alan G. Padgett, 231–45. Malden, MA: Blackwell, 2012.

DiLeo, Daniel R. 'Faithful Citizenship in the age of Climate Change: Why U.S. Catholics Should Advocate for a National Carbon Tax'. *Journal of Catholic Social Thought* 11, no. 2 (2014): 431–64.

Dobzhansky, Theodosius. 'Nothing in Biology Makes Sense Except in the Light of Evolution'. *The American Biology Teacher* 35 (1973): 125–29.

Dudgeon, David, Angela H. Arthington, Mark O. Gessner, Zen-Ichiro Kawabata, Duncan J. Knowler, Christian Lévêque, Robert J. Naiman, Anne-Hélène Prieur-Richard, Doris Soto, Melanie L. J. Stiassny and Caroline A. Sullivan. 'Freshwater Biodiversity: Importance, Threats, Status, and Conservation Challenges'. *Biological Reviews* 81 (2006): 163–82.

Dunham, Scott A. *The Trinity and Creation in Augustine: An Ecological Analysis*. Albany: SUNY, 2008.

Edenhofer, Ottmar, Christian Flachsland, and Brigitte Knopf. 'Science and Religion in Dialogue over the Global Commons'. *Nature Climate Change* 5 (2015): 907–9.

Edenhofer, Ottmar, Christian Flachsland, Kai Lessmann and Michael Jakob. 'The Atmosphere as a Global Commons – Challenges for International Cooperation and Governance'. In *The Handbook on the Macroeconomics of Climate Change*. Edited by Willi Semmler and Lucas Bernard, 260–96. Oxford: Oxford University Press, 2015.

Edenhofer, Ottmar, Michael Jakob, Felix Creutzig, Christian Flachsland, Sabine Fuss, Martin Kowarsch, Kai Lessmann, Linus Mattauch, Jan Siegmeier and Jan Christoph Steckel. 'Closing the Emission Price Gap'. *Global Environmental Change* 31 (2015): 132–43.

Edwards, Denis. '"Sublime Communion": The Theology of the Natural World in *Laudato Si*", *Theological Studies* 77 (2016): 377–91.

Elias, Scott. 'The Problem of Conifer Species Migration Lag in the Pacific Northwest Region since the Last Glaciation'. *Quaternary Science Reviews* 77 (2013): 55–69.

Ellis, Erle. 'Sustaining Biodiversity and People in the World's Anthropogenic Biomes'. *Current Opinion in Environmental Sustainability* 5 (2013): 368–72.

Energy Information Administration (EIA). *Updated Capital Cost Estimates for Utility Scale Electricity Plants*. Washington, DC: U.S. Department of Energy, 2013. Available online: https://www.eia.gov/forecasts/capitalcost/.

Estes, James, Alexander Burdin and Daniel F. Doak. 'Sea Otters, Kelp Forests, and the Extinction of Steller's Sea Cow'. *Proceedings of the National Academy of Sciences* 113 (2016): 880–5.

Etzioni, Amitai. 'The Moral Effects of Economic Teaching'. *Sociological Forum* 30, no 1. (2015): 228–33.

European Union- European Commission-Joint Research Commission. 'CO2 Time Series 1990-2013 Per Capita for World Countries'. Available online: http://edgar.jrc.ec.europa.eu/overview.php?v=CO2ts_pc1990-2013.

European Union- European Commission-Joint Research Commission. 'CO2 Time Series 1990-2014 Per Capita for World Countries'. Available online: http://edgar.jrc.ec.europa.eu/overview.php?v=CO2ts_pc1990-2014&sort=des9.

Finocchiaro, Maurice A. 'The Copernican Revolution and the Galileo Affair'. In *The Blackwell Companion to Science and Christianity*. Edited by J. B. Stump and Alan G. Padgett, 14–25. Malden, MA: Blackwell, 2012.

Francis. Address to the Members of the General Assembly of the United Nations Organization. New York, 23 September 2015.

Francis. *Amoris Laetitia* [Apostolic Exhortation On the Love of the Family], 19 March 2016.

Francis. 'A Big Heart open to God'. *America* 209, no. 8 (30 September 2013). Available online: http://americamagazine.org/pope-interview.

Francis. *Evangelii gaudium* [Apostolic Exhortation on the Proclamation of the Gospel in the Modern World], 24 November 2013.

Francis. *Laudato Si'* [Encyclical On the Care of our Common Home], 29 May 2015.

Francis. Message for the World Day of Migrants and Refugees, 17 January 2016.

Francis. 'Show Mercy to our Common Home', Message for the Celebration of the World Day for the Care of Creation, 1 September 2016.

Francis. Speech at World Meeting of Popular Movements, Santa Cruz de la Sierra, Bolivia, 9 July 2015.

Francis and Andrea Tornielli. *The Name of God is Mercy (A Conversation with Andrea Tornielli)*. Translated by Oonagh Stransky. New York: Random House, 2016.

Futuyma, Douglas. *Evolutionary Biology*. 2nd ed. Sunderland, MA: Sinauer Associates, 1986.

Gaillardetz, Richard R. 'The Ecclesiological Foundation of Modern Social Teaching'. In *Modern Social Teaching: Commentaries and Interpretations*. Edited by Kenneth R. Himes, 72–98. Washington, DC: Georgetown University Press, 2005.

George, William P. 'Catholic Theology, International Law, and the Global Climate Crisis'. In *Confronting the Climate Crisis: Catholic Theological Perspectives*. Edited by Jame Schaefer, 177–98. Milwaukee: Marquette University Press, 2011.

Gerber, P. J., H. Steinfeld, B. Henderson, A. Mottet, C. Opio, J. Dijkman, A. Falcucci and G. Tempio. *Tackling Climate Change through Livestock: A Global Assessment of Emissions and Mitigation Opportunities*. Rome: Food and Agriculture Organization of the United Nations (FAO), 2013.

Global Commission on the Economy and Climate. *Better Growth, Better Climate: The Synthesis Report*, 2014. Available online: http://www.newclimateeconomy. report.

Gordon, Robert. *The Rise and Fall of American Growth*. Princeton: Princeton University Press, 2016.

Gradstein, Felix M., James G. Ogg, Mark D. Schmitz and Gabi M. Ogg. *The Geologic Time Scale 2012*. 2 vol. Oxford: Elsevier, 2012.

Graetz, Michael J. 'Energy Policy: Past or Prologue?' *Daedalus, the Journal of the American Academy of Arts & Sciences* 141, no. 2 (2012): 31–44.

Graham, Ruth. 'An *F* in Science: Why Should America's Crisis of Scientific Illiteracy Concern Catholics?' *U.S. Catholic* 80 (December 2015): 13–17.

Grubb, Michael, Jean Charles Hourcade and Karsten Neuhoff. *Planetary Economics: Energy, Climate Change and the Three Domains of Sustainable Development*. New York: Routledge, 2013.

Grubler, Arnulf. 'The Costs of the French Nuclear Scale-up: A Case of Negative Learning by Doing'. *Energy Policy* 38, no. 9 (2010): 5174–88. doi:10.1016/j. enpol.2010.05.003.

Guardini, Romano. *The End of the Modern World: A Search for Orientation*. London: Sheed and Ward, 1957.

Gutiérrez, Gustavo. 'Friends of God, Friends of the Poor'. In *The Density of the Present: Selected Writings*. Translated by Margaret Wilde 149–50. Maryknoll: Orbis, 1999.

Gutiérrez, Gustavo. *The God of Life*. Maryknoll, NY: Orbis, 1991.

Gutiérrez, Gustavo. 'New Things Today: A Rereading of *Rerum Novarum*'. In *The Density of the Present: Selected Writings* 53–5. Maryknoll, NY: Orbis, 1999.

Gutiérrez, Gustavo. *On Job: God-Talk and the Suffering of the Innocent*. Maryknoll, NY: Orbis, 1987.

Gutiérrez, Gustavo. 'Option for the Poor'. In *Mysterium Liberationis: Fundamental Concepts of Liberation Theology*. Edited by Ignacio Ellacuría and Jon Sobrino. Translated by Robert R. Barr 235–50. Maryknoll: Orbis Books, 1993.

Gutiérrez, Gustavo. 'The Option for the Poor Arises from Faith in Christ'.
Translated by Robert Lassalle-Klein with James Nickoloff and Susan Sullivan.
Theological Studies 70 (2009): 317–26.

Gutiérrez, Gustavo. *A Theology of Liberation*. 15th Anniversary Edition.
Translated by Caridad Inda and John Eagleson. Maryknoll: Orbis, 1988.

Haeckel, Ernst. *Generelle Morphologie der Organismen: Allegemeine Grundzüge
der organischen Formen-wissenschaft, mechanisch begründet durch die von
Charles Darwin reformirte Descendenz-Theorie*. Berlin: Georg Reimer, 1866.

Hammer, Joshua. 'Is a Lack of Water to Blame for the Conflict in Syria?'
Smithsonian Magazine, June 2013. Available online: http://www.
smithsonianmag.com/innovation/is-a-lack-of-water-to-blame-for-the-conflict-in-
syria-72513729/?no-ist.

Hanh, Thich Nhat. *The Heart of Understanding: Commentaries on the
Prajnaparamita Heart Sutra*. Berkeley, CA: Parallax Press, 2009.

Hausherr, Irénée. *Penthos: The Doctrine of Compunction in the Christian East*.
Translated by Anselm Hufstader, OSB. Kalamazoo, MI: Cistercian Publications,
1982.

Hawken, Paul, Amory B. Lovins, and L. Hunter Lovins. *Natural Capitalism:
Creating the next Industrial Revolution*. New York: Little, Brown and Co, 2000.

Hayes, Zachary. *A Window to the Divine: Creation Theology*. Winona, MN:
Anselm, 2009.

Heinberg, R. *The Party's Over*. Gabriola Island, British Columbia: New Society
Publishers, 2005.

Helliwell, John, Haifang Huang, and Shun Wang. '"The Distribution of World
Happiness'." In *World Happiness Report 2016 Update (Vol. I)*. Edited by John
Helliwell, Richard Layard, and Jeffrey Sachs, 8–48. New York: UN Sustainable
Development Solutions Network, 2016.

Honoré, Carl. *In Praise of Slowness: Challenging the Cult of Speed*. New York:
HarperOne, 2005.

'Hope from the Pope'. *Nature* 522, no. 7557 (25 June 2015): 391.

Hopkins, Dwight. 'Holistic Health and Healing: Environmental Racism and
Ecological Justice'. *Currents in Theology and Mission* 36, no. 1 (February
2009): 5–19.

Horan, Daniel P. 'Living la Vida Justicia: Pope Francis and "Liberation Theology"'.
America Magazine (17 March 2013). Available online: http://americamagazine.
org/content/all-things/living-la-vida-justicia-pope-francis-and-liberation-theology.

House, Adrian. *Francis of Assisi*. New York: Paulist Press, 2003.

Howarth, Francis. 'Environmental Impacts of Classical Biological Control'. *Annual
Review of Entomology* 36 (1991): 485–509.

Ignatius. *Ignatius of Loyola: Spiritual Exercises and Selected Works*. Edited by
George E. Ganss. New York/Mahwah: Paulist, 1991.

International Commission on English in the Liturgy. *The Rites of the Catholic
Church, Volume One, Study Edition*. Collegeville, MN: Liturgical Press, 1990.

International Energy Agency (IEA). *Technology Roadmap: Carbon Capture and
Storage*. Paris: International Energy Agency, 2013.

International Energy Agency (IEA). *World Energy Outlook 2015*. Paris, France:
International Energy Agency, 2015.

International Energy Agency (IEA). *World Energy Outlook Special Report 2016:
Energy and Air Pollution*. Paris: International Energy Agency, 2016.

International Union for Conservation of Nature and Natural Resources. 'World
   Conservation Strategy: Living Resource Conservation for Sustainable
   Development'. Available online: https://portals.iucn.org/library/efiles/documents/
   WCS-004.pdf.
IPCC. *Climate Change 2007: The Physical Science Basis. Contribution of Working
   Group I to the Fourth Assessment Report of the Intergovernmental Panel
   on Climate Change*. Edited by S. Solomon, D. Qin, M. Manning, Z. Chen,
   M. Marquis, K. B. Averyt, M. Tignor and H. L. Miller. Cambridge, UK, and
   New York, USA: Cambridge University Press, 2007.
IPCC. *Climate Change 2013: The Physical Science Basis. Working Group I
   Contribution to the Fifth Assessment Report of the Intergovernmental Panel
   on Climate Change*. Edited by T. F. Stocker, D. Qin, G.-K. Plattner, M. Tignor,
   S. K. Allen, J. Boschung, A. Nauels, Y. Xia, V. Bex and P. M. Midgley.
   Cambridge, UK, and New York, USA: Cambridge University Press.
IPCC. *Climate Change 2014: Impacts, Adaptation, and Vulnerability: Working
   Group II Contribution to the Fifth Assessment Report of the Intergovernmental
   Panel on Climate Change*. Edited by C. B. Fields, V. R. Barros, D. J. Dokken,
   K. J. Mach, M. D. Mastrandrea, T. E. Bilir, M. Chatterjee, K. L. Ebi, Y. O.
   Estrada, R. C. Genova, B. Girma, E. S. Kissel, A. N. Levy, S. MacCracken, P. R.
   Mastrandrea and L. L. White. Cambridge, UK, and New York, USA: Cambridge
   University Press, 2014.
IPCC. *Climate Change 2014: Mitigation of Climate Change. Contribution of
   Working Group III to the Fifth Assessment Report of the Intergovernmental
   Panel on Climate Change*. Edited by O. Edenhofer, R. Pichs-Madruga, Y.
   Sokona, E. Farahani, S. Kadner, K. Seyboth, A. Adler, I. Baum, S. Brunner, P.
   Eickemeier, B. Kriemann, J. Savolainen, S. Schlömer, C. von Stechow, T. Zwickel
   and J. C. Minx. Cambridge, UK, and New York, USA: Cambridge University
   Press, 2014.
IPCC. *Climate Change 2014: Synthesis Report. Contribution of Working Groups
   I, II and III to the Fifth Assessment Report of the Intergovernmental Panel
   on Climate Change*. Edited by R. K. Pachauri and L. A. Meyer. Geneva,
   Switzerland: IPCC, 2014.
IPCC. *Special Report on Renewable Energy Sources and Climate Change
   Mitigation*. Edited by O. Edenhofer, R. Pichs-Madruga, Y. Sokona, K. Seyboth,
   P. Matschoss, S. Kadner, T. Zwickel, P. Eickemeier, G. Hansen, S. Schlömer and
   C. von Stechow. Cambridge UK, and New York, USA: Cambridge University
   Press, 2012.
Ivereigh, Austen. *The Great Reformer: Francis and the Making of a Radical Pope*.
   New York: Henry Holt, 2014.
Jackson, Stephen and Jonathan Overpeck. 'Responses of Plant Populations and
   Communities to Environmental Changes of the Late Quaternary'. *Paleobiology*
   26 (2000): 194–220.
Jakob, Michael, Claudine Chen, Sabine Fuss, Annika Marxen, Narashima D.
   Rao and Ottmar Edenhofer. 'Using Carbon Pricing Revenues to Finance
   Infrastructure Access'. Presentation at the 21st Annual Conference of the
   European Association of Environmental and Resource Economists, 2015.
   Available Online: www.webmeets.com/eaere/2015/m/viewpaper.asp?pid=504.
Jakob, Michael and Ottmar Edenhofer. 'Green Growth, Degrowth, and the
   Commons'. *Oxford Review of Economic Policy* 30 (2014): 447–68.

Jenkins, Willis. *Ecologies of Grace: Environmental Ethics and Christian Theology*. New York: Oxford, 2008.

Jensen, Derrick. 'Forget Shorter Showers'. *Orion Magazine*. Available online: https://orionmagazine.org/article/forget-shorter-showers/.

John Paul II. Address to Pontifical Academy of Sciences, 22 October 1996.

John Paul II. *Bula Inter Sanctos Proclaiming Saint Francis of Assisi as Patron of Ecology*. 29 November 1979.

John Paul II. *Centesimus annus* [Encyclical Letter On The Hundredth Anniversary Of Rerum Novarum], 1 May 1991.

John Paul II. 'Deep Harmony Which Unites the Truths of Science with the Truths of Faith'. *L'Osservatore Romano*, 26 November 1979, 9–10.

John Paul II. *Sollicitudo rei socialis* [Encyclical Letter on Social Concern], 30 December 1987.

Johnson, Elizabeth. *Ask the Beasts: Darwin and the God of Love*. New York: Bloomsburg Continuum, 2014.

Kaiser, Christopher. 'Early Christian Belief in Creation and the Beliefs Sustaining the Modern Scientific Endeavor'. In *The Blackwell Companion to Science and Christianity*. Edited by J. B. Stump and Alan G. Padgett, 1–13. Malden, MA: Blackwell, 2012.

Katz, Eric, Andrew Light and David Rosthenberg, eds. *Beneath the Surface: Critical Essays in the Philosophy of Deep Ecology*. Cambridge, MA: The MIT Press, 2000.

Kaufmann, Franz-Xaver. *Der Ruf nach Verantwortung. Risiko und Ethik in einer unüberschaubaren Welt*. Freiburg: Herder, 1992.

Kaufmann, Franz-Xaver. *European Foundations of the Welfare State*. New York: Berghahn Books, 2012.

Klein, Alexandra-Maria, Bernard E. Vaissière, James H. Cane, Ingolf Steffan-Dewenter, Saul A. Cunningham, Claire Kremen and Teja Tscharntke. 'Importance of Pollinators in Changing Landscapes for World Crops'. *Proceedings: Biological Sciences* 274 (2007): 303–13.

Knight, Tiffany, Michael W. McCoy, Jonathan M. Chase, Krista A. McCoy and Robert D. Holt. 'Trophic Cascades across Ecosystems'. *Nature* 437 (2005): 880–3.

Koch, Paul and Anthony Barnosky. 'Late Quaternary Extinctions: State of the Debate'. *Annual Review of Ecology, Evolution, and Systematics* 37 (2006): 215–50.

Krause, R. M., S. R. Carley, D. C. Warren, J. A. Rupp and J. D. Graham. 'Not in (or Under) My Backyard: Geographic Proximity and Public Acceptance of Carbon Capture and Storage Facilities, *Risk Analysis* 34: 529–40 (2014). doi:10.1111/risa.12119.

Lackner, Klaus S., Sarah Brennan, Jürg M. Matter, A.-H. Alissa Park, Allen Wright and Bob van der Zwaan. 'The Urgency of the Development of CO2 Capture from Ambient Air'. *Proceedings of the National Academy of Sciences* 109, no. 33 (2012): 13156–62. doi:10.1073/pnas.1108765109.

Laird, Martin. *Into the Silent Land: A Guide to the Christian Practice of Contemplation*. New York: Oxford, 2006.

Lehnherr, Igor. 'Methylmercury Biogeochemistry: A Review with Special Reference to Arctic Aquatic Ecosystems'. *Environmental Reviews* 22 (2014): 229–43.

Lenton, Timothy M., Hermann Held, Elmar Kriegler, Jim W Hall, Wolfgang Lucht, Stefan Rahmstorf and Hans Joachim Schellnhuber. 'Tipping Elements in the

Earth's Climate System'. *Proceedings of the National Academy of Sciences* 105, no. 6 (2008): 1786–93.

Leonard, Annie. 'The Story of Stuff: Referenced and Annotated Script'. Available online: http://storyofstuff.org/wp-content/uploads/movies/scripts/Story%20 of%20Stuff.pdf.

Leopold, Aldo. *A Sand County Almanac.* New York: Oxford, 1989.

Levertov, Denise. *Sands of the Well.* New York: New Directions, 1998.

Locke, John. *Two Treatises on Government and A Letter Concerning Toleration.* New Haven, CT: Yale University Press, 2003.

Lüthi, Dieter, Martine Le Floch, Bernhard Bereiter, Thomas Blunier, Jean-Marc Barnola, Urs Siegenthaler, Dominique Raynaud, Jean Jouzel, Hubertus Fischer, Kenji Kawamura and Thomas F. Stocker. 'High-Resolution Carbon Dioxide Concentration Record 650,000–800,000 Years before Present'. *Nature* 453, no. 7193 (15 May 2008): 379–82, doi:10.1038/nature06949.

Macy, Joanna. *Mutual Causality in Buddhism and General Systems Theory: The Dharma of Natural Systems.* Albany, NY: State University of New York Press, 1991.

Marcott, Shaun A., Jeremy D. Shakun, Peter U. Clark and Alan C. Mix. 'A Reconstruction of Regional and Global Temperature for the Past 11,300 Years'. *Science* 339, no. 6124 (7 March 2013): 1198–1201. doi:10.1126/science.1228026.

Martin, Claude. *On the Edge: The State and Fate of the World's Tropical Rainforests.* Vancouver, BC: Greystone, 2015.

McClellan, Justin, David W. Keith and Jay Apt. 'Cost Analysis of Stratospheric Albedo Modification Delivery Systems'. *Environmental Research Letters* 7, no. 3 (2012): 1–8. doi:10.1088/1748-9326/7/3/034019.

McCollum, David, Yu Nagai, Keywan Riahi, Giacomo Marangoni, Katherine Calvin, Robert Pietzcker, Jasper van Vliet and Bob van der Zwaan. 'Energy Investments Under Climate Policy: A Comparison of Global Models'. *Climate Change Economics*, LIMITS Special Issue (2014). Available online: http:// www.feem-project.net/limits/docs/04.%20cce%20limits%20special%20issue_ paper3.pdf.

McDonnell, Kilian. *The Baptism of Jesus in the Jordan: The Trinitarian and Cosmic Order of Salvation.* Collegeville, MN: The Liturgical Press, 1996.

McElroy, Bishop Robert W. 'A Church for the Poor'. *America Magazine* 209, no. 11 (21 October 2013).

McMahan, David L. *The Making of Buddhist Modernism.* Oxford: Oxford University Press, 2009.

McNutt, Marcia. 'The Beyond-Two-Degree Inferno'. *Science* 349, no. 6243 (3 July 2015): 7.

McNutt, Marcia. 'The Pope Tackles Sustainability'. *Science* 345, no. 6203 (19 September 2014): 1429.

Meadows, D. and Dennis L. Meadows. *Limits to Growth.* New York: Universe Books, 1972.

Miller, Vincent J. *Consuming Religion: Christian Faith and Practice in a Consumer Culture.* New York: Continuum, 2004.

Miller, Vincent J. 'Slavery and Commodity Chains: Fighting the Globalization of Indifference'. *America Magazine*, 2 January 2014. Available online: http:// americamagazine.org/content/all-things/slavery-and-commodity-chains-fighting-globalization-indifference.

Moevs, Christian. *The Metaphysics of Dante's Comedy*. New York: Oxford University Press, 2005.

Moncrieff, Glenn, Thomas Hickler and Steven I. Higgins. 'Intercontinental Divergence in the Climate Envelope of Major Plant Biomes'. *Global Ecology and Biogeography* 24 (2015): 324–34.

Mora, Camilo, Derek P. Tittensor, Sina Adl, Alastair G. B. Simpson and Boris Worm. 'How Many Species Are There on Earth and in the Ocean?' *PLoS Biology* 9 (2011): 1–8.

Murray, Joyce. 'Liberation for Communion in the Soteriology of Gustavo Gutiérrez'. *Theological Studies* 59 (1998): 51–9.

Nell-Breuning, Oswald von. *Soziale Sicherheit*. Freiburg: Herder, 1979.

Nell-Breuning, Oswald von. *Soziallehre der Kirche*. Vienna: Europa Verlag, 1977.

Nicholás, Adolfo, SJ. 'Depth, Universality, and Learned Ministry: Challenges to Jesuit Higher Education Today'. Mexico City, 23 April 2010. Available online: http://www.sjweb.info/documents/ansj/100423_Mexico%20City_Higher%20 Education%20Today_ENG.pdf.

Nixon, Rob. *Slow Violence and the Environmentalism of the Poor*. Cambridge, MA: Harvard University Press, 2011.

Nordhaus, William. *The Climate Casino: Risk, Uncertainty, and Economics for a Warming World*. New Haven, CT: Yale University Press, 2013.

Norris, Era Dabla, Kalpana Kochhar, Nujin Suphaphiphat, Frantisek Ricka and Evridiki Tsounta. 'Causes and Consequences of Income Inequality: A Global Perspective'. *IMF Staff Discussion Note* 15/13 (2015): 1–39.

Nowak, Martin A. with Roger Highfield. *SuperCooperators: Altriusm, Evolution, and Why We Need Each Other to Succeed*. New York: Free Press, 2011.

Olson, David and Eric Dinerstein. 'The Global 200: Priority Ecoregions for Global Conservation'. *Annals of the Missouri Botanical Garden* 89 (2002): 199–224.

Oreskes, Naomi. 'The Scientific Consensus on Climate Change'. *Science* 306, no. 5702 (Dec 2004): 1686.

Oreskes, Naomi and Erik Conway. *Merchants of Doubt. How a Handful of Scientists Obscured the Truth on Issues from Tobacco Smoke to Issues from Tobacco Smoke to Global Warming*. New York: Bloomsbury, 2010.

Origen. *On First Principles*. Translated by G. W. Butterworth. Glouchester, MA: Peter Smith, 1973.

Orr, David. *The Nature of Design: Ecology, Culture and Human Intention*. New York: Oxford, 2002.

Ostrom, Elinor. *Governing the Commons. The Evolution of Institutions for Collective Action*. Cambridge: Cambridge University Press, 1980.

Ostrom, Elinor. 'Nested Externalities and Polycentric Institutions: Must we Wait for Global Solutions to Climate Change before Taking Actions at other Scales?' *Economic Theory* 49 (2012): 353–69.

Oxfam. '"An Economy for the One Percent".' *Oxfam Briefing Paper* 210 (2016): 1–44.

O'Connor, Clare. 'These Retailers Involved in Bangladesh Factory Disaster Have Yet to Compensate Victims'. *Forbes* (26 April 2014). Available online: http://www.forbes.com/sites/clareoconnor/2014/04/26/these-retailers-involved-in-bangladesh-factory-disaster-have-yet-to-compensate-victims/#2757717657c5.

Patz, Jonathan A., Holly K. Gibbs, Jonathan A. Foley, Jamesine V. Rogers and Kirk R. Smith. 'Climate Change and Global Health: Quantifying a Growing Ethical Crisis'. *EcoHealth* 4 (2007): 397–405.

Peppard, Christiana. *Just Water: Theology, Ethics, and the Global Water Crises.* Maryknoll, NY: Orbis Books, 2014.

Petit, J. R., J. Jouzel, D. Raynaud, N. I. Barkov, J. M. Barnola, I. Basile, M. Bender, J. Chappellaz, J. Davis, G. Delaygue, M. Delmotte, V. M. Kotlyakov, M. Legrand, V. Lipenkov, C. Lorius, L. Pépin, C. Ritz, E. Saltzman and, M. Stievenard. 'Vostok Ice Core Data for 420,000 Years'. *IGBP PAGES/World Data Center for Paleoclimatology Data Contribution Series #2001-076.* Boulder, CO: USA NOAA/NGDC Paleoclimatology Program, 2001.

Piff, Paul, Daniel M. Stancato, Stéphane Côté, Rodolfo Mendoza-Dentona and Dacher Keltnera. 'Higher Social Class Predicts Increased Unethical Behavior'. *Proceedings of the National Academy of Sciences of the United States of America* 109, no. 11 (2012): 4086–91.

Pimentel, David, Lori Lach, Rodolfo Zuniga and Doug Morrison. 'Environmental and Economic Costs of Nonindigenous Species in the United States'. *BioScience* 53 (2000): 53–65.

Pius XI. *Quadragesimo Anno* [Encyclical On the Reconstruction of the Social Order], 15 May 1931.

Pius XII. *Humani generis.* [Encyclical Concerning Some False Opinions Threatening to Undermine the Foundations of Catholic Doctrine], 12 August 1950.

Pontifical Academy of Sciences. *Sustainable Humanity, Sustainable Nature: Our Responsibility.* Citta del Vaticano: Libreria Editrice Vaticana, 2015.

Pontifical Council for Justice and Peace. *Compendium of the Social Doctrine of the Church.* Citta del Vaticano: Libreria Editrice Vaticana, 2004.

Pontifical Council for Justice and Peace. *Energy, Justice and Peace: A Reflection on Energy in the Current Context of Development and Environmental Protection.* Citta del Vaticano: Libreria Editrice Vaticana, 2014.

Power, Mary, David Tilman, James A. Estes, Bruce A. Menge, William J. Bond, L. Scott Mills, Gretchen Daily, Juan Carlos Castilla, Jane Lubchenco and Robert T. Paine. 'Challenges in the Quest for Keystones'. *BioScience* 46 (1996): 609–20.

'Power to the Powerless'. *The Economist* 418, no. 8978 (27 February 2016): 49–50.

Ramanathan, Veerabhadran. 'The Two Worlds Approach for Mitigating Air Pollution and Climate Change'. In *Sustainable Humanity, Sustainable Nature, Our Responsibility, Pontificiae Academiae Scientiarum Extra Series 41/ Pontificiae Academiae Scientiarum Socialium Acta 19.* Edited by Partha S. Dasgupta, Veerabhadran Ramanathan, and Marcelo Sánchez Sorondo, 285–300. Vatican City: Libreria Editrice Vaticana, 2015.

Ramanathan, Veerabhadran, Juliann E. Allison, Maximilian Aufhammer, David Auston, Anthony D. Barnosky, Lifang Chiang, William D. Collins, Steven J. Davis, Fonna Forman, Susanna B. Hecht, Daniel Kammen, C.-Y. Cynthia Lin Lawell, Teenie Matlock, Daniel Press, Douglas Rotman, Scott Samuelsen, Gina Solomon, David G. Victor and Byron Washom. *Bending the Curve: 10 scalable solutions for carbon neutrality and climate stability.* Executive Summary of the Report. University of California, 2015. Available Online: http://uc-carbonneutralitysummit2015.ucsd.edu/_files/Bending-the-Curve.pdf.

Ramanathan, Veerabhadran and Gregory Carmichael. 'Global and Regional Climate Changes Due to Black Carbon'. *Nature Geoscience* 1, no. 4 (2008): 221–7.

Randall, Tom. 'Fossil Fuels Just Lost the Race Against Renewables'. *Bloomberg Business*, 14 April 2015. Available online: www.bloomberg.com/news/articles/2015-04-14/fossil-fuels-just-lost-the-race-against-renewables.

Regaldo, Antonio. 'Brazil Says Rate of Deforestation in Amazon Continues to Plunge', *Science* 329 (2010): 1270–1.

Reiner, David, Tom Curry, Mark de Figueiredo, Howard Herzog, Steven Ansolabehere, Kenshi Itaoka, Makoto Akai, Filip Johnsson and Mikael Odenberger. 'An International Comparison of Public Attitudes Towards Carbon Capture and Storage Technologies'. *NTNU.* 2006. Available online: http://www.ukccsc.co.uk/Publications/Reiner1.pdf.

Rockström, Johan, Will Steffen, Kevin Noone, Asa Persson, Stuart F. Chapin, Eric F. Lambin, Timothy M. Lenton, Marten Scheffer, Carl Folke, Hans Joachim Schellnhuber, Björn Nykvist, Cynthia A. de Wit, Terry Hughes, Sander van der Leeuw, Henning Rodhe, Sverker Sörlin, Peter K. Snyder, Robert Costanza, Uno Svedin, Malin Falkenmark, Louise Karlberg, Robert W. Corell, Victoria J. Fabry, James Hansen, Brian Walker, Diana Liverman, Katherine Richardson, Paul Crutzen and Jonathan A. Foley. 'Planetary Boundaries: Exploring a Safe Operating Space for Humanity'. *Nature* 461, no. 7263 (2009): 472–5.

Rourke, Nancy M. 'The Environment Within: Virtue Ethics'. In *Green Discipleship: Catholic Theological Ethics and the Environment*. Edited by Tobias Winright, 163–82. Winona, MN: Anselm Academic, 2011.

Rubio, Julie Hanlon. 'Toward a Just Way of Eating'. In *Green Discipleship: Catholic Theological Ethics and the Environment*. Edited by Tobias Winright, 360–78. Winona, MN: Anselm Academic, 2011.

Saaristo, Minna, John A. Craft, Kari K. Lehtonen and Kai Lindström. 'Sand Goby (*Pomatoschistus minutus*) Males Exposed to an Endocrine Disrupting Chemical Fail in Nest and Mate Competition'. *Hormones and Behavior* 56 (2009): 315–21.

Sachs, Jeffrey. *The Age of Sustainable Development*. New York: Columbia University Press, 2015.

Salai, Sean, S.J. 'The Faith and Science of Georges Lemaître: 11 Questions for Dr. Karl van Bibber'. *America Magazine*, 25 May 2016. Available online: http://www.americamagazine.org/content/all-things/faith-and-science-georges-lemaitre-11-questions-dr-karl-van-bibber.

Sandel, Michael. *What Money Can't Buy: The Moral Limits of Markets*. New York: Farrar, Straus and Giroux, 2013.

San Martín, Inés. 'Liberation Theology Founder Praises "New Atmosphere" Under Pope Francis'. *Crux*, 12 May 2015. Available online: http://www.cruxnow.com/church/2015/05/12/liberation-theology-founder-praises-new-atmosphere-under-pope-francis/.

Scheer, Roddy and Doug Moss. 'Use it and Lose it: The Outsize Effect of U.S. Consumption on the Environment'. *Scientific American*. Available online: http://www.scientificamerican.com/article/american-consumption-habits/.

Second Vatican Council. *Dei Verbum* [Dogmatic Constitution on Divine Revelation], 18 November 1965. In *The Basic Sixteen Documents: Vatican Council II: Constitutions, Decrees, Declarations*. Edited by Austin Flannery, 97–116. New York: Costello Publishing Company, 1996.

Second Vatican Council. *Gaudium et spes* [Pastoral Constitution on the Church in the Modern World], 7 December 1965.

'Seize the Day: The Fall in the Price of Oil and Gas Provides a Once-in-a-
    Generation Opportunity to Fix Bad Energy Policies'. *The Economist*
    (17 January 2015). Available online: http://www.economist.com/news/
    leaders/21639501-fall-price-oil-and-gas-provides-once-generation-opportunity-
    fix-bad.
Sen, Amartya. *Collective Choice and Social Welfare*. San Francisco: Holden-Day,
    1970.
Sneigocki, John. 'The Social Ethics of Pope John Paul II: A Critique of
    Neoconservative Interpretations'. *Horizons: Journal of the College Theology
    Society* 33, no. 1 (Spring 2006): 7–32.
St. Basil the Great. *Hexaemeron*. Edited by Paul Böer Sr. Veritas Splendor, 2012.
Steffen, Will, Katherine Richardson, Johan Rockström, Sarah E. Cornell, Ingo
    Fetzer, Elena M. Bennett, Reinette Biggs, Stephen R. Carpenter, Wim de Vries,
    Cynthia A. de Wit, Carl Folke, Dieter Gerten, Jens Heinke, Georgina M. Mace,
    Linn M. Persson, Veerabhadran Ramanathan, Belinda Reyers and Sverker
    Sörlin. 'Planetary Boundaries: Guiding Human Development on a Changing
    Planet', *Science* 347, no. 6223 (February 2015): 1–10.
Storr, Anthony. *Solitude: A Return to the Self*. New York: Ballantine, 1988.
Suckling, James and Jacquetta Lee. 'Redefining Scope: The True Environmental
    Impact of Smartphones?' *The International Journal of Life Cycle Assessment*
    20, no. 4 (2015): 1181–96.
Tanner, Kathryn. *God and Creation in Christian Theology*. Minneapolis: Fortress,
    1988.
Taylor, Mark C. *Speed Limits: Where Time Went and Why We Have So Little Left*.
    New Haven: Yale University Press, 2014.
The *Roman Missal*. English translation according to the third typical edition.
    Washington, DC: United States Conference of Catholic Bishops, 2011.
'Trickle Down: Is Access to Clean Water a Human Right?' *Scientific American*, 6
    April 2011. Available online: http://www.scientificamerican.com/article/the-
    right-clean-fresh-water/.
Turkle, Sherry. *Alone Together: Why We Expect More from Social Media and Less
    from Each Other*. New York: Basic Books, 2011.
U.S. Conference of Catholic Bishops. 'Prayer and Worship, the Mass'. Available
    online: http://www.usccb.org/prayer-and-worship/the-mass/order-of-mass/index.
    cfm.
U.S. Conference of Catholic Bishops. 'Two Feet of Love in Action'. Available
    online: http://www.usccb.org/beliefs-and-teachings/what-we-believe/catholic-
    social-teaching/two-feet-of-love-in-action.cfm.
U.S. Department of Energy. 'Advancing Sustainable Materials Management: 2013
    Fact Sheet'. Washington, DC: U.S. Environmental Protection Agency, 2015.
U.S. Department of Energy. 'Energy Consumption by Sector'. Available online:
    http://www.eia.gov/beta/MER/?tbl=T02.01#/?f=A&start=1949&end=2015&ch
    arted=3-6-9-12.
U.S. Department of Energy. 'Energy Explained: Use of Energy in the
    United States for Transportation'. Available online: http://www.eia.gov/
    Energyexplained/?page=us_energy_transportation.
U.S. Department of Energy. 'Renewable Energy Certificates (RECs)'. Available
    online: https://www.epa.gov/greenpower/renewable-energy-certificates-recs#how.

U.S. Department of Energy. 'Solar, Wind, Hydropower: Home Renewable
    Energy Installations'. Available online: http://energy.gov/articles/solar-wind-
    hydropower-home-renewable-energy-installations.
U.S. Department of Energy. 'Sources of Greenhouse Gas Emissions'. Available
    online: https://www3.epa.gov/climatechange/ghgemissions/sources/electricity.
    html.
U.S. Department of Energy. 'Tax Credits, Rebates & Savings'. Available online:
    http://energy.gov/savings.
U.S. Department of Energy. 'Transportation Sector Emissions'. Available online:
    https://www3.epa.gov/climatechange/ghgemissions/sources/transportation.html.
U.S. Environmental Protection Agency & U.S. Department of Energy. 'Benchmark
    Energy Use'. Available online: https://www.energystar.gov/buildings/about-us/
    how-can-we-help-you/benchmark-energy-use.
United Nations. 'International Decade for Action: Water for Life 2005-2015'.
    Available online: http://www.un.org/waterforlifedecade/human_right_to_water.
    shtml.
United Nations. *The Millennial Development Goals Report*. New York: United
    Nations, 2015.
United Nations. *Paris Agreement*. New York: United Nations, 2015.
United Nations. 'Water Scarcity'. Available online: http://www.un.org/
    waterforlifedecade/scarcity.shtml.
United States Government Interagency Working Group on Social Cost of Carbon.
    'Technical Update of the Social Cost of Carbon for Regulatory Impact Analysis
    under Executive Order 12866'. Washington, DC, 2013.
van Bavel, Tarsicius J. 'Love'. In *Augustine through the Ages: An Encyclopedia*.
    Edited by Allan D. Fitzgerald, 509–15. Grand Rapids: Eerdmans, 1999.
van Vuuren, Detlef P., Jae Edmonds, Mikiko Kainuma, Keywan Riahi, Allison
    Thomson, Kathy Hibbard, George C. Hurtt, Tom Kram, Volker Krey,
    Jean-Francois Lamarque, Toshihiko Masui, Malte Meinshausen, Nebojsa
    Nakicenovic, Steven J. Smith and Steven K. Rose. 'The Representative
    Concentration Pathways: An Overview'. *Climatic Change* 109 (2011): 5–31.
    doi:10.1007/s10584-011-0148-z.
von Hirschhausen. Christian, Johannes Herold and Pao-Yu Oei. 'How a "Low
    Carbon" Innovation Can Fail–Tales from a "Lost Decade" for Carbon Capture,
    Transport, and Sequestration (CCTS)'. *Economics of Energy & Environmental
    Policy* 1, no. 2 (2012): 115–23. doi:10.5547/2160-5890.1.2.8.
Warburton, Eve. 'A Right, a Need, or an Economic Good? Debating our
    Relationship to Water'. State of the Planet, Earth Institute – Columbia
    University, 6 June 2011. Available online: http://blogs.ei.columbia.
    edu/2011/06/06/a-right-a-need-or-an-economic-good-debating-our-relationship-
    to-water/.
Ward, Benedicta, ed. and trans. *The Desert Christian: Sayings of the Desert Fathers.
    The Alphabetical Collection*. New York: Macmillan, 1975.
Waters, Colin Jan Zalasiewicz, Colin Summerhayes, Anthony D. Barnosky, Clément
    Poirier, Agnieszka Gałuszka, Alejandro Cearreta, Matt Edgeworth, Erle C. Ellis,
    Michael Ellis, Catherine Jeandel, Reinhold Leinfelder, J. R. McNeill, Daniel deB.
    Richter, Will Steffen, James Syvitski, Davor Vidas, Michael Wagreich, Mark
    Williams, An Zhisheng, Jacques Grinevald, Eric Odada, Naomi Oreskes and

Alexander P. Wolfe. 'The Anthropocene is Functionally and Stratigraphically Distinct from the Holocene'. *Science* 351 (2016): aad2269: 1–10.

Weart, Spencer. *The Discovery of Global Warming*. Available online: http://history. aip.org/climate/index.htm#contents.

White, Lynn, Jr. 'The Historical Roots of Our Ecologic Crisis'. *Science* 155, no. 3767 (1967): 1203–7.

Wigley, Tom M. L. 'Coal to Gas: The Influence of Methane Leakage'. *Climatic Change* 108, no. 3 (2011): 601–8.

Wilson, E. O. *Biophilia*. Cambridge, MA: Harvard University Press, 1984.

Wilson, E. O. *The Creation: An Appeal to Save Life on Earth*. New York: W. W. Norton and Co., 2006.

Wilson, E. O. *The Diversity of Life*. Cambridge, MA: Harvard University Press, 2010.

Wilson, E. O. 'Within One Cubic Foot.' *National Geographic* 217, no. 2 (February 2010): 62–83.

Winemiller, K. O., P. B. McIntyre, L. Castello, E. Fluet-Chouinard, T. Giarrizzo, S. Nam, I. G. Baird, W. Darwall, N. K. Lujan, I. Harrison, M. L. J. Stiassny, R. A. M. Silvano, D. B. Fitzgerald, F. M. Pelicice, A. A. Agostinho, L. C. Gomes, J. S. Albert, E. Baran, M. Petrere Jr., C. Zarfl, M. Mulligan, J. P. Sullivan, C. C. Arantes, L. M. Sousa, A. A. Koning, D. J. Hoeinghaus, M. Sabaj, J. G. Lundberg, J. Armbruster, M. L. Thieme, P. Petry, J. Zuanon, G. Torrente Vilara, J. Snoeks, C. Ou, W. Rainboth, C. S. Pavanelli, A. Akama, A. van Soesbergen and L. Sáenz. 'Balancing Hydropower and Biodiversity in the Amazon, Congo, and Mekong'. *Science* 351 (2016): 128–9.

Worm, Boris and Robert Paine. 'Humans as a Hyperkeystone Species'. *Trends in Ecology and Evolution* 31 (2016): 600–7.

Wykes, Sarah, Ben Garside and Aaron Leopold. 'Energy in the Post-2015 Development Framework'. *Catholic Agency for Overseas Development (CAFOD)*, 2014. Available online: http://pubs.iied.org/pdfs/G03811.pdf.

INDEX